The New City Catechism

Curriculum

52 Questions
& Answers
for Our Hearts
& Minds

The New City Catechism

Curriculum

Volume 2 – Leader's Guide

Christ, Redemption, Grace

Questions 21–35

CROSSWAY®

WHEATON, ILLINOIS

The New City Catechism Curriculum, Vol. 2, Leader's Guide: Christ, Redemption, Grace, Questions 21–35

Copyright © 2018 by The Gospel Coalition

Published by Crossway
        1300 Crescent Street
        Wheaton, Illinois 60187

This publication was made possible through the support of a grant from the John Templeton Foundation. The opinions expressed in this publication are those of the publisher and do not necessarily reflect the views of the John Templeton Foundation.

Cover design: Matt Wahl & Micah Lanier

First printing 2018

Printed in China

Scripture quotations are from the ESV® Bible (The Holy Bible, English Standard Version®), copyright © 2001 by Crossway, a publishing ministry of Good News Publishers. Used by permission. All rights reserved.

Trade paperback ISBN: 978-1-4335-5940-2

Crossway is a publishing ministry of Good News Publishers.

RRDS			29	28	27	26	25	24	23	22	21	20	19
14	13	12	11	10	9	8	7	6	5	4	3	2

Introduction

A very warm welcome to *The New City Catechism Curriculum*! Our prayer is that this curriculum will serve to equip the children entrusted into your care to be theologically robust, confident, virtuous, and courageous followers of Christ. The curriculum consists of fifty-two lessons, and each lesson corresponds to one of the questions in *The New City Catechism*. The curriculum is aimed at children ages eight through eleven, and is designed to be used in a wide variety of contexts—Sunday school, home school, Christian school, or after-school clubs. The catechism will be most effective if it is concurrently taught in the local church and in the context of the family.

What Is a Catechism?

A catechism is a collection of biblical doctrines, assembled into a question-and-answer format. The term comes from the New Testament word *katecheo*, which simply means "to teach or instruct." The process of catechesis has rich Reformation roots. Martin Luther, John Calvin, and other Reformers endeavored to catechize both children and adults in order to combat doctrinal ignorance and biblical illiteracy. This biblically derived process has proven hugely influential at critical points in the history of the church. We believe the church needs this ancient practice more than ever to equip Christ's people to stand fast in the face of an ever-changing, often hostile culture.

What Is This Curriculum Designed to Do?

Catechize Children

Children are constantly learning. Their inquiring minds soak up information at a spectacular rate. They are trying to make sense of a complex and ever-changing world, seeking to acquire the skills to survive—and even thrive—in life. As they learn, a framework of understanding is established in their minds. This is called a worldview. All children and adults observe and interact with the world through their personal worldview. It is a thrilling and great responsibility to raise children and shape their understanding of the world, how it works, and their unique purpose in it. To catechize children is to give them a coherent and extensive system of thought that equips them to confidently interpret the world and their experiences

in the world through a biblical framework. It also nurtures in children a love for and understanding of the essential doctrines for the Christian faith. To catechize children is to lay deep and strong biblical foundations for a lifetime of faith.

Develop Virtue

The New City Catechism Curriculum is designed to help children not only learn sound doctrine but also to learn how to respond to it and live it out in their lives. Each lesson in *The New City Catechism* has a Virtue Vision covering one of ten Christian virtues that connects in some way with the catechism question. The virtues are Awe, Forgiveness, Gratitude, Honesty, Hope, Humility, Joy, Love, Perseverance, and Trust.

The emphasis and intention of *The New City Catechism Curriculum* is to shape and affect the hearts of the children who engage with each lesson, with the hope that the catechism will contribute greatly to the nurture of godly, mature, and virtuous young men and women. This is definitely not about behavior modification, but rather helping children to respond with keen heart awareness to God's Word as they encounter it in and through the catechism and curriculum. The curriculum seeks to develop in children a mature Christian character, shaped by Scripture, that will be countercultural and striking in our world. By cultivating the capacities for character in both the heart and mind, this curriculum prepares children to love God and others. (For more information and research on faith and virtue development in children, visit newcitycatechism.com/virtue.)

How to Use This Curriculum

The New City Catechism Curriculum is designed to be engaging, dynamic, and creative for children ages eight through eleven. It is intended to be taught in order, beginning at Question 1 and working through to Question 52. It can be taught straight through in a year by covering one lesson a week, but it can also be broken up in whatever way fits your church or school schedule best.

The curriculum is divided into three sections and published in three corresponding books.

Part 1: God, Creation & Fall, Law (twenty lessons covering Questions 1–20)

Part 2: Christ, Redemption, Grace (fifteen lessons covering Questions 21–35)

Part 3: Spirit, Restoration, Growing in Grace (seventeen lessons covering Questions 36–52)

Each lesson is intended to be flexible in length to suit a variety of contexts. You'll find three sample lesson outlines on page 12. The sample lesson outlines vary in length, highlighting how the curriculum can be tailored appropriately to serve the needs of a particular classroom. The most essential elements have been included in the shortest outlines. If you have more time, other activities that reinforce the essential components may be chosen from the longer outlines.

Each component has a time allocated to it; this is meant to be only a rough guide. The length of time a component will take depends on a variety of factors, such as the number of children in the class, the age of the children, and the number of teachers. Carefully consider how much time each component may require in your particular context. You may want to go over the allotted time if an activity is going well, or cut it short when it seems wise to you.

Please do not feel obliged to do exactly as the lesson plan prescribes! If you find that your class loves a particular form of catechism recap, then feel free to use that more often than the lesson plans dictate. Similarly, if certain memorization methods work better for your class than others, use the successful methods more.

Some classes will have children who love to work quietly at crafts; others will need more physical activity. The more you seek to illustrate and apply the lessons in a way that specifically works for your class, the more successful you will be at discipling the children through *The New City Catechism Curriculum*.

Memorization is an essential element of this curriculum. There is an emphasis on helping the children to learn the questions and answers of the catechism and the corresponding Scriptures. Each lesson begins with a memory challenge (Catechism Recap) and ends with a memorization game (Memory Activity). The Catechism Recap will help the children recall and reinforce the catechism questions already covered. The Memory Activity can be used either to learn a Scripture verse or to memorize the new catechism question.

The Catechism Recap section sometimes requires questions and answers to be printed out in different sizes for different activities. When you see the abbreviation "DL," it means you can download a pdf prepared for this activity at www.newcitycatechism.com/recap.

Many lessons include visual resources that can be found in the Resource Book (RB). These resources may be photocopied from the book or downloaded at www.newcitycatechism.com /resourcebook. Some resources are worksheets that accompany the activities, and you will need one per child. Others are visual aids for classroom discussion. It would be helpful to enlarge these photos and illustrations before you print or as you photocopy them.

Leading and Loving the Children Well

Children learn best in an environment that is relationally rich and characterized by love. Consistent class leadership facilitates great relationships between the children and their teachers. Though this may not always be possible, some degree of continuity is highly encouraged.

How to Pray
The best way to grow to love the children in your class is to pray diligently for them. Divide the class up into seven groups, and pray for some of the children each day of the week.

Before each class, come together as a group of teachers and pray that God would be at work in the heart and mind of each child that will come into the classroom.

How to Plan a Lesson
Lesson planning is a serious business; don't leave it until the night before the class!

Begin your planning by praying that God would help you to teach the lesson in a way that is faithful and engaging for the children in your care. (Each lesson includes a Leader's Prayer.) Take some time to read through the curriculum material and carefully consider which components you will use to build your lesson plan. Do pay attention to timings, particularly making sure you leave plenty of time to teach the Bible passage well.

Once you have decided which components will be included in your lesson plan, consult the Leader's Tool Kit list and determine what resources you need for the lesson. It's important to check this list in plenty of time in case you need to buy supplies. Most supplies listed can be found at any craft store.

Finally, read through the Bible passage and Teaching Outline multiple times. The Teaching Outline should be only a guide for you. You should expand or amend it to suit your own children and context. Write out the talk in your own words, and include illustrations and applications that you know will connect with the children in your class.

A Discussion and Question Time outline is included in each lesson. These are not meant to be questions leaders ask the children; rather, they are meant to help leaders prepare for the sorts of questions children might ask them. The children in your class may have entirely different questions. Pray that the Holy Spirit will help you answer well and in accordance with God's Word.

How to Manage the Classroom

Children enjoy and thrive in situations where there are clear boundaries. Communicate clearly to the children what your expectations are with regard to behavior in your classroom. For example:

- Raise your hand if you'd like to speak.
- Don't speak if someone else is speaking.
- Don't leave the classroom without permission.
- Be kind and gentle to each other at all times.

Remember, however, that the children are not in school, so while clear boundaries are helpful, the learning environment should be joyful and grace-saturated. Each teacher should strive to clearly model Christian virtue to the children, particularly the ten virtues highlighted in *The New City Catechism Curriculum*.

Mischief usually arises when children are bored or there is a hiatus in the lesson, so good planning and preparation will help manage the classroom.

Make sure to position yourself near the chatty or disruptive children and encourage them to pay attention and participate well. Try not to draw unnecessary attention to a child as you help him or her focus. The less fuss the better.

Work hard to know the names of the children in the class, and call on them by name to contribute. Nurture an active listening stance in the children by encouraging them to be involved in an interactive way throughout the lesson.

Interact individually with children who cause serious disruption. Explain to them how detrimental and distracting their behavior is to the rest of the class. If the disruption continues, involve the child's parents in the discussion.

How to Encourage Memorization

The key to memorization is repetition! It's unrealistic to expect children to remember something if they've heard it only once. Creative repetition is especially helpful in memorization. For example, hearing or singing a song over and over again embeds it in memory. Remember that children learn in a variety of styles, so hearing, seeing, and doing all help children with memorization.

Review is also a very helpful aid to memorization, which is why each of *The New City Catechism Curriculum* lessons begins with a Catechism Recap. Regular review will substantially increase memorization. This is one of the reasons why *The New City Catechism Curriculum* will be most successful if the catechism is concurrently studied in the home as well as the church.

Explanation is also significant in memorization. It is much easier to remember something if you understand it. The children will be better able to commit the catechism questions to memory well if they understand what the question and answer are all about.

How to Nurture Heart Application

The training and instruction of children and the nurture and nature of their hearts are inextricably linked. So as those who presume to teach children, we must be concerned to help them transfer what they're learning from their heads to their hearts. There is a real difference between knowing and understanding something intellectually and having a heart that is deeply affected by the truth.

So how are we going to engage children's hearts as we teach, train, and catechize them? The first thing to acknowledge is that it isn't easy; it takes hard work and great determination. It's reasonably easy to teach the Bible well—providing head knowledge—and reasonably difficult to apply it well to the hearts of children—growing heart knowledge.

It is important to remember that the molding and shaping of the heart is a process. It takes time and will look different depending on the age, stage, and development (physical, emotional, and social) of each individual child. Every child is different; there is no "one size fits all" when it comes to spiritual development.

Try to use "heart language" with children. This will serve to instill in them an awareness that their heart matters and that it affects how they live.

It's much harder to do real heart application with children when leaders change every week, causing the teachers to have underdeveloped relationships with the children. Leaders must know the children well to apply the Word well. Engaging the hearts of children so that they know God, as opposed to simply knowing about God, requires significant relationships. Children need to regularly observe the lives of older Christians who are seeking to apply God's Word to their own hearts and are willing to live honest and transparent lives before the children.

Remember that virtue is not just taught—it is also caught! By displaying Christian character in our own lives as leaders, we are modeling for children how the lessons play out in the real world today. A teacher's authentic faith and embodiment of virtue can be inspiring and instructive to children, so also be sure to attend to your own spiritual growth.

Clear and thoughtful illustration and application in talks is a significant way to engage a child's heart. This is why it's important to work hard to personalize the teaching outlines in *The New City Catechism Curriculum* in a way that resonates deeply with the children in your class.

In order to effectively engage them we need to make every effort to know and understand their hearts, particularly where they're tempted to idolatry. That means we must know and understand their world well—what they're watching, what they're learning, what their friends are saying, and ultimately what worldviews they're encountering in the world.

One-on-one engagement with a child is particularly useful when seeking to involve the heart; this can be done in the classroom and by the parents in the home. This allows us to ask heart-penetrating questions, and it also invites the child to question back.

We have the opportunity to teach children the art of preaching to their own hearts. This is where a catechism is so eternally useful.

Melanie Lacy
Director of Theology for Children and Youth
Oak Hill College

Lesson Outline

- **75-Minute Lesson Outline**
  - Catechism Recap (5 Mins)
  - Introduction to Question (5 Mins)
  - Activity (10 Mins)
  - Teaching Outline (15 Mins)
  - Activity (10 Mins)
  - Discussion and Question Time (5 Mins)
  - Virtue Vision (10 Mins)
  - Memory Activity (10 Mins)
  - Closing Prayer Time (5 Mins)

- **45-Minute Lesson Outline**
  - Catechism Recap (10 Mins)
  - Introduction to Question (5 Mins)
  - Teaching Outline (15 Mins)
  - Discussion and Question Time (5 Mins)
  - Virtue Vision (10 Mins)

- **30-Minute Lesson Outline**
  - Catechism Recap (10 Mins)
  - Introduction to Question (5 Mins)
  - Teaching Outline (15 Mins)

→ Do pick the time frame that works best for your group.

→ Don't be afraid to mix and match the lesson components based on what works best for the children in your group.

Question 21

What sort of Redeemer is needed to bring us back to God?

Answer

One who is truly human and also truly God.

Big Idea
A Redeemer who was fully God and fully human was needed to reconcile man to God.

Aim
To help the children understand that God planned to send a Redeemer who was both fully God and also fully man.

Bible Passage
Isaiah 9:1–7

Memory Verse
"For to us a child is born, to us a son is given; and the government shall be upon his shoulder, and his name shall be called Wonderful Counselor, Mighty God, Everlasting Father, Prince of Peace." (Isa. 9:6)

Virtue
Forgiveness

Leader's Notes

Children are growing up in a world that is diverse and at times confusing. There are a myriad of different religions in the world, and they all have different truth claims. It can be a daunting task for children to try to understand the difference between all the different religions. One of the most important things for children to comprehend is how different world religions understand the nature and status of Jesus. Christians believe that Jesus is fully God and fully man; he is both human and divine. No other faith tradition believes that God left the glory of heaven to be incarnated as the man Jesus. This lesson aims to help the children understand the uniqueness of Jesus the Redeemer and to help them understand that God planned and promised to send a Redeemer who was fully God and fully man to save his people.

Things to remember when planning and teaching:

- Some children will be familiar with the concept of the incarnation but may not have considered just how amazing it is. Help the children to reflect on the uniqueness of the Redeemer.

- The fact that Jesus is fully human and fully God is hard to understand. Reassure those children who find the idea of one person having two natures conceptually challenging.

- Remember to mix and match the activities in the lesson to fit your time frame (see p. 12 for some sample outlines). You won't have time to do them all. Feel free to adapt each activity based on your class's strengths and weaknesses.

Leader's Prayer

Redeeming God, I praise you for the wonder of the incarnation. Please continue to help me to understand the significance of both the humanity and divinity of Jesus. Grant understanding to the children who will hear this lesson. May they find great joy in understanding more about you. In Jesus's name. Amen.

Leader's Tool Kit

- A piece of cardboard or a tray
- Tape
- Twenty plastic cups
- Tissue paper
- Rubber bands
- Candy or small prizes
- Q21 Catechism Recap (DL)
- Q21 Illustrations of World Religions (RB)

- Q21 Human and Divine (RB), one copy for each child

- A copy of the Nicene Creed

- Duplo or Mega Bloks

- Sticky notes

- Paper

Notes

⏱10 Catechism Recap

Stick twenty plastic cups to a piece of cardboard or a tray. Print out and cut up Q21 Catechism Recap (DL). Put one slip in each cup. Once the slips of paper are inside the cups, cover them with tissue paper and secure with a rubber band.

Place the tray at the front of the classroom and explain to the children that they will have an opportunity to win some prizes! Tell the children that some of the cups contain catechism questions that they need to answer. Explain to them that they will get a prize if they answer the question correctly. Also explain that some of the cups do not contain questions—but they do contain prizes to be won. Invite the children up individually to punch a cup and win a prize. If a child doesn't know the answer to one of the catechism questions, invite someone else to answer in his or her place.

⏱5 Introduction to Question 21

You will need Q21 Illustrations of World Religions (RB).

Explain to the children that different world religions believe different things about Jesus. Very briefly describe what Islam, Judaism, Hinduism, and Buddhism believe about Jesus.

Islam
- Jesus was the son of Mary.
- Jesus was a prophet and wise man.
- ! Muslims do not believe that Jesus is God.

Judaism
- Jesus was the son of Mary.
- Jesus was a respected and popular teacher.

- Jesus was a miracle worker.
- Jesus had supernatural power.
- ! Jews do not believe that Jesus is God.

Hinduism
- Jesus was a holy man.
- Jesus was a wise teacher.
- Some Hindus believe that Jesus is a "god" among all the other gods they worship.
- ! Hindus do not believe that Jesus is God.

Buddhism
- Jesus was a holy man.
- Jesus was an enlightened man.

Notes

▪ Jesus was a wise teacher.

! Buddhists do not believe that Jesus is God.

Introduce the children to Question 21: "What sort of Redeemer is needed to bring us back to God?" Explain that a very special kind of Redeemer was required to reconcile humans to God. Highlight for the children that lots of world religions teach that Jesus was human, but they don't teach that Jesus is God. Explain to the children that the claim Christianity makes is that Jesus is both fully human and fully God, and that this kind of Redeemer is the only kind capable of restoring God's relationship with humanity. Acknowledge to the children that this is a difficult concept to understand because Jesus is unique, but that this lesson will help them to understand a little more.

⑩ Activity

You will need to prepare a sticky note for each child in the class. On each sticky note you will need to write the name of a character and what it is in essence. Below are some examples, but you may need to adapt them to your class's age and interests.

▪ Olaf (the snowman)

▪ Winnie the Pooh (the bear)

▪ Woody (the cowboy)

▪ Mr. Tumnus (the faun)

▪ E.T. (the extraterrestrial)

▪ Frodo (the Hobbit)

▪ Ariel (the mermaid)

▪ Chewbacca (the Wookiee)

▪ WALL-E (the robot)

▪ Charlotte (the spider)

▪ Abraham Lincoln (the human)

Explain to the children that, for this activity, everybody will have a sticky note stuck to their forehead. Tell them that each sticky note will have written on it the name of a famous character and also what the character is. Mention that they won't know what is written on their own sticky note. Explain that we call "what something is" its essence or its nature. It would be appropriate to provide an example for the children. Tell the children that they have to figure out who they are by asking other children questions. The questions may only be answered by saying yes or no. Once the children have correctly identified their characters, they can individually try to figure out what their essence is.

This activity should help to identify for the children the concept of what a being's essence is. This question will seek to help the children understand that in essence Jesus is both fully God and fully man.

⑮ Teaching Outline

Begin the teaching time by asking for God's help. Ask that the lesson would be taught faithfully and that the children might listen well.

To begin, ask the children what they are in their essence or nature. Confirm that they are human! Remind the children that Christians believe that Jesus is both fully human and fully divine; clarify that he's not part human or part divine, but that he is one person with two natures.

Acknowledge for the children that it is difficult for humans to understand the concept of Jesus being one person with two natures, because the only point of reference that humans have is our own experience, and we have just one essence or nature.

Explain to the children that the Christian church has always understood that Jesus is both fully God and fully man. Take a little time to look at the Nicene Creed with the children, and invite them to identify the parts that talk about Jesus's divinity (his God-ness) and his humanity.

Read Isaiah 9:1–7. Provide Bibles for the children to read along with you.

Remind the children that Isaiah was written hundreds of years before Jesus was born. Explain that the book was written at a dark and difficult time in the history of God's people. They were rebelling against God. Throughout the book God warns them that

they will face judgment and punishment, but he also promises that he will not abandon his people.

Tell the children that the beginning of chapter 9 is striking because it speaks of a future time that contrasts with the dark and difficult times God's people were experiencing. Isaiah promises times filled with light, joy, and hope.

Explain to the children that those times would be brought about by the arrival of God's promised Savior and Redeemer.

Direct the children's attention to verse 6. Explain that this verse particularly reveals the type of Redeemer who would be sent to save God's people from judgment and punishment.

The beginning of verse 6 identifies that the Redeemer would be human. He would be born into the world as a baby. He would take on human flesh. Isaiah describes him as God's unique gift to the world by using the phrase "a son is given."

Explain to the children that the second part of the verses uses phrases to describe the Redeemer as God. Ask the children to identify the four different titles that are given in this verse to the Redeemer.

The titles used to describe the Redeemer are Wonderful Counselor, Mighty God, Everlasting Father, and Prince of Peace. Tell the children that these titles are all titles used

Notes

in other places in the book of Isaiah, and when they are used they all refer exclusively to God. God is described as wonderful in 25:1 and 28:29. God is described as mighty in 10:21. God is described as everlasting in 40:28. And God is the one who brings peace in 26:3 and 12.

Ask the children if they have figured out what this verse is highlighting about the promised Redeemer.

Help the children to see that the verse is clearly stating that the Redeemer will be both man and God. Remind them that Jesus was fully human and fully God. Explain to the children that everything about a human person and everything about God are found fully in Jesus.

Explain to the children that many people agree that Jesus was fully human; draw their attention back to the various things that world religions believe about Jesus. Tell them that people have a more difficult time believing that Jesus was fully God. Highlight for the children that Isaiah prophesied about the coming Redeemer who would be both man and God.

Conclude the teaching time by helping the children commit Question 21 and the answer to memory.

(These notes are just for guidance. Please expand or amend them to suit your own children and context. Write out your talk in your own words and include illustrations and applications that you know will connect with your children.)

 Activity

You will need a copy of Q21 Human and Divine (RB) for each child. Provide the children with Bibles.

Assign each verse reference to a child. Have the children take turns reading the passages aloud to identify whether they're describing Jesus's divinity or humanity. Invite them to put a *D*, *H*, or *DH* beside each reference.

John 1:14	Titus 2:13
1 Timothy 2:5	Matthew 28:18
John 11:35	John 1:1
Galatians 4:4	Luke 11:17
Hebrews 4:15	Luke 2:7
John 4:6	Matthew 4:2

(5) Discussion and Question Time

Some questions that might arise include:

? How can Jesus be fully human and fully God?

Acknowledge once again that it is a difficult concept for the human brain to understand, but that both the Bible and Christians throughout history agree that Jesus was fully God and fully man.

? Why is Jesus described as God the Son?

Remind the children that Question 3 of the catechism taught them that there are three persons in one God, and that they are each God. Explain to the children that it is God the Son who leaves heaven and becomes incarnate, that he becomes fully man.

Also use this opportunity to help the children to think about their own lives and how this question and answer affects them personally.

- Ask the children if there was anything surprising about today's lesson.

- Ask the children if, in the past, they have thought of Jesus as fully God and fully man.

- Ask the children how they might explain that Jesus is one person with two natures to a person from the Muslim, Jewish, Hindu, or Buddhist faith.

(10) Virtue Vision

Forgiveness

The children have learned in this lesson just how unique Jesus the Redeemer is because he is truly God and truly man. Explain that you are going to spend a few moments talking about why Jesus being fully God and fully man is necessary for our forgiveness.

Tell the children to imagine that Johnny (you may substitute the name of a member of your class) walked up to you and slapped you in the face. While you were still in shock, Susie (substitute with the name of another member of your class) walked up to Johnny and said, "I forgive you." How would that make you feel? Can Susie forgive Johnny for his sin against you? Agree with the children that it is the person who has been sinned against that has the ability to extend forgiveness.

We have all sinned against God because we've broken his holy law. We can't forgive each other for this, only God can. Because Jesus was truly God, he was able to bring forgiveness down to us. We have sinned against him, but he has chosen to forgive us and make us his own!

Ask the children how knowing that God forgives our sins against him will affect them when someone else sins against them. Should it make them more eager to forgive?

(10) **Memory Activity**

Each week, the memory activity can be used to memorize the memory verse, or, if your class is not learning the memory verse, it can be used to reinforce the catechism question and answer.

You will need blocks, such as Duplo or Mega Bloks. Print out the memory verse, cut up the words individually, and stick a word to each block. If you are using the memory verse, you will need thirty-six blocks. If you're doing the catechism question and answer, you will need twenty-one blocks.

Give the children the pile of blocks and invite them to build them into a memory tower. The children will need to put the bricks into the right order and then construct the tower.

Once the tower has been constructed, read through the memory verse or catechism question and answer with the children several times. You can remove blocks to make the task harder.

(5) **Closing Prayer Time**

Pray for the children that, to the extent that their minds will allow, they might grasp that the Redeemer is fully God and fully man. Pray that all who worship false religions will recognize that Jesus is the Son of God.

Question 22

Why must the Redeemer be truly human?

Answer

That in human nature he might on our behalf perfectly obey the whole law and suffer the punishment for human sin.

Big Idea
The substitute sacrificed for our redemption had to be human.

Aim
To help the children recognize that only a fully human Redeemer could fully satisfy God's just demands.

Bible Passage
Hebrews 2:5–18

Memory Verse
"Therefore he had to be made like his brothers in every respect, so that he might become a merciful and faithful high priest in the service of God, to make propitiation for the sins of the people." (Heb. 2:17)

Virtue
Love

Notes

Leader's Notes

Children generally have little problem understanding the humanity of Jesus. They may be comfortable with the fact that Jesus is a historical figure and that he once lived on the earth. But they may still struggle with the concept of Jesus being fully human and fully God. This catechism question, in connection with Question 23, will further enable the children to explore the fact that Jesus is one person with two natures. This lesson will specifically focus on why it was essential for the Redeemer to be fully human, aiming to provide the children with a robust understanding of why Jesus came to earth and took on human nature.

Things to remember when planning and teaching:

- The children will still be trying to comprehend the fact that Jesus is one person with two natures.

- Be careful to maintain some reverence when speaking about Jesus's humanity.

- Remember to mix and match the activities in the lesson to fit your time frame (see p. 12 for some sample outlines). You won't have time to do them all. Feel free to adapt each activity based on your class's strengths and weaknesses.

Leader's Prayer

Father God, thank you for sending your Son to live as a perfect man so that I might be redeemed from sin and death. I praise you for your great love. Grant understanding to the children who will hear this lesson. May they be deeply moved by the great love shown by the Lord Jesus and amazed at your plan of redemption. In Jesus's name. Amen.

Leader's Tool Kit

- Q22 Catechism Recap (DL)

- Clear tape

- Jenga blocks

- Sticky notes

- Markers

- Q22 Body Bingo Grid (RB), one copy for each child

- A picture of Maximilian Kolbe

- Large sheets of paper

⑩ Catechism Recap

Print out and cut up Q22 Catechism Recap (DL). Tape the questions to Jenga blocks and build the Jenga tower. (Not every block needs a question.)

Divide the children into teams. Invite individual children from each team to take turns approaching the Jenga tower and attempt to remove a block (don't continue to build the tower, just place the blocks to the side once they have been removed from the tower). If the block a child removes has a question on it, the child can either answer the question or pass the question back to his or her team. If the team fails to correctly answer the question, another team can jump in and answer it. If they answer it correctly, they get to keep the block. The team with the most blocks whenever the tower falls wins.

⑤ Introduction to Question 22

Ask the children how they came into the world.

- They were born.

Ask the children how they grew from a little baby into a child.

- They were cared for by parents or guardians who fed them and nurtured them.

Ask the children what they do when they're really sad.

- They cry.

Ask the children what they feel when they haven't had any food for a while.

- They feel hungry.

Ask the children how they anticipate their lives ending.

- They will die.

Explain to the children that these are all experiences that are common to human beings. Remind the children that Jesus was fully human as well as fully God. Jesus was born and had parents who nurtured and fed him. Jesus cried when he was sad and felt hungry when he hadn't eaten for a while. Jesus's earthly life ended when he died. Introduce the children to Question 22: "Why must the Redeemer be truly human?" Tell the children that there was a reason that Jesus the Redeemer had to be fully human in order to bring other humans back into relationship with God. Explain that this catechism question will help them to understand why.

Notes

23

(10) Activity

Print out a Q22 Body Bingo Grid (RB) for each child and give everyone a marker.

Ask each child to fill out his or her grid with sixteen body parts in the sixteen squares on the grid. Encourage them not to look at each other's grid. For this game to work, each grid needs to have different parts in different squares.

Read out the body part list below, one at a time. Tell the children that when they hear a body part they have on their bingo sheet, they should cross it off. The first child to get four in a row wins. If a child thinks he has won, tell him to shout, "Body Bingo!"

Foot	*Brain*	*Tongue*	*Skull*	*Ankle*	*Veins*
Hand	*Lung*	*Hair*	*Teeth*	*Nose*	*Wrist*
Ear	*Bone*	*Skin*	*Fingernail*	*Heel*	*Stomach*
Heart	*Nose*	*Knee*	*Belly button*	*Head*	*Shoulder*
Eye	*Elbow*	*Lip*	*Eyebrow*	*Thumb*	*Neck*

Conclude this activity by remarking on the beauty and diversity of the human body. Remind the children that this lesson is about the Redeemer's humanity; explain that Jesus, in his human body, had all the body parts identified just the same as they do.

(15) Teaching Outline

Begin the teaching time by asking for God's help. Ask that the lesson would be taught faithfully and that the children might listen well.

Mention to the children that there is one big difference between Jesus and every other member of the human race that has lived, is living, or will live. Ask the children if they can identify what the big difference is.

The difference, of course, is that Jesus is the only person who has lived a sinless life. Jesus was the perfect human. Explain to the children that this is a crucial thing to understand as they consider why the Redeemer must be truly human.

Read Hebrews 2:5–18. Provide Bibles for the children to read along with you.

Explain to the children that these fourteen verses in the book of Hebrews describe clearly why Jesus had to become fully human.

To help the children understand the significance of Jesus's humanity, bring them back to Genesis and ask them to identify who the first man was. Then ask the children:

- Who has every person on earth descended from?

- Who introduced sin into the human race?

The answer to both questions is Adam. Remind the children that Adam was originally created with the ability to perfectly keep God's law, but he rebelled against God, and so sin and death entered the world.

Tell the children that Jesus, the Redeemer, is sometimes called the second Adam. Briefly compare Adam and Jesus for the children:

1. Adam was created sinless; Jesus is sinless.

2. Adam gave life to all people; Jesus gives eternal life to those he redeems.

3. Adam was given the authority to rule over creation; Jesus is Lord over all.

4. Adam brought spiritual and physical death into the world; Jesus brings eternal life to those who repent of their sins and follow him.

In order for Jesus to be the Redeemer, the second Adam, it was crucial that he was fully human. Ask the children to look back to Hebrews 2:5–18 and see if they can identify from the passage any reasons why Jesus's humanity was so important.

Explain to the children that the writer of Hebrews begins in verses 5–9 by describing how things were meant to be! Humans were made to rule over everything, but because of sin, that had not happened. The earth had not been filled and subdued as God intended. It was messy and out of control. Jesus had to enter this messy world as a man. He left the splendor of heaven to come to earth as man who was intimately involved in the mess that humans had created.

Explain to the children that verse 10 describes how Jesus, the man, became humanity's ultimate champion and deliverer. Tell the children that, in the ancient world, it was quite normal for one man to be chosen to go out and fight another man, each man representing his respective army. The examples of David and Goliath could be used to illustrate this or the fight between the Greek Achilles and the Roman Hector as recorded in Homer's *Iliad*. Tell the children that the way Jesus is described in Hebrews 2 is as the one who has been sent on behalf of humans to fight and overcome sin, the resulting death, and the Devil. Jesus fights to redeem those who have been trapped and enslaved by sin and who face the devastation of death.

Notes

Explain to the children that when Jesus became fully human, with flesh and blood, he became just like those he would count as brothers and sisters after he redeemed them. Ask them if they can identify where it says this in the passage.

Tell the children that Jesus's humanity allowed him to fully understand what life is like in every way. Hebrews especially mentions the struggle of temptation; Jesus was tempted in every way, and yet he was without sin. Explain to the children that Jesus understands what it's like to be tempted to disobey God and tempted to love things other than God. Ask the children if it is helpful and encouraging to know that Jesus understands everything about human life because he lived a life on earth as a human, and still lives as a (glorified) human now.

Explain to the children that God told his people that the penalty for sin is death, but he established a pattern of sacrifice in the Old Testament that allowed people to temporarily atone for their sins. An animal had to be sacrificed and blood had to be shed in order to receive forgiveness. However, an animal sacrifice was not enough; the Bible says that human blood is required to pay the permanent penalty for sin. If there is going to be a substitute, it needs to be sufficiently qualified. Only a human can die in the place of other humans and truly satisfy the penalty. If the Redeemer was not fully human, then he would not have been able to fulfill God's requirements. He is the ultimate mediator between God and humans because he can represent all those who believe and repent. Through his sacrifice, humans find forgiveness for their sins and have a relationship with God. Explain to the children that Jesus in his perfect humanity was able to turn God's anger away from sinful people by taking the full force of the anger and punishment on his own body.

Conclude the teaching time by helping the children commit Question 22 and the answer to memory.

(These notes are just for guidance. Please expand or amend them to suit your own children and context. Write out your talk in your own words and include illustrations and applications that you know will connect with your children.)

Activity

You will need some large sheets of paper and some markers. Write the words below (which are all related to Jesus's earthly life) on slips of paper.

Sleep	Cry	Tired	Walk	Eat	Sad
Baby	Mother	Death	Man	Drink	Love

Divide the children into small teams and give each team some paper and markers.

Explain to the children that each team must send a volunteer to the front of the room to look at a word. The volunteer must then return to his or her team and try to help the team guess the word by drawing pictures. No spoken words or sounds may be used! Once teams have correctly guessed the word, another volunteer should race to the front to read another word and return to draw it for his or her team. The team that is first to guess all their words wins.

Discussion and Question Time

Some questions that might arise include:

? If Jesus was fully human, doesn't that mean that he was a sinner?

Remind the children that God created Adam and Eve without sin. That was what it was to be truly human. They chose to sin, and every human born since has been a sinner. Jesus did not have an earthly father; he had a heavenly Father. This meant he didn't inherit Adam's sinful nature.

? Did Jesus become less God when he lived on earth?

Explain to the children that Jesus did not become less God, but that he did choose to lay aside his heavenly glory when he came to earth, and that he submitted himself fully to the will of God the Father.

Also use this opportunity to help the children think about their own lives and how this question and answer affects them personally.

- Ask the children what it means to know that Jesus fully understands what it is to be human.

- Ask the children if they are struck by Jesus's humility and love, knowing that he willingly left heaven to redeem them.

- Ask the children to sum up why Jesus needed to be fully human.

Virtue Vision

Love

You will need a picture of Maximilian Kolbe.

Tell the children the story of Maximilian Kolbe, a monk who was arrested in Poland in February 1941 and was eventually sent to Auschwitz, a Nazi concentration camp. While he was at the concentration camp, a prisoner escaped, and in retaliation the guards chose ten men to punish by starvation and death. One of the chosen men, Franciszek Gajowniczek (pronounced

Notes

Fran-sis-ek Ga-jown-izek), was deeply distressed at the thought of dying and leaving his family. Maximilian Kolbe offered to take Franciszek's place. After weeks of starvation, Maximilian was eventually murdered instead of Franciszek. He had taken another man's place and had willingly suffered death to save his friend's life. Maximilian Kolbe was motivated by the great humility and love that he saw in Jesus, who left the glory of heaven to come to earth and die so that he might save people from their sins. Maximilian showed the same humility and love when he died for his friend.

Ask the children what feelings they have in response to this story. What feelings might Franciszek have had? (Remind them that he was the man who was spared so that he could remain with his family.) Ask the children what motivated Maximilian, Franciszek's lifesaver.

Also ask: "How is love humble?" and "How might the humility and love of Jesus affect how you live your life and how you love others?"

⑩ Memory Activity

Have the children write out the memory verse or catechism answer on the sticky notes, one word per note. Stick the notes up on the wall, out of order. Task the children with putting the words in order on the wall.

Read the memory verse or catechism answer through with the children several times and then begin to remove some of the sticky notes.

⑤ Closing Prayer Time

Invite the children to praise God for his plan of salvation and praise Jesus for his willingness to come to earth as the Redeemer. They can thank him that he was willing to be sleepy, hungry, and cold, as well as all the other things humans endure, to be their Redeemer.

Question 23

Why must the Redeemer be truly God?

Answer

That because of his divine nature his obedience and suffering would be perfect and effective.

Big Idea
Only God himself is capable of redeeming humanity.

Aim
To help the children understand that only a Redeemer who is fully God could save them.

Bible Passage
Acts 2:22–41

Memory Verse
"God raised him up, loosing the pangs of death, because it was not possible for him to be held by it." (Acts 2:24)

Virtue
Humility

Leader's Notes

Children will understand that Jesus was fully human a little easier than the truth that Jesus was fully God. This lesson will once again focus on the fact that Jesus was one person with two natures. The aim is to help the children further understand that Jesus is fully God and why it was necessary for the Redeemer to be fully God. Given the pluralistic air that surrounds children in everyday life, it will be useful to once again point out that this is where Christianity differs from every other religion that recognizes Jesus. Only Christians believe that Jesus was fully God. This lesson should give children confidence in understanding the divinity of Jesus and the significance of the incarnation for them individually.

Things to remember when planning and teaching:

- This is a hard concept for some children to understand. Reassure them that this lesson should further their understanding.

- Be careful not to be overly critical of other religions, but rather point out the differences clearly.

- Remember to mix and match the activities in the lesson to fit your time frame (see p. 12 for some sample outlines). You won't have time to do them all. Feel free to adapt each activity based on your class's strengths and weaknesses.

Leader's Prayer

Almighty God, thank you that in your great mercy you graciously brought me into a saving relationship with yourself. Thank you, Lord Jesus, for humbling yourself, leaving the glory of heaven to come to earth. Thank you that through your substitutionary death I can know life. Grant understanding to the children who will listen to this lesson. May they fully grasp that Jesus is one person with two natures, and may they be awed by the fact that you came to earth in all your fullness to redeem them. In Jesus's name. Amen.

Leader's Tool Kit

- Q23 Catechism Recap Wheel (RB) printed on cardstock

- Brass paper fastener/brad

- Scissors

- Paper

- Christmas wrapping paper

(10) Catechism Recap

Print onto cardstock the Q23 Catechism Recap Wheel (RB) disc and spinning arm. Cut them out and attach the arrow to the disc with the fastener loosely enough that it can spin. Write the numbers one through twenty-two on slips of paper, and put them in a bowl.

Invite the children to take turns drawing a catechism question or number out of the bowl. After they have their number, let them spin the arrow to see what their assignment is. If they don't know the answer, their classmates can help them. Give as many children a chance to take a turn as your time will allow.

(5) Introduction to Question 23

Briefly tell the children the story of The Prince and the Pauper, in which a prince trades lives with a poor boy who happens to look like him. On the subject of royalty, ask the children if they have seen *Aladdin*, and if they remember when Jasmine ran away from her father's palace.

Ask the children if they lived in the most beautiful place in the world, with perfect relationships and with everything that they could possibly need, would they ever consider leaving their homes? It is unlikely that they would want to leave!

Ask the children if they've ever heard of anyone who left such a beautiful and perfect place to live among their subjects. God left the splendor of heaven to live among his creation when he became man. Introduce the children to Question 23: "Why must the Redeemer be truly God?" Explain to the children that this question will help them to consider more carefully why the one who came to redeem had to be fully God.

(10) Activity ☼

Print or write out the four verses below, which speak of Jesus's divinity. Wrap each verse up as if it were a Christmas present.

John 1:1: "In the beginning was the Word, and the Word was with God, and the Word was God."

John 1:14: "And the Word became flesh and dwelt among us, and we have seen his glory, glory as of the only Son from the Father, full of grace and truth."

John 20:28: "Thomas answered him, 'My Lord and my God!'"

Colossians 2:9: "For in him the whole fullness of deity dwells bodily."

Ask the children what we celebrate at Christmas in the Christian church. It's the

Notes

birth of the baby Jesus! Remind the children that Question 22 helped them to think about the humanity of Jesus, and tell them that this question will help them to learn more about the deity of Jesus—the fact that Jesus was fully God. Help the children consider that when Jesus was born, he was fully human and fully God, one person with two natures.

Ask the children to pick a number between one and twenty. Choose the four students who pick numbers closest to the number five. Give each a package to unwrap, then ask them to read the verse inside. Ask the children what the verses teach about Jesus (you may need to add a little context). The verses clearly indicate that Jesus was God the Son and that he existed eternally before he came to live on earth as a man.

Teaching Outline

Begin the teaching time by asking for God's help. Ask that the lesson would be taught faithfully, and that the children might listen well.

Remind the children that Jesus is one person with two natures. Jesus is fully God and fully human. Acknowledge once again that this is a hard concept to understand because it is unique. Remind the children that this is an area where Christianity differs greatly from other religions. Tell the children that the Jehovah's Witnesses, for example, do not believe that Jesus is God.

Read Acts 2:22–41. Provide Bibles for the children to read along with you.

Tell the children that these verses are part of a speech that Jesus's disciple Peter gave at a time called Pentecost. Pentecost was when God sent the Holy Spirit to his church. Explain to the children that this speech was given to thousands of people in Jerusalem after Jesus's death and resurrection.

Tell the children that Peter clearly proclaims to the listening crowds that Jesus is God. Peter delivers a speech that essentially reminds the people who Jesus was and why he came:

- He was a man whom God the Father used greatly in many ways. Through all the signs and miracles Jesus performed, God the Father was confirming that Jesus was God the Son.

- He was a man destined to die on the cross because God the Father had determined that God the Son would be the Redeemer.

- He died but was raised again because death could not hold God the Son.

- He is now back in heaven at the right hand of God the Father.

Tell the children that Peter had no doubt that Jesus is fully God, and that Peter urged the listening crowd to seek redemption from Jesus.

Explain to the children that Jesus needed to be fully God to redeem humans because:

- Only the Creator God who gave life can recreate and give new life.

- Only God himself can bear the punishment for the sins of all those who trust in him. Jesus's humanity meant that he could be a qualified substitute; Jesus's divinity meant that he was an infinitely valuable substitute.

- If Jesus was not God, he would not have had the authority to pronounce their sins forgiven.

Ask the children to imagine how they'd feel in the following scenario: They stole a toy from a friend, and they were caught.

When they apologized to their friend and asked for forgiveness from the friend, the friend's brother said, "Yes, he forgives you." Explain to them that forgiveness needs to come from the one who has been wronged. Jesus is not a third party. He is God who has been sinned against, and only he has the right to redeem.

Conclude the teaching time by helping the children commit Question 23 and the answer to memory.

(These notes are just for guidance. Please expand or amend them to suit your own children and context. Write out your talk in your own words and include illustrations and applications that you know will connect with your children.)

Notes

---

⑩ Activity

For this activity, you will need a recording of the Christmas carol "Hark, the Herald Angels Sing!"

Tell the children that you are going to pretend it's Christmas for a few minutes. Ask them to sit down. Tell them that you are going to play a Christmas carol, and you want them to stand up every time they hear a line in the song that refers to Jesus as God. They should sit immediately back down so that they will be ready for the next line.

Highlighted below are the lyrics that most clearly refer to Jesus as divine, though the children may hear it in other lines.

Hark! the herald angels sing,
"Glory to the newborn King;
peace on earth and mercy mild,
God and sinners reconciled!"
Joyful, all ye nations, rise;
join the triumph of the skies;
with the angelic hosts proclaim,
"Christ is born in Bethlehem!"
Hark! the herald angels sing,
"Glory to the newborn King!"

Christ, by highest heaven adored,
Christ, the everlasting Lord!
Late in time behold him come,
offspring of the virgin's womb.
Veiled in flesh the Godhead see;

Notes

hail the incarnate Deity,
pleased as man with men to dwell,
Jesus, our Immanuel.
Hark! the herald angels sing,
"Glory to the newborn King!"

Hail the heaven-born Prince of Peace!
Hail the Sun of Righteousness!

Light and life to all he brings,
risen with healing in his wings.
Mild, he lays his glory by,
born that man no more may die,
born to raise the sons of earth,
born to give us second birth.
Hark! the herald angels sing,
"Glory to the newborn King!"

---

⑤ Discussion and Question Time

Some questions that might arise include:

? Why did Jesus not save himself if he was God?

> Remind the children that Jesus, God the Son, was perfectly obedient to God the Father. He was fully God, but chose to do his Father's will.

? Why didn't God redeem people another way?

> Tell the children that this was the only way possible for humans to be freed from sin and brought into a relationship with God.

Also use this opportunity to help the children to think about their own lives and how this question and answer affects them personally.

- How does understanding that Jesus is fully God affect their desire to worship him?

- How might they explain that Jesus is one person with two natures to someone who has never heard about Jesus before?

---

⑩ Virtue Vision

Humility

Ask the children what the opposite of being humble is. Tell them that the opposite of humility is pride.

Ask the children if they can recall a time when they acted proud. Ask if they feel tempted to boast or brag about their greatness when they do something well.

Ask the children if they believe there is a difference between confidence and pride.

Jesus had every reason to act proud—he is God himself! But instead, he humbled himself to become a little human baby in order to save us. Ask the children what it would look like for them to be humble instead of proud.

Memory Activity

On individual pieces of paper write the following instructions:

Croak like a frog.

Squeak like a mouse.

Speak with an accent.

Whisper like the wind.

Divide the children into four small groups and give each group a piece of paper with one of the instructions on it. Tell the children that their challenge is to say the memory verse or catechism answer in the way that their instructions require. After the children have each said the memory verse in one style get them to swap instructions and say it in another style.

Closing Prayer Time

Encourage the children to praise and thank Jesus for his willingness to leave heaven and his humility in coming to earth to redeem humans in desperate need of him.

Question 24

Why was it necessary for Christ, the Redeemer, to die?

Answer

Christ died willingly in our place to deliver us from the power and penalty of sin and bring us back to God.

Big Idea

There is no possible way for people to be reconciled to God except through the atoning death of Jesus.

Aim

To help the children understand that the only way to be reconciled to God is through the substitutionary death of Jesus.

Bible Passage

Colossians 1:15–23

Memory Verse

"And you, who once were alienated and hostile in mind, doing evil deeds, he has now reconciled in his body of flesh by his death, in order to present you holy and blameless and above reproach before him." (Col. 1:21–22)

Virtue

Love

Notes

Leader's Notes

Children don't like the idea of punishment generally, but the concept of someone being wrongly punished for something he didn't do will be deeply offensive! Children have a keen sense of what is fair, and they will question why Jesus had to suffer and die for sins that he didn't commit. This lesson will help the children to comprehend why the sinless Jesus had to be punished for their sins, and why this was the only way God could redeem a people for himself. By highlighting for the children that God was pleased to have his fullness dwell in Jesus and that Jesus himself knew the purpose of his life and death, this lesson should further equip the children to understand substitutionary atonement.

Things to remember when planning and teaching:

- Be careful to communicate to the children that great caution should be taken when questioning God's plans and purposes! The Bible says that God's ways are higher than our ways and warns that we should not lean on our own understanding, or else we might arrive at incorrect assumptions.

- It is important for the children to understand the cost and consequences of sin and rebellion.

- Highlight for the children that they will, on occasion, hear people declare that there are many ways to God. Explain to them that this is not what the Bible teaches. All people need to understand who Jesus is and why he came to earth.

- Remember to mix and match the activities in the lesson to fit your time frame (see p. 12 for some sample outlines). You won't have time to do them all. Feel free to adapt each activity based on your class's strengths and weaknesses.

Leader's Prayer

Redeeming God, thank you that in your great mercy you suffered to bring men and women and boys and girls into relationship with you. Help me to recognize the significance and the cost of the atonement. Grant understanding to the children who will hear this lesson, and cause them to be filled with love for you as they understand the necessity of Christ's death. In Jesus's name. Amen.

Leader's Tool Kit

- Q24 Catechism Recap (DL)
- Sticky Tack
- Scissors
- Q24 One-Way Maze (RB), one for each child
- Markers

- A video clip from *Chitty Chitty Bang Bang* and a way to show it
- Drinking straws
- The memory verse printed out twice and cut up into individual words
- Q24 Love Letter Template (RB), one for each child
- Glue sticks
- Old magazines
- Paper

Notes

(10) Catechism Recap

Print out Q24 Catechism Recap (DL). Cut each question into three parts. Stick the questions up around the classroom with Sticky Tack, but in a jumbled-up way. For instance, put the wrong question with the right number and answer. You could prepare two sets and make this a competition.

The room should be prepared with the various jumbled-up questions stuck up on the wall. Tell the children that the questions are on the wall, but that the number, question, and answer combinations are not correct! Invite the children to move around the room and work together to recall the questions and answers. Tell the children that they can move pieces of the questions to form the correct number, question, and answer combinations. Be sure to keep a master copy of the catechism questions to easily determine if the children have completed their task correctly. Read some of the questions and answers with the children to check that they have been accurately corrected.

(5) Introduction to Question 24

You will need the DVD of Chitty Chitty Bang Bang *set up to play or an online streaming version.*

Play the short clip from *Chitty Chitty Bang Bang* that shows all the children who have been captured by the Child Catcher held in the dungeon. (The scene starts at 2:13:08.)

Explain to the children that the children in the movie need to be freed, but they are not able to do it themselves. Tell the children that the characters need someone to save them, to release them from captivity and to allow them to enjoy freedom. They need a way out. Introduce the children to Question 24: "Why was it necessary for Christ, the Redeemer, to die?" Explain that the children in *Chitty Chitty Bang Bang* would find freedom only through someone releasing them, and that the same is true for those who are held captive by sin and death. Freedom for those who are enslaved by sin and death can be gained only by someone paying a great price for their release. Remind the children that there was only one person who could pay that price, and tell them that this question will help them to understand why Jesus Christ had to die, and that there was no other way sin could be dealt with.

⑩ Activity

Print out the Q24 One-Way Maze (RB), one for each child.

Give each child a pen and a copy of the maze, which only has one way through. Give the children a set amount of time to see if they can work out the way through the maze.

Once the time has finished, tell the children that there was only one way through the maze. Explain that there is only one way to be redeemed and only one way to return to a relationship with God, and that is through Jesus Christ. Acknowledge that people at times question why Jesus had to die, and tell them that this lesson should help them understand more fully why Jesus's life and death provided the only way for us to be made right before God.

Read John 14:6 for the children: "Jesus said to him, 'I am the way, and the truth, and the life. No one comes to the Father except through me.'"

⑮ Teaching Outline

Begin the teaching time by asking for God's help. Ask that the lesson would be taught faithfully and that the children might listen well.

Begin this time by asking the children if they think God had to redeem anyone. Explain to the children that God was not obliged to rescue anyone from sin and death, but that he chose to do so out of love. Remind the children that God does not need humans, but humans need God! God chooses to redeem people because he is loving, kind, and gracious.

Ask the children how this knowledge— that God was not obliged to rescue us— affects their view of God.

Explain to the children that once God determined that he would provide a path to redeem people, the only way he could do that was by sending Jesus to die on the cross.

Read Colossians 1:15–23. Provide Bibles for the children to read along with you.

Explain to the children that Paul is writing to Christians in Colossae, and he wants to help them to understand the supremacy of Jesus Christ.

In verse 19, Paul reminds the Colossians that Jesus is fully God. Paul also declares that through Jesus all things would be reconciled to God. Show the children that Paul says in this verse that God was pleased to be at work in this way. God was pleased that Jesus would be the one Mediator and Redeemer between heaven and earth. The redemption offered by Jesus was the only way out; there was no other way for humans to become friends again with God.

Paul declares in verse 20 that Jesus achieved peace between humans and God through shedding his blood on the cross. Explain to the children that Paul acknowledges clearly that it was necessary for Jesus to die on the cross; this was how God decided he would restore the relationship between himself and humanity. Tell the children that Paul explains to the Colossians that they once were enemies of God who had broken his laws and had done things that displease God—all of which deserve God's judgment and punishment. But Paul says that those who are Christians—those who trust in Jesus Christ for redemption—need not fear God's judgment. They should not fear God's punishment either because when Jesus died on the cross, he freed people from sin and death. How? Tell the children that he stood in the place of sinful man and took judgment we deserved. He suffered their punishment in their place by dying on the cross. Jesus paid the price to redeem sinners so that they could know life in relationship with God.

Tell the children that Jesus said, "For even the Son of Man came not to be served but to serve, and to give his life as a ransom for many" in Mark 10:45. Explain to the children that there is a cost for rejecting God, for rejecting his rule, and for living without regard for him. The cross demonstrates the cost clearly. Sin is serious, and God had to take sin seriously in order to deal with it.

Acknowledge to the children that it does seem unfair when someone has to take the punishment for something that he or she hasn't done. Ask the children if they've ever experienced this, either at school or with their siblings.

Explain to the children that it was Jesus's decision to take the punishment for the sins of others, even though he had never sinned. (You might remind them of the story of Maximilian Kolbe from lesson 21.) God demanded a perfect sin-offering to be sacrificed in order for the punishment to be satisfied. Jesus was the only one who fit the bill. Only the blood of Christ would really be able to redeem people.

Conclude the teaching time by helping the children commit Question 24 and the answer to memory.

(These notes are just for guidance. Please expand or amend them to suit your own children and context. Write out your talk in your own words and include illustrations and applications that you know will connect with your children.)

Activity

You will need some old magazines, sheets of paper, scissors, and glue.

Invite the children to make word collages by cutting out letters from the magazines and sticking them on the paper to make words. Tell the children that the words should sum up their heart's response to God as they consider his amazing love in redeeming his people.

⑤ Discussion and Question Time

Some questions that might arise include:

? If God didn't have to redeem anyone, why did he choose to?

Explain to the children that God longs to be in relationship with his creation. He wants us to know and enjoy his goodness, so he brought us back into friendship with himself.

? Did Jesus die to reconcile and redeem everyone?

Tell the children that Jesus's death redeems only those who turn to him in repentance and faith. Jesus's death does not redeem those who reject him.

Also use this opportunity to help the children to think about their own lives and how this question and answer affects them personally.

- Ask the children if it is clear to them why Jesus's death was necessary.

- Ask them if considering the magnitude of what Jesus did on their behalf increases their love for him.

- Ask them how they might pray for and speak to those who don't understand the necessity of Christ's death.

⑩ Virtue Vision

Love

Print out a Q24 Love Letter Template (RB) for each child and give everyone a pen.

Invite the children to respond to God's great love as displayed in Jesus by writing a love letter to him. They may be able to use some of the words from their collage.

Invite the children to consider how understanding God's love for them affects how they might love others. Remind the children that God's love was costly and sacrificial. Ask them how they might love others sacrificially.

If time allows, ask the children to turn to a neighbor and brainstorm opportunities to love others sacrificially. Have them write down a goal to challenge themselves to love others well in the coming week. Encourage them to be as specific as possible and show enthusiasm about their good ideas.

Memory Activity

You will need drinking straws and two sets of the memory verse or catechism answer cut up into individual words. Cut the verse up into individual words. (Before you assign this challenge, ensure that the size of the words and weight of the paper makes this task possible.)

Divide children into two teams. Place one set of words on a table at the opposite end of the classroom for each team. Explain to the children that they will run a relay race. They must run up to the table and suck one of the words onto the end of their straw and bring it back to their team. As each child returns, the next should run out. The first team to assemble the verse wins. The verse could be read before the relay to provide the children with a little help. Read it through several times after the relay for reinforcement.

Closing Prayer Time

Pray that the children might remember how great is God's love for them and that they would want others to experience the same love by knowing their Redeemer.

Question 25

Does Christ's death mean all our sins can be forgiven?

Answer

Yes, because Christ's death on the cross fully paid the penalty for our sin, God will remember our sins no more.

Big Idea
At the cross, Jesus achieved all that was necessary for the complete forgiveness of sins for those who turn to him in repentance and faith.

Aim
To help the children have confidence and joy in the imputed righteousness of Christ.

Bible Passage
2 Corinthians 5:16–21

Memory Verse
"For our sake he made him to be sin who knew no sin, so that in him we might become the righteousness of God." (2 Cor. 5:21)

Virtue
Joy

Leader's Notes

The greatest transaction the world will ever know occurred on the first Good Friday at the cross of Christ. God in his mercy and kindness chose to place the sins of everyone who repents onto the Lord Jesus who willingly bore the punishment for each of those sins in his own body. Jesus imputed his righteousness to everyone who repents. A swap occurred! Jesus took the sin and gave the righteousness. This lesson will help the children understand exactly what Jesus achieved through his death on the cross. This lesson aims to give them great confidence in the redeeming work of Christ and to help them know that deep and lasting joy comes from being reconciled to God through Christ.

Things to remember when planning and teaching:

- Some of the children will already understand the concept of imputed righteousness. Seek to engage these children by emphasizing the awesomeness of the great swap and the personal implications for everyone who repents and believes.

- For other children the concept of imputed righteousness will be hard to understand because it is outside their experience. Try to explain and illustrate the lesson in a clear and concise way.

- Engage the hearts of the children by emphasizing what imputed righteousness means for each of them individually.

- Remember to mix and match the activities in the lesson to fit your time frame (see p. 12 for some sample outlines). You won't have time to do them all. Feel free to adapt each activity based on your class's strengths and weaknesses.

Leader's Prayer

Righteous God, thank you that because of Jesus I can know the righteousness of Christ and be confident of my standing before you. Help me to know deep joy and have great confidence in the gospel each and every day. Grant understanding to the children who will hear this lesson; may they understand the great exchange that occurred at the cross for all those who trust in Jesus. May they also know great joy in their salvation. In Jesus's name. Amen.

Leader's Tool Kit

- Paneled beach ball
- Permanent marker
- Cardboard
- Three glasses/vases

- Tape or labels
- Iodine
- Bleach
- Two white T-shirts large enough to fit a leader
- Two medium sized boxes
- An assortment of sticks, leaves, and rocks
- Quarters, at least one per child
- Whiteboard/large piece of paper and whiteboard marker

Catechism Recap

On a paneled inflatable beach ball write a selection of catechism questions from one through twenty-four.

Gather the children into a circle and explain that the idea of the game is to keep the beach ball off the floor. Each child must participate to keep the beach ball in the air. If the beach ball drops to the ground, someone must volunteer to answer one of the catechism questions written on the ball, or the whole group gets a penalty. The penalty could be things like twenty jumping jacks or five push-ups, or something silly like walking across the room like a crab.

Introduction to Question 25

In three vases prepare the following solutions:

1. *100 percent water*

2. *80 percent water and 20 percent iodine*

3. *80 percent water and 20 percent bleach*

On the first vase stick a label saying YOU; on the second vase stick a label saying SIN; and on the third vase stick a label saying JESUS.

Tell the children that when we are born, we are in Adam, and that means that we are sinful. Pour some of the second vase (SIN) into the first vase (YOU). The water will become discolored, thus showing the effect of sin. Explain to the children that they are fully corrupted by sin.

Invite some of the children to explain what happens when people put their trust in Jesus Christ for redemption and ask him to forgive their sins. Help them to see that when Jesus forgives our sins, we are covered by his righteousness. To emphasize that Christians are those who are *in Christ*, pour the contents of the first vase (YOU) into the third vase (JESUS), and watch the liquid from the first vase become instantly clear. Ask the children if they can see any trace at all of the old YOU. Introduce the children to Question 25: "Does Christ's death mean all our sins can be forgiven?" and tell them that this lesson will help them to understand that because of Jesus Christ's death, all of their sins can be forgiven. Explain that they are totally dealt with and fully taken away.

(10) Activity

You will need two white T-shirts and some permanent markers. On one shirt write "Sinful," and on the other write "Righteous."

Place a piece of cardboard between the front and back of the T-shirt that has "Sinful" written on it so the marker doesn't bleed through. Invite the children to write as many words as they can on the T-shirt that are related to sinning against God and breaking his commands.

Once the children have finished writing, ask one of the leaders to put the T-shirt on over his or her clothes. Explain that this was what our lives were like before we were redeemed by Jesus Christ. We were sinful, we rejected God's rule, and broke God's laws. Explain to the children that when we turn to Jesus in repentance and faith, something amazing happens. Tell the children it's the greatest swap in history! Take the sin-stained T-shirt off the leader and place the righteous T-shirt

on him or her. Explain to the children that Jesus takes all the sin and guilt and rebellion, and in exchange, he gives the redeemed sinner his perfect righteousness. (Save both shirts. You will need them again for lesson 27.)

Ask the children if they understand what's happened. Explain to them that Jesus gives his perfect righteousness to each person whom he redeems. That means that when God looks at the redeemed sinner, he sees one who is righteous. (Righteousness simply means rightness with God, and Jesus was right with God because he lived a perfect, sinless life.) Explain that the minute a redeemed sinner receives the righteousness of Jesus Christ, he or she is no longer guilty before God, the just Judge, and is reconciled to him in friendship.

Ask the children if they agree that this is the best swap ever!

(15) Teaching Outline

Begin the teaching time by asking for God's help. Ask that the lesson would be taught faithfully and that the children might listen well.

Read 2 Corinthians 5:16–21. Provide Bibles for the children to read along with you.

Explain to the children that Paul is writing to the Christians in Corinth. At this point in the letter, he is explaining the difference

between being in the flesh (a non-Christian) and being in Christ (a Christian). Tell the children that Paul was seeking to correct some false teaching that the Corinthians had heard.

Paul instructs the Corinthians to regard Jesus as not only as a man, but as fully man and fully God. He is the perfect Redeemer who can deal with the sins of humankind once and for all.

Notes

Paul teaches that anyone who has been redeemed by Christ is a new creation; God welcomes believers into his family and makes us citizens of heaven. The old ways of hating and rebelling against God are gone, and a new life of loving God and living for God begins.

Use Paul's life as an example for the children of how radical the change should be. Paul changed from a man who hated Jesus and became a man who lived his whole life to tell people about him.

Tell the children that Paul emphasizes that God is the one who is at work redeeming and reconciling people to himself. Ask the children if this is surprising. Why would God do this? Why would he want to be friends with those who had sinned against him and broken his laws? Explain to the children that it is simply amazing that God is the one who takes the initiative.

Remind the children that God is holy and just, as well as forgiving. Paul explains once again in this passage that God cannot just dismiss sin. He has said that for sin to be dealt with, a price must be paid. For justice to be done, the penalty must be paid. Ask the children to read verse 21 and look at how Paul describes what happened to God the Son.

Explain to the children that Paul declares that Jesus—who was sinless— became sin so that people could be righteous before God.

Ask the children to try to remember what *righteous* means. It means that people are right with God. The way that people could become right with God is by being totally cleansed of all their sin.

Ask the children: If people are to be right with God, what must happen to their sin? Can even a little sin remain? Explain to the children that for people to be presented righteous before God, their sin must be fully removed.

Tell the children that when Jesus died on the cross, God inflicted on him the punishment our sin deserved. He fully experienced God's anger and fully received God's just penalty.

Explain to the children that this is how Christ's death means that all their sins can be forgiven. By way of conclusion, highlight for the children that this doesn't mean they will have an easy life or that they will be free from the temptation to sin, but it does mean that Jesus has dealt with their sin and God has pronounced them not guilty. For this we can celebrate God's grace and thank Jesus!

Conclude the teaching time by helping the children commit Question 25 and the answer to memory.

(These notes are just for guidance. Please expand or amend them to suit your own children and context. Write out your talk in your own words and include illustrations and applications that you know will connect with your children.)

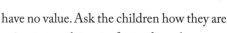

⑩ Activity ☼

Take two boxes. Label one "Adam's Sin" and the other "Jesus's Righteousness." Fill the box labeled "Adam's Sin" with sticks, leaves, and small rocks. Fill the other box with quarters, at least one for each child.

Tell the children that the cost of attending class today is twenty-five cents. Assure them that they don't need to worry if they didn't bring it because they can pay you with what they draw out of the box. Hold the box labeled "Adam's Sin" above each child so they can't see in but are able to draw out a stick, leaf, or rock. Now, ask the children for their payment.

Tell them that you don't want the things that they drew out of the box because they have no value. Ask the children how they are going to pay the cost of attending class.

Probably one of the children will catch on that they need something from the box labeled "Jesus's Righteousness," but if necessary, give them a hint. Allow each child to draw a quarter out of the box. When each child has the quarter, invite them to put their worthless sticks, leaves, and rocks in Jesus's box. Finally, ask the children if they can now pay their debt. As you collect the quarters, explain to the children that Christ exchanged his righteousness, which was of great value, for our unrighteousness, which would only have brought us God's wrath.

⑤ Discussion and Question Time

Some questions that might arise include:

? Does this mean that I will never sin again?

Explain to the children that this doesn't mean that they will never sin again. The temptation to sin is always part of human life. Tell the children that it does, however, mean that when God looks at Christians, he sees the righteousness of Christ not the sinfulness of humans.

? Does this mean I can sin as much as I want then?

Tell the children that when someone is redeemed and becomes a Christian, the Holy Spirit comes to live in him or her. One of the purposes of the Holy Spirit is to help Christians live obediently and therefore glorify God. Explain that this does not earn them any favor with God because Jesus has already given them perfect righteousness, but obedience does please and glorify God. Tell them that you will be talking more about this in future lessons.

Also use this opportunity to help the children to think about their own lives and how this question and answer affects them personally.

- Ask the children what difference knowing that the righteousness of Christ belongs to them makes in their lives.

- Ask the children how they might explain the great swap to a friend who doesn't really understand what Jesus achieved on the cross.

Virtue Vision

Joy

Ask the children if they've seen the movie *Inside Out*. Have those who have seen the movie describe the character Joy. Explain that Joy's main aim is to make Riley happy. She loves fun and tries to find the bright side in every situation! Joy just wants Riley to be happy.

Ask the children if they think that joy is about always being happy. Challenge them by asking, "Can joy be felt even when things are not going so well?"

Ask the children what about today's lesson could bring them joy, even when things aren't going their way. Help them see that Christians can have joy because of what Jesus has done for them. It doesn't matter if everything is going well or if life isn't very fun. Joy can always be experienced by remembering the great swap made on our behalf.

Memory Activity

Write the memory verse or catechism answer on a white board or on a large sheet of paper. Have the beach ball used in the catechism recap on hand.

Divide the children into two groups and have them form two parallel lines.

Read the memory verse through with the children a few times, then put it away or erase it. Hand the child at the top of one line the beach ball. He or she must say the first word of the memory verse or answer and then throw it to the person opposite him or her, who must say the second word of the memory verse and then that person must throw it to the second person in the opposite line, and so on. Repeat the process until the memory verse or catechism answer has been completed. Conclude by saying the memory verse together once more.

Closing Prayer Time

Conclude by praying that the children might understand clearly the significance of the greatest swap ever. Pray that the children would know deep joy by putting their trust in Jesus for redemption.

51

Question 26

What else does Christ's death redeem?

Answer

Every part of fallen creation.

Big Idea
God's redemptive work in Jesus benefits his creation as well as his creatures.

Aim
To help the children understand that all creation will be redeemed through Christ's death.

Bible Passage
Colossians 1:18–20

Memory Verse
"For in him all the fullness of God was pleased to dwell, and through him to reconcile to himself all things, whether on earth or in heaven, making peace by the blood of his cross." (Col. 1:19–20)

Virtue
Hope

Leader's Notes

Children will be increasingly aware that many people believe that this world and this life is all that there is. God is excluded from this worldview and the mantra for many is "Eat, drink, and be merry, for tomorrow we die." Christians understand that God is currently reconciling all things to himself through the redemptive work of Jesus. The Bible clearly teaches that this life is not all there is and that this world will be redeemed and restored. This lesson will help the children understand that Christ's redemptive work includes all of creation and not just humanity. This lesson aims to show the children that God has a saving plan for his world. It should also instill hope in the children as they are caused to consider the new heavens and the new earth.

Things to remember when planning and teaching:

- The world will still look pretty messy to many children. It will be important to highlight the "already/not yet" aspects of redemption.

- Children may get distracted by asking about the different types of things that will be in the new creation. Help them to understand that the new creation includes not just the natural world, but civilization as well. Avoid pursuing too many tangents though!

- For some children the thoughts of the new heavens and new earth may be new and worrying. Be careful to build joy, anticipation, and hope into the lesson.

- Remember to mix and match the activities in the lesson to fit your time frame (see p. 12 for some sample outlines). You won't have time to do them all. Feel free to adapt each activity based on your class's strengths and weaknesses.

Leader's Prayer

Loving God, thank you that you have a beautiful plan of salvation for your world. Thank you that I can anticipate with hope the full redemption and restoration of your creation. May my heart ever anticipate that day. Grant understanding to the children who will hear this lesson. May they be filled with joy and hope as they understand your redemptive work in your world and consider the full restoration of your creation. In Jesus's name. Amen.

Leader's Tool Kit

- Q26 Catechism Recap Memory Game (RB), one copy
- Pictures of beautiful places, people, and things
- Inflatable globe
- Black paint
- Large bucket

- Chalkboard or chalkboard paper and chalk
- Pieces of paper with HOPE printed across the top, one per child
- Alphabet cereal
- Paper

(10) Catechism Recap

Print out Q26 Catechism Recap Memory Game (RB) and cut out the tiles. Arrange them in a grid on the floor.

This is a memory game! Invite the children to gather around and take turns turning over two paper tiles. The aim of the game is to find a matching question and answer. If no match is found, the pieces of paper are turned back over on the floor. The children must try to remember the details as the tiles are turned over so that they can find a match when it comes to their turn.

(5) Introduction to Question 26

You will need pictures of beautiful places, people, and things in the world.

Ask the children to identify the things that they love about the world; perhaps it's a favorite place, a favorite bird, or a favorite building. Show pictures of some of the things that people describe as beautiful in the world.

Highlight for the children that while there is great beauty in the world today, it is not as God originally intended. Explain that everything in the world has been affected by sin; the damaging effects of sin infect every single part of God's creation.

Ask the children to imagine what God's creation might be like if it were unaffected by sin. It would be more beautiful and wonderful than anyone could imagine! Let them talk about what would be different. Introduce the children to Question 26: "What else does Christ's death redeem?" Explain to the children that Jesus's death on the cross was significant for all creation and not just humans. Tell the children that this question will help them to understand what that means a little more.

⑩ Activity

Tell the children that you're going to play a game called "Creation, Fall, Redemption." Identify the left side of the room as creation, the middle as the fall, and the right side as redemption. Tell the children that when you call out one of the words, they have to run to that position in the room. Begin slowly, but then increase the pace!

Then read out the following verses and ask the children to go to the position they think best represents where the verse comes in God's story of the world.

- "In the beginning, God created the heavens and the earth" (Gen. 1:1). **Creation**

- "That the creation itself will be set free from its bondage to corruption and obtain the freedom of the glory of the children of God" (Rom. 8:21). **Redemption**

- "So when the woman saw that the tree was good for food, and that it was a delight to the eyes, and that the tree was to be desired to make one wise, she took of its fruit and ate, and she also gave some to her husband who was with her, and he ate" (Gen. 3:6). **Fall**

- "And God blessed them. And God said to them, 'Be fruitful and multiply and fill the earth and subdue it, and have dominion over the fish of the sea and over the birds of the heavens and over every living thing that moves on the earth'" (Gen. 1:28). **Creation**

- "He drove out the man, and at the east of the garden of Eden he placed the cherubim and a flaming sword that turned every way to guard the way to the tree of life" (Gen. 3:24). **Fall**

- "And through him to reconcile to himself all things, whether on earth or in heaven, making peace by the blood of his cross" (Col. 1:20). **Redemption**

Explain to the children that the big story of the Bible can be divided into these three categories. Tell the children that in this lesson they will learn more about the effects of sin on God's creation and how Jesus Christ's redemption changes things.

⑮ Teaching Outline

You will need an inflatable globe, a large bucket, and black paint.

Begin the teaching time by asking for God's help. Ask that the lesson would be taught faithfully and that the children might listen well.

Ask the children if they remember in the previous lesson how iodine poured into water represented sin's effect on us. Hold up the inflatable globe and ask the children how significantly they think sin affects God's world. Demonstrate to the children that sin affects each and every bit of the world by holding the globe over the bucket and pouring the black paint (representing sin) all over the globe. Explain to the children that sin doesn't affect only humans; it affects every single aspect of God's creation.

Read Romans 8:20–22. Provide Bibles for the children to read along with you.

Ask the children what they think Paul is saying about creation. Explain to children that because of Adam's sin, the world was subject to death and decay. In Genesis 3, God cursed creation as well as Adam and Eve. The world is not as it was when God created it, and it is not how it will be when God fully restores it. Tell the children that currently the world is waiting to be made new, and God has promised that one day he will do that. In the meantime, creation is groaning in anticipation.

Explain to the children that Jesus Christ's death is the beginning of the redemption and renewal of every part of fallen sin-infected creation.

Read Colossians 1:18–20.

Reintroduce the children to Colossians 1. Remind them that they already spent a little time looking at it in lesson 24. Remind the children that God's mission in Christ is to reconcile all things to himself for his glory.

Highlight for the children that in verse 18 Paul says that Jesus is "the beginning." By that, he means that the death and resurrection of Jesus Christ announces

the beginning of the redemption of the whole earth. Jesus's redeeming death has implications for creation as well as for humanity.

In verse 20 Paul explains that the redemption is characterized by making peace. He brings peace in the restoration of God's relationship with humanity and peace in the restoration of the world to perfection.

Remind the children that God the Son was the one who brought the world into creation (lesson 5), and now he is proclaimed Lord over all creation. Jesus is re-creating, making new, both creation and humans. Explain to the children that re-creation has already begun, but that it will not be fully complete until the Lord Jesus returns. At that time God will conclude history, and he will bring all those who have been redeemed in Christ to live with him in a new, perfect creation. Creation will be fully renewed and restored, there will be new heavens and a new earth, and the perfection that was found in Eden will be once again seen in the new creation.

Explain to the children that all of creation belongs to God, and he is concerned to redeem it as well as humans. Creation is still affected by sin, but because of Christ's redeeming work it will one day be free from sin and all its effects.

Read Revelation 21:1–5 to conclude. Tell the children that redemption leads to restoration. The redemption has already been accomplished by Christ's death and

Notes

resurrection, but the creation will not be fully restored until he comes again.

Conclude the teaching time by helping the children commit Question 26 and the answer to memory.

(These notes are just for guidance. Please expand or amend them to suit your own children and context. Write out your talk in your own words and include illustrations and applications that you know will connect with your children.)

Activity

You will need a chalkboard or chalkboard paper and chalk. Draw lines to divide it into four equal sections.

Divide the children into groups of four, and invite each group to draw a pictorial representation of creation, fall, redemption, and restoration (one per group). Encourage the children to depict the various periods of the Bible's storyline.

Discussion and Question Time

Some questions that might arise include:

? Why does the full restoration not happen now?

Explain to the children that when Jesus returns to bring restoration, there will be no more opportunities for people to find redemption through the blood of Christ. Read 2 Peter 3:9: "The Lord is not slow to fulfill his promise as some count slowness, but is patient toward you, not wishing that any should perish, but that all should reach repentance." Redemption has heralded a new age, but it will not be fully realized until Jesus returns. In the meantime, as we wait for the restoration of creation, we should pray that many will be saved.

? What in creation will be redeemed?

Tell the children that many things are included in creation; it's not just the natural things we see. It includes buildings and music, books and bicycles. Give the children a big view of what creation means in this context.

Also use this opportunity to help the children to think about their own lives and how this question and answer affects them personally.

- Ask the children if thinking about the new earth gives them hope.

- Ask the children what this lesson teaches them about God's character.

- Ask the children how this lesson might influence the way they think about creation.

Virtue Vision

Hope

Ask the children to consider what kind of things they hope for. A new bike? Good grades in school? Their best friends to be put in their class?

Ask the children how hope helps them to look forward to the future. Help the children understand that hope allows them to anticipate the future and feel joyful even when their current situation may not be all that they would wish.

Give each child a piece of paper with the word *HOPE* at the top. Ask them to list things that they look forward to in God's restored creation.

Memory Activity

You will need some boxes of alphabet cereal. Give the children some Bibles to consult.

Divide the children into small groups and give each group a bowl of (dry) alphabet cereal. Challenge the groups to write out the memory verse or catechism answer in alphabet cereal. The children may swap letters with the other groups if they need additional letters.

Read the memory verse or catechism answer through with the children to aid memorization.

Closing Prayer Time

Invite the children to give thanks to God for his great plan of redemption that spans all creation. Let them take turns thanking God for some of the things they look forward to about his redeemed and restored creation.

Notes

Question 27

Are all people, just as they were lost through Adam, saved through Christ?

Answer

No, only those who are elected by God and united to Christ by faith.

Big Idea

Only those who are united to Christ, having been elected by God before the creation of the world, will be saved.

Aim

To help the children understand that God chooses those whom he will save.

Bible Passage

Ephesians 1:5–12

Memory Verse

"For if, because of one man's trespass, death reigned through that one man, much more will those who receive the abundance of grace and the free gift of righteousness reign in life through the one man Jesus Christ." (Rom. 5:17)

Virtue

Gratitude

Leader's Notes

Universalism is the belief that everyone will be reckoned righteous on the day of judgment and therefore be admitted to heaven. While this may hold emotional appeal for us, it is not what the Bible teaches. The Scriptures clearly differentiate between those who are in Adam and those who are in Christ. It is those who are in Christ who will be saved and will be granted eternal life to enjoy forever in God's presence. This lesson will consider the doctrines of election and saving grace. Most significantly, this lesson aims to show the children that the doctrine of election is a beautiful thing and something to rejoice in.

Things to remember when planning and teaching:

- This question may be emotional for children who have non-Christian family members.

- The children might be tempted to consider God unkind as they encounter the doctrine of election. Ensure that the emphasis is on the grace and goodness of God throughout the lesson.

- Some children will be anxious about their own salvation; be prepared to support and encourage them by pointing them to Jesus.

- Remember to mix and match the activities in the lesson to fit your time frame (see p. 12 for some sample outlines). You won't have time to do them all. Feel free to adapt each activity based on your class's strengths and weaknesses.

Leader's Prayer

Gracious God, thank you for predestining me to be part of your family and redeeming me through the precious blood of Jesus. I praise you for your saving grace. Grant understanding to the children who will hear this lesson. May they know you as a kind, loving, and gracious God. May they be encouraged by your sovereign grace in the world. In Jesus's name. Amen.

Leader's Tool Kit

- Paper

- Markers

- Balloons

- Q27 Catechism Recap (DL)

- Picture of a sports team

- Video clips of adoptive parents meeting their child for the first time

- Q27 Illustrations A, B, and C (RB)

⑩ Catechism Recap

Print out and cut up Q27 Catechism Recap (DL). Fold the slips of paper up very small and place them inside individual balloons. Inflate and tie the balloons.

Tell the children that the aim of the game is to burst the balloons and locate the pieces of papers enclosed within the balloons.

Once they have a piece of paper, they should work together to form a group that contains the questions, answer, and memory verse for Questions 21–26. A small group should form as the various elements of each question are brought together. Ask each group to read out their question, answer, and memory verse.

⑤ Introduction to Question 27

You will need a picture of a sports team.

Show the children a picture of a sports team. Ask the children if they've ever played a sport or a game in which the team captains chose the team members. Ask them what kind of things make a team captain want to choose a player for his or her team.

Agree with the children that captains usually want the most athletic, coordinated players on their teams. They want the quickest and the strongest—those who will be able to score points!

Ask the children how God picks the members of his family. Does he do it the way that a team captain chooses team

members? Help them to see that, according to the Bible, God *does* choose the members of his family, but he does not choose us based on our ability, intelligence, beauty, or goodness. When we talk about God's choosing, we call it *election*. It is done purely by his own will, not because of anything in us.

Introduce the children to Question 27: "Are all people, just as they were lost through Adam, saved through Christ?" Explain to the children that this question will help them to understand that not everyone is redeemed through Jesus's death and resurrection. Only those God elects will be saved, but our election is not based on our own worth.

⑩ Activity

Find one or more video clips of families meeting an adopted child for the first time (thousands are available on the Internet). If there happens to be *a family in your church who has adopted a child, ask if they would be willing to let you use a video or photo of their adoption.*

Notes

Ask the children if they know what adoption is. Ask them how parents decide what child they will adopt. Do they choose the baby whom they think will be the smartest or the prettiest or the fastest? How could you even tell what people will be like when they are only a baby or young child?

Explain to the children that they are going to learn from today's Bible passage that all who trust Christ for salvation have been adopted by God. They were chosen to be in Christ before the world was even made! We are not chosen based on anything special about us, but because God freely decides to bestow his love on us.

Ask the children if the parents in the video adopted all of the children from the country where they got their child (for example, "Did the Browns adopt all of the children in China?"). Help them see the parallel that God does not adopt every person in the world; he adopts only those he has chosen.

⑮ Teaching Outline

Begin the teaching time by asking for God's help. Ask that the lesson would be taught faithfully and that the children might listen well.

Explain to the children that some people in the world believe in something called universalism. Ask if anyone knows what that is. Tell the children that universalists believe that God will save everybody, regardless of whether people have sought forgiveness from God through the blood of Christ.

Acknowledge that it might be more comfortable to believe in universal salvation, but that it's not what the Bible teaches. Remind the children that everyone is either in Adam's sin or in Christ's righteousness. Whether you are in Christ or in Adam determines your eternal destiny.

Remind the children that God didn't need anyone, but in his grace and kindness he chose to save some people and make them his sons and daughters.

Explain to the children that God does not save everyone, but that he elects that only some will be saved. Everyone will be born in Adam, but then some will be born again in Christ. Reiterate that this isn't like picking a sports team! The men and women who play on sports teams are chosen because of their athletic ability. God chooses those whom he will save even before they're born, so being chosen by God to be in Christ has nothing to do with how good you are or how nice you are. Rather it has everything to do with how good God is and how kind God is.

Read Ephesians 1:3–12. Provide Bibles for the children to read along with you.

Ask the children what the word *predestine* means. Explain to them that it means to determine something beforehand. In this passage, we learn that God predetermined whom he would adopt, even before he created the world.

Ask the children to look at verse 6 and see if they can tell you why God chose to predestine his children before they were even born, rather than waiting to see who would be the best. Draw out the meaning of the phrase "to the praise of his glorious grace." Grace means "unmerited favor." If God had chosen to favor those who deserved it, we would not be the recipients of grace.

Remind the children that Ephesians is actually a letter written to people in the city of Ephesus. Paul seems to assume everyone he is writing to has been chosen by God.

Ask the children why he assumes this. Help them see it is not because every person has been chosen by God. Paul knows that he is writing to those who have trusted Christ for salvation. Anyone who has done this can know that he or she has been elected by God to be adopted as his child.

Conclude the teaching time by helping the children commit Question 27 and the answer to memory.

(These notes are just for guidance. Please expand or amend them to suit your own children and context. Write out your talk in your own words and include illustrations and applications that you know will connect with your children.)

Notes

 Activity

Print out Illustrations A, B, and C (RB).

Introduce the children to the Reformer John Calvin (1509–1564) but begin by simply showing the children the picture and inviting them to try to guess who is in the picture.

A few facts about Calvin:

- He was born in France in 1509.

- He was a lawyer.

- He later became a theologian, pastor, and Reformer

Tell the children (if they've not guessed) that this is John Calvin and that he is an

important historical figure for Christian history. Explain that he is known as a Reformer. Reformers were concerned to make sure the churches actually taught what was in the Bible. Tell the children that Calvin was one of the men who studied the Bible and explained the idea of people being chosen or elected by God.

Now ask the children whether they think Calvin was the first person to teach that God chooses people. Show them the picture of Augustine, and tell them that this is someone who lived earlier than John Calvin. His name was Augustine of Hippo.

A few facts about Augustine:

Notes

- He was not a hippo, but he lived in Hippo, a region of North Africa.

- He was born in 354—just three centuries after Jesus lived!

- For many years he did not believe in God. Then, when he was in his thirties, he became a Christian and a pastor. He wrote many books, including his own autobiography.

Tell the children that just three centuries after Jesus, long before John Calvin, Augustine taught that God elects those that he will save. Ask the children if they think he was the first person to teach this.

Show the children the picture of the apostle Paul. Confess that we do not really know what Paul looked like. But he lived during the time of Jesus, long before Augustine and John Calvin! Tell the children that the apostle Paul taught that God chooses those who will be saved; remind them of the passage that you studied in today's lesson. These are just a few of the many people throughout history who have taught about God's election.

Ask the children if they think Paul was the first person to teach about election. The answer is that election is taught throughout the Bible, from the very beginning of the Old Testament when God chose Abraham.

⑤ Discussion and Question Time

Some questions that might arise include:

? What happens to those who aren't saved through Christ?

Explain to the children that Question 28 will answer the question more fully, but that those who are not saved through Christ will be removed from God's holy presence forever because of their sin.

? How do I know if I'm one of the elect?

Reassure the children that if they believe in God and trust in Jesus for redemption, they can be confident that they are elect. Read John 6:37: "All that

the Father gives me will come to me, and whoever comes to me I will never cast out." All who believe in Jesus and put their trust in him can know that they've been chosen by God.

? Why do we need to bother telling people about Jesus if God has already chosen the elect?

People need to hear about Jesus in order to respond to the gospel. God uses those who already know him as his messengers to get the good news to others so that all who are elect will come to him. The Bible commands believers to spread the good news, and we should joyfully obey that command.

Notes

Also use this opportunity to help the children to think about their own lives and how this question and answer affects them personally.

- Ask the children if they can think of why it is actually comforting to know that God elects some people for salvation.

- Ask the children whether this motivates them to tell others about Jesus.

- Ask the children if knowing that God graciously saves people causes them to praise him.

---

(10) **Virtue Vision**

You will need pens and paper for the children.

Gratitude

Ask the children if there is anything about this lesson that makes them feel gratitude. Why should knowing we were not chosen because there was anything special about us make us even more grateful?

Encourage the children to write a letter of thanks to God for choosing to adopt them into his family.

---

(10) **Memory Activity**

Print out the memory verse or catechism question and answer and cut it up so that every word is on a separate piece of paper. Hide the individual words around the room.

Ask the children to find the words and lay them out in the correct order. Read the memory verse through with the children several times.

---

(5) **Closing Prayer Time**

Invite the children to read some of their letters of gratitude to God aloud.

Question 28

What happens after death to those not united to Christ by faith?

Answer

They will be cast out from the presence of God, into hell, to be justly punished, forever.

Big Idea
Eternal separation and punishment will be the everlasting reality for those who are not united to Christ by faith.

Aim
To help the children understand that those who are not united to Christ by faith will perish eternally.

Bible Passage
John 3:16–18, 36

Memory Verse
"For God so loved the world, that he gave his only Son, that whoever believes in him should not perish but have eternal life." (John 3:16)

Virtue
Honesty

Leader's Notes

This is a difficult topic to broach with children. The lesson must be taught in a way that clearly communicates God's Word but recognizes that the doctrine of hell is particularly unnerving to consider. It must be taught, however, because eternity is at stake, and if children aren't directly taught what the Bible teaches, they will default to what the culture around us believes. Because this is a difficult doctrine to teach to children, many people shy away from it, preferring to leave it until the children are older. That is a mistake because children who fail to understand what happens to those who are not united to Christ will have a lesser understanding of the glorious gospel of God's saving grace. Children must clearly understand what they have been saved from and for.

Things to remember when planning and teaching:

- This lesson has the potential to be scary for the children. Be aware of the language that you use and your tone of voice as you teach these difficult truths.

- Be aware that for some children this lesson may have a very personal effect, particularly if they have non-Christian family members or friends.

- Help the children to consider carefully how to communicate the gospel message with urgency, but also with gentleness.

- Adults as well as children wrestle with this doctrine. If you are troubled by it, take some time to read through the commentary on Question 28 at www.newcitycatechism.com.

- Remember to mix and match the activities in the lesson to fit your time frame (see p. 12 for some sample outlines). You won't have time to do them all. Feel free to adapt each activity based on your class's strengths and weaknesses.

Leader's Prayer

Loving God, thank you that your great love caused you to send your precious Son to die on the cross in my place. I praise you that I am united to him and may have joy and confidence in my salvation, and I look forward to eternity in your presence. Grant understanding to the children who will hear this lesson; may they be struck by how awful perishing apart from you is, but may they not be unnecessarily frightened or concerned. Let them carry from this lesson great confidence in your power to save. In Jesus's name. Amen.

Leader's Tool Kit

Notes

- Whiteboard and whiteboard marker

- Some depictions of hell:

  - The Nether in Minecraft

  - Hell as depicted in the TV
    series *The Simpsons*

  - A diagram of the circles of
    hell in Dante's *Inferno*

- Q28 Code Buster (RB), one per child

- Pencils

- A blank jigsaw puzzle and a marker

(10) Catechism Recap

*You will need a whiteboard and two
whiteboard makers and a copy of the catechism
questions and answers.*

Divide the children into two teams and line
each team up facing the whiteboard. Explain
to the children that this is a head-to-head
challenge! The children should come to the
whiteboard in pairs; the first children from
each team, followed by the second children
from each team, etc.

Read a catechism question out to the
children. Tell them that the first to write
the number associated with the question on
the whiteboard wins a point for their team.
Give that child a chance to say the answer.
If he gets the answer right, he gets another
point for his team. If he can't remember it,
the child from the other team can answer for
one point. Play until every child has had a
turn going head-to-head to guess the correct
number and answer to a question.

(5) Introduction to Question 28

*You will need some pictures that show common
depictions of hell.*

Show the children several ways that hell has
been popularly depicted:

- The Nether in Minecraft

- Hell as depicted in the TV
  series *The Simpsons*

- A diagram of the circles of
  hell in Dante's *Inferno*

Explain to the children that in the world,
many people don't take God or the Bible
seriously. Tell the children that, sadly, that
means they don't understand the reality
of life separated from God. They get their
idea of hell from cartoons rather than
from the Bible.

Introduce the children to Question 28:
"What happens after death to those not
united to Christ by faith?" Explain that
everyone who is in Christ experiences one

Notes

thing after death and everyone who is still in Adam because he or she has not believed the gospel experiences something different.

Tell the children that this question will help them to consider the fate for those who are not united to Christ by faith.

Activity

Have a copy of the Q28 Code Buster (RB) worksheet for each child.

Ask the children to decode some of the key verses where Jesus speaks about the fate of those who are not united to him. When they have finished, ask three children to read out the three different verses. Answers:

- "And do not fear those who kill the body but cannot kill the soul. Rather fear him who can destroy both soul and body in hell." (Matt. 10:28)

- "While the sons of the kingdom will be thrown into the outer darkness. In that place there will be weeping and gnashing of teeth." (Matt. 8:12)

- "Bind him hand and foot and cast him into the outer darkness. In that place there will be weeping and gnashing of teeth." (Matt. 22:13)

Explain to the children that instead of looking to the world to find out what life apart from God is like, it is important to look to Jesus and his words in the Bible. Read through each verse and observe that Jesus teaches that there is a place called hell and that is where those who are not united to Christ go.

Teaching Outline

Begin the teaching time by asking for God's help. Ask that the lesson would be taught faithfully and that the children might listen well.

Read John 3:16–18, 36. Provide Bibles for the children to read along with you.

Ask the children to begin by looking at these verses. Have them consider what they teach about God. Draw out the following points for the children:

- God is loving.

- God gave his precious Son up to death on the cross because he loved the world.

- God will give his people eternal life.

Ask the children what this passage says will happen to those who do not believe in Jesus—who are not united to Christ by faith.

- Explain to the children that verse 16 says all who are not united to Christ will perish.

- Verse 18 says that those who will perish are those who are condemned. They are condemned because of their sin, their rebellion against God, and their rejection of God's laws. They are people who will be judged by God and face the just punishment of God.

Tell the children that in the Bible, *perishing* does not mean that you cease existing, but that you exist in eternal separation from God.

Explain to the children that many people live as if God doesn't exist. They ignore him and fail to acknowledge the many blessings that he provides to everyone on earth. They are blind to the fact that God's presence and grace are blessing them and that he is also holding back and restraining evil.

Explain to the children that in eternity, people who have lived as if God doesn't exist will be separated from him forever.

The main thing that characterizes hell isn't flames or devils. It is separation from God. We can't really imagine what that would be like, but it is the worst thing that could ever happen to someone.

Conclude by confirming for the children that hell is a real place! Share that even though people have come up with various pictorial representations of hell, no one can truly comprehend what it is like. Remind the children that God doesn't want people to perish (2 Pet. 3:9), which is why he sent his Son to save us.

Conclude the teaching time by helping the children commit Question 28 and the answer to memory.

(These notes are just for guidance. Please expand or amend them to suit your own children and context. Write out your talk in your own words and include illustrations and applications that you know will connect with your children.)

Notes

Activity

Have the children turn to Luke 16:19–31 in their Bibles.

Read the parable of the rich man and Lazarus to the children. Divide them into small groups and help them to create a short drama to retell the story.

Ask the children what they observe from this parable that Jesus taught.

- Heaven and hell are real places.
- It is not possible to move between heaven and hell.

Allow some of the children to perform their dramas for the group.

(5) Discussion and Question Time

Some questions that might arise include:

? How do I know if I'm going to heaven?

> Explain to the children that if they believe in God and trust in Jesus for redemption, they need not fear. Reassure them that God will not let his children go.

? What about those who have never had a chance to hear about Jesus?

> Tell the children that this is a good question, and there are a number of things to consider. First of all, God is just and fair. He will not do something wrong, and so he can be trusted to make the right decision about every person's salvation. Second, the Bible tells us that while God's Word is the most important place to learn about God and Jesus, creation also reveals the reality and existence of God. Finally, encourage the children by highlighting that God is kindly providing time for Christians to go and explain the good news about Jesus far and wide.

? If God doesn't want people to perish, why didn't he elect everyone?

> Affirm that this is a good question, but not one that we know the answer to. The Bible clearly teaches that God is just and loving. While it may seem like a good idea to us for God to elect everyone, God's ways are higher than our ways, and we cannot fully understand his purposes. We have to trust that they are good and that one day we will understand.

Also use this opportunity to help the children to think about their own lives and how this question and answer affects them personally.

- Help the children to have a big view of God. Remind them that he is good, trustworthy, and in control.

- Ask the children if this lesson makes them want to tell people about Jesus. Ask them if they would consider going to places and people who haven't yet heard about Jesus.

(10) Virtue Vision

Honesty

Acknowledge to the children that they all know God expects us to be honest. They will remember that the ninth commandment teaches not to lie. But ask them if God expects us to be honest *with him*. Explain to the children that God loves and demands honesty from his children. Remind the children that God sees our hearts, so we couldn't hide anything from him if we tried!

Help the children to consider what it is to be honest with God in light of this lesson.

Psalm 62:8 says, "Trust in him at all times, O people; pour out your heart before him; God is a refuge for us." If any of the children have found today's lesson troubling, the best thing they can do is pour out their hearts to God in honesty. They can tell him if they feel scared or they don't understand. They can be honest with their parents and teachers about it too.

Memory Activity

Write the memory verse or catechism question and answer on the blank jigsaw puzzle.

Give the children the puzzle and ask them to put it together to reveal the memory verse or catechism question and answer.

Read the verse through with the children several times. Slowly remove pieces of the puzzle and see if the children can remember the verse or question and answer. Continue removing pieces until the puzzle is fully broken up.

Closing Prayer Time

Pray that the children may know God's great love and trust him. Pray that they might be eager to tell others about Jesus so that none might perish.

Question 29

How can we be saved?

Answer

Only by faith in Jesus Christ
and in his substitutionary
atoning death on the cross.

Big Idea
Only through faith in the Lord Jesus Christ
can we be saved from the punishment we
rightly deserve from God.

Aim
To help the children understand clearly that
salvation comes through Christ alone and to
give them confidence in the saving work of
Jesus on the cross.

Bible Passage
Ephesians 2:1–10

Memory Verse
"For by grace you have been saved through
faith. And this is not your own doing; it is
the gift of God, not a result of works, so that
no one may boast." (Eph. 2:8–9)

Virtue
Trust

Notes

Leader's Notes

Children in the twenty-first century are growing up in a pluralistic world. They are surrounded daily by a myriad of beliefs, many of which challenge and contradict biblical faith. Children encounter a pluralistic worldview at school, in the movies, on TV, among their friends, and even in their own families. They are taught to tolerate the view that there are many ways to God and many ways to be saved. Today's philosophical climate says it's ok to believe *personally* that salvation is found by faith alone through Christ alone, but it insists that you must not claim exclusivity to the pathway of salvation. Christians believe that salvation is found only through faith in the Lord Jesus Christ and his substitutionary atoning work on the cross. This lesson aims to help children understand what it means to be saved by the grace of God in Jesus Christ and to have confidence in the gospel.

Things to remember when planning and teaching:

- It is quite possible that your children will be familiar with the gospel, so be prepared to work hard to apply this lesson in an engaging and heart-penetrating way. Try to be concrete and practical when applying the catechism question and answer to the lives of your children.

- Big Bible words and theological concepts need to be explained carefully and clearly to children.

- Remember to mix and match the activities in the lesson to fit your time frame (see p. 12 for some sample outlines). You won't have time to do them all. Feel free to adapt each activity based on your class's strengths and weaknesses.

Leader's Prayer

Gracious God, thank you for saving me through the death of the Lord Jesus Christ. Please cause me to rejoice in my salvation and boldly proclaim the gospel to the next generation. Grant understanding to the children who will hear this lesson. May they know joy and confidence as they trust in Jesus for salvation, and may they humbly be prepared to challenge the pluralistic air that surrounds them and point others to Jesus, who is the way, the truth, and the life. In Jesus's name. Amen.

Leader's Tool Kit

- Ping-pong balls

- A permanent marker

- Q29 Who Am I? clues (RB)

- Blank index cards

- A large piece of paper

- Red construction paper cut into large hearts, two for each child

- A large paper cross

- Markers

(10) Catechism Recap

Write the numbers 1–28 on ping-pong balls and put them into a bag or box. If your budget allows, you could purchase a bingo cage or blower to add to the fun, or make your own.

Divide the children into two teams, and explain that you are going to have a quiz to help them remember some of the catechism questions that they've already learned. Let each team pick a numbered ball out for their opponents. The opposing team will get two points if they can remember the catechism question and answer associated with the number. The team with the most points wins!

(5) Introduction to Question 29

Familiarize yourself with the story of the Chilean miners who were trapped underground for sixty-nine days in August 2010, when the San Jose Mine collapsed. Print out some pictures of the scene, the mine, and the rescued men.

Begin by asking the children if they have ever been saved from something terrible happening to them. Try to keep this question grounded in real life, rather than jumping straight to the gospel at this stage. Perhaps they've been saved from:

- Getting lost in the mall

- Running out in front of a car

- Falling and breaking a leg

Ask, "What did it feel like to be saved?"

Ask the children if they've ever heard any stories about people being saved. Once you've exhausted their stories, share the story of the Chilean miners.

Ask, "Who did the saving? What kind of people do you think they were? Were they brave or strong? Why did they want to save someone else?"

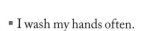

Notes

Introduce Question 29: "How can we be saved?" Commend the children for their participation in the discussion. Remind them that everyone needs to be saved, not from a fire or from drowning or from a car crash, but from the punishment of God that is due to everyone who sins against him.

⑩ Activity ☼

Who Am I?

Print out the Q29 Who am I? clues (RB). Ask your children to guess who the clues describe.

Read the clues in stages, and see how many clues the children need to identify the professions of the lifesavers. For example:

- I work in a team with other people.
- I wash my hands often.
- I often use a scalpel in my work to save people.
- I'm used to seeing lots of blood.
- Nurses work with me.
- I am a **surgeon**!

⑮ Teaching Outline

Cut out two large paper hearts for each child; they must be suitable for writing on. Stick up a cross at the front of your meeting room. Pass out markers.

Begin the teaching time with prayer, asking that God would help you to teach the lesson faithfully and the children to listen well.

Remind your children that in the story of the Chilean miners, you encountered people who really needed a savior. They needed to be saved. They were helpless and unable to save themselves.

Explain that it's not only people who are stuck in a burning building or a collapsed mine who need to be saved. That's why the question "How can I be saved?" is such an important one! The Bible clearly teaches that everyone needs to be saved.

Everyone who has ever lived or will ever live is facing punishment and death because everyone has disobeyed God. Emphasize to the children that this includes you and them. Tell them that there is nothing we can do to save ourselves from this fate.

Briefly discuss what sin is (refer to Question 16) and the consequences of sin for each man, woman, and child. Be sensitive to those children who may be worried by this reality, but also seek to engage well with children who behave as if they've heard it all before. Be prepared to explain sin in a more detailed way to new or visiting children.

Explain that you're going to read a bit more from Paul's letter to the Christians in Ephesus.

Read Ephesians 2:1–3. Provide Bibles for the children so they can read along with you.

Help the children to see that the passage describes those without a Savior as "dead in [our] trespasses and sins," a devastating description that applies to everyone who has lived, is living, and will live. Help them to understand how people can be described as dead, when by all appearances they're living and breathing. Those who have sinned against God are dead spiritually. They have no relationship with God because their sin separates them from God, and therefore they can do nothing to please God.

We need a Super-Savior to save us from this terrible predicament!

Explain to the children that in the passage Paul identifies everyone as a *sinner*— someone who has rejected God's rule and failed to live according to his laws.

Have the children write some of their personal sins on a paper heart. Gently help the children who believe that they're sinless to see where they disobey God. This may be an appropriate time to share a little of your own testimony, highlighting how you came to realize that you were a sinner and dead in your trespasses and sin, one who deserved to be punished by God. Have them fold the heart in half so that no one can see inside.

Read Ephesians 2:4–10.

Tell the children that these verses are truly amazing because they explain that God so loved the world that he sent his only beloved Son to save all those who are dead in their sins, to bring them from death to life.

Jesus is the Super-Savior! He's the only One who is able to save.

Explain to the children that God still had to punish someone for all the sins committed because he is a just God; Jesus took the place of and bore the punishment for sinners. Jesus was the only person who ever lived a perfect, sinless life. He was the only person who didn't deserve punishment and death, because he never disobeyed God. Tell the children that when Jesus died on the cross, he stood in to take the punishment for sin. He paid the price that was required for people to be made alive to God. It is the greatest swap of all time: God takes the repentant sinner's sin and puts it on Jesus. And he takes Jesus's perfect righteousness and imputes it to all those who have faith in him.

Ask the children to bring their sin-stained paper hearts to the foot of the cross and have them pick up a clean, unblemished heart. Explain to them that if they put their faith in the Lord Jesus and confess their sins, he gives them a clean heart. Remind the children that those who don't trust in Jesus are described as dead, but those who trust in Jesus are made alive—they have a heart transplant. The

Notes

Notes

good news is that those who are alive—those who have put their trust in Jesus to deal with their disobedience and sin—will enjoy a relationship with God forevermore.

Remind the children that new life is a free gift from God. The Bible calls that *saving grace*. We don't have to do anything to be saved except repent and believe in Jesus, whose resurrection from the dead ensures our eternal life.

Conclude the teaching time by helping the children commit Question 29 and the answer to memory.

(These notes are just for guidance. Please expand or amend them to suit your own children and context. Write out your talk in your own words and include illustrations and applications that you know will connect with your children.)

---

⑩ Activity ☼

Divide the children into groups and ask them to act out a news report describing what occurred on the cross of Calvary on the first Good Friday and why it needed to happen. You might want to challenge them to include certain words in their report, such as:

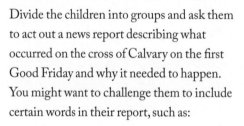

Dead	Alive	Swap
Gift	Saved	

---

⑤ Discussion and Question Time

Some questions that might arise include:

? What happens to those who don't repent and believe in Jesus?

> Explain to the children that the Bible teaches that those who remain dead in their sin will face the punishment of God and separation from his presence eternally (John 3:36). Be mindful that this reality could be distressing to some children.

? How can we be sure that we are saved?

> Encourage the children to have confidence in Jesus and to rejoice in the knowledge that once they have asked Jesus to deal with their sin, they can be sure they are saved. Explain that those who are alive in Christ will have a desire to live for God and to stop sinning. Our confidence is not based on how strong our faith is, but on what a Super-Savior Jesus is.

? Can we lose our salvation?

> No one who has truly put their trust in Jesus will lose their salvation. Share John 6:37: "All that the Father gives me will come to me, and whoever comes to me I will never cast out."

Use this opportunity to help the children think about their own lives and how this catechism question and answer affects them personally.

- Have they repented of their sin and believed in Jesus?

- How will they respond when they hear someone say that there are other ways to be saved, like living a good life?

- What does knowing that they are saved mean for them if they have already chosen to follow Christ?

Notes

Virtue Vision

Trust

Invite the children to reflect back to beginning of the session and the story of the Chilean miners.

Ask them to consider how the trapped miners might have come to the decision to trust those men and women who were attempting to save them.

Similarly, ask the children to consider why people trust firefighters or paramedics to save their lives.

Explain to the children that when you are in a life-threatening situation, you trust the men and women who are equipped and trained to save you. It's easy to place your trust into the hands of another when there is no other way out.

Remind the children that we need a Super-Savior to rescue us from death. Ask them whether Ephesians 2:1–10 has identified someone who is trustworthy and able to save.

Ask the children if they consider Jesus to be trustworthy. Invite them to voice any concerns they may have about trusting Jesus.

Remind them that Jesus is the only one who is able to save them and bring them from death to life.

Memory Activity

Write each word of the memory verse or catechism question and answer on a separate index card. You will need one full memory verse set of cards for each team.

- Divide the children into teams.

- Read the memory verse or question and answer aloud to the children.

- Read it again, inviting the children to repeat each phrase after you.

Notes

- Read it again, inviting the children to say the entire verse along with you.

- Hand out a full set of memory verse cards to each team; make sure the words are not in order! Ask the children to put the words in the correct order. The first team to finish wins!

- Practice the memory verse together one final time.

⑤ **Closing Prayer Time**

Conclude the lesson by reading aloud some of the things that the children wrote on the gratitude wall and thank God for his grace, most perfectly shown in Jesus.

Question 30

What is faith in Jesus Christ?

Answer

Receiving and resting on him alone for salvation as he is offered to us in the gospel.

Big Idea
Faith in Jesus Christ is the belief that Jesus is the Messiah, the one promised by God and revealed in his Word. Faith results in a desire to trust, obey, and worship Jesus wholeheartedly.

Aim
To help the children to understand that faith in Jesus Christ means trusting him as Savior and Lord and living for him alone.

Bible Passage
Galatians 2:15–21

Memory Verse
"I have been crucified with Christ. It is no longer I who live, but Christ who lives in me. And the life I now live in the flesh I live by faith in the Son of God, who loved me and gave himself for me." (Gal. 2:20)

Virtue
Trust

Leader's Notes

Many children may be intellectually able to assent to the truth of the gospel, but they might not have personally committed themselves to Jesus Christ. Their head knowledge may not have reached their hearts. They may say they believe the gospel, but trust themselves, or something else, more than Jesus. This question will encourage the children to embrace the gospel wholeheartedly and to place their faith and trust fully in Jesus. They will learn that believing without exercising faith is insufficient and will be challenged to consider what lives look like that are lived by faith in the Lord Jesus Christ.

Things to remember when planning and teaching:

- Faith is a hard concept to communicate to children! Help them to understand that faith is a gift from God.

- Ensure that your children understand that justification comes through faith alone.

- The children may be familiar with the language of faith, but may not have discovered what a personal faith is yet.

- Remember to mix and match the activities in the lesson to fit your time frame (see p. 12 for some sample outlines). You won't have time to do them all. Feel free to adapt each activity based on your class's strengths and weaknesses.

Leader's Prayer

Saving God, thank you that I have heard and understood the truth about Jesus. Thank you that my faith is in him alone. Help me to continually rest in him. Grant understanding to the children who will hear this lesson; may they know saving faith in Jesus. In his name. Amen.

Leader's Tool Kit

- Q30 Catechism Recap (DL)
- Paper
- Markers
- A small wrapped gift for each child in the class
- Video clips of people parachuting or bungee jumping
- Glue
- Scissors
- Magazines that can be cut up
- Memory verse or catechism question and answer in code, one for each child

(10) Catechism Recap

Have paper and markers ready, along with a bucket or wastepaper basket. Print and cut out the answers from Q30 Catechism Recap (DL) and place them in a bowl.

Divide the children into small groups. Give each group eight pieces of paper and a marker.

Explain to the children that in the bowl are the answers to eight catechism questions. The aim of the game is for them to quickly write down the question that goes with the answer. Draw one of the eight answers from the bowl and read it aloud. Give the teams one minute to write down the question. Once the minute is up, read out the question. The teams that have correctly identified the question get to come forward to a certain point in the classroom, crumple up their piece of paper, and shoot for the basket. And so it begins again—until all answers have been drawn from the bowl. The team with the most scores in the basket wins the game.

(5) Introduction to Question 30

Wrap individual gifts for each child in the class.

As the children settle down for the lesson, hand each child a gift. Tell them that they are free to open their gifts. Allow them a moment to open and enjoy the gifts they have received.

Introduce Question 30: "What is faith in Jesus Christ?" Explain to the children that today's question will help them to understand what faith in Jesus is. Ask the children if they enjoyed receiving the little gifts, and ask them if they generally enjoy receiving gifts for their birthday or Christmas. They will undoubtedly respond affirmatively! Highlight for the children that the gift of faith given by God surpasses all other gifts, and tell them that the significance of such a gift will be explored in the lesson.

Ask them if they did anything to earn the gift you gave them. Although they didn't earn their gifts, they unwrapped them and willingly received them. The same is true of salvation by faith.

(10) Activity

Prepare some video clips of people parachuting or bungee jumping.

Show the children videos of people parachuting or bungee jumping. Ask the children if they would ever want to jump out of a plane or off a cliff. Ask them what people are trusting in when they jump with a parachute or bungee cords. (Although their reflexive answer may be

"God," the right answer is the parachute or bungee cord.)

Draw the children's attention to the fact that these people trust either a parachute or a bungee cord to save their life, noting that if the parachute fails to open or the bungee cord snaps, the results could be messy!

Explain to the children that the people jumping need to have great faith that their equipment is reliable.

Highlight that trust is an essential part of faith, and faith in Jesus Christ means trusting him ultimately with our lives.

⑮ Teaching Outline

Begin the teaching time by asking for God's help. Ask that the lesson would be taught faithfully and that the children might listen well.

Tell the children that sometimes people describe faith as a leap in the dark. This implies that faith is placing your trust in something you know nothing about. Explain that might be what the first ever parachuter did when he jumped out of an airplane with a piece of material strapped to his back. But that isn't what parachuters are doing nowadays. They have faith in their parachute because they know how to use them. They've read the instructions. They know that they're made by reputable companies, and they learn how to use them from experienced instructors. They trust that as they fall to the ground, one tug on a cord will release a parachute that will allow them to fall gently to the ground without being hurt in any way.

Explain to the children that faith is actually trust or confidence that is based on knowledge coming from evidence. It's not a leap in the dark.

Explain to the children that when we put our faith in Jesus Christ, we are placing our trust in him because of all the evidence in Scripture that testifies to him as the promised Savior. He is the one whom God said he would send to save his people from their sins. He is the fulfillment of the Old Testament prophecies.

Tell the children that a Christian is not just a person who simply believes in his or her head that Jesus is the Savior, but someone who, from the heart, is ready to say, "Here, Jesus. Here is my whole life. I am not trusting anything else to save me." Ask the children to think about jumping off a wall into a parent's arms. They might believe that their parent is able and willing to catch them, but they don't exercise that belief as trust until the moment they jump. It's when we "jump" into the arms of Jesus, putting our whole trust in him, that we show faith.

Read Galatians 2:15–21. Provide Bibles for the children to read along with you.

Tell the children that now you are going to look at part of Paul's letter to the churches in Galatia. At this point in the letter, Paul is explaining what it means to be justified by faith. That simply means to be put back in a right relationship with God through faith alone, not by ever doing anything else.

Explain to the children that Paul is clearly arguing that the only way to be saved is by trusting in Jesus Christ. At the time when Paul was writing, and indeed now, people thought that you must keep laws in order to be made right with God. They believed that they had the power to save themselves if they lived in a certain way. But they were deluded; no one except Jesus has been able to keep God's law perfectly. Paul says that the only way to be justified is by acknowledging that we need Jesus in order to be saved, that we can't do it by ourselves. It is putting our full trust confidently in Jesus.

Tell the children that God gives the gift of faith when we become Christians. Our old life dies, and we receive new life in Christ— new life lived through faith in Jesus Christ.

Paul speaks personally in these verses, declaring that Christ loved *him* and died for *him*, and as a result *he* lives by faith in Jesus. He no longer trusts in himself or lives his own way, but trusts Jesus and lives for him, striving to resist the sin that would have been so attractive in his old life.

This is what faith in Jesus Christ looks like!

Finish the teaching time by helping the children commit Question 30 and the answer to memory.

(These notes are just for guidance. Please expand or amend them to suit your own children and context. Write out your talk in your own words and include illustrations and applications that you know will connect with your children.)

Notes

---

⑩ Activity   ☼

Pass out magazines, scissors, glue, markers, and a piece of paper for each child.

Tell the children that they will be making a collage to help them remember what faith is. They should cut up the magazines so that they have the letters *F*, *A*, *I*, *T*, and *H*. Have them glue the letters on their collage and use markers to make an acrostic:

F	Forsaking
A	All
I	I
T	Trust
H	Him

⑤ Discussion and Question Time

Some questions that might arise include:

? Can I be sure I have the gift of faith?

> Explain to them that once they've placed their trust in Jesus, they can be sure God has granted them faith.

? What if I realize I've been trusting in something besides Jesus?

> Any time we realize we have put our trust in something else, we can confess it to God and know that he will forgive us. Faith in him involves believing he will forgive our sin. Seeing our sin (that we've trusted in something else) is the perfect opportunity to put your faith in Jesus, not your own goodness.

Also use this opportunity to help the children to think about their own lives and how this question and answer affects them personally.

- Do they fully and confidently rely on Jesus for salvation?

- Are they determined to live obedient lives for Christ as they hope and trust in him?

- What do they think the world thinks about having faith in Jesus? Are they going to be able to stand when people discredit the gospel?

⑩ Virtue Vision

Trust

Discuss with the children what trust means to them.

Ask them to think about two parachuters. Tell them that one is a confident jumper and has no fear at all. The other is jumping for the first time and is nervous. She is not sure that her parachute will work. She is afraid. Nevertheless, both people jump out of the plane.

The first jumper had a lot of faith, but the second didn't have very much faith. Ask the children which one they think made it safely to the ground. The answer is that they both did! Even though the second jumper had only a little faith, she still exercises trust in the parachute by jumping out of the plane. Her safety was not dependent on the strength of her trust, but on the strength of her parachute.

Tell the children that if they ever get worried they are not trusting God enough or that they don't have enough faith, they can remember that their salvation is not dependent on the amount of faith they have, but on the strength and trustworthiness of Jesus to save them!

⑩ Memory Activity

Give each letter in the alphabet a number, and then write the memory verse or catechism question and answer out in a number code. The children will have to decipher the code in order to crack the memory verse. You could tell the children that A=1, B=2, etc.

Present the children with the coded memory verse or catechism question and answer and ask them to figure out what it says by cracking the code.

Have them read the memory verse through several times after they've decoded it, then ask them to turn their papers over and say it out loud.

⑤ Closing Prayer Time

Encourage the children to thank God for the gift of faith in Jesus. Pray that their trust would grow deeper in full knowledge that they are being lovingly held by a perfectly trustworthy Father.

Question 31

What do we believe by true faith?

Answer

We believe in God the Father Almighty, Maker of heaven and earth; and in Jesus Christ his only Son our Lord, who was conceived by the Holy Spirit, born of the virgin Mary, suffered under Pontius Pilate, was crucified, died, and was buried. He descended into hell. The third day he rose again from the dead. He ascended into heaven, and is seated at the right hand of God the Father Almighty; from there he will come to judge the living and the dead. We believe in the Holy Spirit, the holy catholic church, the communion of saints, the forgiveness of sins, the resurrection of the body, and the life everlasting.

Big Idea
There is one true faith that was handed down by the apostles.

Aim
To help the children embrace and defend the one true faith as taught in the Apostles' Creed.

Bible Passage
Jude 1–4

Memory Verse
"I found it necessary to write appealing to you to contend for the faith that was once for all delivered to the saints." (Jude 3)

Virtue
Awe

Leader's Notes

The Apostles' Creed is a historic statement that contains the essential doctrines of the Christian faith. It has been used for centuries to inform and equip Christians. Children living in a pluralistic world will be encouraged to believe that there are many faiths and many ways to God. This lesson will help the children understand that there is one true faith that has been taught from the time of Jesus until now, and it is encapsulated in the Apostles' Creed. By memorizing the Creed, the children will be able to easily recall the essential doctrines of the true faith. This lesson aims to give children confidence in the historic Christian faith and the ability to contend for it.

Things to remember when planning and teaching:

- The answer to this question is long! Be patient with the children as they endeavor to learn the Creed.

- It's important for the children to understand as well as learn the Creed. Carefully engage with the children to ensure that they understand each statement in the Creed.

- Remember to mix and match the activities in the lesson to fit your time frame (see p. 12 for some sample outlines). You won't have time to do them all. Feel free to adapt each activity based on your class's strengths and weaknesses.

Leader's Prayer

Gracious God, thank you for revealing yourself and your great plan of salvation in and through your Word. I praise you for the courage of the men and women who have contended for the Christian faith all through history. Thank you for the historic creeds of the church, and for the way they clearly articulate biblical doctrine. Grant understanding to the children who will read this lesson. May they be equipped with a knowledge of the true Christian faith, and may they be made ready to stand for you. In Jesus's name. Amen.

Leader's Tool Kit

- A selection of numbers one through thirty-one, printed and cut into individual pieces of paper

- Q31 Martyr Illustrations (RB)

- Q31 Creed Matchup (RB)

- Envelopes

- Q31 Apostles' Creed Bookmark (RB), one per child, printed on cardstock and cut out

- Stickers

- Markers

- Glitter glue

- Cards with the words of the memory verse printed on them

(10) Catechism Recap

Print a selection of numbers one through thirty-one and cut them up so that they are on individual pieces of paper. Place them upside down on the floor around the classroom. Use two fewer numbers than the number of children in your class. For instance, if you have eighteen children, use sixteen numbers; if you have ten children, use eight numbers, etc.

Have the children line up against the wall and tell them that when you say "go," they should run and stand on a piece of paper. The children who don't find a piece of paper to stand on should move to the side of the room. Ask the children to look at their paper and see what number is written on it. If they think they can remember the question and answer, they should stand still, but if they are unsure of the question and answer, they can invite one of the children at the side to switch in for them. Invite a few of the children to recite the question and answer that goes with their number. Play a few rounds of this game, reducing the pieces of paper each time.

(5) Introduction to Question 31

Show the children the pictures The Burning of Latimer *and* Ridley *and* Cranmer's Martyrdom *from Q31 Martyr Illustrations (RB).*

Ask the children to describe what is going on in these two pictures. Let them look carefully at the pictures and notice the details.

Tell the children that these pictures are of three men known as the Oxford martyrs. The first picture shows Hugh Latimer and Nicholas Ridley being burned at the stake

on October 16, 1555. Thomas Cranmer was burned five months later. Each of these men died because he contended for and defended the true Christian faith during a time when the Queen of England wanted her people to follow doctrine not taught in the Bible.

Introduce the children to Question 31: "What do we believe by true faith?" Explain to the children that this question will help them to consider what true Christian faith is and what it means to contend for the faith.

Notes

⑩ Activity

Print a copy of Q31 Creed Matchup (RB). Cut up the verses and phrases from the Creed. Put the twelve pieces of paper in an envelope. Make several sets of the puzzle, each in its own envelope.

Introduce the children to the Apostles' Creed by reading it to them. Tell the children that a creed is a statement of Christian beliefs. All through history people have had to contend (fight) for the true Christian faith, starting soon after Jesus's death and resurrection.

Tell the children that Christians in the fourth century were facing great opposition from a group called the Gnostics, who taught that Jesus didn't really die and rise again. (You may want to write out the word for them and explain that the *G* is silent.) In response to the false teaching, the Apostles' Creed was formulated as a statement of true Christian faith.

This Creed is named for the apostles. Tell the children that it wasn't written by the apostles, but it contains the things the apostles taught.

Divide the children into small teams. Give each team an envelope with twelve slips of paper in it; there should be six Bible verses and six points from Apostles' Creed. Explain to the children that everything that is written in the Apostles' Creed is found in Scripture. Challenge the children to link the statement from the Creed with the Bible verse it's derived from.

⑮ Teaching Outline

You will need Q31 Apostles' Creed Bookmark (RB), one per child.

Begin the teaching time by asking for God's help. Ask that the lesson would be taught faithfully and that the children might listen well.

Read Jude 1–4. Provide Bibles for the children to read along with you. Point out to them that the book of Jude is one of the shortest in the whole Bible. It has only one chapter!

Tell the children that in this small passage, Jude calls Christians to contend for the faith. He wants to make sure that they fight to defend the true Christian message and to maintain the biblical faith that has been passed down from generation to generation.

For some Christians, defending the true faith still involves risking their lives, as Latimer, Ridley, and Cranmer did, but for the millions and millions of others it means knowing all about the faith and being able to tell others why you believe it. It involves resisting people who teach false things about the faith. Everyone who knows and understands the true Christian faith does so because of a long, long line of believers who contended for the faith!

Ask the children what soldiers do before they go into battle. They train and equip themselves in preparation to contend! Inform the children that knowing and understanding the Apostles' Creed is one of the ways God's people can prepare themselves to contend for the true Christian faith.

In verse 3, Jude calls Christians to defend the faith that was "once for all delivered to the saints." Tell the children that the Apostles' Creed contains the core doctrines that Jude is referring to. It communicates the truth of the gospel as understood by the apostles, who learned it from Jesus himself and who taught it to God's people in the church. All but one of the apostles were put to death by people who opposed the message they taught.

Jude also highlights that the Christian faith was handed to the saints "once for all"; the message was given to the church once for everyone, for all time.

The final point to draw out for the children from the passage is that sometimes those who threaten the church and the understanding of the true Christian faith are those who are already inside the church, not simply outsiders.

Close by explaining to the children that in many churches around the world, the Apostles' Creed is said collectively each week. Saying the Creed together is a good way to remind each other what the true Christian faith is as we prepare to contend for it.

Give the children a copy of the Apostles' Creed in a bookmark format. Invite them to read it with you and to take it home and place it somewhere they will see it regularly, like in their Bible or by their bed.

Conclude the teaching time by helping the children commit Question 31 and the answer to memory.

(These notes are just for guidance. Please expand or amend them to suit your own children and context. Write out your talk in your own words and include illustrations and applications that you know will connect with your children.)

Notes

---

(10) Activity ☼

Designate one side of the room as "True" and the other as "False." Read out the statements below. Have the students move to one side or the other depending on whether the statement is true.

1. The Apostles' Creed is found in the Bible word for word. FALSE

2. The Apostles' Creed was written by the apostles. FALSE

Notes

3. The Apostles' Creed is a summary of the true Christian faith. TRUE

4. Everything written in the Apostles' Creed is taught in the Bible. TRUE

5. The Apostles' Creed refers to all three persons of the Trinity. TRUE

6. Jesus is seated at the left hand of the Father. FALSE

7. Only the dead will be judged. FALSE

8. Jesus rose from the dead after two days. FALSE

9. The Apostles' Creed says that Jesus didn't suffer. FALSE

10. The Apostles' Creed declares that Jesus is the Son of God. TRUE

---

(5) **Discussion and Question Time**

Some questions that might arise include:

? Do I just need to know the words of the Creed to be a Christian?

No! Explain to the children that these words are helpful and historically important because they summarize the Christian faith well, but that a Christian is someone who has been redeemed and reconciled to God through the death of Christ.

? Why does the Apostles' Creed say we believe in the catholic church?

Today we often use the word *catholic* to refer to the Roman Catholic Church, but that is not the meaning of the word used in the Creed. *Catholic* here means "universal." When we say we believe in the holy, catholic church, we mean that there is one true church made up of people all over the world who believe in Jesus.

? Did Jesus literally go to hell?

The Bible teaches that Jesus bore the full wrath of God, and thus those who trust him do not have to experience hell—eternal separation from God. We know that Jesus was separated from his Father when he was on the cross (see Matt. 27:46, in which Jesus cries, "My God, my God, why have you forsaken me?"). In that sense, he experienced hell for us. But the Bible doesn't clearly teach that Jesus went to a physical place called hell. When we affirm, "he descended into hell," most people take that to mean that Jesus bore the full wrath of God.

Also use this opportunity to help the children to think about their own lives and how this question and answer affects them personally.

- Ask the children if they're prepared to contend for the faith.

- Ask the children how they would feel if they faced losing their life in order to contend for the gospel.

⑩ Virtue Vision

You will need stickers, markers, and glitter glue to decorate the bookmarks.

Awe

Let the children read and decorate the bookmarks.

While they work on their bookmarks, ask the children what happens to people when they do not have awe for God. Help them see that people who deny the truth given to us in the Bible demonstrate that they have a small view of God; they do not hold him in awe.

People who are willing to die to preserve the faith have a great deal of awe. Their view of God is so big that they will not betray him, even if it costs their lives.

Ask the children if they feel a sense of awe when they think of those who have given their life for the faith.

⑩ Memory Activity

Today's lesson includes two different memory activity options.

To help children learn the memory verse: *Print each word of the memory verse onto a card. You will need one full memory verse set of cards for each team.*

- Separate the children into two teams.

- Read the memory verse out to the children.

- Read the memory verse, inviting the children to repeat each word after you.

- Read the memory verse again, inviting the children to say the entire verse with you.

- Hand out a full set of memory verse cards to each team; make sure they're not in order! Ask the children to put the words in the correct order. Points can be given to the winning team that first completes the verse correctly.

- Practice the memory verse one final time.

To help children learn the catechism answer: *Find Q31 on the Songs from the New City Catechism album (available at newcitycatchism.com or on the NCC app). Because this answer is longer than most, the song will be helpful in memorizing the Apostles' Creed.*

Play "Q31 What do we believe by true faith?" for the class. Encourage the children to make up motions that correspond to the song. Play it as many times as necessary, then invite the children to try to sing it with their motions without the recording.

Notes

⑤ Closing Prayer Time

Give each child a partner, and invite
the children to offer prayers of praise
with their partner.

Question 32

What do justification and sanctification mean?

Answer

Justification means our declared righteousness before God. Sanctification means our gradual, growing righteousness.

Big Idea
God justifies those whom he has chosen and sanctifies his chosen people.

Aim
To help the children understand that justification and sanctification are both part of the Christian life, but that justification comes before sanctification.

Bible Passage
1 Peter 1:1–2

Memory Verse
"To those who are elect exiles . . . according to the foreknowledge of God the Father, in the sanctification of the Spirit, for obedience to Jesus Christ and for sprinkling with his blood: May grace and peace be multiplied to you." (1 Pet. 1:1–2)

Virtue
Joy

Leader's Notes

Justification and *sanctification* are big Bible words that are sometimes hard for children to understand. It is important, however, that children understand these concepts, know the difference between them, and see the significance of their order in the Christian life and experience. This lesson will remind children that people are justified when they become Christians; they are legally declared righteous in the sight of God. The lesson will then explain to the children that sanctification follows justification. Sanctification is an internal supernatural work of the Holy Spirit in the Christians heart. This lesson aims to help the children recall what justification is and begin to understand the process of sanctification.

Things to remember when planning and teaching:

- Children can find the prospect of becoming more like Jesus a little worrying and confusing because they're unsure of how the process happens.

- The concept of the Holy Spirit coming to live in a Christian is puzzling for a child. Take time to explain that it is a supernatural process and not an actual person indwelling us. Children will clearly understand the physical realm, but they will still be growing in their understanding of the supernatural realm.

- Remember to mix and match the activities in the lesson to fit your time frame (see p. 12 for some sample outlines). You won't have time to do them all. Feel free to adapt each activity based on your class's strengths and weaknesses.

Leader's Prayer

Loving God, thank you that you have chosen and justified me. I praise you that you're sanctifying me through the power of the Holy Spirit. Please help me long to be more like Jesus and be obedient to you for your glory. Grant understanding to the children who will hear this lesson. May they understand the significance of justification and long for the work of sanctification in their individual lives. In Jesus's name. Amen.

Leader's Tool Kit

- 8 business size envelopes
- Poster board
- Index cards
- Glue or tape
- Two boxes
- Wrapping paper and tape
- The word *sanctification* printed on a sheet of paper

- The word *justification* printed on a sheet of paper

- Q32 Justification or Sanctification? (RB), several copies

- Wallpaper or butcher paper

- Markers

Catechism Recap

Seal eight business size envelopes, then cut each one in half so that you have sixteen open-ended pockets. Attach them to the poster board with the cut end up—four across and four down. In each pouch place a card. Leave four cards blank and write one of these sentences on each of the others:

- *ZAP—Switch points with the other team.*

- *ZAP—Add two points to your team score.*

- *ZAP—Lose two points from your team score.*

- *ZAP—Both teams lose four points.*

- *ZAP—Your team's score goes back to zero.*

- *ZAP—The other team's score goes back to zero.*

Keep score on two sheets of paper so that the scores can be swapped when that card is drawn.

Divide the group into two teams. Take turns to ask each team to recall the answer to a catechism question. Read a question, and the team must come up with the right answer. They have one chance to recite the answer. If they get the answer right, they get a chance to go to the board and pick a card out of one of the pouches. The teams will end up gaining, losing, switching, or totally zapping out! The team with the most points when all of the cards have been drawn wins. The aim of the game is to help the children have fun while reviewing the answers to the catechism questions.

Introduction to Question 32

You will need two boxes and gift wrap. Print the word justification *on one sheet of paper and* sanctification *on another, and place one in each box. Wrap the boxes up and stick a number one on one box and a number two on the other.*

Place the two boxes at the front of the classroom and ask the children if they're excited to see what's inside. Explain to the children that the boxes contain words that

describe two of God's great gifts to humans. Tell the children that the boxes must be opened in a certain order, though!

Invite a child to the front of the classroom to open box number one and pull out the word *justification*. Tell the children that justification is God's declaration that someone is righteous before him. Only God can justify, and the only reason he can justify

Notes

is because Jesus died on the cross to take the punishment that was due to guilty sinners. Justification is an amazing gift from God!

Invite another child up to open the second box, and remind the children that the boxes had to be opened in a special order. Pull out the word *sanctification*. Explain to the children that sanctification only happens after justification. When people are justified by God and saved from the punishment

they deserve, the Holy Spirit comes to live in them. As he lives in them, the Holy Spirit makes them more and more like Jesus. Sanctification is the process of becoming more like Jesus.

Introduce the children to Question 32: "What do justification and sanctification mean?" Tell them that this lesson will help them to understand the act of justification and process of sanctification further.

Activity

Divide the children into small groups. Print out a copy of Q32 Justification or Sanctification? (RB) for each group.

Give each group a copy of "Justification or Sanctification?" Ask the children to discuss and figure out which relate to *justification* and which relate to *sanctification*. They should write an *S* by the words that refer to

sanctification and *J* by the words that are about justification.

After a few minutes take some time to discuss the words with the children and assess whether they're beginning to understand the difference between justification and sanctification. Note: A few words relate to both.

Teaching Outline

Begin the teaching time by asking for God's help. Ask that the lesson would be taught faithfully and that the children might listen well.

Ask the children why the gift-wrapped boxes needed to be opened in a certain order. Remind the children that only after a person is justified by God, through Christ, does the Holy Spirit comes and live in him or her and begins the process of sanctification. Trying to simply live a good life or become more like Jesus without being justified will never

make anyone right with God. The process of sanctification begins after God has justified.

Ask the children if they often get asked what they want to be when they grow up. Explain to the children that there are lots of wonderful things to do and become in God's world, but the greatest desire Christians can have is to glorify God as they become more like Jesus. Ask the children how they think adults might respond if they answered the "what to do you want to be when you grow up" question with "more like Jesus"?

Read 1 Peter 1:1–2. Provide Bibles for the children to read along with you.

Explain to the children that the apostle Peter is writing a special letter to Christians who are scattered abroad in different places and who are being persecuted because they love Jesus.

Explain that Peter is trying to encourage them by reminding them that they are very special to God. He refers to three works of God in the salvation of each believer:

1. Election

2. Justification

3. Sanctification

Invite the children to look at the two verses to see if they can identify what God the Father does, what God the Son does, and what God the Holy Spirit does.

1. Election: God the Father

2. Justification: God the Son

3. Sanctification: God the Holy Spirit

Remind the children of Question 27 and the fact that God chose which people he would justify and sanctify. That is what Peter is referring to when he addresses the exiled Christians as the "elect." They are the ones that God chose to be his holy people. Peter is comforting the Christians who are being rejected for their faith by reminding them that they have been elected—chosen—by God!

In verse 2, Peter highlights the fact that the exiled Christians have been justified by God through the blood of Jesus. (Romans 5:9 may be a useful verse to refer to at this point in the lesson.) Christians are those who have been declared righteous once and for all. Their sin is fully dealt with. Help the children to imagine a court scene in which a criminal is standing before a judge in fear and trepidation, but the judge declares the criminal "not guilty." Remind the children that's exactly what happens to a Christian. Jesus the Redeemer pays the price for sin, and God declares the repentant sinner not guilty. The righteousness of Christ is given to the repentant sinner in exchange for his or her sin.

Peter also tells the exiled Christians that they are being sanctified by the Holy Spirit. Ask the children if they can remember what sanctification is. Sanctification means our gradual, growing righteousness. Ask the children who does the work of sanctification in the lives of Christians. It is the Holy Spirit who works in the hearts of Christians to make them more like Jesus.

Explain to the children that sanctification is a lifelong process! They won't suddenly wake up one morning and be fully like Jesus. The Holy Spirit will be at work in the heart of Christians until the day they go to be with Jesus.

Ask the children if they can think of why it might be a bad thing to mix up the order of justification and sanctification. Help them

Notes

Notes

to see that if sanctification comes before justification, then they will be trying to work their way into heaven rather than relying on the righteousness of Christ.

The exiled Christians would have received much comfort from this reminder from Peter, and that's exactly what he intended! He concludes verse 2 by saying "may grace and peace be multiplied to you," reminding them that being a Christian and the recipient of God's election, justification,

and sanctification brings continued grace and peace.

Conclude the teaching time by helping the children commit Question 32 and the answer to memory.

(These notes are just for guidance. Please expand or amend them to suit your own children and context. Write out your talk in your own words and include illustrations and applications that you know will connect with your children.)

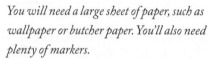 **Activity**

You will need a large sheet of paper, such as wallpaper or butcher paper. You'll also need plenty of markers.

Write "Becoming more like Jesus" across the top of a large sheet of paper. Remind the children that sanctification is the process of being set apart to become more like Jesus and that it begins after people have been justified.

Ask the children to write or draw things on the sheet of paper that signify what Jesus is like. Encourage them to portray Jesus's qualities that we can also have (for example, "loving" rather than "all-knowing.") After

a short period of time invite the children to return to their seats and discuss with them some of the things they've written or drawn on the paper. Explain to the children that Jesus is fully righteous and the process of sanctification is all about becoming righteous.

Remind the children that for all Christians, the purpose of life is to glorify God as we become more like Jesus. Tell the children that in a little while there will be a prayer time during which they can ask God to help them to become more like Jesus through the work of the Holy Spirit.

Discussion and Question Time

Some questions that might arise include:

? How do I know I've been justified?

> Explain to the children that if they've turned to God in repentance and

> trusted Jesus for the forgiveness of their sins, they have been justified.

? I'm a Christian, but I still sin. Why am I not more like Jesus yet?

Remind the children that becoming a Christian doesn't mean that they become sinless, but rather, their desire to sin should be decreasing and their obedience to God increasing. Encourage the children that if they long to become more like Jesus, the Holy Spirit is at work in them.

? Will I be able to feel the Holy Spirit working?

Reassure the children by explaining that the work of the Holy Spirit is a great thing because it's making us more like Jesus. Explain that while there isn't a physical feeling that comes with the Holy Spirit's work, at times they will be aware that the Holy Spirit is at work because they will notice more of their sin and want to turn from it.

Also use this opportunity to help the children to think about their own lives and how this question and answer affects them personally.

- Ask the children if understanding justification and sanctification gives them hope and courage in the same way that Peter intended to encourage the exiled elect by his letter.

- Ask the children how the doctrine of justification might encourage them if people are unkind to them because they are Christians.

- Ask the children how they might explain the process of sanctification to a friend at school.

Notes

Virtue Vision

Joy

Ask the children if they think they would be joyful even if they were being persecuted like the Christians Peter was writing to.

Remind the children that joy is different from happiness. Joy is being confident in who God is and what he has done, is doing, and will do!

The Bible lists joy among the "fruit of the Spirit" (Gal. 5:22). As the Holy Spirit works on Christians through sanctification,

they will have increasing joy, even if their circumstances are not good.

Ask the children if they've ever known someone who showed a lot of joy even though he or she had a hard life.

(10) Memory Activity

Print each word of the memory verse or catechism answer on a piece of paper, and then cut each word in half. Hide one half of each word around your classroom.

Give every child one half of a word from the memory verse or catechism answer. Instruct them to find the other half of their word, which is hidden somewhere in the classroom. Once the children have found the other half of their word, ask them to put the Bible verse or catechism answer in the correct order. Read it through with the children. Then remove half of some of the words and read through it again. Finally remove full words and see if the children can remember the whole verse or answer.

(5) Closing Prayer Time

Invite the children to pray that God would help them to become more like Jesus through the power of the Holy Spirit. Encourage the children to think about specific areas of their lives where they long to become more like Jesus.

Question 33

Should those who have faith in Christ seek their salvation through their own works, or anywhere else?

Answer

No, everything necessary to salvation is found in Christ.

Big Idea
Salvation is through faith alone in Christ alone.

Aim
To help the children confidently know that Jesus's death and resurrection are sufficient for salvation.

Bible Passage
Galatians 2:15–21

Memory Verse
"Yet we know that a person is not justified by works of the law but through faith in Jesus Christ, so we also have believed in Christ Jesus, in order to be justified by faith in Christ and not by works of the law, because by works of the law no one will be justified." (Gal. 2:16)

Virtue
Perseverance

Leader's Notes

The doctrine of salvation by grace alone through faith is essential to the gospel and Christian life. It is one of the defining doctrines of the Protestant Reformation, and it is vital to help children comprehend the implications of this doctrine for Christian life. This lesson will help the children grasp that Jesus's substitutionary and sacrificial death is entirely sufficient for salvation. The children should clearly understand that a works-based mentality is inconsistent with the gospel. This lesson aims to help children trust fully and completely in Christ for salvation.

Things to remember when planning and teaching:

- Children are often people-pleasers and will seek praise and reward through good behavior. They need to understand that their behavior will never be good enough to earn their relationship with God. Conversely, missing the mark will not cause them to fall out of the saving grace of God if they have repentant hearts.

- The children may need help understanding what is meant by the phrase "through their own works."

- Remember to mix and match the activities in the lesson to fit your time frame (see p. 12 for some sample outlines). You won't have time to do them all. Feel free to adapt each activity based on your class's strengths and weaknesses.

Leader's Prayer

Gracious God, thank you for the gift of faith. I praise you for revealing to me that faith and trust in Jesus is sufficient for my salvation. Please make me aware of the places in my life that I'm tempted to rely on works rather than grace. Grant understanding to the children who will hear this lesson. May they fully understand that salvation comes by grace alone through faith in Christ alone and be equipped to persevere in the faith. In Jesus's name. Amen.

Leader's Tool Kit

- Sticky notes

- Q33 Picture of Martin Luther (RB)

- Paper

- Markers

(10) Catechism Recap

You will need one sticky note for each child. The notes should have numbers on them that fall between one and thirty-three.

Gather the children together and put a numbered sticky note on the back of each child. The children should not be told what their number is! Each number represents a catechism question. The task for the children is to figure out which catechism question they represent by asking other children to tell them something about their question. The children can ask as many questions as necessary to gather information about their question. By the end of the activity the children should be able to identify and say their question and answer.

(5) Introduction to Question 33

You will need Q33 Picture of Martin Luther (RB).

Introduce the children to Martin Luther. Explain that he was an important person in something called the Reformation. The Reformation was significant because many people read the Bible for themselves and rediscovered what true faith is.

Tell the children that Martin Luther made a huge personal discovery during his life. Martin Luther originally thought that he had to work his way to peace with God and that eternal life was earned by doing good things. Explain to the children that one day he was reading his Bible, and he read Romans 1:17: " For in it the righteousness of God is revealed from faith for faith, as it is written, 'The righteous shall live by faith.'"

When Luther read, "The righteous shall live by faith," he realized that he had it all wrong! He didn't have to do anything to earn his salvation or work his way into God's favor, but he had to accept God's free gift of salvation.

Introduce the children to Question 33: "Should those who have faith in Christ seek their salvation through their own works, or anywhere else?" Explain to the children that this question will help them to understand why Martin Luther was right: salvation is by grace alone through faith! It is not necessary or even possible to seek salvation through works.

(10) Activity

Ask the children to stand in a line in the middle of the room and explain to them that they need to move to the left side of the room if they think the statement that you read out is wrong and to the right if they think that the statement is right. Remind the

111

Notes

children as the activity begins that salvation means being saved by Jesus from God's judgment and punishment.

Is this statement right or wrong?

- Salvation is found through doing my homework on time.

- Salvation is found through trusting Christ alone.

- Salvation is found through trusting Christ alone and helping the elderly.

- Salvation is found through trusting Christ alone.

- Salvation is found through always obeying my mom and dad.

- Salvation is found through trusting Christ alone.

- Salvation is found through trusting Christ alone and giving money to church.

- Salvation is found through trusting Christ alone.

- Salvation is found through keeping the Ten Commandments.

- Salvation is found through trusting Christ alone.

The intentional movement from side to side should reinforce for the children that everything necessary for salvation is found in Christ. Explain that there is nothing wrong with doing the other things. Many of them are worth doing! But highlight that Jesus Christ is fully sufficient as Savior and Redeemer. Nothing but trusting him is required for salvation.

⏱ Teaching Outline

Begin the teaching time by asking for God's help. Ask that the lesson would be taught faithfully and that the children might listen well.

Introduce the teaching time by telling the children that many people believe that they will get to heaven by living a good life and doing good things. Ask the children how they would respond to someone who said that.

Explain to the children that some people who believe in Jesus *still* think that to get to heaven they need to do good things!

Explain that Galatians 2:15–21 will help them understand that Jesus's work on the cross is enough.

Read Galatians 2:15–21. Provide Bibles for the children to read along.

Tell the children that we are going to look again at Paul's letter to the Galatians. Highlight that this letter is all about helping the Galatians to understand how important it is to believe that Jesus's work on the cross is enough. Faith does not need to be supplemented by good living or law keeping.

In fact, if we trust in those things, we are not trusting in Christ.

Ask the children to look at verse 16 and investigate whether Paul says a person can be justified by keeping the law. Paul says a person is not justified by keeping the law!

Ask the children to identify how Christians are justified. By faith in Jesus Christ!

Explain to the children that it's sometimes difficult to believe that salvation is God's free gift because it is uncommon to get free gifts in life. Most things in life have to be worked for. Ask the children if they can name some things that come as a result of hard work.

Emphasize again that Paul says the only way to be justified is to believe in Jesus Christ. Explain to the children that those who believe that good works are essential in order to have a relationship with God actually have a very low view of what Jesus achieved on the cross (and a high view of their own capabilities)!

The belief that we must add to what Christ has done says that Jesus's death on the cross is not enough. Ask the children whether they think that kind of thinking might

be offensive to God. It is deeply insulting to God to give the impression that Jesus's sacrificial atoning death is not enough.

Also highlight for the children that humans frequently fail to live in a way that pleases God. Believing that living good lives will make them right with God is trusting in abilities that have proven to be untrustworthy. No one is able to fully keep the law of God and thus please God—except Jesus.

Explain to the children that the only way to know salvation is through Christ. Paul says in verse 20 that those who are in Christ have died to law-keeping. That means that Christians should fully trust in Jesus's death and resurrection and resist believing that there are other ways to seek salvation.

Conclude the teaching time by helping the children commit Question 33 and the answer to memory.

(These notes are just for guidance. Please expand or amend them to suit your own children and context. Write out your talk in your own words and include illustrations and applications that you know will connect with your children.)

Notes

---

⑩ **Activity**   ☼

You will need pieces of paper and markers for every child.

Help the children to make signs that say "Jesus + Anything = NOTHING." Give the

children paper and markers and invite them to creatively decorate their signs. As the children are drawing, remind them that the only way to salvation is through Jesus. To add anything to Jesus makes the gospel useless.

113

_____

⑤ Discussion and Question Time

Some questions that might arise include:

? Does this mean that to trust Christ, I shouldn't keep the law?

> Explain to the children that no, this isn't what Paul is saying. The Bible teaches that people must not believe that they can find salvation through any means except faith in Christ. We will talk more next week about why, although we shouldn't *trust* obedience to save us, we should obey God.

Also use this opportunity to help the children to think about their own lives and how this question and answer affects them personally.

- Ask the children why some people don't like to hear that we can't be saved by good works.

- Ask the children how knowing Jesus's death and resurrection is sufficient affects their hearts.

- Ask the children how they might explain the concept of salvation by grace through faith to a school friend who thinks being a Christian is just living a good life.

---

⑩ Virtue Vision

Perseverance

Ask the children if they know what the word *perseverance* means. Help them to understand that to persevere means to keep going no matter how difficult things get, even if you have to wait a long time to see any concrete results.

Ask the children what kinds of activities requires great perseverance.

- Running a marathon

- Trekking across a desert

- Flying into space

Tell the children that the book of Galatians was written to a group of people who needed to be reminded to persevere. They had started out believing that their salvation came by grace alone through faith, but then some people convinced them that they also had to keep the law to be saved. They needed to forsake this wrong teaching and persevere in the truth. Ask the children whether it will be easy or hard to persist in the Christian life trusting that salvation comes through faith alone.

Memory Activity

Divide the children into groups and invite them to act out the different clauses in the memory verse or catechism question and answer. Give them a while to practice, then let the groups take turns saying the verse or catechism question and answer with their motions.

Notes

Closing Prayer Time

Encourage the children to confess to God the things that they might be tempted to trust for their salvation, then thank God that Jesus's death and resurrection are sufficient to save.

Question 34

Since we are redeemed by grace alone, through Christ alone, must we still do good works and obey God's Word?

Answer

Yes, so that our lives may show love and gratitude to God;

and so that by our godly behavior others may be won to Christ.

Big Idea
Christians have been made citizens of heaven, which should affect the way we live in this world.

Aim
That the children might understand clearly where the identity of a Christian is found and what the joyful responsibility of the Christian is.

Bible Passage
1 Peter 2:9–12

Memory Verse
"But you are a chosen race, a royal priesthood, a holy nation, a people for his own possession, that you may proclaim the excellencies of him who called you out of darkness into his marvelous light. Once you were not a people, but now you are God's people; once you had not received mercy, but now you have received mercy. Beloved, I urge you as sojourners and exiles to abstain from the passions of the flesh, which wage war against your soul. Keep your conduct among the Gentiles honorable, so that when they speak against you as evildoers, they may see your good deeds and glorify God on the day of visitation." (1 Pet. 2:9–12)

Virtue
Gratitude

Leader's Notes

Children need to continually be reminded that salvation is found through grace alone by faith alone in Christ alone. Though they must be dissuaded from a works-based mentality, they also need to be taught how to respond to God's saving grace with thankful and obedient lives. This lesson will help children marvel once again at the beauty and privilege of being adopted into God's family and welcomed into heavenly citizenship. They will consider what it is to be chosen, holy, precious, and a member of the royal priesthood. The lesson should cause their hearts to respond in great gratitude to God from which should flow obedient and loving lives. This question will allow the children to consider the role that God has given his people in his world.

Things to remember when planning and teaching:

- Keep emphasizing that salvation is found through faith in Christ alone. Remind the children that Jesus + Anything = Nothing!

- It's important to help the children understand that as citizens of heaven, Christians take on a new identity and a new responsibility to live in a way that represents their God and King.

- It may be necessary to help the children think practically about what obedient and God-glorifying lives look like.

- Remember to mix and match the activities in the lesson to fit your time frame (see p. 12 for some sample outlines). You won't have time to do them all. Feel free to adapt each activity based on your class's strengths and weaknesses.

Leader's Prayer

Gracious God, thank you that you call us to become citizens of heaven. Thank you that I can confidently know that my home is in heaven with you and that I have been chosen to be your precious possession, holy and set apart for your glory. Help me to live a fruitful life of gratitude to you. May my life bear great witness to you. Grant understanding to the children who will hear this lesson. May they clearly understand that salvation is by grace through faith and that the right response to you is a thankful heart. In Jesus's name. Amen.

Leader's Tool Kit

- Q34 Catechism Recap (DL)

- Sticky Tack

- A passport or pictures of passports from different countries

- Stickers or labels with names of famous people written on them

- A large roll of paper, such as butcher paper or wallpaper

- Markers and art supplies to decorate a banner

(10) Catechism Recap

Print out and cut up the questions and answers from Q34 Catechism Recap (DL). Mix up the questions and answers and stick them up around the room with Sticky Tack.

Tell the children that all of the questions and answers for one through thirty-three are stuck up around the walls of the classroom, but that they're not paired correctly! Encourage the children to work together to pair all the questions with the right answers. Run through some of the questions and answers with the children to aid their recall.

(5) Introduction to Question 34

You will need some passports representing different countries or pictures of passports from different countries.

Show the children the passports, and ask them to identify what kind of information passports contain. For example:

- Nationality

- Country of birth

- Date of birth

- Photo

Explain to the children that a passport can reveal a lot about a person. It particularly reveals a person's citizenship. Remind the children of lesson 27 when you talked about adoption. If children from another country are adopted by someone, they become a citizen of their adoptive parents' country. They will receive a new passport, learn the language of their parents, and grow up eating the food that is popular in their new country.

Explain to the children that once a person becomes a Christian, he or she becomes a citizen of heaven. We take on the citizenship that belongs to our heavenly Father, and it will change the way we live.

Introduce the children to Question 34: "Since we are redeemed by grace alone,

Notes

through Christ alone, must we still do good works and obey God's Word?" Explain to the children that citizens of heaven will glorify God and, by their witness, show a watching world what God is like.

---

(10) Activity

You will need a sticker or label for each child with the name of a famous person written on it. Pick cartoon characters or celebrities who will be easily recognizable!

Place a sticker on each child's forehead and tell the children that they have to figure out who they are. They can ask any questions they like to the other children in the group, but they can receive only yes or no answers!

For example, the children could ask:

- Am I a man?

- Am I a woman?

- Am I an animal?

- Do I have black hair?

- Am I old?

- Am I young?

- Do I have glasses?

Once the children have figured out the identity of the character on their stickers, explain to them that the Bible clearly declares who Christians are and what their identity is.

---

(15) Teaching Outline

Begin the teaching time by asking for God's help. Ask that the lesson would be taught faithfully and that the children might listen well.

Read 1 Peter 2:9–12. Provide Bibles for the children to read along.

Remind the children that a few minutes ago, when they had a label on their head, they needed help figuring out who they were. In this short passage, Peter is trying to help some of his Christian friends understand who they are. Invite the children to look at the passage and see if they can find the four different ways that Peter describes Christians.

Remind them that when someone becomes a Christian, he or she becomes a citizen of heaven. Although Christians live on earth for a time, their real home is with God in heaven—that's why Peter calls Christians "sojourners." Peter says that they are members of a chosen race, a royal priesthood, a holy nation, and a people for God's own possession. Highlight for the children that Christians are:

Chosen: God has chosen people to become members of his family, citizens of heaven, and he wants to spend forever with them. Christians are God's possessions, which he bought with the blood of his precious Son.

Holy: Christians are set aside by God to be sanctified—to become more like Jesus.

A royal priesthood: Christians have direct access to God and have been called to serve others for God's glory.

God gives his people an identity, and he also gives his people a purpose in life. Tell the children that as citizens of heaven, God wants Christians to live in a new way, the way of their new adoptive Father and heavenly country. He wants the world to know all about him and about Jesus, and his plan has always been to use Christians to "proclaim the excellencies of him who called you out of darkness into his marvelous light" (1 Pet. 2:9).

Explain to the children that when we do good works and obey God's Word, we are acting like citizens of heaven. We are showing people what our adoptive heavenly Father is like, and we hope that our lives will make them want to join God's family. Be clear with the children that doing good works and obeying God's Word won't make anyone right with God. Instead, Christians will do good works and obey God's Word as a response to God's kindness.

Explain to the children that God clearly teaches through his Word who his people are and what their purpose in life is. They have an identity and a job! Ask the children if they think that being a Christian is exciting and a privilege. Help them to understand that becoming a citizen of heaven is the most wonderful thing that could happen to anyone ever and serving God in his world is an immense privilege.

Finish up by asking the children to consider whether Christians are good witnesses for God in his world. Discuss with the children how they might live for God and bring glory to God in gratitude for his saving grace.

Conclude the teaching time by helping the children commit Question 34 and the answer to memory.

(These notes are just for guidance. Please expand or amend them to suit your own children and context. Write out your talk in your own words and include illustrations and applications that you know will connect with your children.)

Notes

Activity

You will need a long piece of paper (such as butcher paper) and art supplies to decorate it.

Invite the children to make a banner depicting the identity and job of a Christian.

Encourage the children to look back to the passage to draw inspiration for the banner. They should pull words from the passage that tell us who we are in Christ and then draw pictures to represent what behaviors go

Notes

with our identity. Once the banner has been completed, display it on the classroom wall. If the number of children is large, divide the children into smaller groups to make several banners.

⑤ Discussion and Question Time

Some questions that might arise include:

? How do I know if I'm a citizen of heaven?

> Remind the children that all those who put their faith in Jesus alone for salvation are citizens of heaven. Explain that Christians receive the gift of eternal life from God; some of that life is lived on earth and some of it will be lived in heaven and the new creation.

? Will God be angry with me if I'm not good at living a thankful life?

> Encourage the children to focus on the confidence that Christians can enjoy by trusting in the sufficiency of Jesus as Savior and Redeemer. Remind the children that for the Christian, God's anger was borne by Christ on the cross. Encourage them to pray that God would increase their understanding of what he has done so that their thankfulness will grow.

? How do I know if I'm trusting in my good works to save me or if I'm doing them out of gratitude for my salvation?

> We sometimes have trouble getting to the bottom of our own motives, but God sees our hearts perfectly. If the children are concerned they might be trusting their works to save them, they should confess this to God and ask him to help them fully rely on him alone for salvation.

Also use this opportunity to help the children to think about their own lives and how this question and answer affects them personally.

- Ask the children if they have a personal understanding of what it means to be a Christian and become a citizen of heaven.

- Ask the children how knowing that they are chosen, holy, precious, and royal priests might help them to face difficult things in life.

- Ask the children if they think it's easy or hard to live thankful lives for God. Ask them what makes it hard or easy.

⑩ Virtue Vision

Gratitude

Members of God's family will show their gratitude to God by how they live and how they treat others. Divide the children into two groups. Invite the first group to make up a skit that shows how someone lives who doesn't show the gratitude that comes from being a member of God's family. Invite the second group to make up a skit that shows how a grateful member of God's family interacts with the people around him or her. Let both groups perform their skits.

⑩ Memory Activity

You will need to write the memory verse or catechism question and answer out on a large sheet of paper or chalkboard.

Read the memory verse or catechism question and answer with the children several times (since this week's verse is long, you may want to pick a smaller portion to memorize). Ask for a volunteer from among the children who thinks that he can remember the memory verse or catechism question and answer. Explain to the volunteer that you are going to ask him to close his eyes and you are going to point to a word for the rest of the group. The rest of the group should be instructed to clap instead of saying the word as they read the memory verse or catechism question and answer. The volunteer must see if he can identify the missing word as the memory verse or catechism question and answer is read. Repeat the process several times with different volunteers and different missing words.

⑤ Closing Prayer Time

Invite the children to pray prayers of gratitude to God. Close by asking God to make our lives the kind that will make people want to join God's family.

Question 35

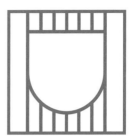

Since we are redeemed by grace alone, through faith alone, where does this faith come from?

Answer

From the Holy Spirit.

Big Idea
The Holy Spirit is the means by which a person is washed, reborn, and regenerated.

Aim
To introduce the children to the role of the Holy Spirit in the life of the believer.

Bible Passage
Titus 3:1–7

Memory Verse
"But when the goodness and loving kindness of God our Savior appeared, he saved us, not because of works done by us in righteousness, but according to his own mercy, by the washing of regeneration and renewal of the Holy Spirit, whom he poured out on us richly through Jesus Christ our Savior." (Titus 3:4–6)

Virtue
Perseverance

Leader's Notes

This is the first of three questions that highlight the role and work of the Holy Spirit in the life of the Christian. It is reasonably hard for children to understand exactly who the Holy Spirit is and what he does. This lesson will remind the children that salvation comes by grace alone through faith alone, and it will emphasize that the Holy Spirit grants faith to the repentant sinner. The lesson will remind the children that no one deserves God's grace and mercy, but in his kindness and great love, God rescues a people for himself through the death and resurrection of his precious Son. This is in contrast to all the other world religions, which require their followers to merit salvation.

Things to remember when planning and teaching:

- The person of the Holy Spirit is sometimes difficult for children to understand.

- Thinking about the work of the Holy Spirit in the life of the believer can be frightening for a child if it is not explained well.

- Remember to mix and match the activities in the lesson to fit your time frame (see p. 12 for some sample outlines). You won't have time to do them all. Feel free to adapt each activity based on your class's strengths and weaknesses.

Leader's Prayer

Gracious God, thank you that, though I am so underserving, you chose to rescue me from sin and death by the power of the Holy Spirit as I was cleansed from my sin and given new life in Christ. I praise you for your grace and mercy. Grant understanding to the children who will hear this lesson. May they understand and rejoice in the work of the Holy Spirit as the agent of salvation. In Jesus's name. Amen.

Leader's Tool Kit

- White board (or large piece of paper) and white board marker
- Pad of large sticky notes
- Papier-mâché letters spelling FAITH (available at any craft store)
- An empty box that the papier-mâché letters will fit in
- A gift tag

- Wrapping paper (preferably gender-neutral baby wrapping paper)
- Q35 What We Were Word Search (RB), one for each child
- A small papier-mâché box for each child in the group
- Markers
- Tape

(10) **Catechism Recap**

On the white board, outline a 4 x 5 grid. Make each box in the grid the same size as your sticky notes, so that the note covers the box. Write on the grid, in random order, both the question and answer for Questions 21–30. Cover each question and answer with a sticky note. Label the sticky notes with letters A–T.

Invite a child to select a letter from the board. Lift the sticky note with that letter on it to reveal a question or an answer. Then ask the child to choose another letter to see if he or she can find the matching question or answer. If the child doesn't successfully find the match, the sticky notes are returned to cover up the words on the grid. If the child gets a match, he or she should hold on to the sticky notes. The aim of the game is to match all the question and answers. Keep playing until all the matches have been revealed.

(5) **Introduction to Question 35**

You will need to place the papier-mâché letters in the box and wrap the box in the wrapping paper. Secure the gift tag to the outside of the box.

Explain to the children that you have a gift in the box. Invite them to guess what's in the box! Ask them if they'd like you to open the box. Once the box is opened, pull out the letters in the wrong order, and ask the children if they can figure out what they spell. Read out the gift tag for the children; it should say "To: New Christian, From: The Holy Spirit." Explain to the children that faith is a free gift from the Holy Spirit, and

it is given to every new Christian. Ask the children if they noticed anything about the wrapping paper. Tell the children that a new Christian is described as someone who has been born again and the Holy Spirit is the one who gives the gift of faith.

Introduce the children to Question 35: "Since we are redeemed by grace alone, through faith alone, where does this faith come from?" Explain to the children that this question will help them to understand a little more about the free gift of faith that comes from the Holy Spirit.

(10) **Activity** ☼

You will need a copy of the Q35 What We Were Word Search (RB) for each child. The children will need to find the following words:

- astray
- disobedient
- envy
- foolish
- hated
- hating
- malice
- slaves

Once the children have found the words in the word search, explain to them that these words are used by Paul in today's Bible passage to describe all those who are not Christians. Ask the children what they think of the words. Ask them whether they think these kinds of people deserve to be saved from God's judgment, anger, and punishment.

Emphasize to the children that no one deserves God's free gift of faith, and no one can earn God's free gift of faith. It is given graciously by the Holy Spirit.

⑮ Teaching Outline

Begin the teaching time by asking for God's help. Ask that the lesson would be taught faithfully and that the children might listen well.

Ask the children to describe one of the best gifts they've ever received. Ask them if the gift changed their lives forever.

Ask the children to think about the occasions when they receive gifts, and ask them if they had to do anything to qualify for the birthday gift or Christmas gift. Gifts are freely given without reason and illustrate the greatest gift a person can ever receive. The gift of faith is the most significant gift ever, and it is life-changing!

Read Titus 3:1–7. Provide Bibles for the children to read along.

Explain to the children that Paul is trying to help Titus understand how to care for and teach the Christians in his congregation. In chapter 3, Paul asks Titus to remind the Christians about what they once were, before they were given faith by the Holy Spirit. He is encouraging Titus to help the Christians live joyful, godly, and obedient lives.

Explain to the children that these verses clearly identify where faith comes from, and they contain a strong reminder that people cannot save themselves. Paul says that salvation comes from God the Savior. God in his great kindness and love reaches out to save those who are undeserving. Invite the children to look at verse 5 and ask them if they can identify what the Holy Spirit does.

The Holy Spirit gives faith through:

- washing

- rebirth

- renewal

Explain to the children that it is God the Holy Spirit who changes people's hearts when they become Christians. In verse 7 Paul explains to Titus that Christians are justified by God's grace; because of Jesus, Christians are declared not guilty by God. At the same time, the Holy Spirit washes away a Christian's sin and makes him or her new. Encourage the children to think back to Question 25: "Does Christ's death mean all our sins can be forgiven?" The iodine/bleach illustration demonstrated the washing away of sin. Christians are born again and become members of God's family. Remind the children of the baby wrapping paper and the fact that when the Holy Spirit gives the gift of faith, a new Christian is born into God's family. Acknowledge to the children that this is a difficult thing to understand and that they will gain a deeper understanding as they get older. They just need to remember that the gift of faith comes through the Holy Spirit to those who are undeserving but greatly loved by God.

Conclude the teaching time by helping the children commit Question 35 and the answer to memory.

(These notes are just for guidance. Please expand or amend them to suit your own children and context. Write out your talk in your own words and include illustrations and applications that you know will connect with your children.)

Notes

Activity

You will need a papier-mâché box for each child and materials to decorate them with.

Give each child a box. Ask the children to write "FAITH" inside the box on the bottom and "FROM: The Holy Spirit" on the lid of the box. Allow the children to decorate the boxes. As they are decorating, remind them that faith is a free gift from the Holy Spirit to everyone who trusts in Jesus for the forgiveness of sins.

Discussion and Question Time

Some questions that might arise include:

? If God has to give faith, does that make me like a robot with no choice about what to believe?

No, people have wills, something robots do not have. It is true that we cannot have faith unless God gives it to us through the Holy Spirit. That gift comes because God reveals to our minds his true glory and goodness, which we had not previously been able to see. This is very different from programming a robot.

? Can I feel the Holy Spirit at work inside me?

Explain to the children that the work of the Holy Spirit is a wonderful thing and not to be feared. Reassure the children that it is not a physical change, but a spiritual change, and so there won't be a tangible physical experience. There will be a spiritual awareness of being made new by the Holy Spirit when someone puts his or her trust in Jesus in repentance and faith.

Notes

? **Do all Christians have the Holy Spirit living inside them?**

> Yes! Explain to the children that everyone who becomes a Christian will receive the gift of faith from the Holy Spirit and the indwelling of the Holy Spirit (see John 16:13; Rom. 8:9).

Also use this opportunity to help the children think about their own lives and how this question and answer affects them personally.

- Ask the children if they acknowledge that they cannot save themselves.
- Ask the children if they can rejoice in the gift of faith personally.
- Ask the children whether they pray for their friends and family to receive faith from the Holy Spirit as they come to understand their need for a Redeemer.

Virtue Vision

Perseverance
Discuss with the children whether it's easy or hard to keep going with something. Ask them if they are more likely to give up quickly if they're on their own or if they've got someone helping and supporting them.

Ask the children if they think marathon runners appreciate having lots of support on the streets when they're running. Support and encouragement helps people persevere.

Tell the class that after the Holy Spirit gives us faith, he doesn't leave us. He stays with us, encouraging and equipping us so that we can persevere as we run the race of faith. Ask the children whether knowing that the Holy Spirit is always with them will help them to persevere in the Christian life. Ask them how they can help one another persevere.

Memory Activity

You will need to print the memory verse or catechism question and answer and cut it up into words or phrases (depending on the number of children in the class). Stick the words/phrases under the children's chairs before the lesson begins.

Read the memory verse or catechism question and answer to the children and then explain to them that words or phrases are stuck under their seats! Invite the children to get the word from under their seat and then encourage them to organize themselves so that the memory verse is in the correct order. Read the memory verse for the children as they as trying to figure out the correct order of the words/phrases.

⑤ **Closing Prayer Time**

Pray that the children would understand and
know personally that faith comes from the
Holy Spirit rather than themselves, and that
this would make them glad.

Acknowledgments

We are grateful to Crossway for publishing this curriculum and would like to extend special thanks to Tara Davis for her keen editorial eye, and to Dave DeWit and Josh Dennis for their oversight.

Redeemer City to City and Redeemer Presbyterian Church gave The Gospel Coalition permission to develop *The New City Catechism*, originally the work of Timothy Keller and Sam Shammas, into *The New City Catechism Curriculum*.

The project was made possible in part through a generous grant to The Gospel Coalition from the John Templeton Foundation. Thanks to Richard Bollinger and Sarah Clement who believed in the character and virtue potential of this project early on. Thanks also to TGC's Ben Peays and Dan Olson, who worked closely with the John Templeton Foundation when this project was just an idea.

We are grateful for the input and ideas of Sarah Schnitker and Kimberly Griswold of Fuller Theological Seminary on virtue development, educator Caitlin Nunery on classroom activities, and psychologist Brent Bounds on psychological development of children.

Betsy Howard of the Gospel Coalition served as managing editor of *The New City Catechism Curriculum*, and Collin Hansen provided theological oversight.

Most importantly, this curriculum would never have come to fruition without its chief writer, Melanie Lacy of Oak Hill Theological College. Melanie's years of experience as a proponent of catechesis and as a practitioner of children's ministry in the church shaped the curriculum and enriched each lesson.

It took many people to produce *The New City Catechism Curriculum*. Together, we hope it will be used to raise up a generation of children who place their only hope, in life and death, in Jesus Christ.

The New City Catechism

Curriculum

52 Questions
& Answers
for Our Hearts
& Minds

The New City Catechism

Curriculum

Volume 1 – Leader's Guide

God, Creation & Fall, Law

Questions 1–20

WHEATON, ILLINOIS

The New City Catechism Curriculum, Vol. 1, Leader's Guide: God, Creation & Fall, Law, Questions 1–20

Copyright © 2018 by The Gospel Coalition

Published by Crossway
    1300 Crescent Street
    Wheaton, Illinois 60187

This publication was made possible through the support of a grant from the John Templeton Foundation. The opinions expressed in this publication are those of the publisher and do not necessarily reflect the views of the John Templeton Foundation.

Cover design: Matt Wahl & Micah Lanier

First printing 2018

Printed in China

Trade paperback ISBN: 978-1-4335-5939-6

Crossway is a publishing ministry of Good News Publishers.

RRDS		29	28	27	26	25	24	23	22	21	20	19
14	13	12	11	10	9	8	7	6	5	4	3	2

Introduction

A very warm welcome to *The New City Catechism Curriculum*! Our prayer is that this curriculum will serve to equip the children entrusted into your care to be theologically robust, confident, virtuous, and courageous followers of Christ. The curriculum consists of fifty-two lessons, and each lesson corresponds to one of the questions in *The New City Catechism*. The curriculum is aimed at children ages eight through eleven, and is designed to be used in a wide variety of contexts—Sunday school, home school, Christian school, or after-school clubs. The catechism will be most effective if it is concurrently taught in the local church and in the context of the family.

What Is a Catechism?

A catechism is a collection of biblical doctrines, assembled into a question-and-answer format. The term comes from the New Testament word *katecheo*, which simply means "to teach or instruct." The process of catechesis has rich Reformation roots. Martin Luther, John Calvin, and other Reformers endeavored to catechize both children and adults in order to combat doctrinal ignorance and biblical illiteracy. This biblically derived process has proven hugely influential at critical points in the history of the church. We believe the church needs this ancient practice more than ever to equip Christ's people to stand fast in the face of an ever-changing, often hostile culture.

What Is This Curriculum Designed to Do?

Catechize Children

Children are constantly learning. Their inquiring minds soak up information at a spectacular rate. They are trying to make sense of a complex and ever-changing world, seeking to acquire the skills to survive—and even thrive—in life. As they learn, a framework of understanding is established in their minds. This is called a worldview. All children and adults observe and interact with the world through their personal worldview. It is a thrilling and great responsibility to raise children and shape their understanding of the world, how it works, and their unique purpose in it. To catechize children is to give them a coherent and extensive system of thought that equips them to confidently interpret the world and their experiences

in the world through a biblical framework. It also nurtures in children a love for and understanding of the essential doctrines for the Christian faith. To catechize children is to lay deep and strong biblical foundations for a lifetime of faith.

Develop Virtue

The New City Catechism Curriculum is designed to help children not only learn sound doctrine but also to learn how to respond to it and live it out in their lives. Each lesson in *The New City Catechism* has a Virtue Vision covering one of ten Christian virtues that connects in some way with the catechism question. The virtues are Awe, Forgiveness, Gratitude, Honesty, Hope, Humility, Joy, Love, Perseverance, and Trust.

The emphasis and intention of *The New City Catechism Curriculum* is to shape and affect the hearts of the children who engage with each lesson, with the hope that the catechism will contribute greatly to the nurture of godly, mature, and virtuous young men and women. This is definitely not about behavior modification, but rather helping children to respond with keen heart awareness to God's Word as they encounter it in and through the catechism and curriculum. The curriculum seeks to develop in children a mature Christian character, shaped by Scripture, that will be countercultural and striking in our world. By cultivating the capacities for character in both the heart and mind, this curriculum prepares children to love God and others. (For more information and research on faith and virtue development in children, visit newcitycatechism.com/virtue.)

How to Use This Curriculum

The New City Catechism Curriculum is designed to be engaging, dynamic, and creative for children ages eight through eleven. It is intended to be taught in order, beginning at Question 1 and working through to Question 52. It can be taught straight through in a year by covering one lesson a week, but it can also be broken up in whatever way fits your church or school schedule best.

The curriculum is divided into three sections and published in three corresponding books.

Part 1: God, Creation & Fall, Law (twenty lessons covering Questions 1–20)

Part 2: Christ, Redemption, Grace (fifteen lessons covering Questions 21–35)

Part 3: Spirit, Restoration, Growing in Grace (seventeen lessons covering Questions 36–52)

Each lesson is intended to be flexible in length to suit a variety of contexts. You'll find three sample lesson outlines on page 12. The sample lesson outlines vary in length, highlighting how the curriculum can be tailored appropriately to serve the needs of a particular classroom. The most essential elements have been included in the shortest outlines. If you have more time, other activities that reinforce the essential components may be chosen from the longer outlines.

Each component has a time allocated to it; this is meant to be only a rough guide. The length of time a component will take depends on a variety of factors, such as the number of children in the class, the age of the children, and the number of teachers. Carefully consider how much time each component may require in your particular context. You may want to go over the allotted time if an activity is going well, or cut it short when it seems wise to you.

Please do not feel obliged to do exactly as the lesson plan prescribes! If you find that your class loves a particular form of catechism recap, then feel free to use that more often than the lesson plans dictate. Similarly, if certain memorization methods work better for your class than others, use the successful methods more.

Some classes will have children who love to work quietly at crafts; others will need more physical activity. The more you seek to illustrate and apply the lessons in a way that specifically works for your class, the more successful you will be at discipling the children through *The New City Catechism Curriculum*.

Memorization is an essential element of this curriculum. There is an emphasis on helping the children to learn the questions and answers of the catechism and the corresponding Scriptures. Each lesson begins with a memory challenge (Catechism Recap) and ends with a memorization game (Memory Activity). The Catechism Recap will help the children recall and reinforce the catechism questions already covered. The Memory Activity can be used either to learn a Scripture verse or to memorize the new catechism question.

The Catechism Recap section sometimes requires questions and answers to be printed out in different sizes for different activities. When you see the abbreviation "DL," it means you can download a pdf prepared for this activity at www.newcitycatechism.com/recap.

Many lessons include visual resources that can be found in the Resource Book (RB). These resources may be photocopied from the book or downloaded at www.newcitycatechism.com/resourcebook. Some resources are worksheets that accompany the activities, and you will need one per child. Others are visual aids for classroom discussion. It would be helpful to enlarge these photos and illustrations before you print or as you photocopy them.

Leading and Loving the Children Well

Children learn best in an environment that is relationally rich and characterized by love. Consistent class leadership facilitates great relationships between the children and their teachers. Though this may not always be possible, some degree of continuity is highly encouraged.

How to Pray

The best way to grow to love the children in your class is to pray diligently for them. Divide the class up into seven groups, and pray for some of the children each day of the week.

Before each class, come together as a group of teachers and pray that God would be at work in the heart and mind of each child that will come into the classroom.

How to Plan a Lesson

Lesson planning is a serious business; don't leave it until the night before the class!

Begin your planning by praying that God would help you to teach the lesson in a way that is faithful and engaging for the children in your care. (Each lesson includes a Leader's Prayer.) Take some time to read through the curriculum material and carefully consider which components you will use to build your lesson plan. Do pay attention to timings, particularly making sure you leave plenty of time to teach the Bible passage well.

Once you have decided which components will be included in your lesson plan, consult the Leader's Tool Kit list and determine what resources you need for the lesson. It's important to check this list in plenty of time in case you need to buy supplies. Most supplies listed can be found at any craft store.

Finally, read through the Bible passage and Teaching Outline multiple times. The Teaching Outline should be only a guide for you. You should expand or amend it to suit your own children and context. Write out the talk in your own words, and include illustrations and applications that you know will connect with the children in your class.

A Discussion and Question Time outline is included in each lesson. These are not meant to be questions leaders ask the children; rather, they are meant to help leaders prepare for the sorts of questions children might ask them. The children in your class may have entirely different questions. Pray that the Holy Spirit will help you answer well and in accordance with God's Word.

How to Manage the Classroom

Children enjoy and thrive in situations where there are clear boundaries. Communicate clearly to the children what your expectations are with regard to behavior in your classroom. For example:

- Raise your hand if you'd like to speak.

- Don't speak if someone else is speaking.

- Don't leave the classroom without permission.

- Be kind and gentle to each other at all times.

Remember, however, that the children are not in school, so while clear boundaries are helpful, the learning environment should be joyful and grace-saturated. Each teacher should strive to clearly model Christian virtue to the children, particularly the ten virtues highlighted in *The New City Catechism Curriculum*.

Mischief usually arises when children are bored or there is a hiatus in the lesson, so good planning and preparation will help manage the classroom.

Make sure to position yourself near the chatty or disruptive children and encourage them to pay attention and participate well. Try not to draw unnecessary attention to a child as you help him or her focus. The less fuss the better.

Work hard to know the names of the children in the class, and call on them by name to contribute. Nurture an active listening stance in the children by encouraging them to be involved in an interactive way throughout the lesson.

Interact individually with children who cause serious disruption. Explain to them how detrimental and distracting their behavior is to the rest of the class. If the disruption continues, involve the child's parents in the discussion.

How to Encourage Memorization

The key to memorization is repetition! It's unrealistic to expect children to remember something if they've heard it only once. Creative repetition is especially helpful in memorization. For example, hearing or singing a song over and over again embeds it in memory. Remember that children learn in a variety of styles, so hearing, seeing, and doing all help children with memorization.

Review is also a very helpful aid to memorization, which is why each of *The New City Catechism Curriculum* lessons begins with a Catechism Recap. Regular review will substantially increase memorization. This is one of the reasons why *The New City Catechism Curriculum* will be most successful if the catechism is concurrently studied in the home as well as the church.

Explanation is also significant in memorization. It is much easier to remember something if you understand it. The children will be better able to commit the catechism questions to memory well if they understand what the question and answer are all about.

How to Nurture Heart Application

The training and instruction of children and the nurture and nature of their hearts are inextricably linked. So as those who presume to teach children, we must be concerned to help them transfer what they're learning from their heads to their hearts. There is a real difference between knowing and understanding something intellectually and having a heart that is deeply affected by the truth.

So how are we going to engage children's hearts as we teach, train, and catechize them? The first thing to acknowledge is that it isn't easy; it takes hard work and great determination. It's reasonably easy to teach the Bible well—providing head knowledge—and reasonably difficult to apply it well to the hearts of children—growing heart knowledge.

It is important to remember that the molding and shaping of the heart is a process. It takes time and will look different depending on the age, stage, and development (physical, emotional, and social) of each individual child. Every child is different; there is no "one size fits all" when it comes to spiritual development.

Try to use "heart language" with children. This will serve to instill in them an awareness that their heart matters and that it affects how they live.

It's much harder to do real heart application with children when leaders change every week, causing the teachers to have underdeveloped relationships with the children. Leaders must know the children well to apply the Word well. Engaging the hearts of children so that they know God, as opposed to simply knowing about God, requires significant relationships. Children need to regularly observe the lives of older Christians who are seeking to apply God's Word to their own hearts and are willing to live honest and transparent lives before the children.

Remember that virtue is not just taught—it is also caught! By displaying Christian character in our own lives as leaders, we are modeling for children how the lessons play out in the real world today. A teacher's authentic faith and embodiment of virtue can be inspiring and instructive to children, so also be sure to attend to your own spiritual growth.

Clear and thoughtful illustration and application in talks is a significant way to engage a child's heart. This is why it's important to work hard to personalize the teaching outlines in *The New City Catechism Curriculum* in a way that resonates deeply with the children in your class.

In order to effectively engage them we need to make every effort to know and understand their hearts, particularly where they're tempted to idolatry. That means we must know and understand their world well—what they're watching, what they're learning, what their friends are saying, and ultimately what worldviews they're encountering in the world.

One-on-one engagement with a child is particularly useful when seeking to involve the heart; this can be done in the classroom and by the parents in the home. This allows us to ask heart-penetrating questions, and it also invites the child to question back.

We have the opportunity to teach children the art of preaching to their own hearts. This is where a catechism is so eternally useful.

Melanie Lacy
Director of Theology for Children and Youth
Oak Hill College

Lesson Outline

- **75-Minute Lesson Outline**
  - Catechism Recap (5 Mins)
  - Introduction to Question (5 Mins)
  - Activity (10 Mins)
  - Teaching Outline (15 Mins)
  - Activity (10 Mins)
  - Discussion and Question Time (5 Mins)
  - Virtue Vision (10 Mins)
  - Memory Activity (10 Mins)
  - Closing Prayer Time (5 Mins)

- **45-Minute Lesson Outline**
  - Catechism Recap (10 Mins)
  - Introduction to Question (5 Mins)
  - Teaching Outline (15 Mins)
  - Discussion and Question Time (5 Mins)
  - Virtue Vision (10 Mins)

- **30-Minute Lesson Outline**
  - Catechism Recap (10 Mins)
  - Introduction to Question (5 Mins)
  - Teaching Outline (15 Mins)

  → Do pick the time frame that works best for your group.

  → Don't be afraid to mix and match the lesson components based on what works best for the children in your group.

Question 1

What is our only hope in life and death?

Answer

That we are not our own
but belong to God.

Big Idea
Certain hope is found only in relationship
with God through Jesus Christ.

Aim
To help your children understand that
children of God belong to him and should
long to live for him.

Bible Passage
Romans 14:7–12

Memory Verse
"For none of us lives to himself, and none of
us dies to himself. For if we live, we live to
the Lord, and if we die, we die to the Lord.
So then, whether we live or whether we die,
we are the Lord's." (Rom. 14:7–8)

Virtue
Forgiveness

Leader's Notes

Children may not be inclined to regularly consider the purpose of their existence, but they will daily encounter messages that seek to teach them about the meaning of life. The media, school, friends, and family are all seeking to shape and focus children for the future. Some will say that the purpose of life is to be successful and earn lots of money; others will teach that the purpose of life is simply to be happy; and still others may insist that the point of life is to make a positive impact on the world. Children's hearts are often nurtured to place their hope either in themselves or in created things, rather than in the Creator. This lesson aims to help the children understand that they were made by God and for God. The lesson will show them that they should put their hope in God as they come to him through the forgiveness won for them by the Lord Jesus Christ and that he alone is trustworthy in life and death.

Things to remember when planning and teaching:

- Children are familiar with the concept of hope, but in a limited way. They may hope for snow tomorrow or a great present at their next birthday. Their understanding of the concept of eternal hope will need to be developed.

- There is of course nothing wrong with enjoying the good gifts that God has provided in life, like money or enjoying the feeling of happiness. The difficulty arises when these good things become god things.

- The ability to hope in God comes only to those who know his forgiveness through the saving work of Jesus.

- Remember to mix and match the activities in the lesson to fit your time frame (see p. 12 for some sample outlines). You won't have time to do them all. Feel free to adapt each activity based on your class's strengths and weaknesses.

Leader's Prayer

Loving God, please give me joy in the knowledge that you are my hope in life and death. Please make me aware of the areas in my own life where I am tempted to substitute hope in created things for hope in you, the generous Creator God.

Please help the children who will hear this lesson to understand clearly how wonderful it is to know forgiveness through the Lord Jesus, so that they may place their hope in you, both now and forever. In Jesus's name. Amen

Leader's Tool Kit

- Two large pieces of paper

- Markers

- Copies of Q1 Illustrations (RB)

- Each word of the memory verse printed on its own card; two sets of cards

(5) Catechism Introduction

This is an opportunity to explain to the children what a catechism is. Explain that a catechism is simply a way to learn more about what the Bible says on many different things. The way it works is by learning questions and answers. Encourage the children by telling them that this is a biblical, fun, and exciting way to grow in the Christian faith. Explain to them that at different times in history, God has used this way of learning about him and his Word to grow, strengthen, and equip his church in different countries around the world.

Pass around copies of *The New City Catechism for Kids* for the children to see.

(5) Introduction to Question 1

Ask the children if they can figure out which stories these sentences refer to:

? **The prince's only hope was to find the owner of the glass slipper.**

| *Cinderella*

? **The rabbit's only hope was that Mr. McGregor would not find him in the watering can.**

| *The Tale of Peter Rabbit* (Beatrix Potter)

? **The children's only hope was Aslan.**

| *The Lion, The Witch and the Wardrobe* (C. S. Lewis)

Then ask the children what they think the phrase "their only hope was" means. They will recognize that each character was in a situation that required some help to escape from it. Highlight for the children that hope often involves trusting somebody or something. Ask the children about the kinds of things they hope for their future.

Introduce Question 1: "What is our only hope in life and death?" Explain to the children that in life people hope for many things, but in actual fact the Bible teaches that there is only one certain hope in life and in death, and that is that we are not our own but belong, body and soul, both in life and death, to God and to our Savior Jesus Christ.

(10) Activity

Lay out two large pieces of paper. On the top of one of the papers write "My Family" and on the other write "God's Family."

Ask the children to identify and list the things that are great about belonging to their particular family. They will perhaps mention the love of their parents, the home that they live in, or the fun vacations they enjoy. Write down their answers. Ask the children what would happen if another child were adopted into their family. Would he benefit from all these great things as well because he would now belong to their family?

Then ask them to identify and list the great things about being part of God's family. Be prepared to offer some prompts, such as, "Think about why Jesus died on the cross," or "What do we look forward to after death?" Write down their answers.

Explain to the children that everybody is born into a human family (it may be worth acknowledging that some of these families are less than ideal), but not everybody is born into God's family. God brings people into his family and makes them his children through adoption! Teach the children that adoption into God's family allows people to have certain hope and that adoption happens after people have realized that they are sinful and turn to Jesus to say they are sorry and ask for his forgiveness.

(15) Teaching Outline

Begin the teaching time by asking for God's help. Ask that the lesson would be taught faithfully and that the children might listen well.

Introduce the children to Romans 14. Explain to them that this letter is written by Paul and that in this chapter he is trying to sort out some disagreements among people in the church in Rome.

Tell the children that this was a family squabble! The people who were arguing were all people who had found forgiveness in Jesus and had been adopted into God's family; they just couldn't agree on how they should live. Paul explains to them that in some situations, people in God's family will do things differently, but that the important thing is that they seek to do things to bring praise and glory to God.

Read Romans 14:7–12. Provide Bibles for the children to read along with you.

Ask the children what they think verse 8 means. What does it mean to belong to the Lord? Is it a good thing or a bad thing?

Help the children to recognize that most people believe that their lives are their own. However, those who have found forgiveness in Jesus and have been adopted into God's family recognize that they have been rescued from God's anger and punishment. The Bible says that those who do not believe in Jesus are slaves to sin. In order for slaves to be freed, a price must be paid for their release. Jesus paid the ultimate price for sinners by sacrificing his own life and paying the price for sin on the cross. The Bible says that those who are adopted into God's family have been bought at a great price, and now their lives belong to God. Tell the children that being God's child is the most wonderful way to live life—the most joyful, freeing, and fulfilling. Paul is helping the Romans understand that their lives are not their own. Everything that they are and have belongs to God.

Ask the children if they think it's easy to live for God. Ask them what might stop them from living for God. Ask them to consider how remembering what Jesus did on the cross might motivate them to live for God. (Be prepared to prompt them in their answers.)

Help the children consider how to live with God as Lord of their lives. Help them see how sometimes they may prefer to be Lord. Offer some examples from their everyday experiences where they might

struggle to submit to the lordship of God. Ask them when they're tempted to put themselves first.

Explain to the children that Paul helps the Christians in Rome to focus on their own lives and not to worry about how others are living. Show the children verse 12. Explain that one day, everybody will answer to God for how they've lived their lives. Help them to understand that, because of the price Jesus paid on the cross, those who've been adopted into God's family should long to live fully for him.

Conclude by reminding the children that being adopted into God's family means that we get all the great things that come with being part of the family. We trust God in life and death, knowing that he is with us and that he alone is where our hope is found.

Finish the teaching time by helping the children commit Question 1 and the answer to memory.

(These notes are just for guidance. Please expand or amend them to suit your own children and context. Write out your talk in your own words, and include illustrations and applications that you know will connect with your children.)

---

⑩ Activity ☼

Around your classroom, post pictures of various things that represent the children's lives. Cut out and use Q1 Illustrations (RB). Feel free to add your own pictures.

- Television
- iPad/Computer
- School
- Sports

Notes

- Music
- Friends
- Money
- Shopping
- Family

Arrange the children in pairs and send a pair to each picture. Ask them to discuss how belonging to God affects how they should use or interact with the various components of their lives. When all the pairs have visited all the pictures, ask them to sit back down and discuss with the group whether they think that belonging to God makes a difference in their day-to-day lives.

⑤ Discussion and Question Time

Some questions that might arise include:

? Does this just mean that we move from being slaves to sin to being God's slave?

Explain to the children that they are made for relationship with God, which is where perfect freedom is found. So while the world might think that Christianity is all about rules and regulations, the truth is that being part of God's family is how best to enjoy life in all its fullness.

? What if I just can't live for God all the time?

Explain to the children that in this life, it will be a struggle to live for God, but that God will help them through his Spirit. They can prayerfully ask for help.

Also use this opportunity to help the children to think about their own lives and how this catechism question and answer affects them personally.

- How will they respond to the messages the world communicates about the meaning of life?
- How will they seek always to have their hope in God?
- How might they explain what their hope is to someone at school?

⑩ Virtue Vision

Forgiveness

Remind the children of the earlier conversation about the benefits of being in a family. When God adopted us into his family, we received forgiveness through Jesus. We belong to God and enjoy all the privileges of being in his family. While it may be easy to *accept* forgiveness, it can be hard to *give* forgiveness. But once we become a part of God's family, we should want to imitate our Father. God showed sinners great mercy when he sent Jesus to die on the cross. God's children must be quick to forgive because we have been forgiven.

Share this short testimony with the children:

> Corrie ten Boom was imprisoned for helping Jewish people during the Holocaust escape from the people who wanted to kill them. Many years later, after she was released, she was at a church service when she saw a man who had been her prison guard. Corrie had spoken all about the forgiveness that God offers through Jesus. The man came up to her after she spoke and told her that he had found forgiveness in Jesus and had been adopted into God's family. He wanted to shake Corrie's hand, but Corrie remembered all of the horrible things that had happened to her and others in prison. She just couldn't bring herself to shake his hand. But then she remembered who she was: a child of God who had been forgiven. As one who belonged to God, she was to live for him. So she prayed and asked God to give her the strength to forgive this former guard and rejoice that he was part of God's family too. God answered Corrie's prayer.

Notes

⑩ Memory Activity

Print each word of the memory verse onto its own card; you will need two sets of cards. If you choose not to do a memory verse, this activity can be used to help the children memorize the catechism question and answer.

- Divide the children into two teams.

- Read the memory verse out to the children.

- Read the memory verse, inviting the children to repeat each word after you.

- Read the memory verse again and invite the children to join in saying it with you.

- Hand out a full set of memory verse cards to each team; make sure the cards are not in order! Ask the children to put the words in the correct order. Points can be given to the team that first arranges the cards correctly.

- Practice the memory verse one final time.

⑤ Closing Prayer Time

Conclude the lesson by inviting the children to say short prayers asking God to help them to live for him and to allow him to be the Lord of their lives.

19

Question 2

What is God?

Answer

God is the creator of everyone and everything.

Big Idea
God can be fully known only through the pages of Scripture.

Aim
To help the children understand who the God of the Bible is.

Bible Passage
Psalm 86

Memory Verse
"There is none like you among the gods, O Lord, nor are there any works like yours. All the nations you have made shall come and worship before you, O Lord, and shall glorify your name. For you are great and do wondrous things; you alone are God.... But you, O Lord, are a God merciful and gracious, slow to anger and abounding in steadfast love and faithfulness." (Ps. 86:8–10, 15)

Virtue
Awe

Leader's Notes

Children, particularly those in the West, are growing up in societies that seek to remove God from life. The atheistic worldview is increasingly popular, with movements aggressively declaring that there is no God. Even where some belief in God remains, it is often not an accurate understanding of who God is as revealed in the pages of Scripture. This lesson will seek to introduce the children to the God of the Bible and to instill in them confidence that there is a God and that we can both know about him and know him personally.

Things to remember when planning and teaching:

- Children who have been raised in a Christian context will hopefully already have a firm belief in God. They will, however, need some help in understanding how to engage with a world that is increasingly keen to erase God.

- Children must be challenged to commit to searching the Scriptures for themselves in order to grow in their knowledge and love of God.

- Remember to mix and match the activities in the lesson to fit your time frame (see p. 12 for some sample outlines). You won't have time to do them all. Feel free to adapt each activity based on your class's strengths and weaknesses.

Leader's Prayer

O great God, thank you that you alone are God. Thank you that you are knowable, and through the pages of the Bible I can understand more about you each day. Please, would you increase my love for you as I prepare this lesson? Would you cause the children who will participate to gain a clear understanding of who you are and what you're like? In Jesus's name. Amen.

Leader's Tool Kit

- Some autobiographies (or pictures of autobiographies) of famous people
- White paper
- Markers
- Magazine articles or TV clips that show an atheistic worldview
- Envelopes
- Tape
- "Fun size" candy bars or small toys
- Q2 Attributes of God (RB)

⏱ Catechism Recap

Quiz the students to see what they remember from the previous lesson.

- What was Question 1?

  What is our only hope in life and death?

- What is the answer to Question 1?

  That we are not our own but belong to God.

- What was the memory verse?

  "For none of us lives to himself, and none of us dies to himself. For if we live, we live to the Lord, and if we die, we die to the Lord. So then, whether we live or whether we die, we are the Lord's." (Rom. 14:7–8)

- What was the name of the lady in the story about forgiveness?

  Corrie ten Boom

Commend the children for their participation and tell them that they're ready to move to Question 2!

⏱ Introduction to Question 2

Have some autobiographies of famous people ready to show the children. They should include people that most of the children will recognize.

Ask the children if they have ever read an autobiography. Explain that autobiographies are books people write about themselves.

Show the children some of the autobiographies you've brought. Explain that it's not usually easy to get to know famous people, but reading an autobiography is one way to find out a little bit more about them.

Introduce Question 2 to the children: "What is God?" Explain that this lesson will focus on getting to know God through his own story, the Bible.

⏱ Activity ☼

Give each child a piece of paper and some markers. Have them fold the paper in half to make it look like a book.

Ask the children to consider what they might include in their own autobiography.

- What would they like people to know about who they are?

- What great deeds have they done that the world should know about?

Get them to design the front cover of their autobiography, and then challenge them to write a brief summary that might be printed on the back cover of their autobiography.

⑮ **Teaching Outline**

Begin the teaching time by asking for God's help. Ask that the lesson would be taught faithfully and that the children might listen well.

Introduce this teaching time by telling the children that some people say there is no God. Others say that we cannot know what God is truly like. Some people even make God what they want him to be. Tell the children that they should expect to encounter these views in the world. It might be helpful to show them some evidence from popular media, magazine articles, or TV clips. (For example, see the famous 1966 *Time* magazine cover story "Is God Dead?" or the *New York Times* article "God Is a Question, Not an Answer.")

Ask the children if they ever encounter these views at school or among their friends.

Draw the children's attention back to their autobiography covers. Comment that even through reading the little that they've written, you have grown to know them more.

Explain to the children that God wants to be known—although God can never be known in all his fullness. He longs that people might know about him and subsequently truly know him. God has kindly revealed himself, and he has done that in and through his Word, the Bible. God has spoken, and his words have been written down so that people throughout all of history might hear God speak. As God speaks through the Bible, he reveals what he is like.

Read Psalm 86. Provide Bibles for the children to read along with you.

Explain to the children that King David wrote this psalm, and it reveals a personal relationship between God and David. In this psalm, David refers to God in a way that reveals he is kind, forgiving, and abounding in great love.

Direct the children's attention to verses 8–10 and ask them what they can learn about God from these verses. Invite them to share their thoughts with the group.

These verses reveal the power and greatness of God. There is no one, in heaven or on earth, who is like God. God is so powerful that one day all nations will bow down before him. He is sovereign, ruling over all things. The beautiful thing for the children to understand from this psalm is that this awesome, all-knowing, powerful, incomparable, sovereign, and great God is approachable. David in this psalm is crying out to God in prayer! Remind the children that this is the God who is eternal, who has no beginning and no end, who has created the whole universe and sustains it each day, and who has performed countless miracles. This big God hears the prayers of his people.

Remind the children that this is God's story, and even in these few short verses God makes himself known.

Show the children from verse 11 that David prayed that he might know God's way and live fully for God (Ps. 86:11). David has understood who God is and what God is like. David longs to follow him with an undivided heart. Tell the children that the purpose of spending time reading the Bible is to come to know God more and to understand more fully what it is to live his way.

Conclude by confirming for the children that there is a God and that they can know him.

Finish the teaching time by helping the children commit Question 2 and the answer to memory.

(These notes are just for guidance. Please expand or amend them to suit your own children and context. Write out your talk in your own words and include illustrations and applications that you know will connect with your children.)

Notes

---

⑩ Activity

Cut up Q2 Attributes of God (RB) so that each attribute is on one slip of paper. Wrap each piece of paper around a small candy bar or small toy, and hide them around the classroom or building.

This activity will introduce the children to even more attributes of God. Let the children go on a treasure hunt. Tell the children not to unwrap the items until they return to their seats. Once the children are seated, invite them to open the items and read the attributes and accompanying definitions aloud. (If you used candy bars, tell the children they must take them home and eat them only with their parents' permission.)

- Eternal—God has no beginning or end
- Righteous—God is right in everything he says, does, and thinks
- Sovereign—God rules over and is in control of all things
- Holy—God is perfect and separate from sin
- Gracious—God is kind
- Infinite—God knows no bounds
- Omniscient—God knows all things
- Wise—God never makes mistakes
- Faithful—God always keeps his promises
- Omnipotent—God is all powerful
- Omnipresent—God is everywhere, all the time
- Immutable—God never changes
- Self-sufficient—God does not need anything or anyone
- Merciful—God is compassionate
- Incomprehensible—God is too grand to understand
- Never-tiring—God never has to sleep
- Patient—God is slow to become angry
- Victorious—God always wins

Notes

(5) Discussion and Question Time

Some of the questions that
might arise include:

? Is the God of the Bible
actually interested in me?

> Reassure the children that God is
> intimately involved in his world and is
> concerned for each of his children.

? Why does God not speak
directly to us today?

> Explain to the children that God speaks
> directly today through his Word. The
> Bible is infallible (never wrong), and
> it is trustworthy. Help the children
> to understand that it would be very
> difficult to discern the authoritative
> voice of God outside the Bible.

? Can we actually believe that
God is who he says he is?

> The whole Bible testifies to God's
> character. Explain to the children that
> God's mighty acts recorded in Scripture
> confirm time and time again that he is
> who he says he is.

Also use this opportunity to help the
children to think about their own lives
and how this catechism question affects
them personally.

- Ask the children to consider how they
  might describe the God of the Bible to
  someone who has never heard about him.
- Ask the children what difference
  having a bigger view of God
  might make in their lives.

(10) Virtue Vision

Awe

*Provide each child with a piece of paper, an
envelope, and some markers.*

Explain to the children that to be filled with
awe is to be amazed and filled with wonder.

Ask the children to write a letter to
themselves and to describe the ways that the
lesson filled them with awe as they learned
more about who God is and what he is like.

Encourage them to be creative in the design
and layout of their letter. Ask the children to
place their letters in the envelope and to seal
the envelope. Tell the children to write their
name and address on their envelope.

Sometime during the week mail the letters
to the children; this will once again cause
them to be filled with awe as they reflect on
their great God.

⑩ Memory Activity

This memory verse is longer than most, and so the memory activity for this lesson will not work for the catechism answer. If your class is not memorizing the verses, use one of the memory activities from another lesson to reinforce the memorization of Question 2.

Divide the children into four groups, and give each of them a sentence of the memory verse to learn. Give the children a little time to learn their sentence.

1. There is none like you among the gods, O Lord, nor are there any works like yours.

2. All the nations you have made shall come and worship before you, O Lord, and shall glorify your name.

3. For you are great and do wondrous things; you alone are God. . . .

4. But you, O Lord, are a God merciful and gracious, slow to anger and abounding in steadfast love and faithfulness. (Ps. 86:8–10, 15)

Call the children together, and have each group say the line assigned to them; you can ask some groups to say their line loudly and some quietly, or some in high-pitched voices and some in low-pitched voices. Conclude by getting the group to recite the verse together.

Notes

⑤ Closing Prayer Time

Have the children call out why they think God is awesome! Join the shouts of praise together by thanking God that he reveals himself and allows himself to be known through the Bible.

Question 3

How many persons are there in God?

Answer

There are three persons in one God: the Father, the Son, and the Holy Spirit.

Big Idea

A correct understanding of the Trinity is essential to right worship of God.

Aim

To help the children understand that God is *three* persons; Father, Son, and Holy Spirit, and that each person is *fully* God and that there is only *one* God.

Bible Passage
2 Corinthians 13:5–14

Memory Verse
"The grace of the Lord Jesus Christ and the love of God and the fellowship of the Holy Spirit be with you all." (2 Cor. 13:14)

Virtue
Awe

Leader's Notes

It is worth acknowledging that the concept of the doctrine of the Trinity is hard to understand for adults as well as children! However, it is important for children to begin to engage with the doctrine of the Trinity, which will expand their knowledge and understanding of who God is and what he is like. Children will be exposed to pantheistic religions through various everyday encounters: at school, with their friends, and via the media. It is important to help them understand that the God of the Bible is one and that Christianity is a monotheistic faith. The examination of the doctrine of the Trinity will help the children to understand that God is one, but also three distinct persons. This lesson aims to begin to help the children to understand the beauty and diversity in the Godhead. It is worth noting that the Trinity is often described as a mystery for a reason; be as clear and concise as you can in this lesson, but do not expect the children to grasp the doctrine fully.

Things to remember when planning and teaching:

- It is quite possible that the children will have heard illustrations that have attempted to teach the doctrine of the Trinity incorrectly (water, steam, ice; a shamrock; an egg). Be prepared to graciously correct any misunderstanding and explain to the children that most of the illustrations people use don't actually teach the doctrine well.

- You may need to reassure the children by telling them that this is a hard concept to understand and that many adults find it tricky. Explain that in our humanness it is sometimes difficult to fully grasp the greatness of God.

- The use and consistency of language in this lesson will be extremely important. Aim to explain this question as simply and clearly as possible.

- Remember to mix and match the activities in the lesson to fit your time frame (see p. 12 for some sample outlines). You won't have time to do them all. Feel free to adapt each activity based on your class's strengths and weaknesses.

Leader's Prayer

Beautiful triune God, thank you for revealing yourself in your Word as God the Father, God the Son, and God the Holy Spirit. I praise you that in learning more about your triune nature, I can further understand what unity in diversity means. Please grant the children who will engage with this lesson a great degree of comprehension, and help me to explain and teach the lesson in a way that glorifies you. I pray that the children would better understand who you are and what you're like after this lesson. In Jesus's name. Amen.

Leader's Tool Kit

- Rolls of chalkboard paper
- Liquid chalk marker pens
- Printouts of the words *God the Father*, *God the Son*, and *God the Holy Spirit*
- A copy of Q3 Trinity Diagram (RB) for each child
- Colored pencils
- Papier-mâché letters (AWE)
- Permanent marker

Catechism Recap

Cover a wall well with chalkboard paper and provide liquid chalk pens for the children to use.

Divide the children into a few groups and give them a designated area to design. Invite the children to design and decorate their chalkboard with as much detail as they can remember of Questions 1 and 2 of the catechism. Encourage them to try to recall the questions and answers. You can award distinctions such as "most creative," "neatest," and "prettiest."

Introduction to Question 3

Print out and cut up the words God the Father, God the Son, *and* God the Holy Spirit,—*you can either cut them into individual letters, or if you have a small group, words. Put all the letters/words into a container.*

Explain to the children that today you're going to learn a really difficult concept about God. At this stage encourage the children to listen carefully, but reassure them that it doesn't matter if they don't gain full understanding. Tell the children to empty the container and to try to assemble the letters into words or phrases.

Depending on the capabilities of the group, you can give them some clues or help. Once the puzzle has been solved, introduce the children to today's question: How many persons are there in God? Introduce the children to the concept of one God and three persons—Father, Son, and Holy Spirit.

Activity

Read the following true/false quiz aloud. Tell the children that if the statement is true, they should run to the right side of the room. They should run to the left side if they think the statement is false.

1. The word *Trinity* is found in the Bible. (False)

2. There is one God. (True)

3. The Father is fully God. (True)

31

Notes

4. God has always existed as three persons. (True)

5. God the Son only came into existence when Mary became pregnant. (False)

6. The Son is not the Father. (True)

7. The persons of the Trinity each have distinct roles. (True)

8. God the Father died on the cross for our sin. (False)

⑮ Teaching Outline

Begin the teaching time by asking for God's help. Ask that the lesson would be taught faithfully and that the children might listen well.

Ask the children if they have learned who the three persons of the Trinity are. Hopefully they will say God the Father, God the Son, and God the Holy Spirit.

Explain to the children that the word *Trinity* means "Tri-Unity"—*Tri* means three, and *Unity* means one. The word acknowledges what the Bible reveals to us about God, that God is three persons who all have the same essence of God.

Highlight for the children these key things they need to understand about God:

1. There is only one God. (Deut. 6:4)

2. God is three persons. (2 Cor. 13:14)

3. Each person is fully God. The Bible speaks of the Father as God (Phil. 1:2), Jesus as God (Titus 2:13), and the Holy Spirit as God (Acts 5:3–4). Emphasize that each person is fully God, not one-third of God.

4. Each person of the Trinity is different from the others. Because the Father sent the Son into the world (John 3:16), the Father cannot be the same person as the Son. Likewise, after the Son returned to the Father (John 16:10), the Father and the Son sent the Holy Spirit into the world (John 14:26; Acts 2:33). Therefore, the Holy Spirit must be distinct from the Father and the Son.

5. The three persons of the Trinity relate eternally as Father, Son, and Holy Spirit.

Read 2 Corinthians 13:5–14. Provide Bibles for the children to read along with you.

Introduce the children to the apostle Paul and his second letter to the Corinthians. Explain that Paul is writing to the Corinthians in preparation for a visit he is planning to make to them. Tell the children that there are lots of problems in the Corinthian church that Paul wants to address and that he's afraid that when he arrives in Corinth, the Christians will be arguing and fighting. Tell the children that in these ten verses, Paul is really challenging the Christians in Corinth to live obedient lives for God's glory. Paul ends this letter with a verse that has become very well-known and is often said as a prayer in church: *"May the grace of the Lord Jesus Christ, and the love of God, and the fellowship of the Holy Spirit be with you all."*

Paul mentions the three persons of the Trinity in this verse; there are three who's and one what! In this prayer, Paul is trying to show the Corinthians how important God is for their lives and relationships with one another. Explain to the children that in this verse we see something of the distinct roles of the Father, Son, and Holy Spirit.

Paul first identifies Jesus, God the Son, as the one who displays God's grace clearly in his life and death. Grace is kindness shown to someone who does not deserve it. Tell the children that when they are kind to someone who has been unkind to them, they are showing grace. Jesus Christ is the person of the Trinity who reveals God's grace to us. Remind them that God shows sinners great grace by allowing the Lord Jesus to take the punishment for sin that was due to them. Those who've experienced such grace should show grace to others.

Paul then prays that the Corinthians would know the love of God the Father. Paul is describing the love of a Father that is

known by those who have been brought into a relationship with him through the sacrificial death of Jesus. Highlight to the children that as those who know the great love of God as Father and those who are made in his image, they should be characterized by love.

Finally, Paul prays that the Corinthians would know the fellowship of God the Holy Spirit. Explain to the children that it is the Spirit who brings sinners into friendship with God and into friendship with one another.

Finish by telling the children that the experience of grace, love, and friendship is the result of being in a relationship with God. The triune God exists in three persons, the Father, the Son, and the Holy Spirit. Each one demonstrates for us a certain characteristic in this verse. Jesus shows us the grace of God. The Father shows us love. The Holy Spirit draws us into fellowship. These three are one.

Conclude the teaching time by helping the children commit Question 3 and the answer to memory.

(These notes are just for guidance. Please expand or amend them to suit your own children and context. Write out your talk in your own words and include illustrations and applications that you know will connect with your children.)

Notes

33

(10) Activity

*Give each child a copy of Q3
Trinity Diagram (RB).*

Invite the children to fill in the blanks, and, if
time allows, have them color the diagram.

Remind the children that:

1. There is only one God.

2. The Father is God.

3. The Son is God.

4. The Holy Spirit is God.

5. The Father is not the Son.

6. The Son is the not the Holy Spirit.

7. The Holy Spirit is not the Father.

(5) Discussion and Question Time

Some of the questions that
might arise include:

? **Why do we believe this doctrine if the
word *Trinity* isn't used in the Bible?**

Explain to the children that the nature
of the triune God is very clearly
shown in the Bible. Although the
word isn't used, the doctrine is present
in Scripture. Also mention that the
Christian church has believed in the
Trinity for several thousand years.

? **This is really hard to understand. If I
don't understand it, am I not a Christian?**

Reassure the children that the Trinity
is hard to understand and that many
adults can't fully comprehend what the
Trinity is. Explain that this is because
we're not God, and he is hard for us to
comprehend. Reassure the children that
a lack of understanding does not mean
that they're not Christians.

? **What does it mean that persons
of the Trinity related eternally as
Father, Son, and Holy Spirit?**

Explain to the children that God wasn't
created like us. God always existed and
always will exist. So God the Father,
God the Son, and God the Holy
Spirit always related to each other in
unity and love.

Also use this opportunity to help the
children think about their own lives and how
this catechism question and answer affects
them personally.

- Help the children think about what
it means to be made in the image of
God when we understand that God
is three persons in one. Remind them
that God exists in perfect unity and
love. Help the children understand the
implications for personal relationships
and the necessity of community.

34

- Help the children to think about what it looks like to have distinct roles but to be equal in value, as God the Father, Son, and Spirit are. Explain to the children that being different or having different roles does not mean people have less value.

Virtue Vision

Awe

Have large papier-mâché letters spelling AWE ready for the children to write on with permanent markers. You may need more than one set depending on the size of your class.

Ask the children if they remember what awe is. To be in awe of something is to be amazed and filled with wonder. We often use the word *awesome* casually, but ask the children if they think it is accurate to describe something like a video game or a toy as "awesome," given the true definition of *awe*.

Explain that awe is a "See-Feel-Do" thing.

First, we use our senses, typically sight, to experience something vast (visiting the ocean or witnessing the live performance of a large orchestra are examples). Next, we feel humbled or small in comparison. We may even get goose bumps, or our jaw may fall open as we are amazed at what we see. Finally, the experience of sensing and feeling awe leads us to action. For instance, awe may lead us to give praise to God who formed all of creation.

Ask the children whether knowing that God is a Trinity makes them feel awe.

Give each group a set of letters (*A, W, E*). Have them write descriptive words of God or how they feel toward God. For an extra challenge give the following special instructions: When they are writing on the letter *A*, they must use words beginning with *A*; on letter *W*, they must use words beginning with *W*; and on letter *E*, they must use words beginning with *E*. Take time to set up a classroom display of the letters so the art can be a reminder for the children to experience awe in the future.

Memory Activity

Print each word of the memory verse or catechism on a piece of paper, and then cut each word in half. Hide one half of each word around your classroom.

Give every child one half of a word from the memory verse or catechism answer. Instruct them to find the other half of their word that is hidden somewhere in the classroom. (If you have a small group of children in your class, give each child responsibility for two words; if you have a big class, have children work in pairs). Once the children have

Notes

found the other halves of their words, have them put the sentence in the correct order. Read it through with the children. Then remove half of some of the words and read through it again. Finally remove full words, and see if the children can remember the whole sentence.

(5) **Closing Prayer Time**

Close the lesson by praying for the children, that God would grant them understanding and that by learning about the Trinity they would have a much bigger understanding of who he is.

Question 4

How and why did God create us?

Answer

God created us male and female in his own image to glorify him.

Big Idea
Men and women are created by God, in his image and for his glory.

Aim
To help children understand that they were made in the image of God and for his glory.

Bible Passage
Genesis 1:26–31

Memory Verse
"So God created man in his own image, in the image of God he created him; male and female he created them." (Gen. 1:27)

Virtue
Love

Leader's Notes

Children are increasingly being exposed to evolutionary theory that is used to discredit the existence of God and the fact that the world was created by God and for his glory. If they are not fully versed in the Christian doctrine of creation, children will find it difficult to stand apart when they face disagreements about the origins of the world and humanity. This lesson will allow the children to engage with the biblical truth concerning the creation of humanity and to understand why God chose to create men and women. This lesson aims to ground children in the knowledge that they were created by a loving God in order to rule over his creation and to show his likeness to the world, while glorifying him with their lives.

Things to remember when planning and teaching:

- The children may be concerned about engaging with this question in relation to the theory of evolution. Help the children to have confidence in the knowledge that God created people in his image and likeness and for his glory.

- The children will be aware that God created men and women, and some of them may have been exposed to some of the popular debates concerning gender. Be sensitive while clearly showing the children that God created two genders and remind them (from Question 2) that God doesn't make mistakes.

- Remember to mix and match the activities in the lesson to fit your time frame (see p. 12 for some sample outlines). You won't have time to do them all. Feel free to adapt each activity based on your class's strengths and weaknesses.

Leader's Prayer

Creator God, thank you for the beauty and design of your world. May my heart be filled with awe and wonder each day as I consider the greatness and power of your creative work. Thank you for creating me in your image and likeness. May I always glorify you.

Please help the children who hear this lesson to have confidence in you, the Creator God. May they trust that your design is good and that your plan for creation is glorious. In Jesus's name. Amen.

Leader's Tool Kit

- Q4 Catechism Recap (DL) printed and cut up
- Markers

- White paper
- Q4 Human Body Outline (RB), several copies

▪ Q4 Illustrations of Ancient Near East Statues (RB)

▪ Play-Doh (4–5 cans)

Catechism Recap

Print out and cut up the answers to Questions 1, 2, and 3 (DL), and lay them upside down on the floor in the middle of the classroom.

Begin the catechism recap by reading Questions 1, 2, and 3 aloud (don't read out the answers!). Tell the children that on the floor are the words that make up the answers to each question. Have the children turn over the words and see if they can work together to correctly assemble the right words into the right order to answer each question. Practice saying each question and answer together to finish the recap.

Introduction to Question 4

Provide the children with paper and markers.

Gather the children into small groups, and ask them to pick one person from their group to pose as a model. Then ask the children to create a Minecraft avatar based on the model.

Introduce Question 4: "How and why did God create us?" Tell the children that the lesson today is all about the creation of men and women, boys and girls. They have just made an image of their friend by drawing an avatar. Highlight the fact that when God created men and women, he made them in his image, to be like him. Tell the children that this catechism question will help them to understand what that means and why it's important.

Activity ☼

Divide the children into groups, and give each group a copy of Q4 Human Body Outline (RB).

Divide the children into groups, and ask them to identify all the ways that humans are different from the rest of God's created beings. Have them fill in the outlines of the human bodies with words or drawings that describe or show the differences.

The aim of this activity is to help the children clearly understand that by being created in the image of God, humans are distinct from the rest of God's creation.

Conclude this activity by highlighting for the children that God not only made humans different from the rest of creation, but he actually made two different genders—male and female. Tell the children that God intentionally made men and women to live in his creation and that he made them equal but different.

(15) **Teaching Outline**

Begin the teaching time by asking for God's help. Ask that the lesson would be taught faithfully and that the children might listen well.

Introduce the teaching by telling the children that there are many people in the world today who sadly do not believe in God and therefore do not believe that human beings were created but rather they developed or evolved accidentally over a long period of time.

Tell the children that Christians disagree with this belief and confidently believe that human beings were made by God, the Creator of all things.

Ask the children to compare the difference between growing up thinking that you're alive because of a random development on earth, and knowing that you were created by a loving and good God. Ask them if this knowledge makes a difference in how they view their worth and value and purpose in life.

The Bible clearly declares that God made human beings not because he was lonely or because he needed some sort of help on earth, but because he is loving and relational. God did not need people, but he decided to create and use people as part of his plan for his world.

Read Genesis 1:26–31. Provide Bibles for the children to read along with you.

Introduce the children to the creation account in Genesis 1–2.

Explain to the children that in the ancient Near East, a king would often set up an image or statue of himself to show his rule over an area. The image would communicate to everyone that the king was in charge of the land. Show the children some pictorial examples from Q4 Illustrations of Ancient Near East Statues (RB).

Genesis 1:26–27 declares that God made human beings in his image and placed them in his world to rule over all other created things. Human beings are not statues, but they are made in the image and likeness of God, to represent him and his rule on earth. Human beings were given authority by God to rule over all the earth.

So human beings were not accidents that just evolved on earth. They were the pinnacle of God's creation—nothing else was created in God's image! At the end of the sixth day God surveyed everything and saw that it was very good.

Ask the children what they think it means to be made in God's image. Ask them to think about all the differences they spotted between human beings and the rest of creation.

Explain to the children that human beings are made in God's likeness. This means that we will be like God in lots of ways—

in character rather than in appearance. We are God's representatives here on earth, and so we are called to reflect his image in our lives. Some of the ways we might do that are by being:

Creative: God is creative. He instructed Adam and Eve in Genesis 1:28 to use their creativity to rule over creation.

Communicative: God is a God who speaks, and so we too are made to communicate.

Relational: God is in perfect relationship as the Trinity, and being made in his image means that we are relational too. Ultimately we are made for relationship with God.

Loving: God's purpose in creating human beings was love, and so we are called to live and rule showing God's loving character to the world.

Help the children to see from the Bible passage that God intentionally created men and women. Clearly explain that God did not make everyone the same, nor did he allow people to choose their gender. He clearly created men and women and boys and girls.

Finish by explaining to the children that their existence is about showing God's existence and about giving him glory.

Ask the children what they think it means to glorify God.

In essence, to glorify God is to acknowledge him as loving Creator, as all-powerful and perfect, and then to live lives of praise to him. We can exalt him in the world. We can show the watching world what he is like. (Tell the children that Question 6 will teach a little more about how to glorify God.)

Conclude the teaching time by helping the children commit Question 4 and the answer to memory.

(These notes are just for guidance. Please expand or amend to suit your own children and context. Write out your talk in your own words and include illustrations and applications that you know will connect with your children.)

🔟 Activity ☼

Help the children to create a rap or hand-clapping rhyme for Question 4. Ask them to name some of the key things that they would like to communicate and then set the words to a beat. This could be done in a large group or in smaller groups.

⑤ Discussion and Question Time

Some of the questions that might arise include:

? Can we really believe that human beings were created by God?

> Yes! Millions of people do and have done so throughout history. Help the children to understand that Genesis wasn't meant to be a scientific book describing every detail of how humans were created, but rather it's about the beginning of God's great creation.

? How did God actually make people?

> The Bible describes how Adam and Eve were made, and everyone else descended from them. We know that God created everything out of nothing. (This might be a good time to have them turn in their Bibles to Hebrews 11:3 and read it aloud.) After he created the earth, he created Adam from the dust of the earth, breathing life into his nostrils (Gen. 2:7, 21–22).

? What about the theory of evolution?

> The theory of evolution—that we are here by accident rather than created—is often taught as fact, but it is just a theory. Tell the children that there are many Christians who are scientists who believe God created us out of nothing.

Also use this opportunity to help the children to think about their own lives and how this catechism question and answer affects them personally.

- How will they reflect God's image in his world?
- Has sin affected their ability to image God?
- What happens when they decide not to glorify God?
- How might they explain to a friend who thinks we are here by accident that they believe God created human beings, and that they have a purpose in his plan for his world?

⑩ Virtue Vision

Love
Remind the children that God created out of love, and to be his image bearers in the world we should be loving too.

Help the children to consider what godly love looks like. Does it mean loving only the people they like or who like them? Does it mean loving only people who act like them

and look like them? Or does loving the way God loves mean something much more?

Discuss with the children what it would look like if they were always concerned to show God's love to siblings and parents at home and to classmates and friends at school.

Ask each child to think of one person in their life that they want to love well.

⏱ Memory Activity

Divide the children into groups and ask each group to create a word of the memory verse or catechism answer in Play-Doh.

Place each word of the verse or catechism answer on a long flat surface. Have the children say the memory verse, and then gradually ball up the Play-Doh to remove words. See which of the children can remember the whole memory verse and recite it to the group.

⏱ Closing Prayer Time

Conclude the lesson by inviting several of the children to give thanks to God for creating them and to ask that God might help them to glorify him. Conclude by asking God that as the children grow in understanding that they are immeasurably precious in the eyes of the Lord, he might help them show love more and more in his image!

Question 5

What else did God create?

Answer

God created all things, and all his creation was very good.

Big Idea

God created everything—through his Son, in the power of the Spirit, and for his glory.

Aim

To help the children have confidence in God as Creator and to understand God's purposes in creation.

Bible Passage

Genesis 1:1–31

Memory Verse

"And God saw everything that he had made, and behold, it was very good." (Gen. 1:31)

Virtue

Joy

Leader's Notes

Some children will never have considered where the world came from or who made it; others will be fully committed to the belief that God created the world. One thing that the children will certainly encounter at some stage during their lives is the belief that the world came into existence by chance and that there is no intelligent design behind the world. This catechism question will enable the children to think more deeply about the doctrine of creation out of nothing. It will help them to understand that the world came into being through purposeful creation. This lesson aims to bring the children a little deeper into the Genesis account and to show them the presence of the triune God at the dawn of creation. Hopefully the children will find joy in understanding more of God's creative purpose in his world and will more clearly recognize that the world was made for God's glory and delight.

Things to remember when planning and teaching:

- The question of evolution will be in the children's minds.

- Conceptually it's hard for children (or anyone for that matter) to understand how God could create something out of nothing.

- The introduction of the Trinity in lesson 3 is foundational to helping students understand that God the Father, God the Son, and God the Holy Spirit were all involved in creation.

- Remember to mix and match the activities in the lesson to fit your time frame (see p. 12 for some sample outlines). You won't have time to do them all. Feel free to adapt each activity based on your class's strengths and weaknesses.

Leader's Prayer

Triune God, thank you for your beautiful creation. May I find joy in it each day. Thank you that you are not distant now from your creation but intimately involved during every second of every day. Please help the children who hear this lesson to be thrilled with a deeper engagement with your creation story. May it increase in them confidence in you. In Jesus's name. Amen.

Leader's Tool Kit

- Three plastic cups
- Two ping-pong balls
- Small prizes

- Q5 Animals in Creation Quiz (RB), one for each child
- A pen or pencil for each child

- Q5 Cake recipe
- A bowl
- A wooden spoon
- An apron or chef's hat

- Q5 Days of Creation Illustrations (RB)
- Legos
- Q5 Joy Grid (RB), one for each child

Catechism Recap

Set up three plastic cups on a table and give each team a ping-pong ball.

Divide the children into two or more teams. Ask each team to pick a number between one and four. The team must then try to collectively remember the catechism question and answer for the number they chose. If the team can do it, they get a chance to throw the ping-pong ball into a cup to claim a prize. Write on the bottom of the cups what the prizes are. Repeat with as many teams as you have. Remind the children of any of the catechism questions not covered.

Introduction to Question 5

Have the children stand in a circle, and starting with the letter *A* ask them to name things alphabetically that God has made in creation. The first child says something beginning with *A*, the second *B*, and so on. Go through the alphabet as many times as possible. If the children can't think of something, they sit down and pass to the next person until only one child is left standing.

Ask the children what listing some of the amazing things that God has made makes them feel. Are they amazed at the variety of God's creation?

Introduce Question 5: "What else did God create?" Explain to the children that this question will be all about God's marvelous creation.

Activity

Print out a copy of the Animals in Creation Quiz (RB).

Give children the creation quiz and ask them to complete it in a set amount of time. Let the children read aloud their answers (or guesses), then tell them the correct answers (found on the Solutions page of the Resource Book). The aim of the quiz should be to induce awe, wonder, and joy as they think about God's amazing creation.

⑮ Teaching Outline

Begin the teaching time by asking for God's help. Ask that the lesson would be taught faithfully and that the children might listen well.

Invite a child to the front of the classroom and give him a mixing bowl, a wooden spoon, a copy of Q5 Cake Recipe (RB), and a chef's hat or apron. Invite him to bake a cake for everyone. Encourage him to get started by reading the recipe out to the class. When he asks for the ingredients, explain to him that he needs to create this cake from nothing!

Explain to the children that it is impossible to make something out of nothing. Ask them to describe the process of creating something, such as a cake or a house.

Highlight that in our experience everything that is created is made out of something; there are raw materials that are used for each and every creation. But when we come to the creation of the world, it is entirely different!! Tell the children that the way the world came into being is totally inconsistent with our experience and in some ways, it's hard to understand. But we must remember that this is God doing the creation and not us: he is all-powerful and all-knowing (refer to lesson 2). Of course he can do things that we can't do.

Read Genesis 1:1–31. Provide Bibles for the children to read along with you.

To involve the children in reading the passage for this lesson, ask different children to read out the creation account for each day.

As the verses are read, show pictures that correspond with the creation account from Q5 Days of Creation Illustrations (RB).

The first startling thing to help the children notice is that God created everything out of nothing; there was nothing that coexisted materially with God eternally. There was a time when the hills didn't exist, when the sand didn't exist, when the stars didn't exist. Creation comes out of God's will and imagination, and he creates everything for himself, with great meaning and purpose.

Remind the children that it's impossible for us to create something out of nothing, but of course everything is possible for God. Genesis records that by speaking, God brought the heavens and the earth into creation. Point out to the children the number of times the Genesis account says "and God said."

Ask the children if they think anyone besides God the Father was involved in the creation of the world. Encourage them to read verse 2 again. Help them to see in Genesis 1:2 that the Spirit of God was hovering over the waters after they were created. The Spirit of God brought life to all that God the Father created.

Show the children that both God the Father and the God the Spirit are involved in creation, but hint to them that there was someone else as well. Ask them to turn to John 1:1–3 to discover who that was.

Ask the children what they think these three verses are saying.

John reveals that Jesus was with God the Father when the world was created. John calls Jesus "the Word," and it was through God's spoken Word that everything was formed. So at the beginning of the world, God the Father, God the Son, and God the Holy Spirit were all involved in creating.

Ask the children how God described his creation.

God described all his creation as very good; each and every thing on earth was made by God. Everything that God created was intended to show his glory. There are lots of ways creation reveals something of the nature and character of God.

Ask the children if there are aspects of creation that bring them joy and cause them to praise God for the beauty of the world. Remind them that God is powerful, creative, and beautiful, and he has an awesome imagination.

Creation is intended to bring God great glory and honor and praise. God delights in his creation, and we are invited to delight in it too. God has created a beautiful world for his children to inhabit.

Tell the children that since the creation of the world, God has been intimately involved in his world; he didn't just set it up and then retreat back to heaven. God is constantly sustaining everything in his world.

Finish the teaching time by helping the children commit Question 5 and the answer to memory.

(These notes are just for guidance. Please expand or amend to suit your own children and context. Write out your talk in your own words and include illustrations and applications that you know will connect with your children.)

Notes

Activity

Borrow or buy some Legos and divide the children into groups that correspond to the days of creation. Invite each group to build a representation of one of the days. Take a photo of each day that the children create and print out a collage of the photos to use next week in review.

Discussion and Question Time

Some of the questions that might arise include:

? **How was Jesus present at the creation of the world?**

Jesus is eternal and all-powerful. Jesus lived with God until he came to earth as a man, and now he is once more with God.

Notes

? What about evolution?

> Explain to the children that some people believe we evolved by accident, but that there are millions of people—even top scientists—who believe that the world came into being when God purposefully spoke it into existence.

Also use this opportunity to help the children think about their own lives and how this catechism question and answer affects them personally.

- How might they explain their belief in a Creator God to their friends?
- Does knowing God as Creator and Sustainer of the world bring them joy?
- Are they able to reflect on all the things they have and enjoy, which ultimately come from God?

 Virtue Vision

Joy
Download and print the Q5 Joy Grid (RB), one per child. Give each child a pen or pencil.

Ask the children to think of something in particular that gives them joy as they reflect on creation. Once the children have had a moment to think of something, ask them to write it down in one square of the grid. Then have them move around the room and find out what parts of creation bring joy to the other children. Tell them to fill in the grid as they exchange the information about what in creation brings them joy. The first student to fill in her grid wins.

Memory Activity

Invite the children to make up some actions for the memory verse or catechism answer in small groups. Allow each group to show their actions to the rest of the children. Finish with all the groups joining together in saying the memory verse or catechism answer.

Closing Prayer Time

Encourage the children to thank God for the great joy they can find in his beautiful creation.

Question 6

How can we glorify God?

Answer

By loving him and by obeying his commands and law.

Big Idea
A right response to God is to glorify him with obedient, thankful, and trusting lives.

Aim
To help the children understand that God longs to be glorified and that obedient lives bring great glory to God.

Bible Passage
Deuteronomy 11:1–13

Memory Verse
"You shall therefore love the LORD your God and keep his charge, his statutes, his rules, and his commandments always." (Deut. 11:1)

Virtue
Trust

Leader's Notes

Children in the twenty-first century are used to seeing the created glorified, rather than the Creator! The children will be able to identify how the world gives glory and praise to celebrities, sport stars, and even politicians. The children will be less familiar with the concept of glorifying God. This lesson aims to help children to consider what a right response to God is. The lesson should help them to consider what it is to have their hearts and lives oriented fully toward God so that he might be number one in their lives. This question will explain to the children that one of the ways God is glorified is through obedient lives.

Things to remember when planning and teaching:

- Children are naturally inclined to legalism. Help them to clearly understand that glorifying God is a response to his grace in Jesus rather than a way to win favor with him.

- Be aware that the idea of glorifying something may be difficult for some children to comprehend. Try to explain it as clearly and concisely as you can.

- Be sure to challenge the children to put God first in their lives and to love and trust him above all else.

- Remember to mix and match the activities in the lesson to fit your time frame (see p. 12 for some sample outlines). You won't have time to do them all. Feel free to adapt each activity based on your class's strengths and weaknesses.

Leader's Prayer

Almighty God, forgive me for the times that I fail to glorify you in my own life. Help me to have a heart that is oriented to you in love and obedience. May my life and witness help the children understand what it is to glorify you. Grant the children in this lesson clear understanding and help them to know you as the One who deserves all the glory. In Jesus's name. Amen.

Leader's Tool Kit

- Balloons
- Paper
- Q6 Catechism Recap (DL), printed out and cut up
- Large sheet of paper
- Markers
- Pens or pencils
- Paper
- Jar

Catechism Recap

Print and cut out the question, answer, and memory verse for questions one to five (DL). Fold the individual pieces of paper up very small, and place them inside individual balloons. Inflate and tie the balloons.

Tell the children that the aim of the game is to burst the balloons and locate the pieces of papers enclosed within them. Once they have a piece of paper, they should work together to form a group that contains the question, answer, and memory verse for each of the first five questions of the catechism. A small group should form as the various elements of each question are brought together. Ask each group to read out their question, answer, and memory verse.

Introduction to Question 6

Ask the children if any of them are fans of a sports team. Let them tell which teams they like, and ask if they are a "sort-of" fan or a "huge" fan. For those who consider themselves huge fans, ask if there are ways we would be able to tell this without asking. Some ways might be wearing fan gear, talking about the team with other fans, bragging about a win, and, of course, going to games.

Ask the children if they've ever been to a game in a large stadium or arena. How do fans act? Point out to the children that shouting, cheering, and singing songs and chants at a sports game are all ways that fans glorify a team. We don't ordinarily use that word, but being a huge fan and letting others know it is "glorifying" a team.

Explain to the children that to glorify people or things is to give them praise, to tell other people who they are and how great they are, and ultimately to love them. Introduce the children to Question 6: "How can we glorify God?" Explain that Question 6 will help them consider how they can glorify God in their lives. It won't be exactly the way we glorify our favorite teams, but it will be by loving him, praising him, telling others about him, and serving him.

Activity

Give the children Bibles, and ask them to look up the following verses. Appoint four children to read aloud one verse each. Ask the class to notice what these verses all have in common.

Psalm 63:3   Psalm 95:6

Psalm 134:2   Psalm 34:8

Ask the children to think carefully about what each verse is saying and what it is teaching them about glorifying God. Did they notice that each verse refers to something they would do with their bodies (praise with lips, lift up hands, kneel, taste, and see)? Glorifying God is something that involves our minds, our hearts, and even our bodies.

(15) Teaching Outline

Begin the teaching time by asking for God's help. Ask that the lesson would be taught faithfully and that the children might listen well.

Ask the children to consider carefully how often they think about God each day. Reassure them that you won't ask them to say anything out loud! Explain to the children that sometimes people become forgetful and forget God. Help the children to reflect briefly on who God is. Ask them to describe who God is and what he's like. You may like to write the children's answers on a large sheet of paper for them to see.

Discuss the greatness, majesty, power, and beauty of God. Ask the children if remembering all the wonderful things about God inclines them to praise him. To glorify him is to acknowledge his greatness and worship him. Explain to the children that God longs for his people to give him glory. Also explain that God is jealous and does not want anyone or anything else to receive glory (Isa. 42:8).

Read Deuteronomy 11:1–13. Provide Bibles for the children to read along with you.

Invite the children to think about the passage, and ask them to identify the mighty acts of God. Help the children to see how God worked to care for, protect, and save his people, Israel. Show the children how, even in this short passage, God is amazing!

Explain that these words were spoken to God's people by Moses. He wanted them to understand that their love for God should be characterized by obedience, by telling others about him, and by commitment to one another. Moses wanted to teach the people how to glorify God. He wanted them to understand how awesome God is and to help them understand that he alone is worthy of their honor, glory, and praise.

Remind the children that we who have also been saved by God through Jesus are now a part of God's people. Invite the children to marvel at the greatness of God as one who continues to save disobedient and rebellious people.

Explain that one of the most effective ways to bring God glory is to obey him, just as Moses explained to the Israelites in the Bible passage.

Explain to the children that this obedience will not win them any favor with God or bring them closer to God; only Jesus can do that. Highlight that obedience to God is a worthy response to his greatness and beauty and that it brings glory to him. Tell the children that obeying God shows thankful hearts. It also displays a trust in him, showing the world that God is great and his ways are good.

Encourage the children to consider once again whether they might need to remember God more in their day-to-day lives. Enquire whether they might be able to consider how they might bring him glory day by day and hour by hour.

Conclude the teaching time by helping the children commit Question 6 and the answer to memory.

(These notes are just for guidance. Please expand or amend to suit your own children and context. Write out your talk in your own words and include illustrations and applications that you know will connect with your children.)

Notes

Activity ☼

Pass out pens and paper to each child.

Invite the children to write a personal prayer asking God to help them love and trust him each day, so that they might glorify him through obedient lives. Prompt them to think of three things they love about God, and three ways they struggle to obey him. Remind them that God loves to answer our prayers and wants to help us obey. Encourage them to look at their prayer and pray it during the week.

Discussion and Question Time

Some of the questions that might arise include:

? Is it wrong to like celebrities or sports stars?

Explain to the children that it is appropriate to appreciate the different ways that God has gifted people in his world, and we can appreciate that. Highlight that God wants to be number one in his people's lives and longs to receive glory from his people.

? I don't fully understand what it means to glorify God.

Remind the children that glorifying God is giving him praise and honor, it is telling him and others that he is great, and it is living trusting lives that reflect his goodness.

? Why does God need to be glorified?

Explain to the children that God doesn't need to be glorified—God doesn't need anything! Glorifying God is part of being in a loving relationship with him, and that is what God longs for with those whom he has created. He knows it is good for us to give him glory.

Also use this opportunity to help the children to think about their own lives and how this catechism question and answer affects them personally.

- What would it look like to be more focused on glorifying God?
- Is it a struggle to give God glory, honor, and praise?
- Do you find it hard to be obedient to God?

(10) Virtue Vision

Trust

Cut up paper so that each child has a slip to write on.

Remind the children that you've been talking about how obedience glorifies God. We usually think of obedience as not doing bad things, but it also includes doing the good things God commands. God has commanded us to *trust* him. Invite someone to read Proverbs 3:5: "Trust in the LORD with all your heart and do not lean on your own understanding."

Ask the children to think of things in their lives that worry them. When they've thought

of something, ask them to write it on their slip of paper if they want to trust that worry to God. Then invite them to fold it up and put it in your jar.

Once all of the slips are put in the jar, point out that you now have their worry slips, and they don't have them any more. This illustrates that when we give our worries to God, he has them, and we don't have them anymore. That's what trust in God looks like! Ask them if the command to glorify God by trusting him is easy or difficult.

(10) Memory Activity

Give every child a piece of paper and some markers. Have them write out the memory verse or catechism answer. Then have them make the words they consider more important bold. Encourage them to decorate

each word in a way that will help them remember it. After a few minutes, ask them to turn over their papers and see if they can remember the verse or answer.

(5) Closing Prayer Time

Invite any of the children who would like to read out the prayers that they wrote during the lesson to do so. Conclude by praying that God might receive the glory that is due to him as people live thankful and obedient lives.

What does the law of God require?

Answer

That we love God with all our heart, soul, mind, and strength; and love our neighbor as ourselves.

Big Idea

God's law is still relevant for the Christian, and it requires obedient and loving lives.

Aim

To help the children understand what it is to live wholeheartedly for God in light of his love and grace.

Bible Passage

Matthew 22:34–40

Memory Verse

"And [Jesus] said to him, 'You shall love the Lord your God with all your heart and with all your soul and with all your mind. This is the great and first commandment. And a second is like it: You shall love your neighbor as yourself. On these two commandments depend all the Law and the Prophets.'" (Matt. 22:37–40)

Virtue

Gratitude

Leader's Notes

This lesson is the first in a section of nine questions that deal with God's law and the response that God demands from his people. Each question will consider an aspect of the law and will engage with its significance for the children today. This lesson will highlight for the children that God's law is still relevant today and that it is an important part of the Christian life. This lesson aims to encourage the children to consider carefully what it means to respond to God's saving grace by living thankful lives characterized by obedience. The children will be encouraged to consider their love for God—and how that is expressed in their lives—as well as their love for others. The role of God's law is often downplayed in the Christian life, but this question will help children to understand that it is meant to guide us in how to respond appropriately to his grace in his world.

Things to remember when planning and teaching:

- Be sure to point out that obeying the law will never make anybody right with God.

- You will need to help the children to think seriously about how this question will practically affect their individual lives.

- Be careful to articulate clearly the fact that wholehearted devotion to God will involve striving to live obedient lives in the power of the Holy Spirit.

- Remember to mix and match the activities in the lesson to fit your time frame (see p. 12 for some sample outlines). You won't have time to do them all. Feel free to adapt each activity based on your class's strengths and weaknesses.

Leader's Prayer

Gracious God, please help me to love you with all my heart, soul, and mind. Help me to love my neighbors as myself. Please illuminate to me the areas of my life where I could be glorifying you more, and help me to live wholeheartedly for you. Grant understanding to the children who will hear this lesson. May they see the beauty of the grace of the gospel, and may they long to love you with their heart, soul, and mind. In Jesus's name. Amen.

Leader's Tool Kit

- Paneled beach ball

- Permanent marker

- Board games

- A long roll of paper (old wallpaper or butcher paper would be ideal)
- Construction paper cut into heart shapes, one for each child

■ Markers   ■ Q7 Tweet Template (RB)

Catechism Recap

On a paneled inflatable beach ball write
Questions 1–6 with a permanent marker.

Gather the children into a circle and explain
that the idea of the game is to keep the beach
ball off the floor. Each child must participate
to keep the beach ball in the air. If the beach
ball drops to the ground, someone must
volunteer to answer one of the catechism
questions written on the ball, or the whole
group gets a penalty. The penalty could be
things like twenty jumping jacks or five
push-ups or something silly. The activity
should encourage the children to search
their memories and remember what they've
learned about Questions 1–6.

Introduction to Question 7

Ask the children to consider what life might
be like if there were no laws.

Initially their response may be oriented
toward positive and exciting possibilities!
Help them reflect on some of the laws that
are created to keep people safe. For example,
what would it be like if cars never stopped
at red lights? Or if people could harm each
other without consequences?

Explain to the children that laws are an
essential part of life and that they are
generally established so that society can
operate safely and well.

Go on to ask the children to consider
what life would be like if there were no
punishment for breaking laws. They will
hopefully observe that the law means
nothing without the threat of punishment!
Help them to see that people would just
break laws constantly if there were no
consequences for breaking them.

Introduce the children to Question 7: "What
does the law of God require?" Explain that
this lesson, and the next eight lessons, all
focus on God's law.

Activity

Set up some board games for the children to play around the classroom.

Tell the children that there are board games placed around the room for them to play. Settle the children down around the games, and get them ready to start. Explain to the children that the rules for today are that there are no rules! Explain that they do not need to observe the normal rules of the various games. Let the children play for a little while, and allow them to feel the frustration of knowing that there are rules for the games but seeing no one obeying them.

Help the children to once again reflect on how helpful rules and laws are. Even in something as simple as a board game, they make playing easy, ordered, and enjoyable!

Teaching Outline

Begin the teaching time by asking for God's help. Ask that the lesson would be taught faithfully and that the children might listen well.

Ask the children if they are good at obeying their parents. Ask them if they are ever perfectly obedient. Why do they disobey? Help them to reflect on whether it is loving or kind to their parents, and ask them to think about how their disobedience affects their parents. Explain to the children that everyone in the world is a lawbreaker and not just because they disobey their parents. Explain that even if we've kept the laws of our country, we have all broken God's laws.

Explain to the children that God has revealed his law to his people, and it is recorded in the Bible. Ask the children if they know what you're referring to (many of the children will be familiar with the Ten Commandments).

Tell the children that in the Old Testament book of Exodus, God clearly handed down his law to his people (the Israelites) at Mount Sinai, which described how God expected his people to live. Explain to the children that God gave his law to his people right after he had miraculously saved them; they had come to know him as a powerful and merciful saving God. God had brought them out of Egypt and then sought to show them how to live as his people and under his rule. God demanded perfect obedience from his people, the Israelites. God wanted his people to respond to him with wholehearted devotion because of his saving grace. But the Israelite people were not able to perfectly obey God's law, and there were consequences for breaking it.

Read Matthew 22:34–40. Provide Bibles for the children to read along with you.

Explain to the children that God's law still remains today and that it is still the standard by which God expects his people to live. Tell the children that the only person to ever keep God's law perfectly was Jesus. This means that everyone else is a lawbreaker, and lawbreakers deserve punishment. Remind the children that those who are Christians are free from the prospect of punishment, however, because when Jesus died on the cross, he did so in order to take the punishment for all lawbreakers who turn to him in repentance for forgiveness.

Help the children to understand that the reason Christians seek to keep God's law is because of his saving grace shown to them in Jesus, not because it will win them favor with God.

Explain that in Matthew 22:34–40 Jesus taught what can be described as a summary of God's law. It is how he expects his followers to live. Jesus commands people to show upward love and sideways love, to love God and to love other people.

Jesus explains to Pharisees and listening crowds that the law can be summarized by commending people to love God with all their heart, soul, and mind and to love their neighbors as themselves.

Ask the children how they generally respond when they've been given a gift or shown some kindness. Presumably they respond in thanks.

Explain to the children that God's greatest gift to them is Jesus, the One who saves those who trust in him from punishment and death. Encourage the children to consider what the right response is to God's great gift. Surely it is living thankful lives, seeking to glorify God by living as he commands.

Conclude the teaching time by helping the children commit Question 7 and the answer to memory.

(These notes are just for guidance. Please expand or amend to suit your own children and context. Write out your talk in your own words and include illustrations and applications that you know will connect with your children.)

Notes

⏺ **Activity** ☼

Prepare a paper heart for each child.

Give every child a paper heart, and ask them to write "upward love" on one side and "sideways love" on the other side.

Invite the children to consider how they can love God with all their heart, soul, and mind, and write down some thoughts on the "upward love" side. Then ask the children how they might love the people that God has placed them among, and encourage them to write down some ideas on the "sideways love" side.

Conclude this time by asking the children to share some of their thoughts with the rest of the group.

Notes ⏱ ⑤ **Discussion and Question Time**

Some of the questions that might arise include:

? Does keeping God's law please God?

Remind the children that living obedient lives is glorifying to God and is pleasing to him, but be sure to clarify that it does not win favor with him.

? I'd like to keep God's law perfectly. How do I do that?

Tell the children that it is impossible to keep God's law perfectly, and that is why salvation through Jesus is essential. Explain that the Holy Spirit will give them the ability to live in increasingly godly ways that are consistent with God's law.

? What happens if I keep breaking God's law?

Help the children understand that if they consider themselves Christians, they can be confident Christ has taken their punishment. Encourage them to continually repent of their lawbreaking and to ask God to help them live for him with wholehearted devotion. For those children who are not Christians, tell them gently but clearly that they face the punishment for being a lawbreaker.

Also use this opportunity to help the children to think about their own lives and how this catechism question and answer affects them personally.

- Ask the children what they think loving God with all their heart, soul, and mind means.

- Ask the children to consider very practically how they can better love their friends, family, and neighbors. Remind them of God's abundant love and ask them how they can model that to others.

- Ask the children how they can seek to be wholeheartedly devoted to God.

⏱ ⑩ **Virtue Vision** ☀

Gratitude

Give each child a copy of Q7 Tweet Template (RB) and a marker.

Remind the children that the reason God's law is still relevant is because it is God's guide for life and it teaches how to live with gratitude in response to his grace. One way that we show upward love is gratitude to God; one way we show sideways love is gratitude toward people around us.

During this time encourage the children to write a tweet (no more than 140 characters!)

that declares their gratitude to God for who he is and what he's done. They may need to practice writing their tweet on the back of the paper to get it down to 140 characters. Then have them write a tweet of gratitude to another person.

🔟 Memory Activity

Write the memory verse or catechism answer out on a long roll of paper. Unroll the paper and invite the children to read the memory verse through several times. With a person at each end of the roll, begin to reroll the memory verse so that words gradually disappear from each end. Ask the children to try saying the memory verse again after some of the verse has been rerolled. Keep going as long as time permits.

5️⃣ Closing Prayer Time

As a closing prayer activity encourage some of the children to expand on their tweets in a prayer of gratitude.

Question 8

What is the law of God stated in the Ten Commandments?

Answer

You shall have no other gods before me. You shall not make for yourself an idol. You shall not misuse the name of the LORD your God. Remember the Sabbath day by keeping it holy. Honor your father and your mother. You shall not murder. You shall not commit adultery. You shall not steal. You shall not give false testimony. You shall not covet.

Big Idea
God revealed his moral law to the people of Israel in the Ten Commandments.

Aim
To help the children understand what the Ten Commandments are.

Bible Passage
Exodus 20

Memory Verse
"You shall have no other gods before me." (Ex. 20:3)

Virtue
Gratitude

Leader's Notes

The children may encounter a number of opinions about the Ten Commandments. They may be told that they are of no relevance today to either the Christian or non-Christian. Or they may be told that they are of every importance to the Christian today and must be obeyed in order to be right with God. Neither of these statements is true! This catechism question will begin a detailed engagement with the subject of the law; eight questions focus on God's law in this curriculum. Question 8 introduces the law in its original context and examines why and how God gave the law to his people Israel.

Things to remember when planning and teaching:

- The Ten Commandments are God's moral law.

- The Ten Commandments reflect God's character.

- The Ten Commandments are given in love.

- The children may be familiar with the concept of the law.

- Caution must be taken when teaching about the law so it doesn't nurture legalism.

- The question of how to address adultery will be handled in lesson 11. You might want to flip ahead and read the "Note to Teachers" on page 93 in case it comes up in this lesson.

- Remember to mix and match the activities in the lesson to fit your time frame (see p. 12 for some sample outlines). You won't have time to do them all. Feel free to adapt each activity based on your class's strengths and weaknesses.

Leader's Prayer

Father God, thank you for your law. Thank you that through it you help me realize my responsibilities to you and to my neighbors. I'm grateful that as I study your law, I can understand more of who you are and what you're like. Grant understanding to the children who will hear this lesson. May their hearts be filled with gratitude as they encounter your law, because they understand that you are a loving God who chooses to reveal himself to his people. In Jesus's name. Amen.

Leader's Tool Kit

- Q8 Catechism Recap (DL)

- Tape

- Jenga game

- One piece of scratch art paper per child (black with color underneath)

- One wooden stylus (or toothpick) per child

- Pictorial representation of the Ten Commandments

- Markers

- Some large pieces of paper

---

⑩ Catechism Recap

Print and cut out Q8 Catechism Recap (DL). Tape the previous seven questions to Jenga blocks and build the Jenga tower.

Divide the children into teams. Invite individual children from each team, in turn, to approach the Jenga tower and attempt to remove a block (don't continue to build the tower, just place the blocks to the side once they have been removed from the tower). If the block they remove has a question on it, the child can either answer the question herself or pass the question back to her team. If the team fails to correctly answer the question, another team can jump in and answer it. If they answer it correctly, they will win a point for their team. The team with the most points wins.

---

⑤ Introduction to Question 8

Read these real laws to the children:

1. In Arkansas, it is illegal to mispronounce the word *Arkansas*.

2. In Carmel, California, it is illegal to wear high heel shoes without a permit.

3. In Nevada, it's illegal to hunt camels.

4. In Gainesville, Georgia, it is legal to eat fried chicken only with your hands, *not* a fork!

5. In New Orleans, Louisiana, it is illegal to curse at a firefighter.

6. Until 2015, it was illegal in Alabama to play cards on Sunday.

7. In Beacon, New York, it is illegal to possess a pinball machine within city limits.

8. Until 2007, it was illegal to fake a wrestling match in Louisiana.

9. In Kentucky, it is illegal to handle a reptile in a religious service.

10. In Quitman, Georgia, it is illegal to let a chicken cross the road.

Notes

11. In Georgia, it is illegal to sell a child younger than twelve to the circus.

Ask the children why they think laws are important.

Laws help society function well, but some of these laws are crazy!

Introduce the children to Question 8: "What is the law of God stated in the Ten Commandments?" Explain to the children that God gave a set of laws to his people that were concerned with helping people to live in a way that was honoring to God; it was all about right and wrong—God's moral law. Tell the children that this question will explain what the law of God as stated in the Ten Commandments is.

---

(10) Activity ☼

Give each child in the group a piece of scratch art paper and a wooden stylus to scratch with.

Show the children a pictorial representation of what the Ten Commandments might have originally looked like. Invite the children to make their own version of the commandments by cutting the scratch paper into a tablet shape and engraving the commandments onto the paper.

Read Exodus 20 aloud as they are making their tablets.

---

(15) Teaching Outline

Begin the teaching time by asking for God's help. Ask that the lesson would be taught faithfully and that the children might listen well.

Ask the children: if they could establish their own country, what kind of laws might they make to help the country run smoothly? Ask the children to imagine that they were establishing laws for people whom they loved very dearly; would that make a difference?

Help the children understand that the intention when any laws are established is to allow humanity to thrive and flourish in a safe and prosperous society. Introduce the children to Exodus 20. Explain that this Bible passage recalls how God gave the law to his rescued people Israel. Highlight that God gave the law to the Israelites because he loved them and wanted the best for them.

Read Exodus 20. Provide Bibles for the children to read along with you.

Emphasize that many people think that laws are harsh and intended to restrict, but in actual fact laws are meant to be for people's good. When God spoke his law directly to Moses for the people of Israel, he did so because he loved them and was concerned that they would live safely and successfully. God's law as stated in the Ten Commandments is loving and is intended to bless rather than burden his people. Explain to the children that each commandment reveals something about the character and nature of God. When we study the law, we begin to understand the mind of God—we know what he loves, and we know what he hates.

Invite the children to read back over the Ten Commandments and see if they can discern God's character in and through the law.

At the beginning of creation, God gave Adam and Eve one law and that was not to eat from the tree of the knowledge of good and evil. Rather than restricting Adam and Eve, God liberated them! There was only one law to keep. But the Devil caused Adam and Eve to break that one law, and so sin entered into the world. The law as stated in the Ten Commandments is necessary because the world and everything in it is affected by sin.

Read Exodus 19:3–6.

Show the children that in these verses God declares that he wanted the Israelite people to be his treasured possession, a kingdom of priests, and a holy nation. God wants the people to remember that he rescued them from slavery, and that he showed them miraculous care and love as he led them out of Egypt. God wanted the people to understand the laws in the context of the great love that he had for them. He gave them the law not so they could be saved, but because they had already been saved. They had been slaves but now they were free, and the law was meant to serve them in their freedom. God made a covenant with Israel, and he promised great blessing to the Israelites if they upheld the law. But he said he would bring curses upon those who break it.

Ask the children why they think their parents have rules for them to obey. For instance, why do they have to go to bed at a certain time or eat fruit or vegetables? Is it because their parents are mean and want to ruin their fun? No! Explain to the children that it's actually because they want them to enjoy life to the fullest.

The law of God as stated in the Ten Commandments is motivated by a Father's love. Non-Christians might think that God is a spoilsport or a big police officer in the sky, but Christians should know and understand that ultimately God wants the best for his people. That is why he has given them a guide or a set of laws for life.

Explain to the children that God's law is still relevant today, and that it focuses specifically on our relationship with God and with our neighbors.

Finish the teaching time by helping the children commit Question 8 and the answer to memory.

Notes

⑩ Activity

☼

Play Ten Commandment Charades. Let the children take turns pantomiming one of the commandments while the other children guess the commandment.

⑤ Discussion and Question Time

Some of the questions that might arise include:

? Are the Ten Commandments relevant for today?

Explain that they are because they help God's people to understand their responsibility toward him and also their responsibility toward other people.

? Did God actually think people could keep the commands?

Help the children to understand that God knows the heart of all people and that nothing surprises God. We will talk more about why we fail to keep the law perfectly when we get to Question 13.

? Why did God give the Ten Commandments to the people in such an unusual way?

Tell the children that God gave the Ten Commandments in such a spectacular fashion to clearly indicate that the law came from him and not from a human source.

Use this opportunity to help the children think about their own lives and how this catechism question and answer affects them personally.

- How do the Ten Commandments help them understand God's character more?

- Can they understand that the Commandments were born out of love?

- How do they measure up according to God's standards as established in the Ten Commandments?

Virtue Vision

Gratitude

Cover with paper an area of wall that can become a "gratitude wall." At the top write, "I am grateful that God is . . ."

This lesson has helped the children to understand that God has lovingly revealed his character in the Ten Commandments. Encourage the children to write on the wall the things that they have learned about God's character from Exodus 20. Help the children reflect on how wonderful it is that God chose to reveal himself in this way.

Memory Activity

Play the song for Question 8 from "Songs from The New City Catechism" (available for free at newcitycatechism.com or on the NCC app). Let the children listen to the song a few times, and then assign a different commandment to each child. Sing the song, allowing the children to sing their assigned commandment. Once they've got that down, have them swap commandments with someone else and repeat.

Closing Prayer Time

Gather the children around the gratitude wall, and encourage them to praise God for who he is and for the way his law allows people to know him more fully.

Question 9

What does God require in the first, second, and third commandments?

Answer

First, that we know God as the only true God. Second, that we avoid all idolatry. Third, that we treat God's name with fear and reverence.

Big Idea
God does not tolerate the worship of false idols. He is a jealous God who demands wholehearted devotion.

Aim
To help children understand that God alone should be worshiped and to teach them how they should worship him.

Bible Passage
Exodus 20

Memory Verse
"It is the LORD your God you shall fear. Him you shall serve and by his name you shall swear. You shall not go after other gods, the gods of the peoples who are around you." (Deut. 6:13–14)

Virtue
Trust

Leader's Notes

Children will likely be aware of the relativistic and pluralistic air of the twenty-first century. They will be conscious that there are people of different religions—and no religion—in their schools, towns, and cities. The media will particularly be training them to be skeptical about the concept of absolute truth. As a result, they may be reluctant to acknowledge that there is only one true God. This question will help the children to engage with God as he reveals himself in the first three commandments. This lesson aims to help the children understand the kind of relationship that God longs to have with his people and recognize the kind of worship God demands from his people.

Things to remember when planning and teaching:

- The children may be familiar with the Ten Commandments, but they need to be reminded that God is a jealous God who will not tolerate any competition.

- The children need to be encouraged to search their own hearts and question whether they are worshiping God in accordance with his Word.

- The children may be uncomfortable critiquing other religions. Explain that God longs for his name alone to be honored and respected.

- Remember to mix and match the activities in the lesson to fit your time frame (see p. 12 for some sample outlines). You won't have time to do them all. Feel free to adapt each activity based on your class's strengths and weaknesses.

Leader's Prayer

Almighty God, please help me to firmly place my trust in you and worship you as God alone. Help me to continue to know you through your Word and to love you with all my heart and soul and mind. Grant understanding to the children that will hear this lesson. May they be challenged to worship, trust, and find joy in you alone. In Jesus's name. Amen.

Leader's Tool Kit

- Q9 Catechism Recap (DL)
- Bowl
- Pens
- Paper
- Bucket or wastepaper basket

- Q9 Images of False Gods (RB)

- The first three of the Ten Commandments cut up into individual words and each word placed in an envelope

- Q9 In My Heart (RB), one for each child
- Scissors
- Magazines and newspapers to cut up
- Gluesticks

---

⑩ Catechism Recap

Have paper and pens ready, along with a bucket or wastepaper basket. Cut out Q9 Catechism Recap (DL) and place the answers in a bowl.

Divide the children into small groups. Give each group eight pieces of paper and a pen.

Explain to the children that in the bowl are the answers to Questions 1–8. The aim of the game is for them to quickly write down the question that goes with the answer. Draw one of the eight answers from the bowl and read it aloud. Give the teams one minute to write down the question. Once the minute is up, read out the question. The teams that have correctly identified the question get to come forward to a certain point in the classroom, crumple up their piece of paper, and shoot for the basket. Begin again, and cover as many questions as time permits. The team with the most scores in the basket wins the game.

---

⑤ Introduction to Question 9

Have the Q9 Images of False Gods (RB) ready.

Begin by showing the children the images of some of the false gods that people have worshiped or still worship. As you show the images, explain which religion the false god is identified with. (1. Golden calf: Baal worship; 2. Artemis: Greek mythology; 3. Shiva: Hinduism; 4. Shango: Yoruba religion.) Explain to the children that many people worship false gods.

Then show the children the pictures of the various idols people in the twenty-first century worship. Explain that people make gods (with a small *g*!) out of all sorts of things. When we worship created things above the Creator, we are worshiping idols. (5. Altar for ancestor worship: Buddhism; 6. Power; 7. Possessions; 8. Family)

Introduce Question 9: "What does God require in the first, second, and third commandments?" Tell the children that when God gave the Ten Commandments to Moses, he gave specific instructions about how his people should relate to him. God is a jealous God and longs to be the number one person in everyone's life; he will not tolerate being relegated to second place or being ignored.

Activity

Print out each word of the first three commandments on individual sheets and put each word in an envelope. Hide the envelopes for the children to find.

Instruct the children to search for the envelopes. When they find an envelope, encourage them to open it, and then begin to work together to put the words of each commandment in the correct order. This could be made easier by printing each commandment on a specific color of paper.

Tell the children that this lesson will cover the first three commandments. Read them aloud to refresh their memories. The first three commandments all address the relationship between God and his people.

Teaching Outline

Begin the teaching time by asking for God's help. Ask that the lesson would be taught faithfully and that the children might listen well.

Ask the children to consider what they love most in their lives. Don't press them to articulate it out loud, but encourage them to search their own hearts.

Read Exodus 20:1–7. Provide Bibles for the children to read along with you.

Remind the children that at this point in Israel's history the people had experienced God's saving power. He brought them out of Egypt and rescued them from slavery. They knew that they had been chosen, called, and loved by God. They knew he was real, and they had every reason to trust him. Yet in spite of this, we encounter in the first command a strong warning from God. He says, "You shall have no other gods before me." God addresses each and every person individually when he says *you*! It's not a general proclamation; it's a personal message for each individual. God knew that Israel had at times worshiped false gods—a bit like the ones worshiped in the other religions today. Despite the fact that they had seen the true and living God work in amazing ways, he was commanding them to love him alone, for he feared they might once again turn to worship created things rather than the Creator. The Creator God longed for his people to know, love, and worship him alone. God was not and is not prepared to tolerate his people worshiping anything or anybody else except him.

Ask the children what they think about the worship of false gods. Help them to understand that there are people who still worship false gods today and to consider how they might engage with those of other faiths.

Highlight for the children the fact that people often worship other things in the place of God as well. Ask them for some examples of things people worship today. Emphasize that God is a jealous God, and he will not share his worship, praise, or glory with anyone else.

Ask the children to once again search their own hearts. Ask them where they find joy. Who or what do they trust above all else? Is it God, or is it something or someone else?

Move the children on to the second commandment by explaining that the first commandment is all about *who* we worship, and the second commandment is about *how* we worship.

God very clearly says he doesn't want people to worship images (pictures) or statues of him or of false gods. Tell the children that God wants to be known through his Word alone. That is how he has chosen to reveal himself, and that is where he can come to be known. When people make an image of God, they are using their imagination to show God the way they want him to be. The problem is that they will either leave things out that they don't like or add things in that aren't true. Even if they try their best, they can never make an accurate image of God using a painting or statue. God can't be reduced to a lump of stone or a colored canvas! God the Father has never been seen, and so any image of him would just be coming from the human imagination.

Worship must be concerned with the God of the Bible, not a human representation of God. Help the children to understand that we mustn't make God who we want him to be but must know him and worship him as he has revealed himself to us.

Finally, move the children on to the third commandment. Invite them to read verse 7 again, and ask them what they think it means. Ask the children how they feel when they hear someone misuse God's name.

God is concerned to protect his name and his reputation, and he takes it very seriously when his name is misused. When God told people his special name, Yahweh, he was revealing his character to them. Tell the children that the use of God's name often says something about a person's relationship with God. If someone loved God above all things, worshiped him, and found great joy in him, then surely they would not misuse his name. Only those who are estranged from God would misuse his name.

Conclude by helping the children to reflect on who they worship and how they worship in their everyday lives.

Finish the teaching time by helping the children commit Question 9 and the answer to memory.

(These notes are just for guidance. Please expand or amend to suit your own children and context. Write out your talk in your own words and include illustrations and applications that you know will connect with your children.)

Notes

Activity

Provide magazines and newspapers that are appropriate for children and that contain lots of glossy advertisements.

Give each child a copy of the Q9 In My Heart (RB). You will see that there is an innermost heart. The children should write "God" in the center heart to remind them that God alone must be worshiped. Ask them to search the magazines and newspapers and cut out pictures of things that people might be tempted to love above God.

Encourage them to paste in the outer heart things that they've cut out that are good things (pictures of family, animals, food, toys). It is right to love these good things God has created, but we should never put them in the place of God. They can also draw things in the outer heart.

Tell the children that if they've cut out any pictures of things that are not good, they can paste them around the edge of the paper to show that they don't belong in our hearts.

Discussion and Question Time

Some of the questions that might arise include:

? **Why would anyone worship a statue?**

Explain that when people worship an idol, they think that statue or image has a god behind it, and that the god has power. They think if they can make a god happy with them, he will give them what they want. It may sound crazy to us, but many people feel desperate for help and don't know where else to turn.

? **What does it mean to misuse God's name?**

There are many different ways to misuse God's name. One would be to use it as a swear word. Another would be to claim the name of Christ when asking

for something, but not to ask in the way that Christ commanded.

? **Is jealousy a good emotion?**

Explain to the children that when God expresses an emotion, it is always pure and not affected by sin. It is not like our own jealousy. Just as it is appropriate for a husband not to want his wife to love anyone else, it's appropriate for God to want us not to worship anyone or anything else.

Also use this opportunity to help the children to think about their own lives and how this question and answer affects them personally:

- Do they love God or do they worship idols?

- Can they clearly describe what biblical worship is? (Worship of God alone as he is revealed in his Word.)

- Are they prepared to live in contrast to the world, where the misuse of God's name is commonplace?

(10) Virtue Vision

Trust

Explain to the children that everyone puts their trust in someone or something at some time. Children trust their parents to care for them. Airplane passengers trust that the pilot will be able to fly the plane. Zoo visitors trust that the fences will keep them safe from man-eating tigers! Ask if they can think of other examples of how people exercise trust.

Help the children to understand that it is important to carefully consider who they put their trust in. The God of the Bible continually shows his people that he is trustworthy. Ask the children if they think that false idols—such as money, power, or even family—are trustworthy.

Help the children to articulate what it personally means to trust in the God of the Ten Commandments.

(10) Memory Activity

Invite the children to act out the different clauses in the verse or catechism question. As the memory verse is said, collectively encourage the children to do their actions.

(5) Closing Prayer Time

Encourage the children to ask for God's forgiveness if they feel that they have been worshiping and placing their trust in false idols.

Question 10

What does God require in the fourth and fifth commandments?

Answer

Fourth, that on the Sabbath day we spend time in worship of God. Fifth, that we love and honor our father and our mother.

Big Idea
God has ordained a pattern of life and relationships that are consistent with who he is and his created order.

Aim
To help the children understand that God institutes his commands for the good of his people.

Bible Passage
Exodus 20:1–17

Memory Verse
"Every one of you shall revere his mother and his father, and you shall keep my Sabbaths: I am the LORD your God." (Lev. 19:3)

Virtue
Joy

Leader's Notes

As they study the commandments, the children should continually encounter the character and nature of God as revealed through his commands. They may be familiar with the idea of the Sabbath, but may observe a Sabbath rest because their families do and may lack a personal purpose of the Sabbath in the individual life of a Christian. Or it may be that their understanding of the Sabbath is limited to attending church. Throughout this lesson the children will be encouraged to remember that God knows what is good for his children, and he has instituted certain practices in his commandments for the good of his children and for his glory.

The children will also be encouraged to consider what it means to honor their parents in light of the joy of a relationship with a loving heavenly Father. This lesson aims to help the children seriously consider the personal impact of both of these commandments.

Things to remember when planning and teaching:

- The children must clearly understand that obeying the commandments is a way to glorify God and respond to his grace rather than win favor with God.

- It is important to help the children consider the general lack of Sabbath observance in society and to help them see that, for children and adults, there's a lot of pressure not to keep it.

- Remember to mix and match the activities in the lesson to fit your time frame (see p. 12 for some sample outlines). You won't have time to do them all. Feel free to adapt each activity based on your class's strengths and weaknesses.

Leader's Prayer

Gracious God, please help me to find joy in your commandments. Thank you that you are a good Father who knows intimately the needs of your children and what is good for us. Thank you for instituting the Sabbath and for providing time for your people to enjoy rest and refreshment in you. Grant great understanding to the children as they consider the fourth and fifth commandments. May they further understand you as a good God who seeks to care for his people well. In Jesus's name. Amen

Leader's Tool Kit

- Q10 Catechism Recap (DL)
- Candy
- Music that can be started and stopped
- Wrapping paper

- Tape
- Whiteboard and pens
- Pictures of famous parents and children
- A piece of paper for each child with the word *LOVE* printed on it
- Markers

(10) Catechism Recap

Prepare a pass-the-present game. Wrap an assortment of candy in ten layers of paper. In between each layer put a catechism question from Questions 1–9 (Q10 Catechism Recap [DL]) and a small piece of candy.

Explain to the children that you're going to play pass the present. The game begins by passing the present in time with the music and stops with someone when the music stops playing. The child who has the present can unwrap one layer and see the candy and the question. The child gets to keep the candy (to be eaten later, only with a parent's permission) if he gets the question right. If he is unable to answer the question, someone else can have the opportunity to answer the question and win the candy. The music is then restarted, and the game continues until all layers have been unwrapped.

(5) Introduction to Question 10

Find pictures of famous children and parents. The ones the children might be most familiar with are from animated movies and TV programs, such as:

- Belle and Maurice (*Beauty and the Beast*)
- Marlin and Nemo (*Finding Nemo*)
- King Agnarr and Elsa (*Frozen*)
- King Peppy and Princess Poppy (*Trolls*)
- Dave Seville and Alvin (*Alvin and the Chipmunks*)
- Mufasa and Simba (*The Lion King*)
- Elastigirl and Invisigirl (*The Incredibles*)
- Papa Bear and Sister Bear (*The Berenstain Bears*)

Place the pictures of children in a stack. Give each child a picture of a parent and ask them to find their child in the stack.

Explain to the children that part of today's lesson will be examining the relationship that God encourages between children and their parents. Introduce them to Question 10: "What does God require in the fourth and fifth commandments?" Explain to the children that the lesson will continue to consider what the Ten Commandments teach with a particular focus on the fourth and fifth commandments. Ask the children what they think honoring their father and mother means. Ask them if they think honoring their parents is easy or hard.

Activity

Have a copy of Question 10 Code Busting Activity (RB) for each child.

Challenge the children to work out what the sentences are, and make it a race against time. The answers are:

1. That on the Sabbath day we spend time in worship of God

2. That we love and honor our father and mother

Once the children have cracked the code, explain that the lesson will focus on two different areas: Sabbath rest and honoring parents. See if any of the children can recite the first five commandments as you begin the lesson.

Teaching Outline

Begin the teaching time by asking for God's help. Ask that the lesson would be taught faithfully and that the children might listen well.

Ask the children who knows them best in the world. Hopefully the children will identify their parents as those who know them best. Ask some of the children to identify the kinds of things a parent knows about their children, such as:

- What they like on their sandwiches

- When they're happy, sad, or anxious

- What kind of TV shows they enjoy

- How much sleep they need

- How to make them feel better when they're sick

Explain to the children that parents generally know and understand their children very well. They know what is good for their children and how to care for them

well. Ask the children what they think God, as their heavenly Father, is like. Ask them if they think that God knows how to care for his children well. Ask them if they think he knows what's good for them.

Reassure the children that he does! In fact, God knows better than anyone else, but he has entrusted children into the care of families here on earth. The relationship of parent to child is one God has established in order for us to thrive, when practiced according to his commands. Another principle God established for human flourishing is the Sabbath.

Read Exodus 20:1–17. Provide Bibles for the children to read along with you.

Ask the children if they know what the Sabbath is or means. Explain to the children that the Sabbath is a day that God has set apart for worship and rest. From the time of Moses until Jesus, the Jews kept the Sabbath on Saturday. Tell the children that after Christ rose from the dead on a Sunday, his followers started observing that day as the Sabbath. God declares in his Word that people should work for six days and then rest on the seventh day. Make the link back to the pattern of creation for the children: God worked for six days and then rested on the seventh. Clarify for the children that the Sabbath isn't a day for lying in bed or going to the mall! But it is a day where Christians can spend more time resting, delighting in, and worshiping God, and enjoying the company of God's people.

Point out to the children that the language God uses in the fourth commandment is that the people are to *remember*. Ask the children why they think the word *remember* is included in the Ten Commandments. Explain that people are inclined to forget to rest and spend focused time with God. Ask the children what they think about the principle of taking a Sabbath rest. Ask them to think about why God made this one of only ten commandments. (It must be important!)

Remind the children that God, the Creator, knows what is best for his creation, for his children. He knows that work and rest are both included in the best pattern for life. God also knows how important it is for people to have spiritual rest as well as physical rest, and spiritual rest is found in and through God the Father and God the Son. Reassure the children that trusting in a sovereign God means that it is easy to

rest knowing that God is in control—that he has the whole world in his hands. Also highlight for them that it is through Jesus that a relationship with God is secured, and no human work is required. This is another great reason to enjoy spiritual rest.

Ask the children if they might be tempted to forget the Sabbath. Ask them what kind of things might draw them away from God and his people. Ask them if God's command challenges them. Ask the children to read verse 8 again and see if the verse says anything else about what the Sabbath should be.

Remind the children that God is a loving heavenly Father who longs to spend time with his children and only institutes what is best for them.

Moving on to the fifth commandment, explain to the children that it is knowing and experiencing God's fatherly love that helps children honor their parents.

Ask the children what honoring their parents well looks like. Ask whether it's easy to honor their parents or what might prevent some people from desiring to honor their parents.

Finally, ask the children to consider what honoring the parents will look like when they're a bit older.

Remind the children that the Ten Commandments were given to be a source of life and joy to God's people and that they

Notes

Notes

were given by a God who knows what his children need. Help the children to once again remember that obedience is a right response to God's wonderful grace.

Conclude the teaching time by helping the children commit Question 10 and the answer to memory.

(These notes are just for guidance. Please expand or amend to suit your own children and context. Write out your talk in your own words and include illustrations and applications that you know will connect with the children in your class.)

---

⑩ Activity ☼

Print out a piece of paper for each child with the word LOVE *printed vertically on it in large letters.*

Help the children to consider what it might mean to honor their parents in love. For example:

L listen to them.

O obey them.

V volunteer to serve and help them.

E eat my food with a cheerful attitude.

Invite the children to write ideas on their paper of how they can honor their parents in love, both in the things they do as well as the things they choose not to do.

---

⑤ Discussion and Question Time

Some of the questions that might arise include:

? **What happens if my sports team plays on a Sunday, and I can't make it to church?**

> Help the children to reflect on the fact that God has instituted the command for the good of his people because he loves them. Explain to the children that Christians should be cautious about taking part in something that will keep them from worship. If this situation comes up, they should talk it over with their parents and practice the fifth commandment by honoring whatever their parents decide.

? **Are people commanded to honor their parents if they're bad parents?**

> See "A Note to Leaders" on page 87 for addressing this question according to your context.

? **What about honoring non-Christian parents?**

> God doesn't ask us to base our honor on whether our parents deserve it. Acknowledge that sometimes it is hard for people to honor their parents

A Note to Leaders

Brent Bounds, PhD

Given the target age group and demographic of this curriculum, it will most likely not be necessary to bring up the question of abuse in the home unless there is knowledge that a child is in an unhealthy or abusive situation, or if a child discloses this in the asking of a question around this commandment.

The Ten Commandments were given to the people of God with the understanding that they were his and were following him. It is safe to assume that this was intended for adults and children of believing parents who seek to follow God. However, teachers may interact with children whose parents are nonbelievers and, in some situations, are abusive. Addressing such situations should be done with wisdom and discernment. Answering a child's question with a question to gain more information and context is typically a good first start. This allows the teacher to get a better understanding of what the child is *really* asking before a quick answer is given. The focus of the response should be on the meaning of the word *honor*. And while obedience is integral to a healthy parent/child relationship, the word *obedience* is not used in the commandment. Respect, esteem, and reverence are the virtues being required in this commandment. This is similar to the instruction given to people under governments that may not submit to God (Rom. 13:1–7). We are to trust the sovereignty of God who puts authorities and governments in place. We are to live with respect and honor for all authority, and yet we are not required to be obedient to these authorities when they require disobedience to God. A great example of this is Daniel (Daniel 6) who, when aware of King Darius's decree, went to his room and continued to pray with his windows open toward Jerusalem. His interactions with King Darius were honoring and respectful based on the king's authority, but his obedience was to God's authority.

Children (and adults) are commanded to respect and honor their parents because God in his sovereignty has placed them in their particular family. However, if a parent is asking or requiring a child to go against God's instructions by stealing, being dishonest, or committing an act that is inappropriate or indecent, the child is not biblically commanded to obey. We never know how God might use a loving, respectful, and honoring response to convict a parent even when it is accompanied by a refusal to comply with an inappropriate demand.

Notes

especially if they're against the gospel. We don't have to agree with someone to act respectfully toward them.

Also use this opportunity to help the children think about their own lives and how this question and answer affects them personally.

- Help the children think of the areas they might be inclined to rebel against their parents and how peer pressure might influence this.

- Encourage the children to regularly ask God for help to honor their parents.

- Help the children to consider what spending more time focused on God on the Sabbath might look like for them. Brainstorm ways to focus on God that aren't monotonous or boring.

 Virtue Vision

Joy

Remind the children that God designed his commandments to be a source of joy for his people, rather than rules to be kept!

Help the children to reflect on what true joy means. Ask them to consider what the world thinks brings joy, and ask them to contrast the joy that comes from living as a child of God.

Have the children recall the "joy grids" they created for Question 5. Next, have them engage with Proverbs 15:13: "A glad heart makes a cheerful face, but by sorrow of heart the spirit is crushed." Point out that it is

impossible to show a frown and smile at the same time. Ask the children to try to do both at once if they do not believe it!

Divide the children into two groups. Have one group act out a short skit in which someone obeys the fourth commandment without joy, then replay the same skit to show what it would look like to obey the fourth commandment with joy. The second group should act out obeying the fifth commandment without joy and then with joy. Point out to the class that in every skit the commandment was obeyed. Ask the children which kind of obedience they prefer.

Memory Activity

Print the memory verse or catechism answer, and cut it up so that each word is on its own slip of paper. Cut each slip of paper in half horizontally. Hide one of the halves around the room. Then, give each child one of the

remaining half pieces (or more than one if you have a small group). Each child is to find her matching piece only. When all are found, have the children put the words in order and read the verse or answer out loud.

⑤ Closing Prayer Time

Conclude the lesson by thanking God for his care for his children and for the provision of his commandments that are established to bring joy to his people. Pray that the children would "remember the Sabbath" and that they would always find great joy in setting aside time to spend with God's people in praise and worship.

Invite the children to give thanks for their parents and pray that they might always honor them.

Notes

What does God require in the sixth, seventh, and eighth commandments?

Answer

Sixth, that we do not hurt or hate our neighbor. Seventh, that we live purely and faithfully. Eighth, that we do not take without permission that which belongs to someone else.

Big Idea
The commandments are all about loving God and loving others.

Aim
To help the children understand that obeying God's commands involves loving him and loving others.

Bible Passage
Romans 13:8–10

Memory Verse
"For the commandments, 'You shall not commit adultery, You shall not murder, You shall not steal, You shall not covet,' and any other commandment, are summed up in this word: 'You shall love your neighbor as yourself.'" (Rom. 13:9)

Virtue
Honesty

Leader's Notes

The Western world is becoming increasingly selfish and self-centered. The concept of community is being eroded, and people are living largely individualistic lives. God is a God of love who longs for his love to be imaged in his world. This lesson will help the children consider what it is to love radically in the context of the sixth, seventh, and eighth commandments. The aim of the lesson is to help the children understand how to love their neighbors as themselves by obeying God's commands. The children will be encouraged to consider their own hearts as they reflect on God's commandments and to remember that the commandments can be broken internally as well as externally.

Things to remember when planning and teaching:

- Be careful to communicate that obedience to God's commandments is a response to his grace and a wonderful way to glorify God.

- It is worth noting that some children have very active consciences and may be aware of the various ways they break God's commandments. Be careful not to induce guilt, but rather point them to Jesus.

- Encourage the children to develop a desire to show radical, others-centered love.

- Remember to mix and match the activities in the lesson to fit your time frame (see p. 12 for some sample outlines). You won't have time to do them all. Feel free to adapt each activity based on your class's strengths and weaknesses.

For help navigating conversations that might arise around the subject of adultery, see the "A Note to Leaders" on page 93.

Leader's Prayer

Loving God, please help me to live in a way that is others-centered. Help me to show radical love to those in my community. Please grant understanding to the children who will hear this lesson and challenge them to be great agents of your love in your world. In Jesus's name. Amen.

Leader's Tool Kit

- Ping-pong balls
- Bag
- Newspaper clippings
- Red construction paper cut in the shape of a heart, two for each child
- Trash can

- Markers, colored pencils, or crayons
- Blank white paper
- Q11 A Silly Story (RB), one copy
- Poster board
- Ball

A Note to Leaders

Brent Bounds, PhD

For this age group, I would suggest using the terms of husband, wife, and marriage to explain adultery. The older children in this age range (ten- to eleven-year-olds) may have more knowledge about sex and terms around these concepts. But the context of a Sunday school or classroom where the child's parents are not present is probably not the best context to go into a lot of detail about adultery. Even words like *lust* and *impure thoughts* can be a bit obtuse and confusing for younger children. This is a perfect lesson to combine the term *honor* used in the previous lesson with the concept in this lesson of a heart of gratefulness. When we are grateful for what God has given us, even though we may see others who have more, we are more able to relate to others around us with honor and respect. In marriage, this looks like being grateful for the spouse God has given us, loving him or her through acts of kindness and service, and honoring him or her by keeping the marriage relationship special—like no other.

If a child asks questions about adultery that would need more detailed answers about sex in general, it is best to respond and affirm that it is a very good question and you are glad that he or she is asking it. Explain that he or she should talk to the parents about that question or that you (the teacher) would be happy to speak to his or her parents first about the question before giving the child an answer. This response doesn't communicate shame to the child and also respects the parents' input and encourages the child to have conversations about this subject primarily with his or her parents.

Catechism Recap

Write the numbers of the questions that have already been taught on ping-pong balls and put them into a bag or box. If your budget allows, you can put the balls into a bingo cage or blower to add to the fun, or make your own.

Divide the children into teams and explain that you are going to have a quiz to help them remember some of the catechism questions they have already learned. Let each team pick a numbered ball out for their opponents. The opposition's task is to remember the question associated with the number drawn, the answer, and the memory verse. The team will get nine points if they remember all the elements associated with

93

the number (the question, answer, and memory verse), or three for each correct element. The team with the most points at the end of the time wins. Remember, this is meant to be a fun and engaging activity.

⑤ Introduction to Question 11

Gather some newspaper articles that highlight the subject matter of the sixth, seventh, and eighth commandments.

Begin by showing the children the reality of how people treat one another in society today. Highlight some recent news stories that focus on people causing harm to one another, people stealing from one another, and people seeking what is not theirs. Wisely choose articles that show the lack of love that is evident in the world today among all sorts of people.

Introduce the children to Question 11: "What does God require in the sixth, seventh, and eighth commandments?" Explain to the children that these commandments focus on how God's people relate to other people, those whom they live with and encounter day by day. Behind each of these commandments (stealing, murder, adultery) is wanting something that isn't yours or that God has not given you. These desires begin from an ungrateful heart. If you steal, you take something that isn't yours. Hating or murdering a person comes from a place of deep anger, which is rooted in either jealousy of what another person has or who they are, or in the fear that what is important to me is being threatened. Adultery is desiring someone that God has not given you. It results when someone is ungrateful for the husband or wife that God has given him or her and wants a relationship with someone else.

Ask the children to consider how the world might be different if, instead of wanting what is not rightfully ours, people were more concerned with loving others well.

⑩ Activity

It is easy for the children to look at news articles and consider the various ways that other people have broken God's commandments and have failed to love their neighbors as themselves. However, it is appropriate to encourage the children to consider their own hearts at the beginning of this lesson. Tell the children that in the Sermon on the Mount found in Matthew 5, Jesus made it clear that we can break God's law in our hearts, even if no one else knows.

Ask the children if they have ever said that they hate someone or if they have thought mean thoughts about someone else. Jesus taught that hating others is like killing them in our hearts. If we imagine doing things to hurt them, we are sinning, even if we never act on our thoughts. We may not have committed the crimes done by people in the newspaper, but we have all sinned in our hearts.

Give each child a large paper heart. Ask them to fold it in half down the middle. Point out that, once it is folded, no one can see what is inside. This is true of our hearts as well—no one else can see inside, except for God.

Invite the children to write a prayer on the inside of the construction paper heart. They can confess to God any thoughts they've had that are hateful or mean. They can ask God to forgive those sins because Jesus paid for them on the cross. When they are finished writing their prayer of confession, invite each child to tear the paper heart into tiny pieces over the trash can. This reminds us that if we confess our sins, God is faithful to forgive us. No one will ever read the sins they wrote on their hearts, and we can thank God that he forgives us even for the sins that only he knows about.

Notes

---

15. Teaching Outline

Begin the teaching time by asking for God's help. Ask that the lesson would be taught faithfully and that the children might listen well.

Ask the children how the world defines love. Highlight that often the world thinks of love in purely romantic ways. Explain to the children that God really wants his people to live in a way that shows radical love to other people.

Explain to the children that the romantic idea of love emphasizes the idea that people fall in love—it's just something that happens. In contrast, the love that God wants his people to show to one another is something that people must *decide* to do.

Read Romans 13:8–10. Provide Bibles for the children to read along with you.

Introduce the children to Paul, and explain that the book of Romans is a letter that he wrote to Christians in a place called Rome. Highlight to the children that Paul's words are as applicable to them as they were to the Christians in Rome in the first century. Tell them that at this point in his letter Paul is explaining to the Christians how they must live. He references the sixth, seventh, and eighth commandments and highlights for the Christians that to live in a way that glorifies God means keeping these commandments. They must not hate or harm other people; they must love the family God has given them; they must not steal; and they must not covet.

95

Notes

Explain to the children that Paul wants to show how Christians should live among their fellow believers and among those who do not follow Christ.

Direct the children's attention to verse 9, and ask them to investigate how this love should be shown. Is it a reserved love or a half-hearted love? No! They are commanded to love others in the same way that they love themselves. Ask the children what they think that means.

Explain to the children that it means that God's people should always be concerned for the safety, health, security, and respect of each and every person. Ask the children to consider what that might look like in everyday life. Tell them that God clearly commands that people should not harm others, desire what is not theirs, or steal from others. To avoid these sins is another way to love people well.

Remind the children of the activity that they did at the beginning of the lesson, and help them see that they need to continuously consider their own hearts. Help them consider how to be honest about the temptations they may face, whether it is to harbor in their hearts hatred, jealousy, or desires for what is not theirs. Encourage them by reminding them that Jesus has taken the punishment for their law-breaking. Also encourage them to be concerned to keep God's commands so that they might glorify God in response to his grace.

Conclude the teaching time by helping the children commit Question 11 and the answer to memory.

(These notes are just for guidance. Please expand or amend to suit your own children and context. Write out your talk in your own words and include illustrations and applications that you know will connect with your children.)

 Activity

Give each child a piece of blank paper. Tell them to draw scenes of people helping their neighbors. In addition, tell them to hide or incorporate the numbers six, seven, and eight somewhere in their drawing to remind them that the sixth, seventh, and eighth commandments are about loving our neighbors. When they finish, have the children swap pictures and try to find the numbers in their classmates' drawings.

⑤ Discussion and Question Time

Some of the questions that might arise include:

? How do I know if I've broken these commandments in my heart?

Explain to the children that the Holy Spirit will help them see their personal law-breaking. They can pray to God to show them their heart sins. When they see them, they don't have to be discouraged. They can take them to the cross!

? Surely God can't expect us to love everyone, can he?

Yes! God expects us to love and care for everyone we have contact with.

? What should I do if I've stolen something?

Tell the children that the first thing they should do is to tell God they are sorry, and then they should seek to make the situation right, either by returning what they stole or paying for the item. It's hard to tell the truth about stealing, but God's commands are always for our good.

Also use this opportunity to help the children to think about their own lives and how this question and answer affects them personally.

- Help the children to think carefully about how to show radical others-centered love.

- Ask the children whether they find it easy or difficult to keep these commands. Help them to identify any real temptation in their hearts.

⑩ Virtue Vision

Honesty
Ask the children to try to define honesty in their own words.

Mention that lies can be told by making up false information *or* failing to share relevant information that a situation calls for. Ask the children if they can think of any examples.

Explain to the children that being honest doesn't just mean telling the truth. It means living in an honest way and keeping the law. After all, if they broke the law, they might be tempted to be dishonest to cover up their transgressions. Honesty is about speaking and acting truthfully.

Have the children fill in the blanks of the Q11 A Silly Story (RB). Don't let them see the story until all the blanks have been filled, then read it aloud.

Notes

Remind the children that while this story sounds very silly, telling lies can never end well.

Conclude by praying with the children and asking God to help them live honest lives and value honesty in the world.

Memory Activity

You will need a ball for this activity.

- Put the memory verse or catechism answer on a poster so the children can read it.

- Divide the children into two teams.

- Have children read aloud the memory verse or catechism answer with you several times.

- Put down the poster so the children can't see the words.

- Get the teams to stand in two straight lines and then face each other.

- Throw the ball to a child who is expected to say the first word of the memory verse. He or she should then throw the ball to a child on the opposite team, who is expected to say the second word of the memory verse, etc.

- If a child doesn't remember the word or gets it wrong, he or she should throw the ball and then sit down. The team with the most team members still standing is the winner at the end.

Closing Prayer Time

Give each child a second paper heart with no writing on it.

Invite the children to write a short sentence of praise to God reflecting on something

they've learned in the lesson. Encourage them to take their prayer home and praise God throughout the week for not only seeing into our hearts, but also for forgiving us when we confess our sin.

Question 12

What does God require in the ninth and tenth commandments?

Answer

Ninth, that we do not lie or deceive.

Tenth, that we are content, not envying anyone.

Big Idea
God desires that his people live in a way that glorifies him and shows his character to the world.

Aim
To help the children understand that God longs for them to be satisfied in him and to become more like him.

Bible Passage
Exodus 20:1–17

Memory Verse
"If you really fulfill the royal law according to the Scripture, 'You shall love your neighbor as yourself,' you are doing well." (James 2:8)

Virtue
Honesty

Notes

Leader's Notes

Children learn to lie at a very young age. Children usually lie to gain some advantage for themselves, whether it's to become more popular or to avoid some sort of punishment. This lesson will help the children to understand that God loves truth and longs for his people to be truth tellers; this will both benefit human relationships and display something of God's nature to a watching world as his people bear his image. The other thing that children learn to do at a very early age is to covet the belongings of others; sadly, this covetousness is nurtured by a vast advertising and marketing industry. This lesson will help the children to consider what it is to be satisfied in God and to not covet things that others have. The catechism question will teach the ninth and tenth commandments to the children.

Things to remember when planning and teaching:

- Remind the children that obeying God's commandments is a response to his grace and a way to glorify him.

- Be aware of how peer pressure affects children in both the areas of lying and coveting. Help the children to understand the effect that peer pressure has on them.

- Remember to mix and match the activities in the lesson to fit your time frame (see p. 12 for some sample outlines). You won't have time to do them all. Feel free to adapt each activity based on your class's strengths and weaknesses.

Leader's Prayer

God of all truth, thank you for your commandments. Thank you that they show me the correct way to live in response to your grace. Help me to guard my tongue and guard my heart against covetousness.

Grant the children who will hear this lesson understanding, and please challenge them to guard their tongues and hearts also. In Jesus's name. Amen.

Leader's Tool Kit

- Q12 Catechism Recap (DL)
- Bowl
- "The Boy Who Cried Wolf" story
- Toy catalogs
- Paper
- Markers
- Uninflated balloons

Catechism Recap

In a bowl, place slips of paper with the catechism Questions 1–11 (from Question 12 Catechism Recap [DL]).

Divide the children into two teams. Invite a child from each team to come to the front and pick out a question for the other team. Keep repeating this process until all the questions have been answered. The team with the most correct answers at the end wins!

Introduction to Question 12

Tell or read the story of "The Boy Who Cried Wolf" to the children.

Ask the children what they think of lying. Ask whether they like being lied to. Ask them if they ever lie.

Explain to the children that the Bible contains many warnings against lying, and the ninth commandment states clearly that God does not want people to lie.

Introduce the children to Question 12: "What does God require in the ninth and tenth commandments?" Tell the children that Question 12 will help them to consider the problem of lying and also what it means to covet.

Activity

Tell the children you are going to read them some statements. If they think the statement is true, they should move to the right side of the room, and if they think it is a lie, they should move to the left side of the room.

1. September has thirty-one days. (lie)

2. Up is the opposite of down. (truth)

3. The sun rotates around the earth. (lie)

4. Cats have nine lives. (lie)

5. Walt Disney's full name was Walter Elias Disney. (truth)

6. Earthworms breathe through their skin. (truth)

7. The Titanic sank in 1932. (lie)

8. Bamboo is the fastest growing plant in the world. (truth)

9. Nashville, Tennessee, is the largest city in the United States. (lie)

10. Thomas Jefferson's face is on the $3 bill. (lie)

Ask the children whether they are more attracted to people who tell the truth or people who lie. Ask the children why they like hearing the truth, but why they're sometimes tempted to lie.

(15) **Teaching Outline**

Begin the teaching time by asking for God's help. Ask that the lesson would be taught faithfully and that the children might listen well.

Introduce this teaching time by telling the children that God is a God of truth. He loves the truth and hates lies. One of the things that it is impossible for God to do is lie! Explain to the children that it makes perfect sense, therefore, for God to want his children to love truth and hate deception.

Read Exodus 20:1–17. Provide Bibles for the children to read along with you.

Help the children to observe in the passage that the ninth and tenth commandments are focused once again on relationships between people. Explain to the children that these commandments are intended to help God's people live wisely alongside one another.

Ask the children what they think the consequences might be if someone told lies about another person. It would be very damaging, and it would cause a breakdown in relationships. Explain to the children that, sadly, people tell lies to one another and about one another all the time, and that brings lots of difficulties and problems.

Ask the children what it means to be like God and to seek to obey God. Highlight for them that if God loves truth and hates lies, then his people should love truth and hate lies. God demands that his people do not tell any kind of lies, even what might be described as little white lies. Help the children to understand that all lying is wrong—despite what other people might say. God even hates the little white lies. Ask the children to reflect on when they are tempted to lie, what makes them lie? To get out of a tricky situation? To avoid being punished? To make people like them?

Help the children to reflect on the motivations of their hearts. Help them to understand that when they lie, they are concerned about themselves and not about God or his glory.

Explain to the children that the Devil is called the father of lies (John 8:44). Highlight for the children that when they lie, they are behaving like the Devil rather than God.

Direct the children's attention back to the Bible passage and ask them what they think verse 17 means. Ask them if they're ever tempted to covet the belongings of another. What kind of things do they wish they had? Highlight for the children the power of advertising, and explain that the purpose of much advertising is to cause covetousness in the hearts of those watching or looking at the ads. Ask the children to identify where they feel that pressure.

Explain to the children that God cares about the hearts of his people. Tell the children that coveting things often causes people to become obsessed about them, and they can take the place of God in the hearts of people.

Ask the children to think quietly and reflect on whether they think too much about stuff they'd like or if they experience jealousy when they see what other people have.

Explain to the children that covetousness can damage relationships between people. Ask them how they will think about people if they just want what they have. Will they be able to love people, or will they simply be jealous and bitter around those people?

Explain to the children that covetousness says to God that he isn't enough or that he hasn't provided enough for his people. It shows dissatisfaction in God, and it definitely doesn't love God with heart, soul, and mind.

Conclude the teaching time by helping the children commit Question 12 and the answer to memory.

(These notes are just for guidance. Please expand or amend to suit your own children and context. Write out your talk in your own words and include illustrations and applications that you know will connect with your children.)

Notes

---

⑩ **Activity** ☼

Provide some toy catalogs for the children to cut up.

Ask the children to cut out pictures from the catalogs of things that they might be tempted to covet. Alternatively, they could draw or write down the names of things that they might covet.

After a short period of time, let each child show what they have cut out. Tell them to imagine that they've been given the object they cut out. Now send them back to the catalog to choose a second choice.

After the children have cut out a second picture, ask them if it was hard to find a second thing they might be tempted to covet. This demonstrates that getting the thing we covet doesn't really satisfy us. We will always want more!

Pray that God would free the children from desiring things that other people have, and ask that God might grant the children contentment in him.

---

⑤ **Discussion and Question Time**

Some of the questions that might arise include:

? Isn't it sometimes necessary to lie?

Remind the children that the Devil is the father of lies and that he loves it when people lie because it shows the world what he's like rather than what God is like. Encourage the children to always seek to tell the truth.

Notes

? **By not having the same stuff that the other children have, I feel left out and lonely. Isn't that why I covet things?**

> Help the children to understand that possessions will not provide satisfaction or fulfillment. Remind them that God alone can satisfy them, and he will provide all that they need.

Also use this opportunity to help the children to think about their own lives and how this question and answer affects them personally.

- Ask the children how they will strive to be truth tellers.

- Ask the children what it means to be truly satisfied with what God provides and to trust him for all things.

- Ask the children how this lesson has helped them to think about how they might love their neighbors, friends, and family.

Virtue Vision

Honesty

Provide each child with a piece of paper and a pen.

Acknowledge that it is often much easier to tell a lie than to tell the truth. Ask the children to think of some situations in which people might be tempted to lie.

Invite the children to write a story about honesty and how lying got someone into trouble. Ask the children to read out their stories, and discuss what each character could have done instead of lying.

Memory Activity

Write out the memory verse or catechism answer. Cut out the words and put the words of the memory verse or answer into some balloons. Blow up the balloons. Let the children have fun popping the balloons and then arrange the memory verse or catechism answer. Read through it a couple of times, then remove one word at a time until they can say the whole thing.

Closing Prayer Time

Encourage the children to pray, giving thanks to God for the Ten Commandments and for all they teach about him.

Question 13

Can anyone keep the law of God perfectly?

Answer

Since the fall, no human has been able to keep the law of God perfectly.

Big Idea
The law of God has been kept perfectly only by Jesus. No other human has, is, or will be able to keep God's law.

Aim
To introduce the children to the concept of original sin.

Bible Passage
Romans 3:9–20

Memory Verse
"None is righteous, no, not one; no one understands; no one seeks for God. All have turned aside; together they have become worthless; no one does good, not even one." (Rom. 3:10–12)

Virtue
Forgiveness

Notes

Leader's Notes

The concept of sin is increasingly alien to modern society, and the belief in the doctrine of original sin will be offensive to many. The world is inclined to believe that children are born innocent and are corrupted only by the adult influences in their lives. This lesson aims to introduce the children to the doctrine of original sin. It will help the children to understand that no one has kept or will be able to keep God's law perfectly, except Jesus. The children will learn that sin affects their relationship with God and with other people. This lesson aims to help them see how sin corrupts everything and how Jesus can provide salvation because he lived the perfect life.

Things to remember when planning and teaching:

- This is a difficult concept for some children to understand. Exercise care and patience in your teaching.

- This can be a frightening topic for children, especially those from non-Christian homes. Be sensitive to those children who may come from non–Christian homes or who are not yet Christians themselves.

- Remember to mix and match the activities in the lesson to fit your time frame (see p. 12 for some sample outlines). You won't have time to do them all. Feel free to adapt each activity based on your class's strengths and weaknesses.

Leader's Prayer

Gracious God, I recognize that I am an unworthy sinner, but rejoice that you have shown me mercy and grace through salvation in the Lord Jesus Christ. May I ever remember your kindness and be aware of what you have saved me from. Grant understanding to the children who will hear this lesson, and help them to recognize their need for a Savior. In Jesus's name. Amen.

Leader's Tool Kit

- Whiteboard

- Whiteboard markers

- Pictures or video of Evel Knievel

- Flashlight

- Smooth stones, one per child (available in craft store floral departments)

- Paint pens

Catechism Recap

Divide the children into small teams. Have a whiteboard at the front of the classroom, and give each team a whiteboard marker. Ask the teams to give themselves a team name. Write the team names on the board.

Tell the children that you will read either the question or the answer of one of the catechism questions and they have to take turns to run to the board and write the number that is linked to what has been read out. Note who is the fastest and who is correct after each round. Give one point to the fastest team and a point to each team that guesses the correct number. The team with the most points at the end wins.

Notes

Introduction to Question 13

Ask the children what they think the worst crimes are. Write their list on a whiteboard.

Once they've listed some crimes, ask them to rank them from the most offensive to the least offensive. Once they have completed the activity, ask them where they would place themselves on the list. They will probably be shocked at the suggestion that they should even be on the list and protest their innocence.

Reassure the children that you're aware that they haven't committed a crime or broken any laws in the eyes of the state, but challenge them to consider whether they've broken God's law. Now ask them once again where they think they should be on the list, given that it's a list being prepared for God. Hopefully they will put themselves right at the top of the list. Eliminate the rankings and tell the children that before God, everyone is equally guilty. Introduce Question 13: "Can anyone keep the law of God perfectly?" Remind the children that God gave his law to show his people how to live, but that everyone except Jesus has failed to keep the law of God perfectly.

Activity ☼

Tell the children about Evel Knievel. Explain that he was a famous motorcyclist who attempted daredevil stunts. Show them some pictures or video footage to illustrate the kind of stunts he performed.

Explain to them that on the September 8, 1974, Evel Knievel planned to jump across the Snake River Canyon in a specially designed Skycycle. All the spectators were disappointed because he didn't make the jump. He fell short. (Reassure the children that, surprisingly, he was not killed and only had minor injuries.) No one was really interested in how far he did get; the reality was that he just couldn't reach the other side. When you're jumping across a canyon, "almost" is not good enough!

107

Notes

Help the children understand that this is an illustration of how humanity is before God's law. Every single person fails to reach the standard of God's law.

Teaching Outline

Begin the teaching time by asking for God's help. Ask that the lesson would be taught faithfully, and that the children might listen well.

Ask the children if anyone here has ever received a perfect score on a test. Congratulate those who say they have! Then ask those children if they always get 100 percent on their tests. Explain that it is very unlikely that anyone will consistently achieve 100 percent on every test throughout his or her life. Reassure the children that it actually doesn't matter whether they get 100 percent on every exam, as long as they try their best. But help them to see that perfection is impossible to live up to.

Read Romans 3:9–20. Provide Bibles for the children to read along with you.

Introduce the children to Paul's letter to the Romans and explain to them that, at this point in the letter, Paul is helping his readers and listeners understand just how bad the situation is for them! Paul clearly explains to them that everyone, both Jews (God's chosen people) and Gentiles, fail to live up to God's standard as revealed in his law— the Ten Commandments. Paul says that everyone is born sinful, and that means that no one can keep the law of God perfectly.

Explain to the children that God designed human beings to be able to keep his law perfectly, but when sin entered the world through Adam, everything changed. Adam rejected God's law in favor of living his own way, and every single person who has lived since is tainted by the sin that first appeared in Adam. Explain to the children that everybody is separated from God by sin and that no one is capable of living the perfect righteous life that God demands. Remind the children that God has declared that he will punish those who fail to keep his law.

Paul explains that no one is right with God. Invite the children to look back through the passage and pull out some of the things it says about people. Ask the students to identify the parts of the body that are mentioned in the passage. There is no part of us that isn't affected by sin. Ask them if they are shocked or surprised or worried.

Help the children to see that it is both relationships with other people and the relationship with God that is spoiled.

Read verse 20 for the children, and explain that it means it is not possible to save oneself by the law, but rather, through the law people become aware of their sin.

Notes

Ask the children if your classroom is dirty or clean. (Hopefully, they will say that it is clean.) Tell them that although it may be tidy, there may be dust on surfaces that we can't see. Let a few children take turns using the flashlight to see if they can find any dust. Help the children see that the law allows us to see where we have failed to live according to God's perfect way, just as the flashlight helps us see dust that we could not see without it.

Tell the children that there is some good news though! Describe how understanding our failure to keep the law helps the beauty of the gospel to shine through. It's like a black piece of velvet that is put behind a diamond to allow the diamond to shine brightly.

Tell the children that there is One who kept God's law perfectly, and that was Jesus. Explain that God intends to punish those who have rejected his rule and broken his law, but Jesus wonderfully, willingly bears God's punishment in order for relationships to be restored between God and man.

Conclude the teaching time by helping the children commit Question 13 and the answer to memory.

(These notes are just for guidance. Please expand or amend to suit your own children and context. Write out your talk in your own words and include illustrations and applications that you know will connect with your children).

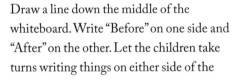

Activity

Draw a line down the middle of the whiteboard. Write "Before" on one side and "After" on the other. Let the children take turns writing things on either side of the line. Everything on the *Before* side should be things that were true before the fall of Adam. Everything on the *After* side should be what is true of our world now.

Discussion and Question Time

Some of the questions that might arise include:

? **Why did God allow sin to enter the world?**

Explain to the children that God knew humanity would sin, but that he allowed it to happen so he could display his amazing love by sending Jesus to die on the cross.

? **What difference does it make if people actually keep the law?**

Explain to the children that because God is just and holy, he will punish those who don't keep his law perfectly

Notes

and fail to repent. People can live as if God doesn't exist and as if his law isn't important, but one day they will stand before God in judgment.

? **I'm not sure I'm a Christian. Will I face God's punishment?**

Help the children understand how to become a Christian by putting their faith in Jesus.

Also use this opportunity to help the children to think about their own lives and how this question and answer affects them personally.

- Ask the children how they might describe the concept of original sin to someone else.

- Ask the children how they might be inspired to obey the law in gratitude for God's saving grace in Jesus.

- Help the children to consider the urgency of sharing the gospel.

 Virtue Vision

Forgiveness
Have the smooth stones and paint pens ready.

Suggest to the children that it would be very bad news for us that we cannot perfectly keep God's law if we did not know that God forgives those who repent. But because the punishment that we deserved was taken by Christ, we can be completely forgiven.

Ask the children how that might make a difference when someone hurts our feelings or sins against us. Does the fact that God has forgiven them make them want to forgive others?

Give each child a small smooth stone. Ask the children what they could draw on the stone to symbolize forgiveness (a cross would be a good choice, but they may have another idea). Let each child decorate his or her own stone. Tell them that this is meant to be a forgiveness stone—a reminder that since God has forgiven us (upward forgiveness), we should forgive other people (sideways forgiveness). When someone sins against them, the forgiveness stone will be a reminder that we forgive because God forgave us.

Don't let the children take the stones home yet. Make a few extra forgiveness stones to keep for next week's Virtue Vision.

Memory Activity

On the whiteboard, write out the memory verse or catechism answer without vowels. Invite the children first to try to read it without the vowels, then to suggest where the vowels should go. Once all the vowels have been inserted, read the memory verse or answer through several times with the children.

Closing Prayer Time

Pray that the children would rejoice in their salvation and that they would be urged to pray for the salvation of others.

Question 14

Did God create us unable to keep his law?

Answer

No, but because of the disobedience of Adam and Eve, we are all born in sin and guilt, unable to keep God's law.

Big Idea

God created Adam and Eve with the ability to perfectly keep his law. Sin now prevents the law from being kept.

Aim

To help the children to understand how sin entered the human race and to understand the contrast of being in Adam and being in Christ.

Bible Passage

Romans 5:12–21

Memory Verse

"Therefore, just as sin came into the world through one man, and death through sin, and so death spread to all men because all sinned." (Rom. 5:12)

Virtue

Forgiveness

Leader's Notes

The question of how sin entered the world is a confusing one that children particularly struggle to understand. This lesson will enable them to recognize that God originally created Adam and Eve with the ability to keep God's law perfectly. However, when Adam decided to reject God's rule in favor of self-rule, sin entered the human race. Since that time it has been passed from generation to generation. The children will learn that no human is able to keep God's law perfectly. This lesson aims to help the children to understand the difference between being in Adam and being in Jesus.

Things to remember when planning and teaching:

- This will be a difficult area for some children to understand. Endeavor to communicate as clearly as possible.

- Help the children to clearly understand what it means to be unable to keep God's law, but be aware of the children who are not Christians or who come from non-Christian homes.

- Remember to mix and match the activities in the lesson to fit your time frame (see p. 12 for some sample outlines). You won't have time to do them all. Feel free to adapt each activity based on your class's strengths and weaknesses.

Leader's Prayer

Sovereign God, thank you that because of Jesus I can be saved from Adam's helpless race. Thank you for bringing salvation and life through Jesus. Please help me to rejoice in my salvation and in your perfect plan. Grant understanding to the children who will listen to this lesson. Help them understand what it is to be in Adam and the contrast of being in Christ. In Jesus's name. Amen.

Leader's Tool Kit

- Q14 Catechism Recap (DL)
- Paper with large hashtags (#) printed on them
- Markers
- Large sheets of white paper
- Red stickers
- Black paint
- A paint brush

Catechism Recap

Print out Q14 Catechism Recap (DL). Stick the questions and answers up around the classroom. With each paper, also stick up a paper with several large hashtags.

Tell the children to go to one of the questions stuck up on the wall and create a hashtag that summarizes the question. Explain that a hashtag is a short summary or comment on something on social media. It is written as words without spaces. If time permits, let the children write hashtags on more than one question. Read out some of their suggestions, and tell the children that hashtags can help them remember the questions and answers.

Example:

Question 2: "What is God?"

Answer: God is the creator of everyone and everything.

Hashtag: #AWESOME

#WhereIcamefrom

Introduction to Question 14

Play a word association game with the children. The rules of the game are that the children must say a word that is directly related to the previous word and that there can be no hesitation or repetition. If there is hesitation or repetition, that child must sit down and another child should be invited to his or her place. The game can carry on for as long as time allows.

Invite two children up to play the game. Give one of the children a word to start.

Below are some words you should use. Every time the players change (through violations of hesitation or repetition), introduce a new word (if it hasn't already been said):

Adam	Fall
Eve	Rejection
Sin	Rule
Good	Serpent

Hopefully this game will bring out many words associated with the creation account and the subsequent entry of sin into the world. Introduce the children to Question 14: "Did God create us unable to keep his law?" Explain to the children that this lesson will consider whether God made humans powerless to obey his laws or if something else happened that affected humanity's ability to keep God's perfect law.

(10) **Activity** ☼

You may use some sheets of red stickers in this game.

Play a game of tag with the children. Explain to the children that the person who is "it" has a deadly virus and if he or she catches you, you too will contract the deadly virus. Give the child who is doing the catching some stickers to attach to the other children as they are caught. Keep one child out of the game, and tell him he will have a special purpose in a minute.

Once the children are infected with the virus, they must sit down as they are unable to help or cure themselves.

Send the remaining child into the game to cure those with the virus by removing the red sticker and placing it on himself. This indicates that the children are free from the virus and are free to run again.

Explain to the children that once sin entered the world, it was like a virus that spread to every single person. No one was immune, and there was a great need for a cure.

(15) **Teaching Outline**

Begin the teaching time by asking for God's help. Ask that the lesson would be taught faithfully and that the children might listen well.

Read Romans 5:12–21. Provide Bibles for the children to read along with you.

Remind the children that when God created Adam and Eve, they were the high point of his creation. God walked with them in the garden of Eden, and they enjoyed his blessing. Explain to the children that Adam and Eve were created with the ability to keep God's law perfectly. But help the children to recall what occurred when the Devil tempted Eve. Remind them that Adam and Eve rejected God's rule and decided to disobey God.

Introduce the children to Romans 5 and explain that, in this part of the letter, Paul is explaining how sin infected the human race and how everyone since the time of Adam now is filled with sin.

Paul teaches the Romans three things in this passage:

1. Sin entered the human race through Adam.

2. Death came into the world because of Adam's sin.

3. The whole world is facing death because everybody is infected with sin.

Ask the children whether they think that God created humanity unable to keep his law. The answer is no! God created humankind with the ability to keep God's law perfectly. That all changed, however, when Adam and Eve rejected God's rule, and sin entered the world.

Ask the children to identify why people are now unable to keep God's law perfectly. It is because everyone is born into Adam's race and so inherits the sin of Adam. Ask what things children inherit from their parents. Hair and eye color? Height and shape? Explain to the children that because humanity descends directly from Adam, each person inherits his sin.

Ask the children if they know the hymn "And Can it Be." Tell the children that it was written by a man named Charles Wesley just after he became a Christian almost three hundred years ago. Read for the children the third verse:

> He left his Father's throne above
> So free, so infinite his grace—
> Emptied himself of all but love,
> And bled for Adam's helpless race.

Ask the children what they think Charles Wesley meant by the words "Adam's helpless race." Explain to the children that because humans are all infected with sin, we are unable to keep God's perfect law.

We are helpless, unable to live according to God's rules and facing punishment for that. Explain to the children that sin affects everyone's ability to love God with their heart, soul, and mind. Everyone is corrupted by sin and death. Highlight for the children that that includes you and them!

But draw the children's attention back to the passage and particularly to Romans 5:15. Help the children to understand that while sin entered the world through one man, salvation also entered the world through one man, and that man was Jesus Christ. Charles Wesley wrote that Jesus left heaven to come to earth because of his great love for Adam's helpless race.

Explain to the children that Adam's sin brought death, but Jesus's salvation brings life.

Conclude the teaching time by helping the children commit Question 14 and the answer to memory.

(These notes are just for guidance. Please expand or amend to suit your own children and context. Write out your talk in your own words and include illustrations and applications that you know will connect with your children.)

117

⑩ Activity ☼

Provide large sheets of paper for the children to draw and write on with markers.

Invite the children to graffiti the sheets of paper with as much information as they can recall about the creation of the first man and woman, Adam and Eve. Encourage them to go back and read the creation account to inform their designs.

Help the children to also reflect on what life may have been like at the beginning of creation. At least one teacher should also create a design.

After the teacher has finished his or her design, with the children watching, paint SIN in big black letters across the picture. Acknowledge that it's a shame to ruin lovely artwork, but explain that you are demonstrating how significantly sin affects God's world. Give the children the option to illustrate the same thing by painting over their own artwork, but let them know it is okay for them to keep their drawings unruined if they prefer.

---

⑤ Discussion and Question Time

Some of the questions that might arise include:

? **Why did God allow Adam and Eve to sin?**

Explain that God created Adam and Eve with a will that allowed them to sin. God knew that they would sin, but he permitted it. Explain that the fall is part of God's salvation plan.

? **By stopping Adam and Eve from sinning, could God have prevented Jesus's death?**

Explain to the children that Jesus's death was part of God's eternal plan of salvation, and remind the children that nothing takes God by surprise.

? **Isn't it unfair for us to inherit sin from Adam?**

Life is not fair. If we insist upon fairness, we must recognize that it is also unfair for Christ's righteousness to be counted on our behalf. Rather than complain about the sinful nature we are born with, we should be grateful that God has provided a way to save us from it.

Also use this opportunity to help the children to think about their own lives and how this question and answer affects them personally.

- How has this question equipped the children to understand the origins of sin?

- How might the children explain what it is to be part of Adam's helpless race to a friend?

- Can the children recognize the contrast between Adam and Jesus?

Virtue Vision

Forgiveness

Explain to the children that our inability to keep the law (which we inherited from Adam), reminds us of our need for forgiveness. Ask the children if they remember talking about forgiveness last week. Why should we be eager to forgive others?

Divide the children into two groups. Ask each group to prepare a skit about forgiveness, incorporating the forgiveness stones they made last week. (Give them the extra stones that you made.) Ask them to see if they can create a skit with the message that we should forgive others because God forgives us.

Memory Activity

Divide the children into two or more teams. The challenge is for each team to outdo the other in saying, singing, or acting out the memory verse or catechism answer in a creative way. Give the children a little time to come up with a plan, and then invite them to show the rest of the group what they've come up with.

Closing Prayer Time

Encourage the children to share short prayers reflecting on God's grace and mercy shown in Jesus.

119

Question 15

Since no one can keep the law, what is its purpose?

Answer

That we may know the holy nature of God, and the sinful nature of our hearts; and thus our need of a Savior.

Big Idea
The law serves to reveal sin, to guide, and to communicate the character of God.

Aim
To help the children understand that the law is valuable in the life of the Christian.

Bible Passage
Romans 3:19–20

Memory Verse
"For by works of the law no human being will be justified in his sight, since through the law comes knowledge of sin." (Rom. 3:20)

Virtue
Awe

Leader's Notes

The question of the usefulness of the law in the life of the Christian is a valid one. Why is the law necessary, when it has already been established that no human can live perfectly according to God's law? Children are very astute and will quickly spot this apparent discrepancy. This will be a useful lesson to encourage them and excite them about the goodness of the law in the life of the Christian. This lesson should encourage the children to anticipate the importance of the law throughout their lives. This lesson aims to show the children that God's law is incredibly valuable to both the non-Christian and the Christian. To non-Christians it reveals their inability to live according to God's standards and exposes their need of a Savior, and to Christians it helps them live in a way that is glorifying to God. The law also reveals the character of God, and that is beneficial for all people.

Things to remember when planning and teaching:

- The children will be inclined to think that the law is superfluous in the life of the Christian; care must be taken to help the children see the usefulness of the law.

- Be aware of the danger of nurturing legalism in children; continue to explain that obedience to the law is a right response to God's saving grace.

- Help the children to remember that living obedient lives is glorifying to God.

Leader's Prayer

Awesome God, thank for your law. Thank you that by examining your law, I can see my own sinfulness and can reorient my heart and life toward you. Thank you that you kindly allow me to look into the law to see a reflection of myself. Thank you that you also reveal yourself through your law. I praise you that you are holy, sovereign, loving, and just. Grant understanding to the children who will hear this lesson. Help them to understand the purpose of the law in your saving plan and reveal more of yourself to them as they peer into your word. In Jesus's name. Amen.

Leader's Tool Kit

- Q15 Catechism Recap (DL)
- Large pieces of paper or a roll of butcher paper
- Markers
- A large mirror
- Chalk pen or dry erase marker
- UV pen set with light included
- Index cards

(10) Catechism Recap

Print out and cut up each of the words that make up the Q15 Catechism Recap (DL), and lay them upside down on the floor in the middle of the classroom.

Begin the catechism recap by reading out Questions 12, 13, and 14 (don't read out the answers!). Tell the children that on the floor are the words that make up the answers to each question. Have the children turn over the words and see if they can work together to correctly assemble the right words in the right order to answer each question. Practice saying each question and answer together to finish the recap.

(5) Introduction to Question 15

You will need a large mirror for this introduction.

Hold up the mirror and ask the children what they see in the mirror. Invite some of the children to come closer and investigate their reflections in the mirror. Ask the children to explain what a mirror is used for. Tell them to imagine that they're explaining the concept of a mirror to someone who has never seen one before.

Put the mirror down for a minute and write "THE LAW" across it in chalk pen or dry erase marker. Explain to the children that the law of God functions like a mirror for the Christian. Tell them that as Christians look into the law, they see what they are really like. Explain that the law does not show us our outward appearance as a mirror does. It shows us what our hearts look like.

Introduce the children to Question 15: "Since no one can keep the law, what is its purpose?" Explain to the children that this question will allow them to understand the purpose of the law. They've already seen that it can act as a mirror and that it reveals God's character. Encourage the children to consider how the law might be revealing something about their own hearts to them.

(10) Silent Interviews ☼

This get-to-know-you exercise is designed to frustrate the children and help them realize that the best way to get to know someone is to hear him or her speak.

1. Give each child a partner.

2. Ask the partners to introduce themselves.

3. Tell the children that starting now, they must be absolutely silent. They can't even whisper or try to mouth words silently. They must communicate without words.

4. Have each child "tell" his partner three things about himself using gestures, as if they were playing charades.

Notes

5. After both partners have had a turn, bring everyone back together.

6. Invite each child to explain what he learned about his partner—speaking is now allowed! It is quite likely that not every child will have gotten his message across, and communicate that that's okay.

Tell the children that it's hard to find out about someone in silence. The best way to get to know someone is when they speak to make themselves known.

Explain to the children that one of the functions of the law is to help people understand more of who God is and what he's like. The law reveals God's character.

Teaching Outline

You will need a UV pen and light for this section.

Begin the teaching time by asking for God's help. Ask that the lesson would be taught faithfully and that the children might listen well.

Write *SIN* multiple times in UV pen on a piece of paper. Show the children the paper and ask them what they can see. They won't be able to see anything because the UV pen is invisible until the UV light is shone on it. Shine the UV light on the pen and reveal the word *SIN*.

Explain to the children that God's law reveals personal sin.

Read Romans 3:19–20. Provide Bibles for the children to read along with you.

Remind the children that they've engaged with this passage recently. Ask them to look at verse 20 and discover what Paul is teaching the Romans about the law. He is telling the Romans that through the law comes the knowledge of sin. When Christians read and reflect on the law, the Holy Spirit helps them identify areas of their lives that are not in step with God's law. Explain to the children that reading the law can help Christians to understand their own hearts and see where they are not meeting God's standards. The law reveals sin, just like the UV light revealed the word sin. So one of the purposes of the law is to remind sinners that they will never be able to live up to God's standards, and because of that they deserve to be punished for breaking the law. The law essentially shines a light on the need for a Savior.

For Christians, the law can also act as a guide to show us how to live. Remind the children that one of the ways Christians can glorify God is by obeying his commands. It's like the family rules for those who are members of God's family. Living by God's good commands helps his children glorify him and also shows the watching world what he is like.

Explain to the children that one of the most significant things about the law is that it communicates what God is like; it reveals his character to the world.

Explain to the children that each of the Ten Commandments reveals something about God. Unlike the game at the beginning of the lesson, God's children can hear his voice through his Word to understand what he is like. No one needs to guess.

Tell the children that the law is important because it reveals the sinful nature of man, it guides God's children in life, and it shows God's character to the world.

Conclude the teaching time by helping the children commit Question 15 and the answer to memory.

(These notes are just for guidance. Please expand or amend to suit your own children and context. Write out your talk in your own words and include illustrations and applications that you know will connect with your children.)

Notes

Activity

Cover a portion of a wall with butcher paper or large pieces of paper side by side. Write AWE in big letters across the top of the paper.

Invite the children to read the Ten Commandments and consider what the commandments teach about God's character.

Encourage the children to write the attributes on a Wall of Awe. If time allows, let children take turns writing words of praise on the Wall of Awe with the UV pen and then reveal them with the UV light.

Discussion and Question Time

Some of the questions that might arise include:

? **How do I know if the law is helping me to understand my heart?**

Reassure the children that if they are conscious of their sin and have a desire to change, then the Holy Spirit is using the law to guide and make them more like Jesus.

? **Why do non-Christians describe the Bible as all rules and regulations and God as a grinch?**

Explain to the children that the world does not see the usefulness of the law in the way that Christians do, and they also do not know God in the way that Christians do. Clarify for the children that the people who live away from God are fooled into thinking that they are

Notes

free, when in actual fact they are slaves to sin. It is in and through Jesus that perfect freedom is found.

Also use this opportunity to help the children think about their own lives and how this question and answer affects them personally.

- Do you think the law can help you glorify God?

- How might you try to explain the usefulness of the law to a non-Christian?

- How does the law expand your view of God?

Virtue Vision

Awe

God's law shows us his holiness. It also shows us how short of that holiness we fall.

Direct the children to the Wall of Awe and encourage them to consider the different attributes of God that are detailed on the wall. Ask the children how studying the character of God helps them to love him more. Ask them if it inclines them to live more for his glory.

Ask the children if anyone can think of a song that is appropriate to sing when we stand in awe of God. Sing as many songs together as your time allows.

Memory Activity

Print each word of the memory verse or catechism answer onto a card; you will need one full set of cards for each team.

- Divide the children into teams.

- Read the memory verse or catechism answer aloud to the children.

- Read the memory verse or catechism answer aloud again, inviting the children to repeat each phrase after you.

- Read the memory verse or catechism answer again, and invite the children to join in saying it with you.

- Hand out a full set of cards to each team; make sure they're not in order! Ask the children to put the words in the correct order, setting it up as a race against the clock.

- Practice the memory verse or catechism answer one final time.

Closing Prayer Time

Encourage the children to praise God for who he is and how he works in light of this question relating to the usefulness of his law.

Question 16

What is sin?

Answer

Sin is rejecting or ignoring God in the world he created, not being or doing what he requires in his law.

Big Idea
Sin is rejecting or ignoring God's moral law and rebelling against him.

Aim
To help the children understand what sin is and how it affects their relationship with God.

Bible Passage
1 John 3:4–10

Memory Verse
"Everyone who makes a practice of sinning also practices lawlessness; sin is lawlessness." (1 John 3:4)

Virtue
Forgiveness

Leader's Notes

The concept of sin is increasingly foreign in today's world. God is consistently erased from society, and life now seems to happen without any reference to his existence. The Western world generally buys into the belief that children are inherently good and are gradually corrupted by external influences. Original sin is an alien doctrine to those both inside and outside the church.

This question will encourage the children to investigate the doctrine of sin and to more fully understand the devastating effects of sin on God's creation. The children will more fully appreciate the fact that everything in the world is tainted by sin and deepen their understanding of the significance and beauty of the sacrificial, atoning death of Jesus on the cross.

Things to remember when planning and teaching:

- The children may be familiar with the concept of sin and mistakenly believe that they have nothing more to learn.
- Some children may feel heavily burdened by their personal sin; leaders must therefore communicate with wisdom, gentleness, and grace.
- The children will need encouragement to grasp the fact that humanity can never deal with the problem of sin without God's intervention.
- Remember to mix and match the activities in the lesson to fit your time frame (see p. 12 for some sample outlines). You won't have time to do them all. Feel free to adapt each activity based on your class's strengths and weaknesses.

Leader's Prayer

Gracious God, please forgive me for sinning against you. Thank you that you sent Jesus to deal with my lawlessness. Please help me to put to death my sinful desires and live a life that is glorifying to you. Please grant understanding to the children who hear this lesson. May they be acutely aware of their need for forgiveness and rejoice in the forgiveness that Jesus alone offers through his death on the cross. In Jesus's name. Amen.

Leader's Tool Kit

- Q16 Catechism Recap (DL)
- Newspapers suitable for children to look at
- Duct tape
- Permanent marker
- Markers or pens
- Paper
- Scissors
- Either a guest to share a testimony or a video testimony

Catechism Recap

Print out every question and answer from one to fifteen (Q16 Catechism Recap [DL]). Print the question on one sheet of paper and the answer on another. Print out one full set of the questions and answers for each group of children.

Divide the children into two groups. Place a pile of mixed-up questions and answers for each team at one side of the room—there should be thirty sheets of paper for each team. Each team should stand opposite their pile of paper on the other side of the room. The team members should take turns running up to collect a piece of paper and bringing it back to their team. The team that collects all the pieces of paper and correctly matches each question and answer is the winner. Make it a race! Keep the task lighthearted and fun for all.

Introduction to Question 16

Have plenty of newspapers available to give the children.

Divide the children into groups and give each group a newspaper. Ask the children to identify something from the news that they might describe as lawless (you may need to ascertain if they understand what *lawlessness* is).

Introduce Question 16 to the children: "What is sin?" Explain to the children that sin is described in today's Bible passage as lawlessness. Most people think of bad criminals when they think of lawless people, people who break laws established by the governments. Highlight for the children that Question 16 will facilitate a big examination of the doctrine of sin.

Activity ☼

Set up a jumping game by placing two lines of tape on the floor. Make sure the lines are a good distance apart. The idea is that the children will not be able to reach the mark. Write Romans 3:23 on the tape that the children are trying to jump to.

Have the children stand along one line; make sure the line is long enough to accommodate all the children in the group or else divide the children into smaller groups.

Invite the children to jump from one line to the other. Give the leaders a chance after the children try.

The jump should be just beyond the reach of the children. Explain to them that when Scripture describes sin as lawlessness, it is referring to the keeping of God's law. Tell them that Romans 3:23 (which is written on the tape) declares that everybody has sinned. Everyone has fallen short of God's

Notes

standards. Every single person fails to make the grade. So when we consider what sin is, we must realize that it affects each and every person who has lived, is living, or will live on earth.

🕙 Teaching Outline

Begin the teaching time by asking for God's help. Ask that the lesson would be taught faithfully and that the children might listen well.

Ask the children if they can see ways that the world tries to push God out of the picture and live as if he doesn't exist. Do they ever live without giving God a thought?

Explain to the children that God is deeply saddened when people ignore him as the Creator and sustainer of the world. God hates when people rebel against his law, and he calls it sin. People sin when they break God's law. God's law can be broken actively by doing something or even by thinking something. The first sin occurred in the world in the garden of Eden with Adam and Eve. Since that time all people have been born with a sinful nature. We are all prone to sin. That is why Paul says in Romans 3:23 that "all have sinned and fall short of the glory of God." We are never able to keep God's law fully because we all fail to meet the mark. When we fail to live in the way that God intended us to, we break his law and our sin separates us from God. Breaking God's loving law leads to death and destruction, for God clearly states in his Word that he will punish sin.

Ask the children to name the kinds of sins that they might be guilty of committing.

Read 1 John 3:4–10. Provide Bibles for the children to read along with you.

Introduce the children to John and his first letter to the churches in Asia Minor (modern-day Turkey). John is writing to the people of God in order to help them live in a way that glorifies God.

John reminds those he's writing to that every time they sin, they are breaking God's law.

Sin is a conscious decision to choose to do things our own way instead of God's way. It says "I know best" rather than "God knows best."

John does, however, highlight the solution to sin! Remind the children that we do not always have to be separated from God by sin or face death and destruction because of sin.

Have the children read verse 5 and identify who John is writing about.

It's Jesus! Jesus is the only one who can deal once and for all with sin. Humans can try to live better lives, they can try to keep God's law, but even the best efforts will be unsatisfactory. But Jesus, the only sinless man ever to live, can deal with our sin. Jesus never broke any of God's laws, he never pushed God out of the picture, he never thought, "I'll do this my way instead of God's way." He submitted to God and was perfect in every way—in how he acted and in what he thought. Because of his perfection, he was the only one that could restore our relationship with God and bear our punishment, death, and destruction. The perfect Jesus died on the cross to take the punishment that was due for our sins.

Explain to the children that when Jesus died on the cross, he made the way for the forgiveness of sins and for a relationship with God. When we ask Jesus for forgiveness, a great exchange happens. Our sins are taken by Jesus, and his perfection comes to us (sometimes it's described as the righteousness of Christ). We are made right with God when we trust in Jesus.

Help the children to understand that if we are "in him," as John says, if we are forgiven and righteous because of Christ, surely our love for sin, for living our own way, must be

Notes

banished. Out of great love and gratitude to God for our forgiveness in Christ, we will try to live like Jesus. We won't stop sinning, but we will stop loving sin.

Explain that it is like when sports players change teams. They leave behind the old team's uniform, songs, cheers, and behavior and move to the new team. They put on the new team's uniform and learn the new team's way of doing things. Sometimes they may slip back into their old ways, but they'll try to act successfully as members of the new team.

Finish the teaching time by helping the children commit Question 16 and the answer to memory.

(These notes are just for guidance. Please expand or amend to suit your own children and context. Write out your talk in your own words and include illustrations and applications that you know will connect with your children).

---

⑩ Activity ☼

Invite a guest to come and share his or her testimony with the group or show a video of an appropriate Christian testimony.

Encourage the focus to be on the devastating effects of sin and the salvation and restoration that can be found in Jesus alone.

---

⑤ Discussion and Question Time

Some of the questions that might arise include:

? Aren't some sins worse than others?

  No! Tell the children God declares that all sins are offensive to him.

? What about those who don't ask Jesus for forgiveness?

  Explain to the children that the only way to be made right with God is to ask Jesus for forgiveness. Those who

Notes

don't repent of their sins and seek God's forgiveness will be separated from him forever.

Also use this opportunity to help the children to think about their own lives and how this question and answer affects them personally.

- Have they personally repented of their sin and sought forgiveness in Jesus?
- Are they striving to live in a God-glorifying way?
- Are there particular ways that they sin or are tempted to sin?

⑩ Virtue Vision

Forgiveness

Ask the children to consider what being forgiven means to them. Begin by focusing initially on their personal experience of forgiveness in their home or school setting. Then ask them to consider the enormity of the forgiveness that Christians have because of Jesus's death on the cross. Remind the children of God's incredible mercy and grace.

Conclude by asking them to consider how being forgiven might affect their relationships with other people, friends, siblings, and even enemies. Having experienced such monumental forgiveness

in Jesus, could they possibly have a right to withhold forgiveness from anyone?

Invite the children to spread around the room. They are going to be statues portraying three different postures related to forgiveness. Read out each pose, give students a couple of minutes to think about it, then say "go" when they are meant to change poses. The three statue poses should represent someone:

- In need of forgiveness
- Receiving forgiveness
- Forgiving others

⑩ Memory Activity

Bring back the newspapers that were used earlier.

Read the memory verse or catechism answer with the children a couple of times.

Then give them the newspapers, and ask them to cut out the words of the memory verse or catechism answer from the newspapers and

put them in the right order. If they can't find exactly the right words, they can join letters or words together. Once the children have created a memory verse montage, ask them to say the memory verse together a number of times. Gradually remove words from the verse to help the children commit the verse or catechism answer to memory.

⑤ **Closing Prayer Time**

Notes

Provide pens and paper for the children.

Encourage the children to write down
a prayer of repentance, telling God that
they are sorry for their personal sin.
Encourage the children to take their
written prayers home.

Question 17

What is idolatry?

Answer

Idolatry is trusting in created things rather than the Creator.

Aim

To help the children to understand that their hearts can be tempted to love and treasure earthly things more than God.

Big Idea

Idolatry is loving something in the created world more than God, the Creator.

Bible Passage

Romans 1:18–25

Memory Verse

"For although they knew God, they did not honor him as God or give thanks to him, but they became futile in their thinking, and their foolish hearts were darkened.... They exchanged the truth about God for a lie and worshiped and served the creature rather than the Creator." (Rom. 1:21, 25)

Virtue

Joy

Leader's Notes

Children are particularly susceptible to the lure of the world, and they can be distracted and seduced by created things that look exciting and promise great things. This catechism question will help the children to understand more fully what idolatry is and to personally consider whether they are tempted to worship created things instead of the Creator. It is often relatively easy to spot the idols of children because they become so enthralled and entangled with them; however, it is best for the children's spiritual maturity if they can identify their own idols as they consider their hearts.

Many things may become idols for children, but be careful when listing potential idols to clarify that your list is not exhaustive! Children are quick to excuse themselves if their particular idol is not named.

Things to remember when planning and teaching:

- The children are all worshipers; they are either worshiping God or idols.

- The concept of idolatry may be new for some children.

- Some children may feel acutely aware of personal idols and may be burdened by guilt from their sin.

- Some children will be unable to do the heart searching without individual help.

- Remember to mix and match the activities in the lesson to fit your time frame (see p. 12 for some sample outlines). You won't have time to do them all. Feel free to adapt each activity based on your class's strengths and weaknesses.

Leader's Prayer

O Great God, please help me to love and worship you above all other worthless idols. May I find my joy and satisfaction in you alone. Please help me to see areas in my own life where I'm tempted to idolatry, and protect me from wandering away from you. Grant understanding to the children who will hear this lesson; may they long to love and serve you as Lord of their lives and flee from worthless idols. In Jesus's name. Amen.

Leader's Tool Kit

- Whiteboard

- Whiteboard marker

- Empty bag

- Markers

- Q17 Thought Bubble (RB), one per child

- A selection of toys

- Tray
- Dish towel
- Paper

- Q17 Comic Strip Template (RB), one per child
- Sticky notes

Catechism Recap

On the whiteboard, draw a grid that is four squares wide and four squares down. Leave room on the board to keep score. In a bag, put slips of paper numbered one to sixteen.

Divide the children into small teams and invite them to name their teams. Set up a score board. Invite each team to pick a number out of the bag. Make sure they can't see what number they're picking! Explain that each time a team picks a number, they will write it on the grid. They will get ten points if they can remember the question that goes with the number, twenty points if they can remember both the question and the answer. Repeat the process until the grid is filled with numbers or you run out of time. The team with the highest score wins.

Introduction to Question 17

Give each child a copy of Q17 Thought Bubble (RB) and some markers.

Ask the children to reflect on what they think about or daydream about often. Get them to write or draw their answers in the thought bubbles.

- Do they daydream about their future?
- Do they daydream about things they'd like to buy?
- Do they daydream about people?

Tell the children that reflecting on their daydreams can sometimes reveal something about their hearts.

Introduce Question 17: "What is idolatry?" Explain to the children that idolatry is loving something more than God. An idol is something that takes the place of God in our lives. It is something or someone we look to for joy and satisfaction, instead of our great Creator God. We all have idols, whether we realize it or not.

Analyzing our daydreams can sometimes help us to identify the things that we're tempted to love and trust more than God. Most of the time, idols are not bad things. They only harm us when they go from their proper place into God's place.

Activity

Gather a selection of things that people are tempted to turn into idols. This activity will work well with a selection of miniature toy things. For example, you could use a toy car or some clothes made for a Barbie. Find things to represent:

Money	Celebrities
Adventure	Education
Cars	Technology
Food	Fashion
House	Sports
Romance	Travel
Friends	

Give each child a piece of paper and a marker.

Explain to the children that this activity will help them to think about some modern-day potential idols.

Place the representative items on a tray or table under a cover. Invite the children to come and look at the items on the table for thirty seconds. Then cover the items up on the table again. Have the children write down as many things as they can remember in a set period of time.

Uncover the items again, and see how many items the children remembered. Highlight to the children that these items represent some of the things that people idolize (or put before God) in the world today. Comment that the people who idolize these things would never forget them though, because they love them and mistakenly trust them to bring lasting happiness. Things that are loved so much can never be far from a person's mind.

(Explain that none of these things are wrong in and of themselves. They become a problem when they take the place of God in our lives.)

Teaching Outline

Begin the teaching time by asking for God's help. Ask that the lesson would be taught faithfully and that the children might listen well.

Explain to the children that in the Bible we can see example after example of people turning away from God to worship idols instead. They rejected God, the Creator, in favor of something created. Highlight to the children that nowadays people may not worship things like a golden calf, but they still are predisposed to worship something created rather than the Creator.

Clarify for the children that we are all worshipers. We are made to worship, and if we're not worshiping God as number one in our lives, we will be worshiping something or someone else.

Ask the children to identify ways that the prevailing culture may tempt them to idolatry.

Explain to the children that an idol will be the object of a person's affections; it will be what they spend their money on or where they spend their time. A passion for an idol will be obvious to the world; it will be where people turn to when they feel sad or lonely or when they are worried. People trust idols to make them feel better, and they mistakenly think that they will make them truly happy.

Tell the children that everyone directs their love and loyalty toward someone or something, but clearly remind them that God longs to be number one in everyone's life. He doesn't want to be downgraded to second place by something or someone he has created!

Read Romans 1:18–23. Provide Bibles for the children to read along with you.

Ask the children whether they remember who Paul was and to whom he wrote letters.

In this passage, Paul tells the Romans that God is angry. He's angry because he looks at the world and sees people who don't honor him, who don't love one another, and who deny God's existence—despite the fact that plenty of evidence in the world points to the existence of a great Creator God.

In verses 22 and 23, Paul describes those who worship images rather than the immortal God as fools! This is what God thinks about those who worship idols. If you love money more than him, he thinks you're a fool; if you love sports more than him, he thinks you're a fool; if you love learning more than you love him, he thinks you're a fool.

Remind the children that God is loving, but he is also jealous for our affection. He wants to be number one in our lives because this is ultimately best for us. He wants us to find joy and satisfaction and hope in him alone. He wants us to realize that when we worship and love created things, we're exchanging the truth for a lie, as we read in verse 25. The lie is that anything other than God can satisfy, that anything other than God can save.

Ask the children to examine their own hearts once again. Encourage them to honestly repent if they think that there are things in their lives that compete with God.

Finish the teaching time by helping the children commit Question 17 and the answer to memory.

(These notes are just for guidance. Please expand or amend to suit your own children and context. Write out your talk in your own words and include illustrations and applications that you know will connect with your children).

(10) Activity

One way to figure out what our idols are is to ask what makes us angry if it is taken away. Do they fight with their siblings over toys? Do they fight with friends at school over another person? These may be clues to potential idols.

Print out a Comic Strip Template for each child (RB). Have the children draw a comic-style story in which someone gets into a fight and then realizes he or she has made something or someone an idol.

(5) Discussion and Question Time

Some of the questions that might arise include:

? Have you mentioned all the things that can become idols?

No. Explain to the children that there isn't an exhaustive list of idols anywhere, and that is why it's important for them to consider their own hearts and discern whether they're loving something more than God.

? What does finding joy and satisfaction in God mean?

Help the children to remember that true happiness and satisfaction can be found only through relationship with God, and that is because that is what we're made for. Nothing else will bring lasting happiness or satisfaction.

? Does God punish idolatry?

Remind the children that God longs to be number one in everyone's life and that he will punish those who worship other gods before him. If we repent of our idolatry and ask God's forgiveness, he will forgive us.

Also use this opportunity to help the children to think about their own lives and how this question and answer affects them personally.

- Have they grasped the fact that idols will always disappoint?

- Do they need to consider what it means to love God wholeheartedly?

- How might they deal with the temptation of idolatry?

⑩ Virtue Vision

Joy

Read Romans 15:13: "May the God of hope fill you with all joy and peace in believing, so that by the power of the Holy Spirit you may abound in hope."

Rehearse for the children all the ways and places that the world suggests we will find joy and happiness. Ask the children to identify where joy comes from and who alone gives joy as you read Romans 15:13 again.

Ask the children what difference it will make in their lives knowing that joy comes from God and that he will fill them with joy.

- Will external, created things provide joy?

- Is joy dependent on circumstances? In other words, can you choose to be joyful and reflect on God's goodness during difficult times?

- Can all Christians experience joy?

⑩ Memory Activity

Write the memory verse or catechism answer on sticky notes, one word per note. Make sure there are enough sticky notes with words on them for each child. You may need to make multiple sets if you have a big group of children.

Give each child a sticky note, and then ask everyone to stick them to their foreheads. Help the children to work out the verse or answer and get themselves in the right order. Have them shout out their words individually, and then have the group say it together.

⑤ Closing Prayer Time

Encourage the children to ask God to help them to love him above all things and for God to help them to see where they may be tempted to worship idols.

Question 18

Will God allow our disobedience and idolatry to go unpunished?

Answer

No, God is righteously angry with our sins and will punish them both in this life, and in the life to come.

Big Idea
God will judge and punish all those who sin against him.

Aim
To help the children understand that God will judge all people, and he will punish those who have sinned against him.

Bible Passage
Ephesians 5:5–14

Memory Verse
"For you may be sure of this, that everyone who is sexually immoral or impure, or who is covetous (that is, an idolater), has no inheritance in the kingdom of Christ and God. Let no one deceive you with empty words, for because of these things the wrath of God comes upon the sons of disobedience." (Eph. 5:5–6)

Virtue
Awe

Leader's Notes

It will be obvious to the children that many people today live lives that are inconsistent with God's Word and God's standards. It may appear to the children that these people are enjoying great lives; they are living the way they want to with idols occupying the place of God. The children may wonder how people get away with living this way. Does God allow it? Are there no consequences for disobeying God? The apparent lack of consequences may be attractive for some children! This question will help them to understand that God hates sin and idolatry and that he has clearly stated in the Bible that he will judge and punish all those who turn away from him. This lesson aims to help the children to have a greater understanding of how God will deal with those who disobey him and encourage them to be concerned for those who have not yet responded to the gospel.

Things to remember when planning and teaching:

- For some children this will be a difficult and worrying topic, particularly if they have family and friends who are not Christians. Children will be anxious to talk about what God's punishment is like.

- Wisdom must be employed when explaining the concepts of justice, judgment, and punishment. Be careful to reinforce the understanding that God is a just judge.

- The world will think that the idea of eternal punishment is nonsense.

- Remember to mix and match the activities in the lesson to fit your time frame (see p. 12 for some sample outlines). You won't have time to do them all. Feel free to adapt each activity based on your class's strengths and weaknesses.

Leader's Prayer

Gracious God, thank you that I have found forgiveness through Jesus Christ, and that I am now in a living relationship with you. Help me to glorify you in my life through obedience. Grant understanding to the children who will hear this lesson. May they be conscious of areas in their lives where they disobey you, and may we all have a greater concern for the lost. In Jesus's name. Amen.

Leader's Tool Kit

- Pieces of paper with numbers one to eighteen printed individually on them
- Newsclips from newspapers or TV news reports about a crime
- A gavel
- Markers
- Paper
- Large piece of paper

Catechism Recap

Print numbers one to eighteen on individual pieces of paper and place them upside down in the room. If you have fewer than twenty children in your class, use fewer numbers. If you have eighteen children use sixteen numbers; if you have ten children use eight numbers, etc.

Have the children line up against the wall, and tell them that when you say "go" they have to run and stand on a piece of paper. The children who don't find a piece of paper to stand on must move to the side of the room. Ask the children to look at their paper and see what number is written on it. If they think they can remember the question and answer, they should stand still. If they don't remember it, they can swap places with one of the children at the side of the room. Invite a few of the children to recite the question and answer that links to their number. Play a few rounds of this game, reducing the pieces of paper each time. Try to work your way through as many questions as time allows.

Introduction to Question 18

Prepare some newsclips that detail a crime and show the perpetrator of the crime. (RB)

Play or read a newsclip for the children, and ask them to decide if the criminal should be punished. Ask the children why they think that the criminal should be punished.

Ask the children if they've ever been punished for anything. Ask them if they think the punishment was justified.

Explain to the children that in both cases, punishment was imposed because a law has been broken.

Introduce Question 18: "Will God allow our disobedience and idolatry to go unpunished?" Remind the children that God hates sin and idolatry, and explain that this question will help them to understand what God is going to do about all the sin and idolatry in his world. Acknowledge to the children that sometimes it seems as if God is not doing anything, and that he's letting people get away with disobedience and idolatry, but reassure them that God will do something about it.

Activity

Tell the children that you are going to set up a courtroom. Assign one child to be the accused, one to be a guard, and one to be his or her lawyer. Pick a child to be the prosecuting attorney. Lastly, pick a child to be the judge, and give him or her a gavel. Arrange your chairs and tables to make it feel like a courtroom, and let anyone

Notes

who is not assigned a part be the audience (there is no jury).

Ask the child who is the defense attorney what his or her role in the courtroom is. Ask the prosecutor what his or her role is. Ask the same of the guard and the accused, and end with the judge. Emphasize to the children that it is the judge's role (in cases where there is no jury) to decide, based on

evidence, if the accused is innocent or guilty. If he or she is guilty, the judge decides what the punishment should be.

Explain to the children that the Bible clearly tells us that God will punish those who are disobedient to him. God is a just God and will deal accordingly with everyone who has sinned against him.

---

⑮ Teaching Outline

Begin the teaching time by asking for God's help. Ask that the lesson would be taught faithfully and that the children might listen well.

Highlight to the children that throughout history, all over the world and right up to the present day, the practice of punishment has been observed. Those who have been caught committing crimes have always been punished.

Explain to the children that we generally like the idea of justice, except sometimes when it's applied to ourselves. Help the children to understand that because we are made in the image of a just God, it makes sense that we are people who like to see justice prevail.

Remind the children that God is indeed just and that the Bible clearly states that he will punish those who disobey him and those who worship idols. Of course, God looks at the heart, and so he

is the only person who can fully know the disobedience and idolatry that a person is guilty of.

Explain to the children that although many people think they're getting away with living godless and idolatrous lives, that isn't actually the case. God is watching and will punish every sin against his sovereignty, holiness, and goodness.

Read Ephesians 5:5–14. Provide Bibles for the children to read along with you.

Introduce the children to Paul's letter to the Ephesians, and explain that Paul is encouraging the Ephesian Christians to live in a way that is consistent with being members of God's family. He is encouraging them to put off the old lifestyle and put on the new. He is exhorting them to live holy lives that are glorifying to God, and one of the ways he does that is by explaining to them the certainty of judgment and punishment.

When Paul says in verse 5, "For you may be sure of this," basically he's saying, "Make no mistake, guys, this is definitely going to happen. No one who is living a life that is ignoring God and loving idols will escape God's anger and judgment."

Explain to the children that Paul says to his readers, "Don't let anyone tell you otherwise," because he knows that some people will say that there is no God. Others will say, "Oh, don't worry. God is a God of love, and therefore he will not judge or punish anyone. Surely everyone will go to spend eternity with God in heaven." Paul warns that this is simply not true! At the end of verse 6, Paul says God's wrath will come on those who are disobedient.

These verses in Ephesians 5 contain a clear warning. Those who have put their trust in Christ, however, can be grateful for the great exchange that occurred when we received salvation through Jesus. We received Jesus's righteousness and became right with God. Jesus took all our sin into his own body and bore the wrath of God on our behalf.

In response, we should sing of gratitude in our lives, and we should be battling against idolatry and disobedience.

Paul reminds us in the next few verses that, as Christians, we must live as members of God's family, as children of light. That means our lives should shine with goodness and righteousness and truth.

God's ultimate judgment will occur at the end of history. At that time he will punish all those who have sinned against him and have denied the truth of the gospel of the Lord Jesus Christ. The final punishment will be eternal separation from God and eternal punishment.

Finish the teaching time by helping the children commit Question 18 and the answer to memory.

(These notes are just for guidance. Please expand or amend to suit your own children and context. Write out your talk in your own words and include illustrations and applications that you know will connect with your children.)

Activity

Give each child a piece of paper and a marker.

Have the children write down three or four crimes that would get someone arrested and taken to court. Then have them write down what they believe would be a suitable punishment if the accused were found guilty.

Next, have them write down three or four things that they or their peers might get into trouble for. Ask them to write down an appropriate punishment for each. Ask them if there's a connection between the sort of punishments they might receive for disobeying their parents and those that people receive for major crimes.

Notes

Help them see that it is only when we understand the certainty and necessity of punishment for sin that we can understand how wonderful it is to escape the punishment we were owed.

 Discussion and Question Time

Some of the questions that might arise include:

? When will the judgment happen?

Explain to the children that the final judgment will be at the end of history when Jesus returns.

? What will the punishment be?

Tell the children that punishment will be separation from God. They will learn more about this when you cover the lesson on Question 28.

? What will happen to those who aren't Christians?

Remind the children that only God really knows and understands where people stand in relation to him, but that those who have lived as if he isn't there will experience eternity without him.

Also use this opportunity to help the children to think about their own lives and how this question and answer affects them personally.

- Is their understanding of God big enough? Are they filled with awe when they consider the greatness of God?

- How might they use the world's love of justice as a way to speak about the justice of God?

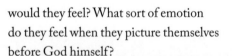 **Virtue Vision**

Awe

Give the children a piece of paper and a marker.

Encourage the children to reflect on the character of God as revealed through this lesson. Ask them to think about the enormity of the punishment that is owed for even one sin against a perfectly holy God.

Ask the children if they were taken before a judge as a guilty party, what sort of emotion would they feel? What sort of emotion do they feel when they picture themselves before God himself?

Ask them to write a brief letter to God explaining what they've learned about today. Help them to focus on God's power and justice. Remind them that the more we learn about God's character, the more we will be filled with awe of him. Encourage the children to take their letters home.

Memory Activity

Write out the memory verse or catechism answer on a large piece of paper without any spaces between the words.

Read the memory verse or catechism answer out to the children, and then invite the children to draw lines between the letters where they think there should be spaces. Have the children read the verse or answer together a few times, and then hide the words. Ask the children if anyone would like to say it individually.

Closing Prayer Time

Encourage the children to silently read their letters to God again and thank him that he is awesome.

Question 19

Is there any way to escape punishment and be brought back into God's favor?

Answer

Yes, God reconciles us to himself by a Redeemer.

Big Idea
God has made provision to bring people into a right relationship with him.

Aim
To help the children understand that there is a clear way back into God's favor through Jesus the Redeemer.

Bible Passage
Isaiah 53:10–11

Memory Verse
"Yet it was the will of the
    LORD to crush him;
    he has put him to grief;
when his soul makes an
    offering for guilt,
he shall see his offspring; he shall
    prolong his days;
the will of the LORD shall
    prosper in his hand.
Out of the anguish of his
    soul he shall see
    and be satisfied;
by his knowledge shall the righteous
    one, my servant,
    make many to be
        accounted righteous,
    and he shall bear their iniquities."
    (Isa. 53:10–11)

Virtue
Gratitude

Leader's Notes

The world appears to be increasingly content to remove God from public life and to ignore the idea that there is a God who is not only intimately involved with his world but who also longs to be in relation with those who have been created in his image and likeness. This lesson will help the children to consider the seriousness of sin. There is amazing joy, hope, and comfort to be found in this lesson for the children. They will be reminded that God is in control, and that God had a plan of how to bring people back into his favor. This lesson aims to give Christian children increased confidence and hope in God and his plan of redemption through Jesus. It will also challenge those who aren't yet believers to consider the reality of their situation very carefully.

Things to remember when planning and teaching:

- Some children will be frightened or overwhelmed at the thought of God's punishment. Help the children to engage with the question in a sensitive and caring manner.

- The children may not all have a good Bible timeline in their minds. You may need to help them understand the chronology of the Bible and show them where Isaiah fits in.

- Some children will be familiar with the gospel story and may seem to take it for granted. Work hard to engage their hearts and cause them to experience renewed gratitude as they encounter God's redemption plan.

- Remember to mix and match the activities in the lesson to fit your time frame (see p. 12 for some sample outlines). You won't have time to do them all. Feel free to adapt each activity based on your class's strengths and weaknesses.

Leader's Prayer

Redeeming God, thank you that you made a way for unworthy sinners like me to escape punishment and death. Thank you, Jesus, for humbling yourself even to death on the cross so that I might know and enjoy God's favor.

Loving God, please grant understanding to the children who will hear this lesson. May they be amazed at your plan of redemption and incredibly grateful for your loving-kindness. In Jesus's name. Amen.

Leader's Tool Kit

- Ping-pong balls
- Bag or bingo cage
- Blank paper
- Markers
- Cardstock or construction paper

Catechism Recap

Write the numbers five to fifteen onto ping-pong balls and put them into a bag or box. If your budget allows, you could put the balls into a bingo cage or blower to add to the fun— or make your own.

Divide the children into teams, and explain to them that you are going to have a quiz to help them remember some of the catechism questions that they've already learned. Let each team pick a numbered ball out for their opponents. The opposition's task is to remember the question associated with the number drawn, the answer, and the memory verse. The team will get nine points if they remember all of the elements associated with the number (the question, answer, and memory verse), or three for each correct element. The team with the most points at the end of the time wins. Remember, this is meant to be a fun and engaging activity; it is up to the leaders to ensure that this spirit is fostered among the children.

Introduction to Question 19

Ask the children to imagine what it would be like to be sentenced to death and placed on death row to wait for execution. There is no doubt that it would be terrifying! Ask the children to then imagine what it would be like for someone else to take their place just at the last minute, just as they were about to be executed. Exclaim to the children that that would be the most amazing feeling ever! Ask them if they think anybody would ever do that.

Introduce the children to Question 19: "Is there any way to escape punishment and be brought back into God's favor?" Explain to the children that this question is going to consider what it would take to free people from the punishment due to them for disobeying God.

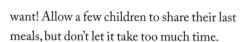

⑩ Activity

Explain to the children that when people are sentenced to death, they are given the chance to choose their last meal before their execution. Ask the children to draw or list on paper what they would want for their last meal. They can ask for anything they want! Allow a few children to share their last meals, but don't let it take too much time.

Tell the children that while it is fun to imagine the best meal ever, it would be a very sad meal. We need a Redeemer!

⑮ Teaching Outline

Begin the teaching time by asking for God's help. Ask that the lesson would be taught faithfully and that the children might listen well.

Introduce this time by explaining to the children that this question is considering whether there is any way for those who are under the judgment of God to escape and be brought back into God's favor. Ask the children if they think a man on death row could save himself. Ask whether sinners under God's judgment can save themselves. The answer is definitely no. Ask the children why men and women and boys and girls cannot save themselves. Clarify that there is no possible way that people can make themselves right with God. Explain to the children that the situation is deadly. It is just like being sentenced to death—the chances of saving oneself are nonexistent!

Read Isaiah 53:10–11. Provide Bibles for the children to read along with you.

Explain that Isaiah was written hundreds and hundreds of years before Jesus left heaven to come to earth as a man, and yet the words tell a story that is wonderfully familiar. Give the children time to look over chapter 53 and identify who they think the words are referring to.

Explain to the children that this passage of Isaiah is often referred to as a Servant Song because it refers to one who would come as God's Servant to redeem and deliver. The children will hopefully be aware that the passage is referring to Jesus, who is the Redeemer. Point out that this was written hundreds of years before Jesus was born.

Tell them that the amazing truth is that God always had a plan. He had determined a way by which people who deserved judgment and death would know freedom and life.

God always knew that he would send Jesus to earth to live a sinless life in perfect obedience to God's law so that he might become the sin offering. God demanded someone without sin to die in order to satisfy his judgment, and Jesus was the perfect spotless One who was sent to be the Redeemer.

Help the children to realize how amazing this is! Help them to appreciate that

Jesus left the glory of heaven to come humbly to earth in order to do what his Father commanded.

Help the children to observe that Isaiah 53 not only talks about Jesus's death but also his resurrection. Isaiah was talking about an entirely new kind of sin offering. Usually an animal was offered, and once it died, it stayed dead. But verse 10 explains that the One who would die would also live again.

Help the children to understand that Jesus is the One who saves the sinner on death row. He is the One who steps in to take his punishment and redeem him.

Conclude the teaching time by helping the children commit Question 19 and the answer to memory.

(These notes are just for guidance. Please expand or amend to suit your own children and context. Write out your talk in your own words and include illustrations and applications that you know will connect with your children.)

Notes

Activity

Invite the children to plan a TV news report that tells the story of the Servant who came to earth to redeem and save. Help the children to explain the significance of the prophecy and to highlight the fact that God always had a plan of how he would save his people.

Discussion and Question Time

Some of the questions that might arise include:

? Why did Jesus have to die?

Help the children to understand that Jesus died in order to fulfill the prophecy and to be obedient to his Father's command. He trusted his Father and knew he must die in order to bring people into a restored relationship with God.

? How did Isaiah know about Jesus's life and death?

Remind the children that all Scripture is God-breathed and that God caused Isaiah to write down the words that he did. Highlight once again that God had a plan!

Also use this opportunity to help the children to think about their own lives and how this question and answer affects them personally.

- Ask the children how their understanding of God's plan is enlarged by this passage.

- Ask the children if they are confident that they have been rescued from

Notes

their own death sentence and have been brought back into God's favor.

▪ Ask the children to consider how they might explain this to a non-Christian.

Virtue Vision

Gratitude

You will need blank greeting cards— construction paper folded in half will do— and markers for this activity.

Ask the children how it makes them feel when they think about Jesus taking their death sentence for them. They may list joy, sadness, or other emotions, but wait for

someone to say that they are thankful. Invite the children to design and decorate a card of gratitude to Jesus for being their Redeemer. Display the cards around the classroom.

Help the children to consider how their gratitude to God might flow over into other areas of their lives.

Memory Activity

This memory verse is longer than most, and so the memory activity for this lesson will not work for the catechism answer. If your class is not memorizing the verses, use one of the memory activities from another lesson to reinforce the memorization of Question 19.

Divide the children into four groups, and assign each of them a quarter of the memory verse to learn. Give the children a little time to learn their sentence, then have the groups recite the verses in order.

Closing Prayer Time

Pray that the children may know God's favor because they have put their trust in Jesus.

Who is the Redeemer?

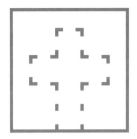

Answer

The only Redeemer is the Lord Jesus Christ.

Big Idea

Every person is a slave to sin. In order to be freed, we must be redeemed; a price must be paid in order to secure a release.

Aim

To help the children understand that Jesus Christ is the Redeemer and that he alone can secure their freedom from sin.

Bible Passage

1 Timothy 2:1–7

Memory Verse

"For there is one God, and there is one mediator between God and men, the man Christ Jesus." (1 Tim. 2:5)

Virtue

Humility

Leader's Notes

Today's world is deeply affected by pluralistic thought. Many believe that there is one God, but that there are many ways to reach him. Children will be breathing in pluralistic air in schools and absorbing it as a worldview from many different media influences. This question will clarify for the children that there is only one God and there is only one way to God: through the God-man Jesus Christ. The children will understand that to enjoy a restored relationship with God and to be freed from the burden of sin, they must put their faith and trust in the saving work of Jesus on the cross. The children need to clearly understand that Jesus is not simply the Christian route to God, but that he is the one and only Redeemer. He alone, in his life and death, made reconciliation with God possible.

Things to remember when planning and teaching:

- Children may be affected by pluralism and relativism and be resistant to saying Jesus is the only Redeemer.

- Children may struggle with the concept that someone had to suffer because of their sin.

- Children may have difficulty understanding the concept of the incarnation. Help them to understand that the fact that Jesus was both God and man made him uniquely appropriate to act as the Redeemer.

- Remember to mix and match the activities in the lesson to fit your time frame (see p. 12 for some sample outlines). You won't have time to do them all. Feel free to adapt each activity based on your class's strengths and weaknesses.

Leader's Prayer

Righteous Father, I owed you a debt I could never have paid. Thank you for sending Jesus to take my place and pay my debt. Forgive me for the times I've thought I was self-sufficient and did not need a Redeemer. Grant the children understanding of the debt that they owe to you because of their sin, but give them joy in accepting Jesus as their Redeemer. In Jesus's name. Amen.

Leader's Tool Kit

- Q20 Catechism Clues (RB)

- Whiteboard and marker (or chalkboard and chalk)

- Sticky notes in two different colors

- Plastic cups

- Paper

- Markers
- Index cards

- *The Lion, the Witch and the Wardrobe* (book)
- Q20 Opportunities for Humility (RB)

Catechism Recap

Draw a grid on the whiteboard that is seven spaces across and six spaces down. Give each team a cup with a selection of clues from Q20 Catechism Clues (RB). Each clue is a scrambled version of a catechism question. Also give each team four sticky notes in one color; each team should have a different color.

Divide the children into teams. Give each team a cup with clues based on the various catechism questions. Invite the children to draw one clue from their cup. The children must try to work out which catechism question their clue relates to. If they unscramble the words correctly, they can place one of their sticky notes on the grid. The idea of the game is to get four matching sticky notes in a row. Each team is able to block their opponents, however! Every time a team gets a question right, they can place a sticky note on the grid or move one of their sticky notes. This game will simply allow the children to recall the questions and answers in a different way.

Introduction to Question 20

Explain to the children that people borrow money from others for many different reasons. A person who borrows money is called a *debtor*. Usually debtors pay back the money they borrow, but sometimes people get into situations where they cannot pay it back. They may spend all the money they have borrowed and have no way to repay it.

Tell the children that, in earlier times, if people were deeply in debt, they would have to go to debtor's prison. They would be locked up until the debt was paid. Ask them if they see any problem with putting someone in debtor's prison. (Give them hints until they realize that someone in prison can't work and so will never pay off a debt.)

Debtor's prison was not a pleasant place to be. People often got sick and died there. Ask the children if they can think of a way people could get out of debtor's prison. Someone would need to pay their debt for them. A person who pays another person's debt to set them free is a redeemer.

Introduce Question 20: "Who is the Redeemer?" Explain to the children that the reality of everyone who lives on earth is that they owe a debt they can never repay and have become slaves to sin. The Bible describes each human being as someone who is captive to sin. Ask the children what they think is needed in order for us to be freed from sin. The answer is a Redeemer, someone to purchase our freedom.

⑩ Activity ☀

Give each child an index card.

Ask each child to draw on the card his or her favorite possession. Don't take long. Have the children give you their drawings and tell you what the possession is and why it is precious to them.

Now tell the children to imagine that you have stolen their prized possession. They cannot call the police. They must pay a ransom to get it back. Tell the children to think about how much money they have. Start low and ask if they would give twenty-five cents to redeem their favorite possession. Move up in increments. Would they pay one dollar? Five dollars? Ten? See if you can find each child's limit, but cut off the bidding once most children have reached their limit.

Give back the drawings, and tell the children that sometimes redemption is costly!

⑮ Teaching Outline

Begin the teaching time by asking for God's help. Ask that the lesson would be taught faithfully and that the children might listen well.

Ask the children to imagine what it would be like to be held in debtor's prison.

Explain to the children that because God is our maker, we owe him obedience. Because of our sinful nature, we do not always obey him. Our sin has put us in debt to God. The debt gets greater and greater because we cannot stop sinning. Everyone who has not trusted Christ is a slave to sin! If we can't pay that debt of obedience, we will be sentenced to something even worse than debtor's prison. Tell the children that we deserve death.

Tell the children that it's a pretty awful situation, which appears to have no way out. People are slaves to sin and are powerless to save themselves, so what they need more than anything is a Redeemer. Explain to the children that a Redeemer is someone who can pray a price—a ransom—in order for a debt to be paid and a slave to be freed.

Read 1 Timothy 2:1–7. Provide Bibles for the children to read along with you.

Tell the children that now Paul is writing a letter to Timothy, and to the churches that Timothy is caring for. In this passage, Paul is encouraging the church to be concerned for all people. Why? Because they are slaves to sin, and God wants everyone to be saved from the consequences of sin.

Tell the children that there is something remarkable in verses 5 and 6. Explain that God has provided a way out of captivity. God has provided a Redeemer! The Redeemer is Jesus Christ.

Ask the children if they noticed that Paul says there is only one God and one Mediator. That implies that there is only one possible way to be freed from sin and to have a restored relationship with God.

Explain to the children that God is both loving and just. In his great love he wants to save people, but justice demands that someone must bear the punishment and pay the price for sin.

Jesus Christ is a unique and perfectly qualified Redeemer. He is the only one who can redeem a people for God.

What makes him unique and perfectly qualified? Remind the children that he is God who left heaven and came to earth as a man. He is God, the eternal Son, and he is man. He can perfectly mediate between God and us. Jesus lived an earthly life that perfectly obeyed God in every way.

Ask the children to reflect on how amazing Jesus's perfect life was. Encourage them to recall all the various ways they sin against God day by day. Highlight for the children that Jesus always honored his father God above everything else, that he always trusted God and followed his instructions for life.

Jesus did not pay money to God to redeem Christians, though. Despite the fact that he lived a perfect life and never sinned against God, he willingly went to die on the cross. In doing so, he paid the price to set Christians free. The price that Jesus paid was his own life; he died a horrific death, so that Christians could know freedom. The remarkable thing is that Jesus humbled himself and did what his Father requested. He made himself nothing. He gave up everything for the sake of those called to faith in God.

Finish the teaching time by helping the children commit Question 20 and the answer to memory.

(These notes are just for guidance. Please expand or amend to suit your own children and context. Write out your talk in your own words and include illustrations and applications that you know will connect with your children.)

Notes

(10) Activity

Bring out a copy of The Lion, the Witch and the Wardrobe.

Ask the children if they are familiar with the story of Edmund and Aslan from *The Lion, the Witch and the Wardrobe.* What was Edmund's problem? (He betrayed his siblings. According to the ancient laws of Narnia, he must be executed as a traitor.) How was Edmund's problem solved? Why wasn't he put to death?

Ask the children whether Aslan was a Redeemer. How was his redemption of Edmund like or unlike Jesus's redemption of us?

(5) Discussion and Question Time

Some of the questions that might arise include:

? **If everyone is born sinful, how can Jesus have lived a sinless life?**

Tell the children that the Bible says Jesus was born without original sin, and so he was able to live a sinless life. Remind the children of the special conditions of Jesus's miraculous birth. He was both God and man.

? **Is Jesus the Redeemer for everyone in the world?**

Explain to the children that only people who accept the redemption Jesus offers will be saved.

? **Why did God choose to make Jesus, his own Son, suffer?**

Help the children understand the reason God allowed Jesus to suffer

so much was because of his great love for us. Jesus was willing to take our place to make a way for us to be with him forever.

Also use this opportunity to help the children think about their own lives and how this question and answer affects them personally.

- Have they realized their own need for redemption in Christ?

- How will they respond when they hear someone say that there are other ways to God?

- How might Jesus's humility, love, and sacrifice affect their everyday lives?

Virtue Vision

Notes

Humility

Print and cut out Q20 Opportunities for Humility (RB). It may be helpful to glue each one onto an index card.

Remind the children of the remarkable humility Jesus showed when he left heaven, submitting to his Father's will, to come to earth as the Redeemer. Ask them to think about how they can model such humility in their own lives.

Hand out the cards with the scenarios on them to nine children. Take turns reading them aloud. Ask the children how a person showing Christlike humility might respond. It may also be helpful to think through what a proud, self-centered response to each scenario might look like.

Memory Activity

Divide the class into two teams, perhaps girls against boys, and ask them to say the memory verse or catechism answer through a few times together. Then take turns having the teams say the verse or answer. You could ask them to say it as quietly as possible or as loud as possible. Declare a winner at the end of the team wars, and then say the verse again together.

Closing Prayer

Conclude the session by thanking God for sending Jesus to be our Redeemer. Be sure to include a word of prayer for those who are still imprisoned by sin, that they might turn to Christ in faith.

Acknowledgments

We are grateful to Crossway for publishing this curriculum and would like to extend special thanks to Tara Davis for her keen editorial eye, and to Dave DeWit and Josh Dennis for their oversight.

Redeemer City to City and Redeemer Presbyterian Church gave The Gospel Coalition permission to develop *The New City Catechism*, originally the work of Timothy Keller and Sam Shammas, into *The New City Catechism Curriculum*.

The project was made possible in part through a generous grant to The Gospel Coalition from the John Templeton Foundation. Thanks to Richard Bollinger and Sarah Clement who believed in the character and virtue potential of this project early on. Thanks also to TGC's Ben Peays and Dan Olson, who worked closely with the John Templeton Foundation when this project was just an idea.

We are grateful for the input and ideas of Sarah Schnitker and Kimberly Griswold of Fuller Theological Seminary on virtue development, educator Caitlin Nunery on classroom activities, and psychologist Brent Bounds on psychological development of children.

Betsy Howard of the Gospel Coalition served as managing editor of *The New City Catechism Curriculum*, and Collin Hansen provided theological oversight.

Most importantly, this curriculum would never have come to fruition without its chief writer, Melanie Lacy of Oak Hill Theological College. Melanie's years of experience as a proponent of catechesis and as a practitioner of children's ministry in the church shaped the curriculum and enriched each lesson.

It took many people to produce *The New City Catechism Curriculum*. Together, we hope it will be used to raise up a generation of children who place their only hope, in life and death, in Jesus Christ.

Build a framework for understanding core Christian beliefs.

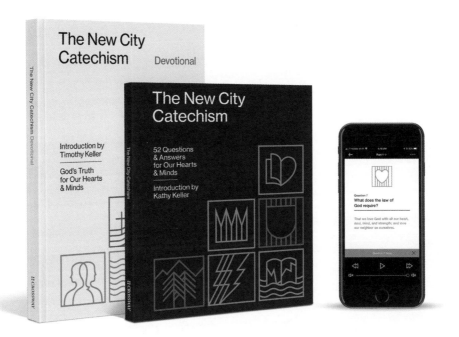

Designed to be memorized over the course of a year, *The New City Catechism* is a valuable resource for building a foundation of important concepts in the minds and hearts of children and adults alike.

For more information, visit
newcitycatechism.com

The New City Catechism

Curriculum

52 Questions
& Answers
for Our Hearts
& Minds

The New City Catechism

Curriculum

Volume 3 – Leader's Guide

Spirit, Restoration, Growing in Grace

Questions 36–52

WHEATON, ILLINOIS

The New City Catechism Curriculum, Vol. 3, Leader's Guide: Spirit, Restoration, Growing in Grace, Questions 36–52

Copyright © 2018 by The Gospel Coalition

Published by Crossway
        1300 Crescent Street
        Wheaton, Illinois 60187

This publication was made possible through the support of a grant from the John Templeton Foundation. The opinions expressed in this publication are those of the publisher and do not necessarily reflect the views of the John Templeton Foundation.

Cover design: Matt Wahl & Micah Lanier

First printing 2018

Printed in China

Scripture quotations are from the ESV® Bible (The Holy Bible, English Standard Version®), copyright © 2001 by Crossway, a publishing ministry of Good News Publishers. Used by permission. All rights reserved.

Trade paperback ISBN: 978-1-4335-5941-9

Crossway is a publishing ministry of Good News Publishers.

RRDS			29	28	27	26	25	24	23	22	21	20	19
14	13	12	11	10	9	8	7	6	5	4	3	2

Introduction

A very warm welcome to *The New City Catechism Curriculum*! Our prayer is that this curriculum will serve to equip the children entrusted into your care to be theologically robust, confident, virtuous, and courageous followers of Christ. The curriculum consists of fifty-two lessons, and each lesson corresponds to one of the questions in *The New City Catechism*. The curriculum is aimed at children ages eight through eleven, and is designed to be used in a wide variety of contexts—Sunday school, home school, Christian school, or after-school clubs. The catechism will be most effective if it is concurrently taught in the local church and in the context of the family.

What Is a Catechism?

A catechism is a collection of biblical doctrines, assembled into a question-and-answer format. The term comes from the New Testament word *katecheo*, which simply means "to teach or instruct." The process of catechesis has rich Reformation roots. Martin Luther, John Calvin, and other Reformers endeavored to catechize both children and adults in order to combat doctrinal ignorance and biblical illiteracy. This biblically derived process has proven hugely influential at critical points in the history of the church. We believe the church needs this ancient practice more than ever to equip Christ's people to stand fast in the face of an ever changing, often hostile culture.

What Is This Curriculum Designed to Do?

Catechize Children

Children are constantly learning. Their inquiring minds soak up information at a spectacular rate. They are trying to make sense of a complex and ever-changing world, seeking to acquire the skills to survive—and even thrive—in life. As they learn, a framework of understanding is established in their minds. This is called a worldview. All children and adults observe and interact with the world through their personal worldview. It is a thrilling and great responsibility to raise children and shape their understanding of the world, how it works, and their unique purpose in it. To catechize children is to give them a coherent and extensive system of thought that equips them to confidently interpret the world and their experiences

in the world through a biblical framework. It also nurtures in children a love for and understanding of the essential doctrines for the Christian faith. To catechize children is to lay deep and strong biblical foundations for a lifetime of faith.

Develop Virtue

The New City Catechism Curriculum is designed to help children not only learn sound doctrine but also to learn how to respond to it and live it out in their lives. Each lesson in *The New City Catechism* has a Virtue Vision covering one of ten Christian virtues that connects in some way with the catechism question. The virtues are Awe, Forgiveness, Gratitude, Honesty, Hope, Humility, Joy, Love, Perseverance, and Trust.

The emphasis and intention of *The New City Catechism Curriculum* is to shape and affect the hearts of the children who engage with each lesson, with the hope that the catechism will contribute greatly to the nurture of godly, mature, and virtuous young men and women. This is definitely not about behavior modification, but rather helping children to respond with keen heart awareness to God's Word as they encounter it in and through the catechism and curriculum. The curriculum seeks to develop in children a mature Christian character, shaped by Scripture, that will be countercultural and striking in our world. By cultivating the capacities for character in both the heart and mind, this curriculum prepares children to love God and others. (For more information and research on faith and virtue development in children, visit newcitycatechism.com/virtue.)

How to Use This Curriculum

The New City Catechism Curriculum is designed to be engaging, dynamic, and creative for children ages eight through eleven. It is intended to be taught in order, beginning at Question 1 and working through to Question 52. It can be taught straight through in a year by covering one lesson a week, but it can also be broken up in whatever way fits your church or school schedule best.

The curriculum is divided into three sections and published in three corresponding books.

Part 1: God, Creation & Fall, Law (twenty lessons covering Questions 1–20)

Part 2: Christ, Redemption, and Grace (fifteen lessons covering Questions 21–35)

Part 3: Spirit, Restoration, Growing in Grace (seventeen lessons covering Questions 36–52)

Each lesson is intended to be flexible in length to suit a variety of contexts. You'll find three sample lesson outlines on page 12. The sample lesson outlines vary in length, highlighting how the curriculum can be tailored appropriately to serve the needs of a particular classroom. The most essential elements have been included in the shortest outlines. If you have more time, other activities that reinforce the essential components may be chosen from the longer outlines.

Each component has a time allocated to it; this is meant to be only a rough guide. The length of time a component will take depends on a variety of factors, such as the number of children in the class, the age of the children, and the number of teachers. Carefully consider how much time each component may require in your particular context. You may want to go over the allotted time if an activity is going well, or cut it short when it seems wise to you.

Please do not feel obliged to do exactly as the lesson plan prescribes! If you find that your class loves a particular form of catechism recap, then feel free to use that more often than the lesson plans dictate. Similarly, if certain memorization methods work better for your class than others, use the successful methods more.

Some classes will have children who love to work quietly at crafts; others will need more physical activity. The more you seek to illustrate and apply the lessons in a way that specifically works for your class, the more successful you will be at discipling the children through The New City Catechism Curriculum.

Memorization is an essential element of this curriculum. There is an emphasis on helping the children to learn the questions and answers of the catechism and the corresponding Scriptures. Each lesson begins with a memory challenge (Catechism Recap) and ends with a memorization game (Memory Activity). The Catechism Recap will help the children recall and reinforce the catechism questions already covered. The Memory Activity can be used either to learn a Scripture verse or to memorize the new catechism question.

The Catechism Recap section sometimes requires questions and answers to be printed out in different sizes for different activities. When you see the abbreviation "DL," it means you can download a pdf prepared for this activity at www.newcitycatechism.com/recap.

Many lessons include visual resources that can be found in the Resource Book (RB). These resources may be photocopied from the book or downloaded at www.newcitycatechism.com/resourcebook. Some resources are worksheets that accompany the activities, and you will need one per child. Others are visual aids for classroom discussion. It would be helpful to enlarge these photos and illustrations before you print or as you photocopy them.

Leading and Loving the Children Well

Children learn best in an environment that is relationally rich and characterized by love. Consistent class leadership facilitates great relationships between the children and their teachers. Though this may not always be possible, some degree of continuity is highly encouraged.

How to Pray

The best way to grow to love the children in your class is to pray diligently for them. Divide the class up into seven groups, and pray for some of the children each day of the week.

Before each class, come together as a group of teachers and pray that God would be at work in the heart and mind of each child that will come into the classroom.

How to Plan a Lesson

Lesson planning is a serious business; don't leave it until the night before the class!

Begin your planning by praying that God would help you to teach the lesson in a way that is faithful and engaging for the children in your care. (Each lesson includes a Leader's Prayer.) Take some time to read through the curriculum material and carefully consider which components you will use to build your lesson plan. Do pay attention to timings, particularly making sure you leave plenty of time to teach the Bible passage well.

Once you have decided which components will be included in your lesson plan, consult the Leader's Tool Kit list and determine what resources you need for the lesson. It's important to check this list in plenty of time in case you need to buy supplies. Most supplies listed can be found at any craft store.

Finally, read through the Bible passage and Teaching Outline multiple times. The Teaching Outline should be only a guide for you. You should expand or amend it to suit your own children and context. Write out the talk in your own words, and include illustrations and applications that you know will connect with the children in your class.

A Discussion and Question Time outline is included in each lesson. These are not meant to be questions leaders ask the children; rather, they are meant to help leaders prepare for the sorts of questions children might ask them. The children in your class may have entirely different questions. Pray that the Holy Spirit will help you answer well and in accordance with God's Word.

How to Manage the Classroom

Children enjoy and thrive in situations where there are clear boundaries. Communicate clearly to the children what your expectations are with regard to behavior in your classroom. For example:

- Raise your hand if you'd like to speak.
- Don't speak if someone else is speaking.
- Don't leave the classroom without permission.
- Be kind and gentle to each other at all times.

Remember, however, that the children are not in school, so while clear boundaries are helpful, the learning environment should be joyful and grace-saturated. Each teacher should strive to clearly model Christian virtue to the children, particularly the ten virtues highlighted in *The New City Catechism Curriculum*.

Mischief usually arises when children are bored or there is a hiatus in the lesson, so good planning and preparation will help manage the classroom.

Make sure to position yourself near the chatty or disruptive children and encourage them to pay attention and participate well. Try not to draw unnecessary attention to a child as you help him or her focus. The less fuss the better.

Work hard to know the names of the children in the class, and call on them by name to contribute. Nurture an active listening stance in the children by encouraging them to be involved in an interactive way throughout the lesson.

Interact individually with children who cause serious disruption. Explain to them how detrimental and distracting their behavior is to the rest of the class. If the disruption continues, involve the child's parents in the discussion.

How to Encourage Memorization

The key to memorization is repetition! It's unrealistic to expect children to remember something if they've heard it only once. Creative repetition is especially helpful in memorization. For example, hearing or singing a song over and over again embeds it in memory. Remember that children learn in a variety of styles, so hearing, seeing, and doing all help children with memorization.

Review is also a very helpful aid to memorization, which is why each of *The New City Catechism Curriculum* lessons begins with a Catechism Recap. Regular review will substantially increase memorization. This is one of the reasons why *The New City Catechism Curriculum* will be most successful if the catechism is concurrently studied in the home as well as the church.

Explanation is also significant in memorization. It is much easier to remember something if you understand it. The children will be better able to commit the catechism questions to memory well if they understand what the question and answer are all about.

How to Nurture Heart Application

The training and instruction of children and the nurture and nature of their hearts are inextricably linked. So as those who presume to teach children, we must be concerned to help them transfer what they're learning from their heads to their hearts. There is a real difference between knowing and understanding something intellectually and having a heart that is deeply affected by the truth.

So how are we going to engage children's hearts as we teach, train, and catechize them? The first thing to acknowledge is that it isn't easy; it takes hard work and great determination. It's reasonably easy to teach the Bible well—providing head knowledge—and reasonably difficult to apply it well to the hearts of children—growing heart knowledge.

It is important to remember that the molding and shaping of the heart is a process. It takes time and will look different depending on the age, stage, and development (physical, emotional, and social) of each individual child. Every child is different; there is no "one size fits all" when it comes to spiritual development.

Try to use "heart language" with children. This will serve to instill in them an awareness that their heart matters and that it affects how they live.

It's much harder to do real heart application with children when leaders change every week, causing the teachers to have underdeveloped relationships with the children. Leaders must know the children well to apply the Word well. Engaging the hearts of children so that they know God, as opposed to simply knowing about God, requires significant relationships. Children need to regularly observe the lives of older Christians who are seeking to apply God's Word to their own hearts and are willing to live honest and transparent lives before the children.

Remember that virtue is not just taught—it is also caught! By displaying Christian character in our own lives as leaders, we are modeling for children how the lessons play out in the real world today. A teacher's authentic faith and embodiment of virtue can be inspiring and instructive to children, so also be sure to attend to your own spiritual growth.

Clear and thoughtful illustration and application in talks is a significant way to engage a child's heart. This is why it's important to work hard to personalize the teaching outlines in *The New City Catechism Curriculum* in a way that resonates deeply with the children in your class.

In order to effectively engage them we need to make every effort to know and understand their hearts, particularly where they're tempted to idolatry. That means we must know and understand their world well—what they're watching, what they're learning, what their friends are saying, and ultimately what worldviews they're encountering in the world.

One-on-one engagement with a child is particularly useful when seeking to involve the heart; this can be done in the classroom and by the parents in the home. This allows us to ask heart-penetrating questions, and it also invites the child to question back.

We have the opportunity to teach children the art of preaching to their own hearts. This is where a catechism is so eternally useful.

Melanie Lacy
Director of Theology for Children and Youth
Oak Hill College

Lesson Outline

■ **75-Minute Lesson Outline**

- Catechism Recap (5 Mins)
- Introduction to Question (5 Mins)
- Activity (10 Mins)
- Teaching Outline (15 Mins)
- Activity (10 Mins)
- Discussion and Question Time (5 Mins)
- Virtue Vision (10 Mins)
- Memory Activity (10 Mins)
- Closing Prayer Time (5 Mins)

■ **45-Minute Lesson Outline**

- Catechism Recap (10 Mins)
- Introduction to Question (5 Mins)
- Teaching Outline (15 Mins)
- Discussion and Question Time (5 Mins)
- Virtue Vision (10 Mins)

■ **30-Minute Lesson Outline**

- Catechism Recap (10 Mins)
- Introduction to Question (5 Mins)
- Teaching Outline (15 Mins)

→ Do pick the time frame that works best for your group.

→ Don't be afraid to mix and match the lesson components based on what works best for the children in your group.

What do we believe about the Holy Spirit?

Answer

That he is God, coeternal with the Father and the Son.

Big Idea
The Holy Spirit is God, and he is an eternal member of the Trinity.

Aim
To help the children understand that the Holy Spirit is a divine person, not a force, and that God has sent him to be our helper.

Bible Passage
John 14:15–31

Memory Verse
"And I will ask the Father, and he will give you another Helper, to be with you forever, even the Spirit of truth, whom the world cannot receive, because it neither sees him nor knows him. You know him, for he dwells with you and will be in you." (John 14:16–17)

Virtue
Love

Leader's Notes

The doctrine of the Holy Spirit must be explained to children simply and often in order for them to understand the Spirit's importance within the Godhead and his role in the Christian's life. This lesson will expand the knowledge that the children already have from Question 3. This lesson aims to reinforce in the children's understanding that the Holy Spirit is God and that he is coeternal with the Father and the Son.

Things to remember when planning and teaching:

- The doctrine of the Holy Spirit is hard to understand; be patient, clear, and concrete in your explanation. Some children will understand this doctrine quicker than others will. Make sure you engage both groups in the lesson. Try to communicate, by your tone and engagement with the lesson, just how amazing the concept of God living within his people is.

- Remember to mix and match the activities in the lesson to fit your time frame (see p. 12 for some sample outlines). You won't have time to do them all. Feel free to adapt each activity based on your class's strengths and weaknesses.

Leader's Prayer

Triune God, I give you great praise as Father, Son, and Holy Spirit. Thank you for your amazing work in your world and in my life. Thank you, God the Father, for sending the Holy Spirit and for his indwelling presence in my life. I rejoice that each day he is at work helping me to see more of Jesus and become more Christlike. Grant understanding to the children who will hear this lesson. May they be filled with joy and wonder as they behold the Triune God. In Jesus's name. Amen.

Leader's Tool Kit

- Q36 Recap (DL), printed out and cut into individual words
- Envelopes
- Whiteboard and marker
- A recording of "Triune Praise" by Shai Linne and a means to play the song
- Paper
- Crayons
- Large piece of construction paper

Catechism Recap

Print out and cut up Q36 Catechism Recap (DL). Place the words in an envelope. Make enough sets for the children to work in small groups of four or five.

Divide the children into small groups and give each group an envelope containing the question and answer for catechism Question 3. Tell the children that each envelope contains a full question and answer and that they need to figure out the question and answer by placing the words in the correct order. Give the children a set amount of time to work out the question and answer. Tell the children that Question 3 links closely with the question in this lesson.

Introduction to Question 36

Ask the children what it means to help someone. Invite them to name members of the helping professions. They will most likely think of:

- Doctor
- Nurse
- Firefighter
- Police Officer
- Paramedic
- Teacher
- Soldier

Explain to the children that this lesson is all about the special helper that God sends to his people in his world. God knew that his people would always need his help, and so he promised to be with them to the end of the age. Introduce Question 36: "What do we believe about the Holy Spirit?" Remind the children that Question 3 of the catechism teaches that there are three persons in one God: the Father, the Son, and the Holy Spirit. Tell the children that this question will help them to learn more about God the Holy Spirit, who is the promised helper.

Activity ☼

Explain to the children that you are going to make some statements about the Holy Spirit and they must decide whether the statement is true or false. Instruct the children to go to the left-hand side of the room if they think the statement is true and the right-hand side of the room if they think the statement is false. Tell the children they can stand in the middle of the room if they are unsure of the answer.

1. The Holy Spirit first appears in the New Testament. **False**

   The Holy Spirit is coeternal with God and was present at the creation of the world (Gen. 1:1).

15

2. The Holy Spirit is a person. **True**

> The Holy Spirit is the third person of the Trinity.

3. The Holy Spirit lives in all people. **False**

> The Holy Spirit dwells in those who have been born again (Rom. 8:9–10).

4. The Holy Spirit first appeared on the day of Pentecost. **False**

> The Holy Spirit came upon believers on the day of Pentecost (Acts 2:1–13), but he has existed eternally and been active throughout history (1 Sam. 16:13).

5. The Holy Spirit is the promised helper. **True**

> Jesus promised to send someone in his place when he ascended into heaven (John 14:15–17). The Holy Spirit is that promised helper.

6. The Holy Spirit is equal to the Father and the Son in the Trinity. **True**

> Yes, the Holy Spirit is equal to the Father and the Son in the Trinity. The Trinity is made up of three equal persons in one God.

7. The Holy Spirit loves the Father and the Son. **True**

> The members of the Godhead have always existed in a loving relationship (1 John 4:16).

To conclude this activity, ask the children to finish these statements:

- The Father is God, the Son is God, the Holy Spirit is ____? (Answer: God)

- The Son is not the Father, the Father is not the Holy Spirit, the Holy Spirit is not the ____? (Answer: Son or Father)

Teaching Outline

Begin the teaching time by asking for God's help. Ask that the lesson would be taught faithfully and that the children might listen well.

Read John 14:15–31. Provide Bibles for the children to read along.

Explain to the children that in this passage in John, Jesus is speaking to his disciples. He is explaining that one day he will have to leave them, but he promises that he will send someone else to be with them.

Jesus describes the One who will come as another helper, a person like Jesus.

In verse 17, Jesus makes it clear who this helper will be; he calls him the Spirit of truth. The Holy Spirit is the promised helper. Tell the children that sometimes people think the Holy Spirit is just a life force or strange power, but in the Bible, the Holy Spirit is always portrayed as a person. That means he has a will and he acts. Even more, the Holy Spirit is described as God (Acts 5:3–4).

The disciples were very sad at the thought of Jesus leaving them, but he reassured them that they would never be alone in life because of the indwelling presence of the Holy Spirit. And they would one day be in Jesus's presence again.

Highlight for the children that this is a most amazing gift to Christians! The Holy Spirit lives in them at Jesus's request. The people in the helping professions assist others only on occasions of need, but the Holy Spirit is with God's people all the time to help because he lives in them!

Ask the children how significant they think the presence of the Holy Spirit is in the life of the Christian. Explain that there is no similar idea in any other religion. The fact that God the Holy Spirit lives in Christians is truly unique.

God the Holy Spirit comes to live in Christians to help them learn more about Jesus and understand more about Jesus. The Holy Spirit is the teacher of truth (v. 26) and he is a bringer of peace (v. 27).

Conclude this teaching time by explaining to the children that the Holy Spirit

- is personal

- is God

- is a gift for Christians, but the rest of the world cannot see or understand him

- reveals more of Jesus to God's people

Conclude the teaching time by helping the children commit Question 36 and the answer to memory.

(These notes are just for guidance. Please expand or amend them to suit your own children and context. Write out your talk in your own words and include illustrations and applications that you know will connect with your children.)

 Activity

You will need to be able to play Shai Linne's "Triune Praise" for the children to listen to. You will also need paper and crayons for each child.

Play "Triune Praise" and invite the children to write down words that stand out to them about the Trinity—especially about the Holy Spirit. Let them decorate and embellish the words with crayons as they listen to the song.

⑤ Discussion and Question Time

Some questions that might arise include:

? When does the Holy Spirit come to live in Christians, and can they feel it?

Explain to the children that the Holy Spirit comes to live in a person the moment he or she becomes a Christian. The new Christian may not feel anything, but the Holy Spirit will start to make a difference in his or her life by helping him or her to follow Jesus.

? If the Holy Spirit is a person, why can't I see him?

Like God the Father, the Holy Spirit is not visible. He is Spirit and does not have a body, yet we should not confuse him with an impersonal force.

Also use this opportunity to help the children think about their own lives and how this question and answer affects them personally.

- Ask the children if they find joy in understanding more about the Holy Spirit and his role in the Christian's life.

- Ask the children how they might explain the concept of the Holy Spirit to someone who's never heard about him before.

- Ask the children if they've ever experienced the help of the Holy Spirit.

⑩ Virtue Vision

Love

Point out to the children that we usually associate love with Valentine's Day, puppies, our favorite sports teams, or other things that make us feel good. Some things and people are easy to love. But some are not so easy to love. Ask the children to describe a situation in which it is hard to show love.

Tell the children that one reason God has given us the Holy Spirit is to help us learn how to love when it isn't easy. The Holy Spirit has always been in relationship with the Father and Son. They have a perfect relationship of love, even though they are three different persons with different roles.

Because the Holy Spirit lives in us, he is willing to coach us through difficult situations to help us love difficult people.

Take a couple of the scenarios the children mentioned in which it is difficult to show love and imagine with the children some of the ways the Holy Spirit, our helper, might coach them through a loving response to a difficult person. If time permits, you could role play the scenarios.

Notes

Memory Activity

You will need to write out the memory verse or catechism question and answer on a large piece of construction paper. Cut the memory verse up into puzzle pieces and hide them around the classroom before the lesson starts.

Tell the children that the memory verse is hidden around the classroom and ask them to find the pieces. As the children begin to bring the pieces back, encourage them to start making the puzzle to reveal the memory verse. Once the puzzle is completed, say the memory verse together several times. Then start removing pieces of the puzzle to see how much the children can recall.

Closing Prayer Time

Invite the children to thank God for his loving gift of the Holy Spirit. Invite them to mention specific areas of their lives where they need his help.

Question 37

How does the Holy Spirit help us?

Answer

The Holy Spirit convicts us of our sin, and he enables us to pray and to understand God's Word.

Big Idea
God the Holy Spirit is at work in his people convicting them of sin, helping them understand and apply the Word, and helping them pray.

Aim
To help the children understand how the Holy Spirit helps Christians in everyday life.

Bible Passage
Ephesians 6:10–20

Memory Verse
"And take the helmet of salvation, and the sword of the Spirit, which is the word of God, praying at all times in the Spirit, with all prayer and supplication. To that end keep alert with all perseverance, making supplication for all the saints." (Eph. 6:17–18)

Virtue
Honesty

Leader's Notes

The children will understand that the various people in their lives play different roles. They daily see their parents, teachers, and coaches perform their particular duties and responsibilities. This lesson should help the children understand the role of the Holy Spirit in the life of the Christian and illuminate the kind of work that the Holy Spirit does in equipping, enabling, nurturing, and teaching God's people. His role has strong similarities with that of parent, teacher, and coach. This lesson aims to continue to teach the children about the Holy Spirit and to help them grow in their understanding of who he is and what he does.

Things to remember when planning and teaching:

- Remember that some children may have a good grasp of who the Holy Spirit is and what his role is; try to stretch them while also being sensitive to those who are struggling to comprehend.

- Remember that some of the children will have a personal faith and others will not. Be sure to communicate that the indwelling of the Spirit occurs at the moment of personal conversion.

- Remember to mix and match the activities in the lesson to fit your time frame (see p. 12 for some sample outlines). You won't have time to do them all. Feel free to adapt each activity based on your class's strengths and weaknesses.

Leader's Prayer

Gracious God, thank you for your kindness in sending your Spirit to dwell in the hearts of your people. I praise you that he is my helper and counselor. Thank you that he shows me more of Jesus as I study your Word and that he intercedes for me. May I continue to be refined by the sword of the Spirit, and may I use the sword of the Spirit to point others to Jesus. Grant understanding to the children who will hear this lesson. May they gain a deeper understanding of your work. In Jesus's name. Amen.

Leader's Tool Kit

- Whiteboard and markers
- Sticky Tack
- Paper
- Markers
- Q37 Illustrations of Roman armor (RB)
- Construction paper

22

- Tape
- Scissors

- Ball

Catechism Recap

Have Question and Answer 36 on hand.

Ask the children if they remember the answer from last week's question. Ask, "What do we believe about the Holy Spirit?" and let students take turns answering until someone gets it exactly right. Divide the children into pairs. Have them take turns asking and answering the question in the voice of a mouse, then a frog, a giant, and a whale. They can look at the words to jog their memory if they need to.

Introduction to Question 37

You will need a whiteboard divided into three sections. Section 1 should have "The Role of a Teacher" written at the top; section 2 should have "The Role of a Parent" written at the top; and section 3 should have "The Role of a Soccer Coach" written at the top.

Write the following on individual slips of paper:

- Teaching children to read
- Organizing school events
- Teaching children how to behave in the classroom
- Planning lessons
- Training players
- Developing new ball skills
- Teaching team members how to be good sports
- Giving pointers on how to score
- Planning match tactics
- Providing pregame nutritional advice
- Doing the laundry
- Cooking meals
- Teaching children to obey
- Comforting children when they have a bad dream
- Keeping the family safe

Lay out the fifteen different pieces of paper and invite the children to stick them on the whiteboard (using Sticky Tack) in one of the three sections. Encourage the children to consider which action is consistent with the role of a parent, teacher, or soccer coach. The aim of this activity is to help the children understand the role and responsibilities that come with a job title. Introduce Question 37: "How does the Holy Spirit help us?" Explain to the children that this lesson will help them understand more about the role of God the Holy Spirit in the life of the Christian.

Activity

The Bible references below speak of the role of the Holy Spirit. Stick the Bible references up around the classroom. Do not include the job titles.

- John 14:16 (helper)
- John 14:27 (giver of peace)
- John 15:26 (helper and teacher)
- John 16:7-8 (helper and convictor of sin)
- John 16:13 (teacher of truth)
- Romans 8:11 (giver of life)
- Romans 8:26 (helper in prayer)

Divide the children into small groups and assign each group one or two verses.

Give each group a Bible. Tell the children that they need to figure out the role or job description for the Holy Spirit by looking up their Bible verses and figuring out what they say about the role of the Holy Spirit.

Once the children have had sufficient time to investigate their verses, ask them to share what they've discovered about the Holy Spirit. Write a job description list for the Holy Spirit on the whiteboard. Ask the children if anything surprised them or confused them.

Assure them that the teaching time will bring more clarity.

Teaching Outline

Have Q37 Illustrations of Roman Armor (RB) ready.

Begin the teaching time by asking for God's help. Ask that the lesson would be taught faithfully and that the children might listen well.

Remind the children that God the Holy Spirit is the third person of the Trinity and that he has a vital role in bringing people to faith in God and also in helping God's people to live for him in the world. The Holy Spirit indwells Christian believers the moment they put their trust in Jesus, and from that time onward he is at work in Christians, helping them to understand more about Jesus and to become more like Jesus. Highlight for the children all the different things detailed on the Holy Spirit's job description (which they listed when they looked up the Bible references) to emphasize how significant he is for Christians. Particularly remind the children that the Holy Spirit convicts people of their sin, helps Christians to pray, and helps them understand the Bible.

Read Ephesians 6:10–20. Provide Bibles for the children to read along. Hold up the illustrations of Roman armor while you read.

Explain to the children that Paul is writing to the Christians in Ephesus and is preparing them to contend for Jesus in the world. He uses the imagery of Roman armor to help them understand how to equip themselves for war against the Devil, who works to keep people away from Jesus. Paul writes about putting on the belt of truth, the breastplate of righteousness, the shoes of peace, the shield of faith, and the helmet of salvation. Paul also speaks about taking up the sword of the Spirit, which is the Word of God; this is the only weapon Paul identifies as necessary for facing the battle.

Ask the children what a sword is capable of. It can do real damage; it can pierce and wound and even kill. Ask the children what they think Paul is saying by describing the Bible as the sword of the Spirit.

Explain to the children that God describes his Word as a sword (Heb. 4:12). God also declares that his Word was written down by men inspired by the Holy Spirit (2 Pet. 1:20–21). So, the sword of the Spirit comes from God.

God's Word protects Christians from spiritual attack as they study it and believe God's promises. It cuts away the truth from the lies told by the world.

Paul also commands the Ephesian Christians to pray in the Spirit. This is a great reminder that the Holy Spirit is an essential component of a Christian's prayer life. Explain to the children that to pray in the Spirit means to pray in a way that is consistent with God's Word. Ask the children to think of ways people might pray that are not consistent with God's Word. Ask them to give examples of ways to pray in line with God's Word. Remind the children that the Holy Spirit lives in each Christian and that he also prays for each Christian (Rom. 8:26).

Explain to the children that God knew his people would struggle with prayer, so he didn't leave his people without help. He sent the Holy Spirit to teach, encourage, and expose the hearts and minds of Christians. He leads, instructs, and inspires the prayers of Christians.

Conclude the teaching time by helping the children commit Question 37 and the answer to memory.

(These notes are just for guidance. Please expand or amend them to suit your own children and context. Write out your talk in your own words and include illustrations and applications that you know will connect with your children.)

Notes

 Activity

You will need some construction paper, scissors, markers, and tape.

Invite the children to make a paper sword. Encourage them to be as creative as possible—there's no wrong way to do it.

Ask them to write the words "the sword of the Spirit—Ephesians 6:17" on the sword. The children could also write the sixty-six books of the Bible on their swords, or one of their favorite Bible verses.

Notes

As the children are making the swords, discuss with them what the sword of the Spirit is and how it will help them to stand firm for Jesus in his world.

Display the swords around the classroom before letting the children take them home.

⏱ Discussion and Question Time

Some questions that might arise include:

❓ Why do I need the help of the Holy Spirit?

Explain to the children that without the help of the Holy Spirit, humans would be inclined to live in ways that focus on themselves and not on Jesus. Also remind the children that the Holy Spirit helps Christians to understand what God's Word means.

❓ What is the difference between the Holy Spirit and my conscience?

Every person alive has a conscience, but only those who have been born again have the Holy Spirit dwelling in them. A conscience can alert us when we've broken God's law, but the Holy Spirit has the power to change our hearts and make us people who want to do what is righteous.

❓ Why do I need to pray if the Holy Spirit is praying for me?

Explain to the children that God loves to hear the prayers of his people and has instituted prayer as a way for his people to respond to his Word and to talk to him. The Holy Spirit is the Christian's guide and help.

Also use this opportunity to help the children think about their own lives and how this question and answer affects them personally.

- Ask the children if they are determined to know God's Word so it might be the sword of the Spirit in their lives.

- Ask the children if it is a comfort to know that the Holy Spirit aids them in prayer.

- Ask the children if they understand the role of the Holy Spirit more fully.

⏱ Virtue Vision

Honesty

Ask the children if they appreciate honesty. Ask them how they feel when people lie to them or hide the truth from them.

Hebrews 6:18 says that God cannot lie. Since we have learned that the Holy Spirit is himself God, what do we know about the Holy Spirit? (He cannot lie.)

Explain to the children that an honest and truthful character is evidence of the work of the Spirit in the life of the believer influencing our actions.

Point out to the children that the answer to today's catechism question says that the Holy Spirit convicts us of sin. We use the word *convict* when someone is arrested and found guilty of a crime. When people are convicted, they are given a punishment.

Ask the children, if the Holy Spirit "convicts" you of lying or telling a half truth, is he going to send you to jail like a judge would? The answer is no. Help the children consider why that is. Help them to see that Jesus has taken our punishment. But though our punishment has been taken, we still need the conviction of the Holy Spirit so that we can confess our sin to the person we have sinned against. It is hard to tell someone else we've lied to him or her, but the Holy Spirit is in us to give us courage to do the right thing.

Notes

Memory Activity

You will need a ball and the memory verse or catechism question and answer written on a piece of poster board. Have some pieces of paper and Sticky Tack handy that you can place over the words of the verse to cover them up.

- Put the poster board with the memory verse or catechism question and answer on the wall.

- Divide the children into two teams.

- Invite the children to read through the memory verse with you several times.

- Gradually cover up the words.

- Have the teams stand in two straight lines and then face each other.

Throw the ball to a child. He is expected to say the first word of the memory verse or catechism question. He should then throw the ball to a child on the opposite team, who is expected to say the second word of the memory verse. Continue down the lines. If a child doesn't remember the word or gets it wrong, he should throw the ball and then sit down. The team with the most team members still standing is the winner at the end.

Closing Prayer Time

Invite a volunteer to lead the class in prayer, asking God to use his Holy Spirit to convict us of sin, to help us pray, and to make us more honest and loving, even when it isn't easy.

Question 38

What is prayer?

Answer

Prayer is pouring out our hearts to God.

Big Idea
Prayer is talking to God in
response to his Word.

Aim
To help the children understand the concept
of prayer and to encourage them to develop
a prayerful relationship with God.

Bible Passage
Psalm 62

Memory Verse
"Trust in him at all times, O people; pour
out your heart before him; God is a refuge
for us." (Ps. 62:8)

Virtue
Gratitude

Leader's Notes

Children's understanding of prayer is generally limited. They likely have experienced corporate and formal prayer times, but the beauty and intimacy of a prayerful relationship with God is rarely modeled well to children. Children often approach personal prayer as if they're communicating with Santa Claus. They present a wish list to God in the hope that he might provide all that they desire. For many children prayer is about getting things from God rather than developing a personal relationship with him. In today's world, self-sufficiency is praised, so the concept of fully relying on God is increasingly difficult for adults. The good news is that children are used to being dependent, so they more easily take their needs to God. Instead, the challenge for children is recognizing the ways God has blessed them. This lesson aims to help children to know that prayer is a wonderful gift from God, that God is listening, and that he loves to hear their prayers—especially their thanks.

Things to remember when planning and teaching:

- The children likely will know what prayer is and will be familiar with certain types of prayer. A clear emphasis should be placed on the development of personal prayer practices. Communicate that prayer is about having a relationship with God.

- Help the children to understand that prayer should be in response to God's Word, and that praise, petition, confession, and thanksgiving are all part of a praying life.

- Some children may be nervous when praying aloud and in an extemporary fashion. It may be useful to encourage the children to begin by writing their prayers down.

- Modeling and demonstrating prayer will be hugely helpful throughout this lesson.

- Remember to mix and match the activities in the lesson to fit your time frame (see p. 12 for some sample outlines). You won't have time to do them all. Feel free to adapt each activity based on your class's strengths and weaknesses.

Leader's Prayer

Loving God, thank you that I can know you in a deep and personal way through your Word and in prayer. Thank you that you delight in having a relationship with me. Grant the children who hear this lesson a deeper understanding of what prayer is and why you have granted us access to you through prayer. In Jesus's name. Amen.

Leader's Tool Kit

- Jumbo craft (popsicle) sticks (42)
- A cup
- Timer (cell phone timer will do)
- Markers
- Q38 Question Mark (RB), one per child

- Scissors
- Tape or Sticky Tack
- Paper and stapler
- Whiteboard and marker

Catechism Recap

Write numbers one to thirty-seven on the jumbo craft sticks. Place the sticks in a cup with the number side down so the children can't see what they're pulling out. Also place five sticks with the word RESET written on them into the cup. Set a timer for five minutes.

Invite the children to take turns pulling a stick from the cup. Challenge them to see if they can remember the question and answer that goes with the number. If they can answer it correctly (don't be too much of a perfectionist!), they get to keep the stick. The person with the most sticks at the end gets a prize. Explain to the children that there's a catch: if someone pulls a RESET stick from the cup, everyone must return their sticks to the cup and start over (but keep the time running). Save the craft sticks to use again with Question 49.

Introduction to Question 38

Using the Q38 Question Mark (RB), cut out a question mark for each child.

Explain to the children that the focus of the lesson is the question "What is prayer?" As part of the introduction to the question, ask the children to write any questions they may have about prayer on the question marks. Stick the question marks up somewhere clearly visible. Assure the children that you'll engage with their thoughts and questions throughout the next few weeks.

Follow by asking the children to think about these questions:

- How did how they get to know their friends and build relationships with them?
- How do they usually communicate with their parents?

Explain to the children that the way people build relationships is by talking to one another. Tell the children that God longs to have a relationship with his people and so he has enabled us to talk to him through prayer. God is not distant or uninvolved in his world or with his people. He is very present and is always listening to the prayers of his people.

Tell the children that prayer is simply talking to God. Explain that when we pray, we give God his rightful place in our lives. We acknowledge gratefully that he gives and sustains life, and we trust him in all circumstances. In the same way that we build relationships with friends and family through talking, our relationship with God will grow and mature as we spend time talking to him.

Activity

Give each child a turn to come to the front. Whisper in his or her ear one of the types of communication listed below. They should use motions but no speech to act out the word. When one word is guessed, let another child come up and act out the next word on the list.

- Talking
- Letter
- Email
- Phone call
- Text message
- Facebook
- Skype
- Facetime
- Message in a bottle

Explain to the children that we have many types of communication in the world today; the game included just a small selection. Remind them that God loves to communicate with his people through the Bible and prayer. God speaks to his people through his Word and then invites us to speak in response to him in prayer.

Teaching Outline

Begin the teaching time by asking for God's help. Ask that the lesson would be taught faithfully and that the children might listen well.

Explain to the children that prayer is an essential part of the Christian life. Yet sometimes Christians don't know how to pray in any way other than bringing lists of wants and needs to God. Ask the children whether they ask their parents for things they need. Of course, they do! But is that the only thing they ever talk about with their parents? Do they ever tell their parents that they love them or share the interesting things going on in their lives? A good relationship includes many different kinds of communication.

Tell the children that prayer is talking to God, our heavenly Father, in response to his Word.

Read Psalm 62. Invite the children to join you in reading aloud. Provide Bibles for the children.

Explain that this psalm was written by a man named David, who was king in Israel. It is found in the book of Psalms in the Old Testament. Tell the children that in this psalm, David encourages his hearers to pray, and in verse 8 he describes prayer by saying, "Trust in him at all times, O people; pour out your heart before him; God is a refuge for us." In this psalm, David encourages God's people to pour out their hearts to the Lord.

Ask the children what they think pouring out their heart would look like.

Tell them it is telling God everything about our lives and what we are thinking and feeling. Ask the children if this kind of prayer would be easy or hard, and have them elaborate on why they think so.

David isn't encouraging God's people to pour out their hearts to just anyone, but to a most amazing God! Have the children search Psalm 62 to identify the different ways David describes God. (A rock, a fortress, a refuge, and the One who saves.)

Tell the children that David builds a picture of a great God who is the completely reliable and trustworthy Creator, in contrast with created people and things (vv. 4 and 10), both of which will disappoint and fail. God longs for honest and regular communication with his children. Help the children to consider what talking with such a trustworthy God is like. Does it mean they can talk to him at any time and in any place? Does it mean they can tell him anything and everything? This psalm shows David trusting fully in God, and therefore relying fully on his strength.

Tell the children that the way we live is often different from the picture David paints for us. Explain that people rely on themselves, doing things in their own strength, until they can't do it on their own anymore, and only then they turn to God. David says that if he relies on his own strength, he will be as easy to knock down as a badly built wall, but when he is relying fully on God he will not be shaken. The kind of relationship David has with God brings him rest; he doesn't have to worry about anything.

Remind the children that prayer is gratefully recognizing that God is God, that he is in control, and that he is completely trustworthy. It is responding to all that we know of and learn about God in his Word, the Bible. When we pray this way, we demonstrate that we trust God to take care of our lives. This is a vital part of a life of faith.

Finish the teaching time by helping the children commit Question 38 and the answer to memory.

(These notes are just for guidance. Please expand or amend them to suit your own children and context. Write out your talk in your own words and include illustrations and applications that you know will connect with your children.)

Notes

Activity

Make a booklet for each child by cutting standard letter-size paper in half (so that it becomes 8.5 x 5.5). Stack five or six sheets together and fold them in half (so that they are now 5.5 x 4). Staple in the fold so that it holds together. Have crayons available.

Give each child a booklet and tell them it is a prayer journal. Invite them to decorate the cover with crayons, and suggest that they may want to put the phrase "Pour out your hearts to him" on the cover to remind them what prayer is. Tell them that they can write anything they like in their prayer journals. It is not meant for any eyes besides their own. It is a private place for them to share their thoughts with God.

Collect the booklets and save them for next week, but assure the children you will not read their prayers. (You may want to make a few extra booklets for any children who might not be in class this week.)

Discussion and Question Time

Some questions that might arise include:

? **If God knows everything, why do we need to pray?**

Explain to the children that prayer is the means God has chosen to allow us to participate in his work. Prayer is a blessing because it allows us to build a relationship with our heavenly Father.

? **Does prayer actually change anything?**

Yes! James 5:16 says, "The prayer of a righteous person has great power as it is working." We don't always understand the way that God uses our prayers, and he doesn't always answer in the way we would expect, but we can joyfully obey his command to pray.

? **Members of other religions pray. What makes Christian prayer different?**

Explain to the children that someone hears us when we pray. Christians pray to the true and living God.

Also use this opportunity to help the children think about their own lives and how this question and answer affects them personally.

- Does the fact that we know God listens to our prayers make a difference when we pray?

- When would be a good time in the day to spend time pouring out their hearts to God?

Virtue Vision

Gratitude

Prepare the whiteboard for a list sixty-two items long. You will probably need to write small and make multiple columns.

Explain to the children that in a good relationship, we can give thanks for lots of things. Thanksgiving is a kind of prayer in which we express our gratitude to God. In Psalm 62, today's Bible passage, David wrote down the things that caused him to praise God.

Show the children the whiteboard with numbers one through sixty-two. Ask the children to see how many things they, as a group, can come up with that they are grateful for. Can the class make it to sixty-two? To get there, they may need to be very specific about the things they are grateful for. Nothing is too small or insignificant to give thanks for!

Memory Activity

You will need to print the memory verse or catechism question and answer and cut it up into words or phrases (depending on the number of children in the class). Stick the words/phrases under the children's chairs before the lesson begins.

Read the memory verse or catechism question and answer to the children, and then explain that there are words or phrases stuck under their seats. Invite the children to get the word from under their seat, and then encourage them to organize themselves so that the memory verse is in the correct order. Read the memory verse for the children as they try to figure out the correct order of the words/phrases. Have the whole class read the verse aloud together several times.

Closing Prayer Time

Have the children pray quick prayers based on their gratitude list. They can be as simple as "Thank you, Father, for _____." Invite the other children to say "Amen" if they are also grateful for the thing their classmate mentions. (Encourage the children not to be silly in their prayers, but don't worry too much if they giggle during the prayer time. You are teaching children to pour out their hearts to God, and sometimes children have a lot of silliness in their hearts!)

Question 39

With what attitude should we pray?

Answer

With love, perseverance,
and gratefulness.

Big Idea
When we pray, our attitude matters.

Aim
To help the children consider how what
we know about God should influence the
attitude with which we pray.

Bible Passage
Philippians 4:4–9

Memory Verse
"Do not be anxious about anything, but in
everything by prayer and supplication with
thanksgiving let your requests be made
known to God." (Phil. 4:6)

Virtue
Perseverance

Notes

Leader's Notes

Last week, we learned that God wants to communicate with us. He commands us to pray to him, but prayer is not drudgery; it's an amazing privilege! Some people may pray to God as if he were their servant who must do whatever they ask. Others approach in fear and doubt that God would ever listen to them. The Bible teaches us to approach God as a loving Father who always hears us. He will not always give us what we ask, but when he doesn't, it's because he knows better than we do what we need.

Things to remember when planning and teaching:

- While this lesson deals with the proper attitude for prayer, the aim is not to discourage students from praying until their hearts are perfect. Rather, this lesson should inspire them to pray with hope and confidence that God hears.

- Children will be familiar with the concept of prayer but may not have discovered what a personal prayerful relationship with God is.

- The children need to understand that God hears the prayers of his people because of Jesus, and through him they can freely approach God.

- Children may be nervous about praying out loud and in an extemporary fashion.

- Remember to mix and match the activities in the lesson to fit your time frame (see p. 12 for some sample outlines). You won't have time to do them all. Feel free to adapt each activity based on your class's strengths and weaknesses.

Leader's Prayer

Father God, please let all that you have revealed about yourself influence the attitude with which I pray. May I pray with love, perseverance, and gratefulness, knowing that you are a good Father who gives his children good gifts. Grant the children who will hear this lesson great understanding. May they be excited about the possibility of coming to you in prayer and challenged to come with humble hearts. In Jesus's name. Amen.

Leader's Tool Kit

- Q39 Catechism Recap (DL)
- Pieces of paper with hashtag signs printed on them
- Pictures of world leaders and famous people
- Q39 Emoticon Template (RB) for each child
- Crayons and markers
- Drinking straws

⑩ Catechism Recap

Print out Q39 Catechism Recap. Stick the questions and answers up around the classroom. With each paper, also stick up a paper with several large hashtags.

Tell the children to go to one of the questions on the wall and create a hashtag that summarizes the question. If time permits, let the children write hashtags on more than one question. Read out some of their suggestions, and tell the children the hashtags can help them remember the questions and answers.

Example:

> Question 14: Did God create us unable to keep his law?
>
> No, but because of the disobedience of Adam and Eve we are all born in sin and guilt, unable to keep God's law.
>
> #Unable
>
> #BorninSin

⑤ Introduction to Question 39

Collect some pictures of world leaders and people you know the children will admire.

Introduce Question 39: "With what attitude should we pray?" by explaining to the children what the word *attitude* means. Help them to understand that it is a response to knowledge about an idea, person, or situation that can affect behavior.

Show the children some pictures of famous people and ask them to describe what attitude they might have if they were to meet them. For example, if they met the Queen of England, would they have a humble or sincere attitude? If they encountered a famous sports personality, would they have an enthusiastic attitude? If they met

someone who had been in an accident, would they have a sympathetic attitude?

Ask the children what kinds of attitudes they express

- To their teachers in school
- To their siblings
- To the school principal
- To an old person

Remind the children that Question 39 is "With what attitude should we pray?" Highlight that this lesson will help them consider how they approach God and what their heart response to God is when they come to him in prayer.

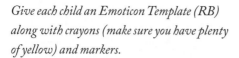

Activity

Give each child an Emoticon Template (RB) along with crayons (make sure you have plenty of yellow) and markers.

Have the children design their own emoticons showing four different attitudes. Encourage them to show the rest of the group their emoticons and let the others guess what attitude each one represents.

Ask the children what sort of attitude they usually have when they pray. Are they bored? Hopeful? Silly? Distracted?

Teaching Outline

Begin the teaching time by asking for God's help. Ask that the lesson would be taught faithfully and that the children might listen well.

Explain to the children that what we know about people affects our attitude around them. God has revealed himself to us in his Word, and what we know about him should determine our attitude when we talk to him.

Read Philippians 4:4–9. Provide Bibles for the children to read along with you.

Explain to the children that Philippians is found in the New Testament and that Paul wrote to Christians in Philippi. Explain to the children that Paul wrote this letter while he was in prison enduring difficult circumstances.

Ask the children if they would be able to write words like Paul's if they were in prison.

Explain to the children that these few verses will teach a lot about God and how to approach him in prayer.

In verse 4 Paul says, "Rejoice in the Lord always; again I will say, rejoice." Explain to the children that Paul is encouraging Christians to find joy in the Lord. This is because he is a trustworthy, sovereign, and good God who loves his people and saves them from judgment, death, and hell through the sacrificial death and resurrection of Jesus. Despite the fact that Paul is in prison, he is able to say "Rejoice!" not because his life or circumstances are good, but because he fully places his trust in God. Encourage the children to look at the second part of verse 5 and to realize that God is near to his people. He is not a far-off distant deity, but he is near, intimately and lovingly involved in the lives of his children. Help the children to see how amazing it is that the Creator of the universe wants to know his creatures and longs for a relationship with them.

In verse 6 Paul encourages Christians to bring their prayerful requests to God. Explain to the children that this should encourage them to recognize that God loves to hear and answer his people's prayers: "Do not be anxious about anything, but in everything by prayer and supplication with thanksgiving let your requests be made known to God."

Ask the children if they can imagine living a life without ever worrying about anything. You might want to ask them what kind of things they worry about.

Paul knows firsthand that life can be difficult, and yet he says that we can bring our worry and anxiety directly to God. Things might still feel scary, and we might want to give in to worry, but God wants us to let him take care of the things that make us anxious. Paul is encouraging Christians to trust God in each and every situation, from the really tricky ones to the everyday occurrences. The passage encourages Christians to be *frequent* and *persistent* in prayer. The way to fight off our anxiety is to pray about everything and ask God to replace worry with his peace.

Ask the children if they noticed the attitude Paul is encouraging Christians to have in bringing their prayers and petitions to God.

Notes

Christians are to have an attitude of thanksgiving in their relationship with God. Christians should have hearts that are thankful that God saves, that God is in control, that God is near, and that God hears and answers the prayers of his people.

What does Paul say will happen as we pray and trust God? Ask the children to read verse 7 aloud with you: "And the peace of God, which surpasses all understanding, will guard your hearts and your minds in Christ Jesus." Explain to the children that as Christians learn to pray and understand God's will, they will be able to know peace, because they are confident that God is in control and that he is working for their good and his glory.

Finish the teaching time by helping the children commit Question 39 and the answer to memory.

(These notes are just for guidance. Please expand or amend them to suit your own children and context. Write out your talk in your own words and include illustrations and applications that you know will connect with your children.)

Activity

Give each child the prayer notebook they decorated the previous week. Have a few extras on hand for any children who were absent.

Read aloud Phil. 4:8: "Finally, brothers, whatever is true, whatever is honorable, whatever is just, whatever is pure, whatever

is lovely, whatever is commendable, if there is any excellence, if there is anything worthy of praise, think about these things." Ask the children to write these words in their prayer journal, leaving space between each word (this will take up several pages):

Notes

True, honorable, just, pure, lovely, commendable, excellence, worthy of praise

Ask the students if there are any words in that list they don't understand, and define them. Invite the children to spend a few minutes listing below each word some things that they associate with it. For example, God's word is true, a soldier who lays down his life is honorable, etc.

Tell the children that God knows that what we think about influences our attitude. Thinking on these things, as God commands, is one way to prepare ourselves for prayer.

Keep the prayer journals to be used again with Question 41.

⑤ Discussion and Question Time

Some questions that might arise include:

? Why does it sometimes seem like God isn't hearing or answering our prayers?

Read Matthew 7:7–11 with the children. This passage teaches us to believe that God hears us and we can expect him to answer us. He wants to give us good gifts. Ask the children, based on the analogy that God is a good Father, what a good father does when a child asks for something harmful or that would be too old for them. In the same way, God sometimes tells us "no" or "wait," but he always hears us.

? Are some situations too unimportant to pray about?

There is nothing too insignificant for prayer. God loves to hear from us about the smallest details of our lives.

? What will having the peace of God feel like?

Explain to the children that the peace of God means our worries and fears get crowded out by faith in God and hope in his goodness. Explain that the peace of God is sometimes immediate, but sometimes it grows slowly, like a seed turning into a tree. We need to continue persevering in prayer to feel God's peace.

Also use this opportunity to help the children think about their own lives and how this question and answer affects them personally.

- Ask the children what an ungrateful prayer would sound like. Ask them if they've ever prayed without gratitude.

- Ask the children what kind of prayers they might pray that would require perseverance on their part.

Virtue Vision

Perseverance

Ask the children if they remember what perseverance means. Help them recall that to persevere means to keep going, even if you have to wait a long time to see any concrete results.

Share this story about George Müller, a passionate evangelist, with the children:

> In 1844, a man named George Müller began praying every day for five of his friends. After many months, one of them became a Christian. Ten long years went by, but then two others were converted. The fourth man became a Christian after Müller prayed for him for twenty-five years! Still the fifth friend did not believe. Müller persevered in prayer for him until Müller died, which meant he prayed for him for fifty-four years. He never gave up hoping that he would accept Christ. His faith was rewarded, for soon after Müller's funeral the fifth friend believed!

Now that is persistence that paid off!

Memory Activity

You will need a drinking straw for each child and two sets of the memory verse or catechism question and answer cut up into individual words. (Before you assign this challenge, ensure that the size of the words and weight of the paper makes this task possible.)

Divide children into two teams. Place one set of words on a table at the opposite end of the classroom for each team. Explain to the children that they will run a relay race. They must run up to the table and suck one of the words onto the end of their straw and bring it back to their team. As each child returns, the next should run out. The first team to assemble the verse wins. The verse could be read before the relay to provide the children with a little help. Read it through several times after the relay for reinforcement.

Closing Prayer Time

Encourage the children to write another prayer in their personal prayer journal. Conclude by praying that God would help the children (and you) to pray with an attitude that reflects his goodness.

Question 40

What should we pray?

Answer

The whole Word of God directs us in what we should pray.

Big Idea
The prayers of God's people should develop in response to God's Word.

Aim
To help the children understand that God's own words in Scripture should inform their prayers.

Bible Passage
Ephesians 3:14–21

Memory Verse
"For this reason I bow my knees before the Father, from whom every family in heaven and on earth is named, that according to the riches of his glory he may grant you to be strengthened with power through his Spirit in your inner being, so that Christ may dwell in your hearts through faith." (Eph. 3:14–17)

Virtue
Trust

Notes

Leader's Notes

Children learn by example. They emulate the behavior of significant people in their lives. One of the ways that children will learn what to pray is by following the example of others. As a teacher, you must be aware that the children will be observing and imitating your prayers. This lesson will also set biblical examples of prayer before the children on which they may model their personal prayers.

When children begin to pray personally, they sometimes struggle to know what exactly to say. This lesson should help the children to think effectively about what to pray, as it examines some concrete biblical examples.

This lesson should once again encourage the children to have great confidence in our trustworthy God. It should help them to consider what it means to pray according to

God's will and for God's glory. Hopefully this lesson will broaden the children's language of prayer and praise.

Things to remember when planning and teaching:

- This is the third lesson focused on prayer; make sure the lesson does not become repetitive.
- The focus of the lesson must be that God teaches his people to pray through his Word.
- Remind the children that God loves to hear his people's prayers.
- Remember to mix and match the activities in the lesson to fit your time frame (see p. 12 for some sample outlines). You won't have time to do them all. Feel free to adapt each activity based on your class's strengths and weaknesses.

Leader's Prayer

Gracious God, please help me to grow in my own prayer life as I spend time in your Word. Grant that the children who hear this lesson may better understand the practice of

praying. May they become people who love to spend time with you in your Word and in prayer. In Jesus's name. Amen.

Leader's Tool Kit

- Q40 Catechism Recap (DL)
- Q40 God Speaks to Me (RB), one for each child
- Pens

⟨10⟩ Catechism Recap

Print out Q40 Catechism Recap (DL). Mix up the sheets and place them upside down in a grid on the floor.

This is a memory game. Invite the children to come forward and turn over two pieces of paper. The aim of the game is to find a matching question and answer. If no match is found, the pieces of paper are turned back over on the floor. The children must try to remember the details as the pages are turned over so that they can find a match when it comes to their turn. The child with the most matches wins!

⟨5⟩ Introduction to Question 40

Give each child a copy of Q40 God Speaks to Me (RB).

Introduce Question 40: "What should we pray?" Remind the children that Christians are in a relationship with God, and because of Jesus's death and resurrection, they can come directly to God in prayer. Highlight for the children that prayer is having a conversation with God. The more Christians know and understand God, the easier it will be to know what to pray.

Explain to the children that good conversations go two ways. When we converse with God, he speaks through his Word, and we respond in prayer.

Tell the children that God has already started the conversation with us by speaking to us in his Word. The Bible verses on the page are all things God has said to them.

⟨10⟩ Activity ☼

Give each child a pen or marker.

Invite the children to respond to the conversation God has started. Have them spend a few minutes writing out prayers in response to each Bible verse from Q40 God Speaks to Me (RB). If it is a command, they may want to ask God to help them keep the command. If it is a promise, they may want to thank God for the promise and claim it for themselves.

47

(15) **Teaching Outline**

Begin the teaching time by asking for God's help. Ask that the lesson would be taught faithfully and that the children might listen well.

Introduce the children once again to Paul. Paul was a man of prayer, and he recorded many of his prayers in the letters he wrote to God's people. Explain to the children that they will begin to learn what to pray as they study Paul's prayer in Ephesians 3:14–21.

Ask the children to consider what they pray for most often (reassure them that you don't expect them to answer out loud). Tell the children that a great way to find out what someone loves most is by examining what he or she prays.

Read Ephesians 3:14–21. Provide Bibles for the children to read along with you.

Explain to the children that just before Paul prays this prayer in Ephesians 3, he clearly explained God's purpose in his world. That purpose is to draw together a people for himself through Jesus Christ. That's why Paul says, "For this reason" at the beginning of his prayer (v. 13). Because Paul clearly understood God's will, he fell to his knees in prayer for the Ephesian Christians.

Ask the children how they might more clearly understand God's purposes for his world and his people. A right understanding of God's will for his world will fiercely fuel

prayer. Help the children to realize that it is through reading God's Word that we understand God's character and mission.

Paul prays that God would help the Ephesian Christians grow in their Christian life, that they would become mature believers. He prays that Jesus would be allowed to rule the hearts of the believers and that he would strengthen them for a lifetime in God's service. It is worth noting to the children that Paul prays to the Father, for the power of the Spirit, and for the sake of the Son.

Paul also prays that the Christians would know the great love that Jesus has for them. Paul wants the Ephesians to know the love of Jesus deep, deep down in their hearts—not just in their heads. And Paul is asking for God's power to help believers understand how wide and long and high and deep the love of Jesus is, because without God's help understanding is limited.

Paul approached God fully trusting that he would hear and answer his prayers (which is the kind of attitude last week's lesson addressed).

Ask the children what this passage teaches us about the content of our prayers.

Finish the teaching time by helping the children commit Question 40 and the answer to memory.

(These notes are just for guidance. Please expand or amend them to suit your own children and context. Write out your talk in your own words and include illustrations and applications that you know will connect with your children.)

 Activity

Ask the children to line up side by side and put their arms around each other's backs. They will need this support to keep their balance.

Tell the children that people often pray in ways that go *against* what the Bible teaches instead of what the Bible commands. Tell them that you are going to read out some prayers. If the prayer you pray agrees with what the Bible teaches, then they should stand on their right foot. If the prayer goes against something the Bible teaches, then they should stand on their left foot. Make sure everyone knows which is the left foot and which is the right. Practice a few times switching from the right to left foot while supporting one another. Then read out these sample prayers:

- Father, I know I won't be happy unless I can have an American Girl doll, so please give me one. (L)

- Father, help me to be content with what I have. If it would be good for me, I would like a new bike. (R)

- Father, don't let my mom find out that I stole money from her purse. (L)

- Father, forgive me for lying to my dad. Help me to have the courage to confess to him. (R)

- Father, I know you have the power to heal. Please heal my grandmother's pneumonia. (R)

- Father, thank you that it is always your will to heal us. Thank you that if we believe you have healed us, we won't ever need medicine. (L)

- Father, I know you are too busy to be bothered. So I won't ask for your help on the test I am about to take. (L)

- Father, I know that you love me and care about every detail of my life. Would you please send a friend to sit with me at lunch? (R)

- Father, my little sister has messed up my room for the fifth time this week. I know you can't expect me to forgive her. (L)

- Father, help me to forgive my big brother for shouting at me. Help me to remember that because you have forgiven me, I should forgive others. (R)

⑤ Discussion and Question Time

Some questions that might arise include:

? Is it wrong to pray for physical or material things?

> No, God wants us to bring all of our needs and desires to him.

? Must we always copy prayers found in the Bible?

> No, but biblical prayers give us helpful patterns to follow.

? How do we pray for non-Christians?

> Tell the children that the most important thing to pray for non-Christians is that they might trust Jesus for their salvation. Reassure the children that we can and should pray for those outside God's family.

Also use this opportunity to help the children think about their own lives and how this question and answer affects them personally.

- Do they enjoy praying? Praying is a bit like riding a bike. The more you do it, the easier and more enjoyable it becomes.

- How might a greater understanding of the love of Jesus affect their prayers?

⑩ Virtue Vision

Trust

Tell the children that James 5:16 says, "Pray for one another." It takes trust to ask someone to pray for you. Read this brief story to the children:

> "What's the matter, Heidi?" Sarah asked. She could tell that Heidi was upset about something. Instead of playing with the other girls, she was sitting in a swing during recess, and she wasn't even swinging!
>
> "Oh, it's kind of embarrassing," said Heidi. "I don't think I want anyone to know."
>
> "You can tell me," said Sarah. "Then I can pray for you about it."

> "I guess you're right," Heidi began. "Last night, my mom found lice in my little sister's hair. I'm so embarrassed. I don't have it, but my mom still made me use a special shampoo that smelled really bad. Will you pray that I won't get lice?"
>
> "Sure I will!" said Sarah, and she ran back to her other friends who were sitting on the monkey bars. Heidi felt better until she realized that all the other girls were looking in her direction. Their eyes were wide. Then they started laughing. Sarah had told them about the lice!

Ask the children if Sarah really wanted to pray for Heidi. Was Sarah a trustworthy person? What is the trustworthy way to respond when someone shares a prayer request in confidence?

Memory Activity

Divide the class into two groups. Read the memory verse or catechism question and answer aloud for the children a couple of times.

Each group must come up with a creative way to perform the memory verse or catechism answer. They could perhaps sing it or say it with an accent. They could do some actions or even a mime. Give the children artistic license and see what they come up with!

Conclude by saying the memory verse through again all together.

Closing Prayer Time

Pray that the children would be able to learn how to pray effectively as they spend time reading the Bible and that their relationship with God might grow.

Question 41

What is the Lord's Prayer?

Answer

Our Father in heaven, hallowed be your name, your kingdom come, your will be done, on earth as it is in heaven. Give us today our daily bread. And forgive us our debts, as we also have forgiven our debtors. And lead us not into temptation, but deliver us from evil.

Big Idea
Jesus gave all believers a model of prayer when he taught his disciples the Lord's Prayer.

Aim
To further equip the children with a pattern of everyday prayer.

Bible Passage
Matthew 6:5–15

Memory Verse
"Pray then like this: 'Our Father in heaven, hallowed be your name....'" (Matt. 6:9)

Virtue
Humility

Leader's Notes

Some of the children may already know the Lord's Prayer by heart. What they may not realize is that the prayer contains a beautiful pattern of prayer, which should be followed by all believers. Sometimes familiarity causes the essence of this prayer to be overlooked. It is not wrong to learn and recite the Lord's Prayer, but it is important to clearly understand the model contained in the prayer. This lesson should further form the children's understanding of what and how to pray. This is the conclusion of the questions in *The New City Catechism* that specifically focus on prayer.

Things to remember when planning and teaching:

- Beware of the children's familiarity with the Lord's Prayer. It will mean that you need to work especially hard to engage the children in this lesson.

- The lesson should show the children that Jesus provides an excellent pattern of prayer to personally follow.

- Remember to mix and match the activities in the lesson to fit your time frame (see p. 12 for some sample outlines). You won't have time to do them all. Feel free to adapt each activity based on your class's strengths and weaknesses.

Leader's Prayer

Father God, help me to be inspired and challenged as I come to study the prayer that Jesus himself taught. Help me to read it with fresh eyes. Please teach me to pray in a way that is consistent with your Word and glorifying to your name. May the children who will hear this lesson be challenged to learn from the patterns of prayer that you institute through your Word. In Jesus's name. Amen.

Leaders Tool Kit

- Ping-pong balls
- Bag or bingo cage
- Q41 Illustrations of Learned Skills (RB)
- Markers
- Q41 Lord's Prayer Bookmark (RB), printed on cardstock, one for each child

- Stickers for decorating the bookmarks
- A printout of Matthew 6:9–13 for each child
- Prayer notebooks from previous weeks
- Whiteboard and marker

Catechism Recap

Write the numbers of a random assortment of the questions that have already been taught on ping-pong balls and put them into a bag or box. If your budget allows, purchase a bingo cage or blower to add to the fun, or make your own.

Divide the children into two teams and explain that you are going to have a quiz to help them remember some of *The New City Catechism* questions they've already learned. Let each team pick a numbered ball out for their opponents. The opposing team will get two points if they can remember the catechism question and answer associated with the number. The team with the most points wins! Remember, this is meant to be a fun and engaging activity!

Introduction to Question 41

Show the children Q41 Illustrations of Learned Skills (RB). Ask them to identify what each person is doing. (Skiing, skydiving, playing the cello, fencing, driving a car.) Tell the children that these are all things that are fun to learn how to do. How would a person go about learning to do one of these things?

Help them to realize that to learn any of these skills, you would need a teacher.

Explain to the children that many things in life need to be taught. The Christian life is all about teaching and learning; we need to be taught to learn and grow as Christians. Introduce Question 41: "What is the Lord's Prayer?" and explain that it allows us to see Jesus teaching his friends how to pray. They said to him, "Lord, teach us to pray," and Jesus used the prayer that we now know as the Lord's Prayer as a model for them.

Activity

Print on cardstock and cut out the Lord's Prayer Bookmark (RB) for each child. Have markers and stickers available to decorate the bookmarks.

Encourage the children to decorate the bookmark and take it home to keep in their Bible or prayer journal. As they decorate, take turns reading the prayer out loud to help with memorization.

(15) **Teaching Outline**

Print a copy of Matthew 6:9–13 for each child in the group. Have lots of markers available.

Begin the teaching time by asking for God's help. Ask that the lesson would be taught faithfully and that the children might listen well.

Introduce the children to Matthew's Gospel. Tell the children that the Gospels record much about Jesus's life and ministry. Explain to them that chapter 6 is part of a long sermon (called the Sermon on the Mount) from Jesus. Tell the children this lesson will focus on the part of the sermon that addresses the practice of prayer.

Jesus reminds those listening to his sermon that prayer is about a personal relationship with God. Remind the children that our attitude matters! Tell them that what we know about God—that he is a loving, all-powerful Father—should affect the way we approach him in prayer.

Pass out the copies of Matthew 6:9–13.

Explain that Jesus taught his disciples how to pray in Matthew 6:9–13, and this prayer should now be used as a pattern of prayer for each believer.

Have the children read the Lord's Prayer and ask them to do the following things on their paper:

▪ Circle the part of the prayer where Jesus addresses God.

▪ Put a squiggly line under the part where Jesus praises God the Father.

▪ Underline every request Jesus makes for himself and his disciples.

Ask the children some questions to help them see what Jesus is teaching us about prayer.

1. Based on the way Jesus prays, how should we address God in prayer?

Jesus teaches us to address our prayers to God the Father. Christians have been adopted into God's family and therefore can call him Father. The more we get to know him as Father, the easier it will be to pray!

2. What does Jesus mean when he prays that God's will would be done?

Jesus is asking that many people would become Christians and love God with their whole hearts, and that they would act in accord with his Word.

3. Why does Jesus ask for God's name to be hallowed?

This is a way of praising God and saying he should be respected and worshiped above anyone else.

4. Why does Jesus pray for daily bread?

He encourages us to pray for our essential daily needs. This helps us to remember that every good gift is from God. Without him, we wouldn't even have food!

5. What does this model prayer teach us about forgiveness?

> If we are seeking God's forgiveness, we must forgive those who have wronged us.

6. Why does Jesus pray that we will not be led into temptation?

> Because of our sinful nature, we are easily led astray by sin. We need

God's help to recognize temptation and run from it.

Finish the teaching time by helping the children commit Question 41 and the answer to memory.

(These notes are just for guidance. Please expand or amend them to suit your own children and context. Write out your talk in your own words and include illustrations and applications that you know will connect with your children.)

Activity

Pass out the prayer notebooks. Make sure each child gets the one he or she started, and have extras on hand for any students who were absent the week they were made.

Ask the children to write a prayer inspired by the model of the Lord's Prayer. It should include words of praise, requests about God's work in the world, requests for your needs, a

request for forgiveness, and a request for help. They can make their prayers more specific than the Lord's Prayer. For example, they can list out more needs than just bread. They can also ask forgiveness for specific sins. Assure them that this is meant for God's eyes alone.

The prayer journals can be sent home with the children this week.

Discussion and Question Time

Some questions that might arise include:

? **Can we pray for things not mentioned in the Bible?**

> Yes, reassure the children that we can bring all our praises and requests to God.

? **Do we always have to use the pattern of the Lord's Prayer?**

> No, but remind the children that it's a helpful tool to learn to pray in a biblical way.

? **Will God always answer our prayers?**

> Yes, tell the children God does answer his people's prayers, but it may not always be in the way people want or expect. Sometimes he says no,

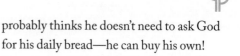

Notes

sometimes he says yes, and sometimes he tells us to wait.

Also use this opportunity to help the children think about their own lives and how this question and answer affects them personally.

- How might they use this pattern of prayer in their own prayer life?

- Ask the children to think of specific ways they could pray for God's will to be done on earth.

- What does it mean to ask God for our daily bread?

Virtue Vision

Humility

In the Lord's Prayer, Jesus asked his Father to provide daily bread. Ask the children to think about where bread comes from. Help them think through the steps that happened before it came to them.

- Someone bought it at a grocery store or bakery.

- Someone baked the loaf.

- Someone mixed the ingredients.

- Someone ground wheat into flour.

- Someone picked the wheat from the field.

- Sun and rain made the wheat grow.

- Someone planted the wheat.

A lot of steps go into providing our daily bread. The richest person in the world probably thinks he doesn't need to ask God for his daily bread—he can buy his own! But ask the children which of those steps is something that all the money in the world can't make happen.

Help the children see that only God can send the sun and rain. No matter how wealthy or powerful we get, we could never even provide our own bread without God sending us what we need. Realizing this should make us humble.

Ask the children if there's anything else in the Lord's Prayer that reminds us to be humble. Help them see that when we pray "forgive us our debts, as we also have forgiven our debtors," it reminds us that none of us is any better than another. We all need God's forgiveness. That should humble us!

Memory Activity

Write the memory verse or catechism answer on a whiteboard large enough so every child can read it.

Tell the children that you are going to read the memory verse or catechism answer together while you do a series of different actions:

- Read the words out loud while patting your own head.

- Read the words out loud while hopping on one foot.

- Read the words out loud while doing jumping jacks.

- Read the words out loud while clapping your hands.

- Say the words out loud while keeping your eyes closed.

⑤ Closing Prayer Time

Pray the Lord's Prayer together to conclude the lesson.

Question 42

How is the Word of God to be read and heard?

Answer

With diligence, preparation, and prayer; so that we may accept it with faith and practice it in our lives.

Big Idea
The Word of God should be read and heard prayerfully and with reverence and humility.

Aim
To help the children understand how to approach the Bible in a way that pleases God.

Bible Passage
2 Timothy 3:10–17

Memory Verse
"All Scripture is breathed out by God and profitable for teaching, for reproof, for correction, and for training in righteousness, that the man of God may be complete, equipped for every good work." (2 Tim. 3:16–17)

Virtue
Hope

Leader's Notes

Reading Scripture is a most precious process. Through Scripture God has chosen to reveal himself to men and women, and as the Word is heard, God the Spirit transforms the hearts and minds of those with ears to hear. Many approach the reading of Scripture in a careless way. Some treat the Bible as any other book, approaching it in a casual and unthinking manner. This question will encourage the children to approach God's Word in a serious fashion. It will cause them to remember that when we read God's Word, we believe that God is actually speaking to us. This lesson aims to equip children to approach the reading and hearing of the Word with prayerful anticipation and hope. It will encourage the children to spend time in God's Word and to hide it in their hearts.

Things to remember when planning and teaching:

- Be careful not to encourage worship of the Bible, but rather worship of God as revealed in the Bible.

- Help the children to be excited about the thought of meeting God as they hear his Word. Clearly communicate to the children that God speaks through his Word.

- Remember to mix and match the activities in the lesson to fit your time frame (see p. 12 for some sample outlines). You won't have time to do them all. Feel free to adapt each activity based on your class's strengths and weaknesses.

Leader's Prayer

Gracious God, I praise you for the gift of your Word. Thank you that you have revealed yourself through it and that it contains all things necessary for life and salvation. Please develop in me the right attitude as I come to study Scripture; may I be teachable, humble, and eager to meet you in your Word. Grant understanding to the children who will hear this lesson. May they to be challenged to approach Scripture in faithful expectation. In Jesus's name. Amen.

Leader's Tool Kit

- 8 business size envelopes
- Poster board
- Glue
- Index cards
- Red construction paper
- Scissors
- Slips of paper with 2 Timothy 3:16–17 printed on them
- Pens or pencils

Catechism Recap

Seal eight business size envelopes, then cut each one in half so that you have sixteen open-ended pockets. Attach them to the poster board with the cut end up—four across and four down. In each pouch place a card. Leave four cards blank and write one of these sentences on each of the others:

- *ZAP—Switch points with the other team.*

- *ZAP—Add two points to your team score.*

- *ZAP—Lose two points from your team score.*

- *ZAP—Both teams lose four points.*

- *ZAP—Your team's score goes back to zero.*

- *ZAP—The other team's score goes back to zero.*

Keep score on two sheets of paper so that the scores can be swapped when that card is drawn.

Divide the group into two teams. Take turns to ask each team to recall the answer to a catechism question. Read a question, and the team must come up with the right answer. They have one chance to recite the answer. If they get the answer right, they get a chance to go to the board and pick a card out of one of the pouches. The teams will end up gaining, losing, switching, or totally zapping out! The team with the most points when all of the cards have been drawn wins. The aim of the game is to help the children have fun while reviewing the answers to the catechism questions.

Introduction to Question 42

Explain to the children that before we get into today's Bible lesson, they will need to do some imagining. Ask them to pretend that they are the citizens of a small kingdom. Their land is in the middle of a famine, but their king has been wisely storing food for years so that, should a famine come, his people will not starve. However, he has only enough food to feed his own people.

Tell the children that word reaches your city that other kingdoms are plotting to steal your kingdom's food. For this reason, the king has stored the food in a secret location outside the city walls, far away. He knows that when the other kingdoms attack, he

may be killed, so he calls his citizens into his throne room.

"Listen carefully," he says. "We are about to face a great battle. I don't know which of us will survive the attack on our city. I am going to tell you where I have hidden our food. Without that food, you will not survive the famine. But it is hidden far away. If you do not listen carefully and follow every word of my directions, you will never find it."

Ask the children: What kind of listeners would those citizens be? Do you think they would be distracted? Would they be thinking about other things? Would they talk to each other while the king was talking?

Confirm to the children that when you know someone is telling you a message of life-or-death importance, you will listen attentively. God has spoken to us in his Word, and his message is the most important that there ever has been. We should listen with as much attentiveness and respect as those citizens would have listened to their king!

Activity

Divide the children into small groups. Invite the children to come up with a movie trailer for a film about the Bible. Tell them that the trailer should tell the audience a bit about the story of the Bible (but not the ending!) and also all the many reasons why people should be interested in the Bible. After a little while, invite each of the groups to act out their movie trailers while you film them on a smartphone.

Teaching Outline

Begin the teaching time by asking for God's help. Ask that the lesson would be taught faithfully and that the children might listen well.

Remind the children that God speaks. God has caused his words to be written down by human writers so that people can know everything necessary for life and salvation. Try to encourage the children to grasp the magnitude of the truth that God revealed himself in his Word. He is not an unknown deity, nor is he some thoroughly mysterious being. God delights in making himself known, and he longs to be known.

Explain to the children that the Bible is the most important book ever written because it is God's primary way of communicating with humanity. God still speaks through his Word to his world today.

Ask the children to consider whether they think they should listen to the Bible in the same way as every other book. Ask the children if they think that any preparation is needed before reading the Bible.

We need to think carefully about how we read and hear the Word of God.

Explain that Paul's letter to Timothy will help the group think about how to approach God's Word.

Read 2 Timothy 3:10–17. Provide Bibles for the children to read along.

Explain to the children that as they prepare to read the Bible, they must realize that they are about to hear from the living God and they need to be ready to listen to his Word.

Explain to the children that in this section of 2 Timothy, Paul is encouraging Timothy to be different from the world, to stand for what he believes in the face of doubters and critics. Paul is encouraging Timothy to have confidence in the truth he has come to believe, which he observed in Paul's life and encountered in God's Word.

Paul tells Timothy that all Scripture is God-breathed, fully inspired by God. He identifies God as the origin of Scripture. But he also describes the purpose of Scripture: it is "profitable for teaching, for reproof, for correction, and for training in righteousness." Tell the children that the Bible is God's means of bringing Christians to maturity.

Remind the children that when someone becomes a Christian, the Holy Spirit comes to live in him or her. When a Christian reads the Bible, the Holy Spirit applies it to his or her life. So every time Christians read the Bible, they are hearing God's Word. We must determine to listen well and allow the Holy Spirit to work in our life.

Ask the children to give some examples of what they think "teaching, reproof, correction, and training in righteousness" means.

Ask them where they will encounter God's Word in their lives each week.

Ask them how and why they should prepare to listen to God's Word.

These are some of the attitudes we adopt as we come to God's Word:

Prayerful

- Thanking God that he speaks

- Rejoicing that he has given his Holy Spirit to apply the Word
- Asking that God would teach, reprove, correct, and train us

Reverent

- Remembering that it is God who speaks through Scripture

Humble

- Expecting God to work and sanctify
- Thanking God that he wants to change and mature his people

Help the children to understand that we should be eager to meet God in his Word, and in order to do that, we must approach reading the Bible respectfully. We should prepare to hear God's Word. We should pray before we hear God's Word, and we should seek to listen carefully to what God is saying to us by his Spirit.

God longs to see his people transformed as they seek to glorify him. When we have listened well to God's Word, we will respond in how we live.

Finish the teaching time by helping the children commit Question 42 and the answer to memory.

These notes are just for guidance. Please expand or amend them to suit your own children and context. Write out your talk in your own words and include illustrations and applications that you know will connect with your children.)

Activity

Give the children red construction paper, a pen or pencil, scissors, and glue. Have ready the slips of paper with 2 Timothy 3:16–17 printed on them.

Instruct the children to place two pieces of construction paper together and fold them down the middle. Next draw a half heart against the fold. Cut through all the pages at once along the lines they've drawn so that when you unfold the paper, there are two identical heart shapes. Fold one heart back up and cut a tiny slit along the fold. Run a small line of glue only around the outside edge of one heart, and glue the two hearts together.

Hand out the slips of paper with 2 Timothy 3:16–17 and have the children slip one inside their heart through the slit.

Ask the children what they think these hearts are meant to represent. If they can't figure it out, invite someone to look up Psalm 119:11.

Discussion and Question Time

Some questions that might arise include:

? **What should I do when I don't understand the Bible?**

First, we should pray and ask the Holy Spirit to give us understanding. Then, we can ask other Christians, including our pastor or our parents, what a Bible passage means. There are also many books called commentaries that have been written to help us understand the Bible.

? **Can I admit that I find the Bible boring?**

Many people assume that the Bible is boring, but that's usually because they don't know it well. If someone watches a baseball or soccer game for the first time, he may find it boring because he doesn't know what's going on. But if he continues to watch baseball or soccer and learns the rules, he will start to enjoy the game more and more. His interest will grow as his knowledge grows. If we find the Bible boring, we should keep reading and trust that as we start to understand it better, we will learn to love and enjoy it.

Also use this opportunity to help the children think about their own lives and how this question and answer affects them personally.

- Are they challenged to think about how they prepare to listen to God's Word?

- Will they approach reading and hearing God's Word differently?

- Are they excited and hopeful that God will work through his Word in their lives?

Virtue Vision

Hope

Have a Bible on hand.

Ask the children if they can think of a time that they or their friends have felt a lack of hope. Perhaps it may have been before a sports game against a really good opposing team. Maybe it was before a difficult test that they did not study for. Maybe their pet was lost, and they gave up all hope of finding it.

Encourage the children that in times like these, we can turn to God's Word to restore our hope. Tell them that God's Word will not promise any particular outcome to the kind of situations you've talked about. It does not promise you will win your game or that your dog will find its way home safely. But it gives us hope that God will use every circumstance for the good of his children.

Ask for a volunteer to look up Romans 8:28 in the Bible. How does Romans 8:28 encourage us to hope, even in hard times?

Memory Activity

Ask the children to read the memory verse or catechism question and answer out loud, together. Next, divide the children into two groups. Have them say the words of the verse or catechism question and answer by alternating between groups. The first group says the first word, the second group says the second word, the first group says the third word, and so on. Go through the verse several times, getting faster each time.

Closing Prayer Time

Encourage the children to give thanks to God for his Word and to pray that God would help them hear his Word with great attentiveness.

Question 43

What are the sacraments or ordinances?

Answer

Baptism and the Lord's Supper.

Big Idea
The sacraments were established by God, for his church, to be a spiritual help to believers.[1]

Aim
To help the children to begin to understand what the sacraments are and why they're important.

Bible Passage
Matthew 28:16–20 and Luke 22:14–23

Memory Verse
Choose one.

"And he took bread, and when he had given thanks, he broke it and gave to them, saying, 'This is my body, which is given for you. Do this in remembrance of me.' And likewise the cup after they had eaten, saying, 'This cup that is poured out for you is the new covenant in my blood.'" (Luke 22:19–20)

"We were buried therefore with him by baptism into death, in order that, just as Christ was raised from the dead by the glory of the Father, we too might walk in newness of life." (Rom. 6:4)

Virtue
Awe

---

1. If your church tradition uses the word *ordinance* instead of *sacrament*, feel free to substitute throughout the lesson.

Leader's Notes

Question 43 is the beginning of five questions that consider the sacraments of the church. The children will be familiar with the concept of baptism and the Lord's Supper, but they most likely will not understand the significance of the sacraments for the believer. It would be wonderful if the children gained a deep and significant understanding of the sacraments through the study of these questions. There will undoubtedly be some confusion and many questions about the sacraments. It will be important to tread carefully in your engagement with the children.

This curriculum has been written to be used in a variety of different Protestant denominations and traditions. It may be helpful for you to talk with your pastor about your church's teaching on baptism and the Lord's Supper to make sure you present this lesson in a way that reinforces your church's teaching. You might also consult the booklet *Baptism and the Lord's Supper* (Crossway 2011).

Things to remember when planning and teaching:

- Children will have all sorts of interesting questions about the sacraments. Be prepared to engage in a wide variety of discussions! It's okay to be honest if you don't know the answer to a question.

- It would be good to make sure the children are able to observe and participate in (where appropriate) both a baptism service and service of the Lord's Supper. It is important to give them an observable experience to engage with this question.

- Remember to mix and match the activities in the lesson to fit your time frame (see p. 12 for some sample outlines). You won't have time to do them all. Feel free to adapt each activity based on your class's strengths and weaknesses.

Leader's Prayer

Almighty God, I praise you that, in your great kindness, you established the sacraments as a means of grace for your church. Thank you that through them you strengthen and nurture my faith and make me more like the Lord Jesus. Grant understanding to the children who hear this lesson. May they be struck by the goodness of your provision and the beauty of your care for your people. In Jesus's name. Amen.

Leader's Tool Kit

- Whiteboard and marker
- Sticky notes in two different colors (at least four of each color)
- Q43 Catechism Recap (DL)

- A cup
- One copy of Q43 Picture Clues (RB)
- A green leaf and a leaf that has changed color, or pictures of leaves changing color

Catechism Recap

Print out and cut up Q43 Catechism Recap (DL). Put the slips in a cup. Draw a grid on the whiteboard that is seven spaces across and six spaces down. Make the spaces roughly the size of your sticky notes. Give each team four sticky notes in one color; each team should have a different color.

Divide the children into teams. The teams will take turns drawing a question. They must appoint one person to answer. If they guess the answer correctly, they can place one of their sticky notes on the grid. The other team follows suit by drawing a question and appointing a team member to answer. On their next turn, each team must choose a child that has not answered.

The goal of the game is to get four matching sticky notes in a row. Each team can block their opponents! Every time a team gets a question right, they can place a sticky note on the grid or move one of their sticky notes. The game ends when one team gets four in a row or all of the questions have been drawn.

Introduction to Question 43

You will need a copy of Q43 Picture Clues (RB). Cut out each clue. Write the letters ECNANIDRO on the whiteboard.

This lesson needs to begin with the explanation of some big words! Tell the children that this lesson involves some big words, and that you want them to figure out what the words are before you explain them.

Tell the children that they should say what they see as you show the pictures. Show them the pictures in order (Sack, Ram, Mints) and see if they can work out that the word is *sacraments*. Help them if they get stuck! Tell them that *sacraments* is the first word to remember for the lesson.

Show the children the letters on the board and explain that they form the second word. Ask the children if anyone can rearrange the letters to figure out the word. Give them a clue by telling them this is the word spelled backwards. Once someone has gotten it, write "ordinance" on the whiteboard and

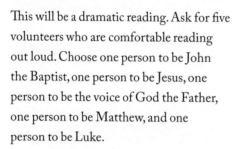

tell the children that this is the second important word for the lesson.

Introduce question 43: "What are the sacraments or ordinances?" Explain to the children that these big words describe things that are done in the church, among the gathered people of God. Tell them that some churches use the word *sacrament*, some use the word *ordinance*, and explain which one your church uses.

The sacraments are baptism and the Lord's Supper. God has given these sacraments to his people to encourage and strengthen them. Explain to the children that the sacraments do not give anyone faith; they are outward signs that someone is a part of God's family.

Activity

This will be a dramatic reading. Ask for five volunteers who are comfortable reading out loud. Choose one person to be John the Baptist, one person to be Jesus, one person to be the voice of God the Father, one person to be Matthew, and one person to be Luke.

Pass out Bibles to all the children, including the five volunteers. Ask them to turn first to Matthew 3:13–17. John should read John's line. Jesus should read what is attributed to Jesus. Tell the person who reading the voice of God to hide out of site, but not out of earshot. Matthew should read everything that isn't in quotes.

After this passage is finished, John may sit back down and the voice of God can come out of hiding. Ask Luke and Jesus to turn to Luke 22:14–20. Again, Luke will read everything that is not in quotes, and Jesus will read whatever Jesus speaks. If he is willing, Jesus should read his part lying down, propped on one arm, which was a common Middle Eastern way to eat.

When they finish, ask the children to give the volunteers a round of applause.

Teaching Outline

Begin the teaching time by asking for God's help. Ask that the lesson would be taught faithfully and that the children might listen well.

Read Matthew 28:16–20 and Luke 22:14–23. Provide Bibles for the children to read along.

Explain that an "ordinance" is a rule or command. Tell the children that lots of organizations have ordinances. Illustrate this point by explaining that a Girl Scout observes the ordinances or rules of the Scouts when she joins by pledging her allegiance to God and her country. Ask the children if they can think of any other groups that have ordinances.

Ask the children: Who commanded the church to baptize and celebrate the Lord's Supper? In other words, who established the ordinances of the church? It was Jesus! He commanded his church to go and baptize, and he also commanded his people to celebrate the Lord's Supper in remembrance of him. Highlight for the children that the sacraments are not human creations, but were instituted by Jesus for the church.

Remind the children that the sacraments are intended to be for those who have faith; they will not give faith.

Ask the children why they think Jesus instituted the sacraments. Was it to keep Christians busy? Or to make sure they're clean?

Tell the children that God knew his people would sometimes struggle to continue to trust in his promises and remember all that he achieved in Christ. God in his kindness established regular ways by which Christians can have their faith in Jesus strengthened during gathered worship.

Explain to the children that the sacraments are not just about remembering. Because they are the Word of God in visible forms, the Holy Spirit works through them to cultivate faith and encourage glad obedience. The sacraments help people grow in their confidence and trust in God. Explain to the children that the sacraments are two

of the ways God, through the Holy Spirit, sanctifies his people.

Ask the children to think about the different senses involved when experiencing baptism or the Lord's Supper. There are words spoken, there are visible signs, there's bread and wine to taste, and there is the washing of water to feel. Ask the children if they think it is significant that the sacraments involve so many senses. God understands that the meaning of the sacraments can more easily be understood when apprehended through various senses.

Tell the children that, as we will learn in future lessons, the sacraments are signs pointing to Christ's death and resurrection on our behalf. We must always look beyond the sign to the thing it is pointing to. If you got excited about baptism and the Lord's Supper but never realized that Christ died for your sins, the signs of the sacraments will have been of no use to you.

Try to nurture an appreciation and gratitude in the children as they begin to understand the significance of the sacraments in the church.

Conclude the teaching time by helping the children commit Question 43 and the answer to memory.

These notes are just for guidance. Please expand or amend them to suit your own children and context. Write out your talk in your own words and include illustrations and applications that you know will connect with your children.)

Notes

Notes

⑩ Activity

Invite a pastor, elder, or other member of your church's leadership to be interviewed about the sacraments. Provide the interview questions in advance.

Some questions to ask:

1. How did you become a Christian?

2. When did you first learn about the sacraments?

3. Why are the sacraments important for our church family?

4. How does our church decide who will be baptized?

5. How does our church decide who can take the Lord's Supper?

6. Can unbelievers participate in the sacraments?

⑤ Discussion and Question Time

Some questions that might arise include:

? Does it matter if people who aren't Christians take the Lord's Supper?

> Explain to the children that the sacraments are meant to be a family meal, only available to those who have been adopted in Christ. If people want to take the Lord's Supper, we can welcome them to do so if they will first repent and believe the gospel.

? Do the bread and wine become Jesus's actual flesh and blood?

> Tell the children that they do not, and that we will talk more about this point, as well as what happens in baptism, in the next few lessons.

Also use this opportunity to help the children think about their own lives and how this question and answer affects them personally.

- Ask the children if they understand what the sacraments are.

- Ask the children why the sacraments are important for God's church.

- Ask the children if God's generous provision of the sacraments increases their awe, love, and gratitude for him.

⑩ Virtue Vision

Awe

You will need a bright green leaf and a leaf that has changed its color. If you can't find colored leaves because it's the wrong season or you live in a place where leaves don't change colors, use pictures of green and changing leaves.

Show the children a green leaf and a leaf that has changed colors. Ask the children if they have ever noticed leaves changing color as the seasons change.

Tell the children that every year leaves appear to change colors when it becomes cooler outside and days become shorter. It can be beautiful—so beautiful that people feel a sense of awe and wonder at God's amazing creation.

Not only can the beauty inspire awe, but understanding why the leaves seem to change color is also amazing. Ask the children if anyone knows what chemical makes leaves green. Tell them that chlorophyll is the chemical that helps convert sunlight and carbon dioxide into energy for the plant and is also green in color. However, chlorophyll is not the only chemical in leaves. Other chemicals in

leaves, such as carotenes or xanthophyll, are also found in carrots and give them an orange color.

When the days become cooler, the chlorophyll in the leaves begins to break down and the green color disappears. Once the green is gone, you can see the other colors that were in the leaf all along—the yellows, oranges, or reds. It is amazing to uncover what was once hidden by the green pigment.

Similarly, our participation in the sacraments doesn't create something new. Instead, it reveals the work that God has already done in our lives. Just like the change in seasons allows us to see the red, orange, and green colors that were always in the leaves, so too the sacraments help us to see God's saving grace in our lives. It is truly amazing!

Notes

Memory Activity

Invite the children to make up some actions for the memory verse or catechism question and answer in small groups. Have each group show their actions to the rest of the children. Finish with all the groups joining together in saying the memory verse.

Closing Prayer Time

Lead the children in praying that the sacraments would help them better understand and remember what salvation means.

Question 44

What is baptism?

Answer

Baptism is the washing with water in the name of the Father, the Son, and the Holy Spirit.

Big Idea
Baptism is an outward sign of an inward reality—cleansing from sin.

Aim
To help the children understand what the sacrament[1] of baptism is.

Bible Passage
Matthew 28:16–20

Memory Verse
"Go therefore and make disciples of all nations, baptizing them in the name of the Father and of the Son and of the Holy Spirit. . . ." (Matt. 28:19)

Virtue
Forgiveness

1. If your church does not use the word *sacrament*, feel free to substitute the word *ordinance*.

Leader's Notes

Baptism is a sign and seal that someone is part of God's family. It is an outward sign of ownership; it is like a royal seal declaring that a person belongs to God. The children will be familiar with the concept of baptism. Whether they have been baptized or not, they will have witnessed the baptism of a family or church family member. This question will help the children dig deeper into the meaning and significance of baptism. This lesson aims to help the children understand how the sign of baptism is applied to the child of God in the name of the Father, Son, and Holy Spirit.

Things to remember when planning and teaching:

- The discussions around this question may take on a denominational form; be prepared to answer the children's questions and be patient with any confusion.

- Continue to work hard to help the children understand abstract concepts in a concrete way.

- It would be helpful if the children could witness a baptismal service as they engage with these questions.

- Remember to mix and match the activities in the lesson to fit your time frame (see p. 12 for some sample outlines). You won't have time to do them all. Feel free to adapt each activity based on your class's strengths and weaknesses.

Leader's Prayer

Heavenly Father, I praise you that you have cleansed me from my sin through the precious blood of Jesus. Thank you that you have instituted the sacrament of baptism in your church and ordained an outward visible washing with baptismal water that portrays my salvation to the world. Grant understanding to the children who will hear this lesson. May they further understand the meaning of baptism and continue to gain great confidence in the gospel. In Jesus's name. Amen.

Leader's Tool Kit

- Paneled inflatable beach ball and a marker
- A wedding ring
- Q44 What Do Theses Signs Mean? (RB), one copy

- Q44 Photos (RB), one copy
- A large sheet of paper and some markers

Catechism Recap

On a paneled inflatable beach ball write a selection of catechism questions from questions twenty-five through forty, one per panel.

Gather the children into a circle and explain that the idea of the game is to keep the beach ball off the floor. Each child must participate to keep the beach ball in the air. If the beach ball drops to the ground, someone must volunteer to answer one of the catechism questions written on the ball, or the whole group gets a penalty. The penalty could be things like twenty jumping jacks or five push-ups, or something silly like walking across the room like a crab.

Introduction to Question 44

You will need a wedding ring.

Show the children the wedding ring and ask them what a wedding ring is a sign of. A wedding ring is a visible sign of promises made when someone is married.

Place the wedding ring on the ring finger of an unmarried person (make sure it will fit before the lesson). Ask the children if simply putting a ring on someone's finger makes him or her married. Of course it doesn't, because the ring is only a sign of what happens in the marriage ceremony. It's not the ring that makes someone married.

Introduce the children to question 44: "What is baptism?" Explain to the children that this lesson will help them to think about the sacrament of baptism. Highlight for the children that baptism is one of the ordinances that Jesus instituted in his church. Explain that just like the wedding ring, baptism is a sign of something promised. It doesn't actually save someone. But it is still an important outward sign of new birth and cleansing inside a person's heart.

Activity

Cut out the four illustrations from Q44 What Do These Signs Mean? (RB)

■ An FBI badge indicates someone is an FBI agent.

■ A purple heart medal indicates that someone was wounded or killed in battle.

■ A baby on board button indicates someone is pregnant.

■ A skull and bones label indicates that something is poisonous.

Pass around the pictures and ask the children if they can identify what they mean. The

Notes

pictures are all signs that reveal something about the owner of the sign (badge, medal, etc.). Invite the children to describe what each sign communicates about the owner.

Point out to the children that the FBI badge doesn't make someone an FBI agent (otherwise everyone would be buying them on the internet!). The badge signifies that the person has trained very hard for many years to serve his or her country and he or she has the power of the United States government backing them.

Ask the children if receiving a military medal makes the owner a brave solider. No, it is because they have been courageous that they have been awarded the medal.

The baby on board button doesn't make someone pregnant. It is an outward sign revealing a very real inward physical reality.

Likewise, a poison label doesn't make something poisonous. It's simply put on the outside of a bottle or box to indicate what is inside.

Explain to the children that baptism is a sign. It says to the world that God is faithful to forgive the sins of those who put their trust in Jesus and live as God's children for his glory.

Be very sure to communicate to the children that the physical act of baptism doesn't save anyone from anything.

⑮ Teaching Outline

Begin the teaching time by asking for God's help. Ask that the lesson would be taught faithfully and that the children might listen well.

Read Matthew 28:16–20. Provide Bibles for the children to read along.

Contextualize this passage for the children by informing them that it comes right at the end of Matthew's Gospel. This event happened after Jesus had been crucified and before he ascended back into heaven to sit at the right hand of God the Father. Explain to the children that this is the moment that Jesus ordains baptism as a sign for all believers. Up until this point

in the Bible, various people had been baptized, but now at this point in salvation history, Jesus commands that all those who trust in him for the forgiveness of sins should be baptized.

Explain to the children that the word *baptize* means to immerse, dip, or submerge, or more generally, cleanse; the word is used of someone coming under water and paints a picture of cleansing and new birth. Ask the children if they can identify with that experience, either from swimming in the sea or a pool or from standing in a refreshing rain or cleansing shower. Explain to the children that the water signifies dying to their old self and rising to new life in Christ.

Notes

Baptism simply symbolizes that a Christian is someone who is united with Christ, someone who has been made new by the Holy Spirit and has turned away from his or her old ways.

Highlight for the children that baptism is a sign with a message. It shows that righteousness is by faith alone, but water baptism doesn't make someone a Christian. Remind the children that the only thing that can save a person from God's righteous anger and judgment is Jesus's substitutionary atonement on the cross, received by faith.

Ask the children if they noticed how Jesus said people should be baptized. It is in the name of the Father, Son, and Holy Spirit—the three members of the Trinity. Explain to the children that being baptized in the name of the Father, Son, and Holy Spirit is important because it shows the role and work of all of the members of the Trinity in the life of the believer.

Being baptized is a sign that shows the world that salvation is by grace alone through faith alone in Christ alone. In salvation, a person's sins are forgiven, and he or she becomes a member of God's family.

Show the children from the passage that the call for all Christians is to go out to the ends of the earth, proclaiming the good news of Jesus and baptizing people in the name of the Father, Son, and Holy Spirit. God calls his church to go out and make disciples; this is a command for every one of us!

Conclude the teaching time by helping the children commit Question 44 and the answer to memory.

(These notes are just for guidance. Please expand or amend them to suit your own children and context. Write out your talk in your own words and include illustrations and applications that you know will connect with your children.)

 Activity

You will need Q44 Photos (RB).

Tell the children that you are going to tell them a true story. Show the picture of Nate Saint's family.

Nate Saint was an American missionary, who along with Jim Elliot, Ed McCully, Roger Youderian, and Pete Fleming went to share the good news of Jesus with the Waodani people in Ecuador. The Waodani

had never heard about Jesus, and this team of men went to fulfill Jesus's command to make disciples of all nations, baptizing them in the name of the Father, Son, and Holy Spirit.

The Waodani people had little contact with outsiders. The five missionaries could not speak much of the Waodani language, but they tried to get to know them through friendly gestures. They thought they had been successful, but to everyone's shock, all

Notes

five men were speared to death by members of the Waodani people on the banks of the Curaray River.

But the story didn't end there! Nate Saint's sister Rachel and Elisabeth Elliot, the widow of missionary Jim Elliot, went back to live and work among the Waodani people. In time, many of the Waodoni became Christians. It was a beautiful testimony to the power of forgiveness and the power of the gospel.

Several years later, Nate Saint's two children, Kathy and Steve, were baptized in the same river where their father had been killed. They were baptized by two of the men who had killed him. Kimo and Dyuwi had become Christians; they had repented of their sin and had found forgiveness in Jesus's name. Steve and Kathy knew that they, too, were sinners, and needed forgiveness. By asking their father's killers to baptize them, they testified that there is no sin that cannot be cleansed by Jesus's blood.

⑤ Discussion and Question Time

Some questions that might arise include:

? **If someone is a Christian but isn't baptized, would he or she go to heaven after death?**

Yes! Explain to the children that baptism does not save, but is a sign of salvation. Every Christian should seek to be baptized, but if something prevents the outward sign, it doesn't take away the inner reality.

? **Why do people need to be baptized then?**

Explain to the children that the most important reason is because

Jesus commanded that his disciples should be baptized.

Also use this opportunity to help the children think about their own lives and how this question and answer affects them personally.

- Ask the children if they understand that baptism is a sign and therefore doesn't by itself save anyone.

- Ask the children if they would be willing to go and make disciples.

- Ask the children how they might explain baptism to a non-Christian.

Virtue Vision

Forgiveness

Invite the children to reflect on Nate Saint's story, and ask if they think they might be able to forgive in the way that the families of the murdered men did.

Ask them what parts of the story show that the families of the murdered men had forgiven the Waodani people. Rachel Saint and Elisabeth Elliot went back to live with the Waodani to share the gospel with them, and Steve and Kathy Saint chose to be baptized by them.

Ask why Steve and Kathy, even though they had been raised by missionaries, needed to be baptized. (We are all sinners and in need of God's forgiveness.)

Ask if anyone can remember the part of the Lord's Prayer that speaks of forgiveness. Do they think Steve's and Kathy's baptisms are a good illustration of "forgive us our debts, as we forgive our debtors"?

Notes

Memory Activity

Write out the memory verse or catechism question and answer on a large piece of paper without any spaces between the words.

Read the verse or catechism question and answer out loud to the children, and then

invite the children to draw lines where they think there should be spaces. Ask the children to read the memory verse or catechism question and answer together a few times, and then ask if anyone would like to say it individually.

Closing Prayer Time

Pray with gratitude for the sacrament of baptism and the beautiful sign that it is of God's forgiveness and rescue, bringing people from life to death.

Question 45

Is baptism with water the washing away of sin itself?

Answer

No, only the blood of Christ can cleanse us from sin.

Big Idea
Only the blood of Jesus can save.

Aim
To help the children understand that salvation is found in Christ alone, not through baptism.

Bible Passage
Luke 3:15–22

Memory Verse
"John answered them all, saying, 'I baptize you with water, but he who is mightier than I is coming, the strap of whose sandals I am not worthy to untie. He will baptize you with the Holy Spirit and fire.'" (Luke 3:16)

Virtue
Honesty

Leader's Notes

Children are inclined to have a works-based theology, mistakenly believing that they can do something to secure their salvation. They must be continually reminded that salvation is a free gift from God and that there is nothing they can do to earn their salvation. This lesson aims to clearly explain to the children that only the blood of Jesus cleanses people from their sin, and the waters of baptism simply signify that internal cleansing. This lesson will allow the children to further explore and understand the sacrament of baptism.

Things to remember when planning and teaching:

- Churches have different policies on baptism and age. This lesson is designed to be used in any context, but it will be stronger if you adapt it to your church's baptismal policy and have the ability to clearly explain it to your class.

- Rather than simply repeating information from Questions 43 and 44, try to build upon previous material.

- Remember to mix and match the activities in the lesson to fit your time frame (see p. 12 for some sample outlines). You won't have time to do them all. Feel free to adapt each activity based on your class's strengths and weaknesses.

Leader's Prayer

Saving God, I recognize that salvation comes through faith in the saving blood of Jesus Christ. Thank you that I am cleansed by his sacrificial death on the cross. Thank you that you give us the sacraments to remind us of that cleansing. Help us to rejoice in them without trusting in them. Grant understanding to the children who will hear this lesson. May they clearly understand that the blood of Jesus cleanses sinners, and that the waters of baptism signify an inward transformation. In Jesus's name. Amen.

Leader's Tool Kit

- Ping-pong balls
- Bag or bingo cage
- A small, inexpensive dry-erase board
- Permanent marker
- Red dry-erase marker
- Water
- Tissues
- Picture of a crucible
- Blank index cards

Catechism Recap

Write the numbers of the questions that have already been taught on ping-pong balls and put them into a bag or box. If your budget allows, purchase a bingo cage or blower to add to the fun, or make your own.

Divide the children into two teams, and explain that you are going to have a quiz to help them remember some of the *NCC* questions that they've already learned. Let each team pick a numbered ball out for their opponents. The opposing team will get two points if they can remember the catechism question and answer associated with the number. The team with the most points wins. Remember, this is meant to be a fun and engaging activity!

Introduction to Question 45

You will need a small, inexpensive dry-erase board, a permanent marker, a red dry-erase marker, water, and some tissues. Before the class begins, draw a heart on the dry-erase board in permanent marker and in the heart write SIN also in permanent marker. It's worth having a trial run of this illustration to make sure it works!

Draw the children's attention to the heart on the dry-erase board and tell them that you're going to try to erase the sin with water. The permanent marker will not be erasable with water. Highlight for the children that this question considers whether baptism with water is the washing away of sin. Explain to them that the baptism with water is not what deals with sin.

Thoroughly color over the word SIN with the red dry-erase marker and explain to the children that it is only the blood of Jesus Christ that cleanses people from their sin. The word *sin* will now rub off with a tissue, clearly illustrating that the water of baptism is not what cleanses people from their sin but rather the blood of the Lord Jesus Christ

Introduce Question 45: "Is baptism with water the washing away of sin itself?" Explain to the children that this lesson is another opportunity to consider carefully what the sacrament of baptism is.

Activity

Play a word association game with the children. The rules of the game are that the children must say a word that is directly related to the previous word and that there can be no hesitation or repetition. If there is hesitation or repetition, that child must sit down and another child should be invited to take his or her place. The game can carry on for as long as time allows.

Invite two children up to play the game. Give one of the children a word to start.

Notes

Below are some words you should use. Every time the players change (through violations of hesitation or repetition), introduce a new word (if it hasn't already been said):

- Baptism
- Water
- Jesus
- Sin
- Forgiveness
- Washed
- Sign

Hopefully, the game will bring out lots of words related to baptism and help the children to remember what they learned during the lessons associated with Questions 43 and 44.

Teaching Outline

Begin the teaching time by asking for God's help. Ask that the lesson would be taught faithfully and that the children might listen well.

Remind the children that baptism is a sign with a message, something external that signifies an internal change.

Read Luke 3:15–22. Provide Bibles for the children to read along.

Explain to the children that in this passage John the Baptist is preparing the way for Jesus. He was preaching repentance and baptizing people. Draw the children's attention to verse 16, and ask what strikes them about the verse. John says that he is baptizing with water but One is coming who will baptize with the Holy Spirit and fire. Explain to the children that John is referring to cleansing of sin that happens when someone turns to Jesus in repentance and faith; remind the children that at that moment the Holy Spirit indwells people's hearts, cleanses them from sin, and brings them to new life in Christ.

John was clearly declaring that it is not water that cleanses, but rather the blood of Jesus through the power of the Holy Spirit. There is no external act necessary for salvation.

Read Luke 23:39–43.

The thief who died on the cross next to Jesus declared his faith in Jesus, and Jesus assured him of his salvation by saying, "Truly, I say to you, today you will be with me in paradise" (v. 43). Point out to the children that the thief had not been baptized, and yet Jesus confirmed his faith. This account shows that while Jesus established the sacrament of baptism in his church to be the normal experience of every believer, baptism is not necessary for salvation.

Conclude the teaching time by helping the children commit Question 45 and the answer to memory.

(These notes are just for guidance. Please expand or amend them to suit your own children and context. Write out your talk in your own words and include illustrations and applications that you know will connect with your children.)

Activity

Divide the children into small groups, and invite them to make up a short skit that could be shown to other children to help them understand the meaning of baptism. Give the groups different prompts, such as:

- Having a discussion at the lunch table at school about baptism with a kid who's never heard of it

- Someone becomes a Christian on her deathbed and asks about baptism

- A conversation with someone who thinks he needs to be baptized again every time he commits a sin

If time permits, invite some of the groups to perform their skits.

Discussion and Question Time

Some questions that might arise include:

? **Can people who are not baptized be saved?**

Yes, absolutely! Remind the children that baptism is an outward sign of something that happens inside a person's heart. Highlight that Jesus has ordained that Christians should be baptized, but they will still be saved if something prevents that.

? **Why does baptism need to happen in public?**

Explain to the children that baptism is a public declaration made before the church family. It is a great encouragement to the church and will also help the church community to support those who profess faith and also their families.

Also use this opportunity to help the children think about their own lives and how this question and answer affects them personally.

- Ask the children if there is anything they find confusing about baptism.

- Ask the children what they might say to someone who believed that the water of baptism brings salvation.

Virtue Vision

Honesty
Have ready a picture of a crucible (a pot in which metals can be melted).

Remind the children that today's Bible passage says that we will be baptized "with the Holy Spirit and fire." Ask the children what they think it might mean to be baptized with fire.

Explain that one way to think about it is to think about the purifying qualities of fire. Normally we think that fire only destroys, but

89

that is not always the case. Explain that when precious metals like gold are taken out of the ground, they have impurities in them that need to be removed. Tell the children that one of the best ways to remove these impurities is to put the raw gold into a crucible and then melt it in a hot fire. (Show picture of crucible.) The impurities would separate from the gold so that only the pure gold was left. In other words, the fire would help separate the true gold from that which was not true gold.

Tell the children that the Holy Spirit does the same thing in our lives, and baptism is a sign of that process. Just as the fire separates out the true gold, the Holy Spirit helps us to know the truth and to remove all falsehood from our lives. The Holy Spirit helps us to have honesty and integrity. Sometimes, we don't even know the lies in our lives. We believe lies that tell us we can't control our temper or lies that tell us we can be good without God's help. We may even start to tell other people these lies. When we are saved by God's grace, which is demonstrated through baptism, God begins to wash away these lies. Suggest that he may even use difficult circumstances that feel like fire to show us the truth, but in the end, we will know what is true from what is not true.

Memory Activity

Write each word of the memory verse or catechism question and answer on a separate index card. You will need one full memory verse set of cards for each team.

- Divide the children into teams.

- Read the memory verse or question and answer aloud to the children.

- Read it again, inviting the children to repeat each phrase after you.

- Read it again, inviting the children to say the entire verse along with you.

- Hand out a full set of memory verse cards to each team; make sure the words are not in order! Ask the children to put the words in the correct order. The first team to finish wins.

- Practice the memory verse together one final time.

Closing Prayer Time

Pray that the children would have great confidence in the saving power of the blood of Jesus.

Question 46

What is the Lord's Supper?

Answer

Christ commanded all Christians to eat bread and to drink from the cup in thankful remembrance of him.

Big Idea
One of the purposes of the Lord's Supper is to nurture thankful remembrance among God's people.

Aim
To help the children understand that Jesus instituted the Lord's Supper so that Christians would remember all that he achieved through his death on the cross.

Bible Passage
1 Corinthians 11:17–34

Memory Verse
"For I received from the Lord what I also delivered to you, that the Lord Jesus on the night when he was betrayed took bread, and when he had given thanks, he broke it, and said, 'This is my body which is for you. Do this in remembrance of me.' In the same way also he took the cup, after supper, saying, 'This cup is the new covenant in my blood. Do this, as often as you drink it, in remembrance of me.' For as often as you eat this bread and drink the cup, you proclaim the Lord's death until he comes." (1 Cor. 11:23–26)

Virtue
Humility

Notes

Leader's Notes

Teaching children about the Lord's Supper can be difficult and a little abstract, particularly if they have seen the sacrament but not participated in it. This lesson will explain to the children the purpose of the Lord's Supper and why it has been instituted as a sacrament in God's church. The children will understand the Lord's Supper in the context of the biblical story and will begin to comprehend the difference between the old covenant and the new covenant. This lesson should encourage an appreciation of the Lord's Supper in the children.

Things to remember when planning and teaching:

- The celebration and meaning of the Lord's Supper is generally quite abstract for many children. Be patient with the children as you seek to teach them about this sacrament and correct any misunderstandings.

- Be aware that there might be a degree of frustration among the children who would like to be actively participating in the Lord's Supper. Help them to understand and to respect their church leadership. Be sure to support the practices of your church throughout the lesson.

- Remember to mix and match the activities in the lesson to fit your time frame (see p. 12 for some sample outlines). You won't have time to do them all. Feel free to adapt each activity based on your class's strengths and weaknesses.

Leader's Prayer

Gracious Lord, thank you for instituting the Lord's Supper so I may be reminded of my union with Christ and encouraged in my faith. Thank you that I am part of the new covenant and can confidently trust in Jesus's blood as it covers me. Grant understanding to the children who will hear this lesson. May it be relevant and inspiring for them, and may they delight in understanding the sacrament of the Lord's Supper. In Jesus's name. Amen.

Leader's Tool Kit

- Q46 Catechism Recap (DL)
- Jenga blocks
- Dishtowel
- Tray
- Wine or juice
- Bread
- Cloth
- Plate or communion tray

- Communion cup or cups
- Bible
- A recording of "Behold the Lamb" (by Keith and Kristyn Getty and Stuart Townend) and a way to play it

- Paper
- Markers and crayons

Catechism Recap

Print and cut out Q46 Catechism Recap (DL). Tape a selection of the catechism questions already covered to Jenga blocks and build the Jenga tower. (Not every block needs a question.)

Divide the children into teams. Invite individual children from each team to take turns approaching the Jenga tower and attempt to remove a block (don't continue to build the tower; just place the blocks to the side once they have been removed from the tower). If the block removed has a question on it, the child can either answer the question herself or pass the question back to her team. If the team fails to correctly answer the question, another team can jump in and answer it. If they answer it correctly, they get to keep the block. The team with the most blocks whenever the tower falls wins.

Introduction to Question 46

Explain to the children that during the last week of Jesus's life, he ate the Passover meal. This is a special meal that Jewish people have celebrated every year from the time of Moses until today.

Ask the children if they know the story of the first Passover, found in Exodus 12. It is likely children will know the story; appoint one to tell it. Make sure they mention the death of the firstborn son, the blood of the lamb on the doorpost, and the unleavened bread.

Explain that every year when Jewish families celebrate Passover, they remember how the blood of the sacrificed lamb kept them from death. Jesus and his disciples were Jewish, and that is why they ate the Passover meal together. But Jesus helped them to see that this meal not only represented the lamb that had been sacrificed so long ago in Egypt. It also represented Jesus himself, the Lamb of God, who would take away the sins of the world.

Jesus told his disciples that after he died, they should remember his death by eating bread and drinking wine together. The Passover Feast helped the Jewish people remember their salvation from Egypt, and the Lord's Supper helps Christians remember our salvation from sin and death.

Notes

Introduce Question 46: "What is the Lord's Supper?" Explain to the children that the church still eats together a special meal of bread and wine to remember that Jesus laid down his life for his people and covered those who trust in him with his blood.

Activity

You will need to gather together items used in the Lord's Supper. Pick the items that are commonly used in your church, such as:

- Wine or juice
- Bread
- Cloth
- Plate or tray
- Communion cup or cups
- Bible

Place all the items on a tray.

Invite the children to come and look at the items on the table for five seconds; then cover them up quickly with a dishtowel.

Ask the children to name as many things as they can remember.

Uncover the items again and see how many items the children remembered. Tell them that this was an exercise in remembering, and the Lord's Supper is also meant to be an exercise in remembering, that is, remembering Jesus's death.

Teaching Outline

Begin the teaching time by asking for God's help. Ask that the lesson would be taught faithfully and that the children might listen well.

As you begin this teaching time remind the children that the sacraments are signs.

Read 1 Corinthians 11:17–34. Provide Bibles for the children to read along.

Remind the children that the apostle Paul was writing this letter to Christians in the city of Corinth. It seems from these verses that there was a problem among the Christians when they gathered to celebrate the Lord's Supper. Paul is rebuking some of the Christians for eating before others; he is saying that the Lord's Supper should be eaten together as the family of God.

In verse 23, Paul starts to remind the Corinthian Christians what the Lord's Supper is. Explain to the children that Paul clearly declares that the tradition of the Lord's Supper came from the Lord himself; he instituted it for his church. In these verses, Paul relates the details of the Passover meal that Jesus celebrated with his disciples on the night before he was put to death.

Invite the children to look at verses 23–25 and ask them to look at the details of what happened. Ask the children if there is anything they don't understand.

Tell the children that at this special meal, Jesus explained to his disciples what would happen to him in his death. His body would be broken and his blood would be shed. Highlight for the children that Jesus didn't just use the meal to teach the disciples but to institute a practice for his church that would help them to remember him until he comes again.

Explain that Jesus describes the breaking of bread and the drinking of wine as a sign of the new covenant. Tell the children that a new covenant means a new agreement. The new covenant is the promise that God makes with humans declaring that he will forgive sin and become friends with all those whose hearts are turned toward him. Jesus Christ is the Mediator of the new covenant, and his death on the cross is the foundation of the promise.

The Passover Feast helped the Jewish people remember how they had been delivered by the blood of the lamb. The Lord's Supper helps Christians remember we have been delivered by the blood of Jesus.

So Paul reminds the people of the new covenant that they should remember Jesus's death by eating bread and drinking wine together.

Tell the children that God's people continue to celebrate the Lord's Supper together to remember Jesus and his death on their behalf.

Conclude the teaching time by helping the children commit Question 46 and the answer to memory.

(These notes are just for guidance. Please expand or amend them to suit your own children and context. Write out your talk in your own words and include illustrations and applications that you know will connect with your children.)

Notes

 Activity ☼

You will need to be able to play a recording of "Behold the Lamb" by Keith and Kristyn Getty and Stuart Townend. Give each child a blank piece of paper along with markers and crayons.

Play "Behold the Lamb" for the children to listen to. Ask them to doodle pictures that represent the Passover Feast and the Lord's Supper. They should include words from the song that stand out to them.

This should be a time of quiet reflection; encourage the children to sit and listen.

(5) Discussion and Question Time

Some questions that might arise include:

? I've heard someone say that the bread and wine literally turn into Jesus's body and blood. Is that right?

> Explain to the children that people of the Roman Catholic faith believe that the bread and wine miraculously turn into Jesus's actual body and blood. Protestant churches do not believe there is biblical evidence for this view.

? Can everyone partake in the Lord's Supper?

> Tell the children that the Lord's Supper is for those who have trusted Christ for salvation. Explain to the children that many churches have guidelines around what age children or young people can begin to take communion. Share your church's guidelines.

? Do all Christians have to celebrate the Lord's Supper?

> Remind the children that this is one of the ordinances or sacraments of the church that Jesus instituted for the good of his people. Christians should partake in the Lord's Supper regularly. As is the case with baptism, if something prevents a Christian from taking the Lord's Supper, it does not prevent them from being saved.

Also use this opportunity to help the children think about their own lives and how this question and answer affects them personally.

- Ask the children if they look forward to participating in the Lord's Supper.

- Ask the children if there's anything about the Lord's Supper that confuses them.

(10) Virtue Vision

Humility

Ask the children what it means to be humble. Does it mean that you are weak? Does it mean that you are not very good at what you do?

Ask for a volunteer to read Philippians 2:5–8.

Help the children see that this passage clearly states that although Jesus is God—he could do anything—he chose to take the humble step of going to death on the cross. He allowed himself to be beaten and mocked, even though he could have spoken one word and put to death all of those who were tormenting him. That's an amazing example of humility.

Tell the children that people who truly understand the Lord's Supper participate in it with humility. By eating the bread and drinking from the cup, you are acknowledging that you cannot save yourself. Only the humble know that they need Jesus!

Ask the children: What is something that you cannot do alone without help from someone else?

Just as we acknowledge our limitations and need for help in these daily activities, we acknowledge on a much bigger level that we need God as our Savior when we take the Lord's Supper. It is easy to forget our need, so this sacrament helps us to remember.

Notes

Memory Activity

Print each word of the memory verse or catechism question and answer on a piece of paper, then cut each word in half. You may want to shorten it and concentrate on one verse. Hide one half of each word around your classroom.

Give every child one half of a word from the memory verse. Instruct them to find the other half of the memory verse that is hidden somewhere in the classroom. Once the children have found the other half of their word, have them put the verse or question and answer in the correct order. Read it through with the children. Then remove half of some of the words, and read through it again. Finally remove full words, and see if the children can remember the entire thing.

Closing Prayer Time

Invite the children to kneel in a posture of humility. Ask them to close their eyes and spend a few minutes praying silently, thanking Jesus for giving us the Lord's Supper.

Question 47

Does the Lord's Supper add anything to Christ's atoning work?

Answer

No, Christ died once for all.

Big Idea
There is nothing that can be added to Christ's atoning work.

Aim
To help the children confidently know that Christ was the complete and perfect sacrifice.

Bible Passage
1 Peter 3:18

Memory Verse
"For Christ also suffered once for sins, the righteous for the unrighteous, that he might bring us to God." (1 Pet. 3:18)

Virtue
Perseverance

Leader's Notes

This question provides another opportunity to teach the children about the sacrament of the Lord's Supper and also reiterates for them that nothing can be added to Jesus's atoning death on the cross. This lesson aims to help the children understand that Jesus Christ was the complete and perfect sacrifice sufficient for all time and all people who turn to him in repentance and faith. There is a delicate balance required in this lesson to continue to communicate the importance of the sacraments in the church while also teaching the sufficiency of Christ Jesus.

Things to remember when planning and teaching:

- The children will have encountered this truth in various ways throughout the curriculum and in other places. Work hard to make the lesson relevant and dynamic for those entrusted into your care.

- Continue to work hard to make those things that are abstract understandable to the children.

- Remember to mix and match the activities in the lesson to fit your time frame (see p. 12 for some sample outlines). You won't have time to do them all. Feel free to adapt each activity based on your class's strengths and weaknesses.

Leader's Prayer

Saving God, thank you that in your great kindness and mercy you sent Christ to die once for all. I praise you that when I join with my brothers and sisters around the Lord's table, I remember all that you have achieved for me through Christ. Thank you that his death is sufficient for my salvation. Grant understanding to the children who will hear this lesson. May they grow ever more confident in the truth of the gospel, and may you be at work bringing many to faith and maturity. In Jesus's name. Amen.

Leader's Tool Kit

- Q47 Catechism Recap (DL)
- Q47 Mural Template (RB), one per child
- Q47 Letter from a Concerned Friend (RB), one copy
- Envelopes
- Paper
- Pens
- Duplo or Mega Bloks (forty blocks)

Catechism Recap

Print out and cut up Q47 Catechism Recap (DL). Mix up the sheets and place them upside down in a grid on the floor.

This is a memory game. Invite the children to come forward and turn over two pieces of paper. The aim of the game is to find a matching question and answer. If no match is found, the pieces of paper are turned back over on the floor. The children must try to remember the details as the pages are turned over so that they can find a match when it comes to their turn. The child with the most matches wins!

Notes

Introduction to Question 47

Ask the children if they can figure out what all these experiences have in common:

1. Having a first birthday

2. Donating a kidney

3. Seeing Hale-Bopp Comet

4. Regrowing a full set of teeth

5. Dying

These are all things that a person can do only once. (People have two kidneys, so they can donate only one kidney and stay alive. Hale-Bopp appears roughly only every 2,500 years. After you lose your baby teeth, you grow only one more set of teeth.)

Tell the children that this lesson will focus on something that Jesus could do only once, and that was suffer death on the cross. Explain to the children that Jesus's death was all-sufficient, perfect, and complete.

Introduce Question 47: "Does the Lord's Supper add anything to Christ's atoning work?" Explain to the children that people are sometimes tempted to believe that things like the Lord's Supper can save them, but that the Bible clearly states that absolutely nothing can be added to the death that Jesus died, once for all.

Activity

Give each child a copy of Q47 Mural Template (RB) and crayons.

Ask the children to design and draw a mural that would creatively make the point that Christ died once for all.

⑮ Teaching Outline

You will need a copy of Q47 Letter from a Concerned Friend (RB) and an envelope with your mailing address on it.

Begin the teaching time by asking for God's help. Ask that the lesson would be taught faithfully and that the children might listen well.

Tell the children that in previous lessons, you've read letters that the apostles wrote to strengthen the churches. Today you have a letter that you'd like to share with them. It's not from the Bible, but it's the kind of letter that the apostles often wrote to Christians in the first century. Take Q47 Letter from a Concerned Friend (RB) out of the envelope and read it to the class.

Read 1 Peter 3:18. Provide Bibles for the children to read along. Encourage them to read the verse for themselves. Once the children have had a chance to read it, repeat it out loud together.

Explain to the children that this verse clearly speaks about the great suffering that Christ endured in order to reconcile sinners to God. Peter explains that Jesus died once, and in that death, Jesus achieved everything necessary for their salvation. Nothing more, nothing different, or nothing new needs to be added to Jesus's once-for-all-time death.

Ask the children what adding something onto Jesus's death (like thinking you must take the Lord's Supper to be saved) says about what Jesus achieved on the cross. Tell the children that Jesus + Something = Nothing, but Jesus + Nothing = Everything!

Peter clearly declares that Jesus died once and for all to forgive sins, to make the unrighteous righteous and secure their membership in God's eternal family.

Conclude the teaching time by helping the children commit Question 47 and the answer to memory.

(These notes are just for guidance. Please expand or amend them to suit your own children and context. Write out your talk in your own words and include illustrations and applications that you know will connect with your children.)

---

⑩ Activity

You will need paper, pens, and envelopes.

Invite the children to write a letter to themselves. Encourage them to write things that they'll need to be reminded of in a few weeks' time. Ask them if there are things they could write down that they might otherwise forget about the Lord's Supper and baptism. Ask them what the questions about the sacraments have helped them to learn about God. Allow the children sufficient time to write a brief letter and place it in an envelope. Ask the children to seal and address it. Tell them that you will mail it back to them in a few weeks' time.

Discussion and Question Time

Some questions that might arise include:

? Are you saying the Lord's Supper isn't that important?

> No! Explain to the children that the Lord's Supper is important; that's why Jesus instituted it in his church. But by itself it cannot make people into Christians.

? Why do some churches call the Lord's Supper "Communion"?

> When people eat and drink the bread and wine together as a church family, they come together into community with one another and into closer fellowship with God.

Also use this opportunity to help the children think about their own lives and how this question and answer affects them personally.

- Ask the children if they believe in their own hearts Christ died once for all.

- Ask the children if they believe that Jesus's death on the cross is sufficient.

- Ask the children if they will remember that the Lord's Supper strengthens Christians but doesn't make Christians.

Virtue Vision

Perseverance

Explain to the children that 1 Peter 3:18 comes in the middle of Peter's letter that is mostly about suffering. Explain to the children that suffering is to be expected as part of the Christian life, and the truth that Christ died once for all should help people endure suffering and keep going in their Christian life.

Peter says that although life may be full of difficult battles, Christ has won! He has secured the Christian's heavenly home and has brought us into God's family.

Ask the children how they feel about suffering. Ask what would help them persevere through suffering. Ask them if having an eternal home to look forward to makes a difference.

Memory Activity

You will need blocks, such as Duplo or Mega Bloks. Print out two copies of the memory verse or catechism question and answer, cut up the words individually, and stick a word to each block, making two sets of blocks. If you are using the memory verse, you will need forty blocks total (include the reference as a block). If you're doing the catechism question and answer, you will need thirty-two blocks total.

Divide the children into two teams. Give each team a pile of blocks and invite them

Notes

to build them into a memory verse tower. The first team to complete the tower should win a prize. The children will need to put the bricks into the right order and then construct the tower.

Once the tower has been constructed, read through the memory verse or catechism question and answer with the children several times; you can remove blocks to make the task harder.

Closing Prayer Time

Invite the children to pray that they will never put their trust in anything but Christ for their salvation. Lead them in giving thanks that Jesus died once for all!

Question 48

What is the church?

Answer

A community elected for eternal life and united by faith, who love, follow, learn from, and worship God together.

Big Idea

God has called people with saving faith in Jesus to unite together as a body called the church.

Aim

To help the children to understand what the church is as well as its purpose.

Bible Passage

2 Thessalonians 2:13–17

Memory Verse

"But we ought always to give thanks to God for you, brothers beloved by the Lord, because God chose you as the firstfruits to be saved, through sanctification by the Spirit and belief in the truth." (2 Thess. 2:13)

Virtue

Love

Leader's Notes

If you ask children what the church is, most will describe a building. Many children have an undeveloped understanding of the church. Adults often inadvertently aid the confusion by speaking about going to church or an event happening at church. However, the church is not a building! It is a people chosen by God and called together into one body. In order to love and serve the people of God, otherwise known as the church, children need to have a rich and robust understanding of it. This lesson aims to help correct any misunderstandings children may have about church and also to help them see the importance of the church for God's plan.

Things to remember when planning and teaching:

- Use language that encourages children to think of the church as people rather than a building.

- Endeavour to help the children understand that the church exists for God, its members, and those outside.

- Communicate to the children that the church is for all those who have put their faith and trust in Jesus— and that includes children!

- Remember to mix and match the activities in the lesson to fit your time frame (see p. 12 for some sample outlines). You won't have time to do them all. Feel free to adapt each activity based on your class's strengths and weaknesses.

Leader's Prayer

Sovereign God, thank you for instituting the church for your people on earth. I praise you for uniting believers together in both the universal and local church. Thank you for the church that I am privileged to belong to, for the opportunity to enjoy fellowship with brothers and sisters in Christ, and the gift of being discipled through your Word. Grant understanding to the children who will hear this lesson. May they develop a deeper and richer understanding of what the church is and rejoice in being part of a church family. In Jesus's name. Amen.

Leader's Tool Kit

- Lots of different individual types of candy, one piece for each child in the class (it is probably best to avoid candy with nuts in case a member of your class is allergic).

- Q48 Illustrations of the Church (RB), cut out

- Paper doll chains made from Q48 Paper Chain Template (RB), at least one per child

- Shoebox or similar size box

- Markers

- Whiteboard and marker

- Sticky notes, two different colors

- Scotch tape

Catechism Recap

Put as many different types of candy as you can in a bucket; ideally there should be a different type of candy for each child in the group. Give each piece of candy a number. Make a key, but don't show it to the children.

Invite each of the children to pick a piece of candy from the bucket. Give the children the opportunity to swap with other people. Once all the children have settled on the piece of candy they'd like, tell them that they can keep the candy if they can correctly remember the question and answer that is linked to that particular candy:

For example:

Hershey Bar = 1	What is our only hope in life and death?

Sweet Tart = 2	What is God?
Peppermint = 3	How many persons are there in God?
M&M's = 4	How and why did God create us?

Surprise the children by allowing them to ask for help from the other children in the class; this will link nicely into the concept of the church and the unity that is found in the body of Christ. Make sure every child has a piece of candy at the end of the recap (to be eaten later, only with parents' permission).

⑤ Introduction to Question 48

Cut out the Q48 Illustrations of the Church (RB) and pass them around. Hold back the illustration of a church building.

Ask the children to examine the first set of pictures (body, bride, group of people, flock of sheep) and see if they can find anything in common in the pictures (be prepared for some odd answers!).

Introduce Question 48: "What is the church?" Explain to the children that the commonality between the pictures is that the Bible uses each of the pictures to describe what the church is like: a body, a bride, a chosen people, and a flock.

Explain to the children that we often think about the church as a building—now show the picture of the church building—but when we look at what the Bible says about the church, it definitely isn't talking about a building. The Bible always talks about the church as people rather than a place.

⑩ Activity ☼

Using Q48 Paper Chain Template (RB), make lots of paper doll chains (enough so that each child can have at least one chain), and place them in a box along with lots of markers.

Tell the children that they are going to make a model of a church, and that you have all the supplies they will need in the box. Ask them to guess what kind of supplies you have in the box.

They may guess popsicle sticks, glue, or other supplies you would need to model a building.

Open the box and explain that, since the church is made of people, a model of the church needs to be made of people.

Pass out paper chains and markers to each child, and ask them to draw faces and clothes to represent the people who make up a church. They should include young and old and people of every ethnicity. (If the children get detailed in their work, you may need to set the project aside and come back to it after the lesson.)

⑮ Teaching Outline

Begin the teaching time by asking for God's help. Ask that the lesson would be taught faithfully and that the children might listen well.

Ask the children if they enjoy the process of being chosen to be on a team. Some children love it because they'll be picked first; others despise the process because they know they'll be chosen last. The process of being chosen for a team is usually influenced by athletic ability, popularity, or relationships—that's what makes it such a tricky process. The Bible tells us that the way God builds his church is by choosing people to be on his team, to become members of his family. But being on God's team has nothing to do with how good we are at anything, how popular we are, or who our friends are. It has everything to do with Jesus Christ and his sacrificial death and resurrection on our behalf. God calls us to put our trust in Jesus for forgiveness of sin and the gift of new life; when we do that, we automatically become members of God's church.

Read 2 Thessalonians 2:13–17.
Provide Bibles for the children to read along with you.

Introduce the children to Paul's letter to the Thessalonians; explain that Paul was writing to the church in Thessalonica, and that meant he was writing to the people and not to a building!

Tell the children that God's purpose in his world is to draw together a people for himself. In this passage, we can see how God works. The first thing to notice in verse 13 is that God chose the people who became part of his church in Thessalonica, and he chose them to be saved. They are saved from God's anger and judgment; they are saved to faith in Jesus and the hope of eternal life. Paul says this process occurs as the Holy Spirit works in their hearts as they hear the truth of the gospel and realize they need a personal Savior. This is God's gospel call to share in the joy and hope of being a member of God's family. God is still building his church today. He is gathering together a

chosen people for himself, and the process is just the same. God chooses and calls people, and by his Spirit opens their eyes to the truth of the gospel.

Explain to the children that when we are united to Jesus, we become united to one another in the church. This means we get new brothers and sisters! As Christians, we have brothers and sisters all over the world, most of whom we'll never even meet. That's the big *universal* church that includes all Christians. Members of that universal church meet in smaller groups where we live, and that's called the *local* church.

Ask the children what kind of people, then, are members of the church. The answer is, all sorts! Young and old, rich and poor, people from all different ethnicities, and people with different jobs. The church is like a big family Christmas dinner, where there are children and old folks, teenagers and young adults all gathered together around the one table.

In a letter that Paul wrote to the church in Corinth, he described the church as a body (1 Corinthians 12). A body is made up of all different parts, but each part is essential for the body to work well. The church is just the same; we are all different, but when we come together to love each other and serve with the gifts God has given us, the church works well.

God desires for his church to do three things:

Notes

1. To love and worship God

2. To love and encourage each other as we live for God

3. To love those outside the church and show them the grace of God

Help the children to understand that coming together as members of God's church is really important. The church is where we learn to love God more, where we can love and encourage one another well, and where we can understand how to love

those in the world in the same sacrificial way that Jesus loved us.

Finish the teaching time by helping the children commit Question 48 and the answer to memory.

(These notes are just for guidance. Please expand or amend them to suit your own children and context. Write out your talk in your own words and include illustrations and applications that you know will connect with your children.)

Activity

Give the children pieces of paper and markers.

Ask the children to design the cover of a book about the church. They can choose the title

and create the cover art. Encourage them to think about the way the Bible portrays the church and depict that in some way.

Discussion and Question Time

Some questions that might arise include:

? Can people who do not trust in Jesus be members of God's church?

Explain that people who do not trust in Jesus can come to the church building and discover more about Jesus and God. They may even pretend to be a Christian. But for God to consider people members of his church, they must trust in him for salvation.

? Aren't there some countries where it's illegal for Christians to meet together?

Tell the children that when it is illegal for some Christians to meet

together, they often do so in secret. This is how important it is to come together as the church.

Also use this opportunity to help the children think about their own lives and how this question and answer affects them personally.

- How can they better love the brothers and sisters in their church?

- How might they explain to someone what the church is?

- How might they pray for their church family?

Virtue Vision

Notes

Love

Create an ideas board. You can make it on a whiteboard by drawing a large light bulb. Have ready two different colors of sticky notes and some pens.

Ask the children to think of ways they could love their church family better. Encourage them to write down their ideas on a sticky note, and then stick it on the ideas board. Remind them that there are all different types of people at church and that they should think of ways to love all kinds of people.

On a different color sticky note, ask the children to write down some ways they might be able to show God's love to those outside the church. Have them stick their ideas on the ideas board.

Thinks of ways you can help the children to put some of their ideas into practice.

Memory Activity

Cut the memory verse or catechism question and answer into individual words. Put Scotch tape on the back of each word, and stick the words up on the wall in order.

Invite the children to read through the memory verse or catechism question and answer with you. Take one word away, and invite the class to read the verse again. Remove one word at a time until there are no words left. Say the verse together from memory!

Closing Prayer

Encourage the children to thank God for his church and ask him to help them love and serve his people in the church more.

Question 49

Where is Christ now?

Answer

Christ rose bodily from the grave on the third day after his death and is seated at the right hand of the Father.

Big Idea
Jesus Christ rose from the grave and, in his resurrected body, ascended into heaven.

Aim
To help the children understand that Jesus lives and reigns even though he is not on earth.

Bible Passage
Ephesians 1:15–23

Memory Verse
"He raised him from the dead and seated him at his right hand in the heavenly places, far above all rule and authority and power and dominion, and above every name that is named, not only in this age but also in the one to come." (Eph. 1:20–21)

Virtue
Perseverance

Leader's Notes

Children can understand that Jesus had a body while he lived on earth because they are familiar with his earthly ministry. They may not have considered that Jesus's resurrection and ascension involved a physical body. Children appreciate the concrete, but struggle a little more with abstract thoughts. This question will introduce the children to the fact that Jesus rose from the dead physically and should help them see that Jesus's bodily resurrection and ascension are core doctrines for Christians. This lesson aims to help children understand the physical nature of Jesus's resurrection and ascension, to clarify for them where Jesus is now, and also to show how the resurrection gives Christians great hope.

Things to remember when planning and teaching:

- This may be a new concept for some of the children. Work hard to creatively help them understand the reality that Jesus is now in heaven at the right hand of God.

- Be sure to explain that the bodily resurrection of Jesus is key to the Christian faith.

- Remember to mix and match the activities in the lesson to fit your time frame (see p. 12 for some sample outlines). You won't have time to do them all. Feel free to adapt each activity based on your class's strengths and weaknesses.

Leader's Prayer

Powerful God, thank you for displaying your greatness by raising Jesus from the dead and seating him at your right hand in heaven. May he receive my rightful praise and honor as ruler over all. Grant understanding to the children who will hear this lesson. May they be thrilled by your power, encouraged by the bodily resurrection and ascension of Jesus, and filled with hope as they understand the implications for each of us. In Jesus's name. Amen.

Leader's Tool Kit

- Jumbo craft (popsicle) sticks (53)

- Permanent marker

- Timer (a cell phone timer will do)

- Cup

- Q49 Illustrations of Famous Homes (RB)

- List of Bible references

- Pens and paper

- Q49 Seats of Power (RB), one per child

- Sticky Tack or tape

- The memory verse or catechism question and answer written on a poster

Catechism Recap

Write numbers one to forty-eight on the jumbo craft sticks. Place the sticks in a cup with the number side down so the children can't see what they're pulling out. Also place five sticks with the word RESET written on them into the cup. Set a timer for five minutes.

Invite the children to take turns pulling a stick from the cup. Challenge them to see if they can remember the question and answer that relates to the number. If they get it right (or come close), they get to keep the stick. The person with the most sticks when the timer goes off gets a prize. Explain to the children that there's a catch: if someone pulls a RESET stick from the cup, everyone must return their sticks to the cup and start over (but keep the time running).

Introduction to Question 49

Have on hand the Q49 Illustrations of Famous Homes (RB)

- *The White House*

- *Cinderella's Castle*

- *Gingerbread House from Hansel and Gretel*

- *Rapunzel's Tower*

Show the children the homes one by one and invite them to guess who resides in each one. Tell the children that each house is where someone lives; it is the physical location that they inhabit. Introduce the children to Question 49: "Where is Christ now?" Explain to the children that this question will help them to understand where Jesus Christ has been since leaving this earth.

Activity

Give each child a Bible. Print out several copies of the following list of references (Q48 Activity [DL]):

- *John 14:28*

- *Luke 22:69*

- *Colossians 3:1*

- *Hebrews 1:3*

- *1 Peter 1:8*

Divide the children into small groups, and give each group a list of references. Appoint

Notes

a notetaker for each group and give him or her a pen and paper. Tell the children to take turns looking up and reading the references while the notetaker writes down everything these verses tell you about where Jesus is now. Once the children have had some time to read the verses, ask them to share what they've discovered. Particularly highlight for the children the truth that Jesus was resurrected bodily and that he now lives in heaven seated at the right hand of God the Father.

Teaching Outline

Begin the teaching time by asking for God's help. Ask that the lesson would be taught faithfully and that the children might listen well.

Read Ephesians 1:15–23. Provide Bibles for the children to read along.

Explain that this part of the letter to the Ephesians is actually a prayer. The writer of the letter, Paul, is praying that the Ephesian Christians would know more and more about the power and greatness of God.

Ask the children to identify people they think are really powerful. Ask them why they perceive some people to be powerful.

Explain to the children that there is no one as powerful as God, and this passage highlights just how powerful God is. God displayed his incredible power when he raised Jesus from the dead on the third day after he was crucified. Show the children where Paul says this in verses 19 and 20. God the Father also did more than raise Jesus from the dead; he caused him to ascend into heaven! Emphasize to the children that when Jesus rose from the dead, he had a body. People walked and talked with Jesus,

and he ate food. In those respects, his body was just like ours. But after his resurrection, he could do things we could not do, such as walk through walls!

It is probably worth mentioning to the children that the bodily resurrection of Jesus is one of the most disputed but also most investigated aspects of Christianity. Christians throughout the ages have confidently believed that Jesus was raised from the dead and that we too will one day receive a resurrected body.

Remind the children that Jesus stayed on earth for only forty days after his resurrection. Jesus (in his body) went back to heaven to sit at the right hand of God the Father. Ask the children what they think it means to sit at someone's right hand. Explain that it is a position of special honor. When Jesus sat at God's right hand, God gave him authority over all things.

Ask the children what Jesus was made the head of in verse 22. Jesus is head of the church, which is described in verse 23 as Christ's body. God gives his precious Son Jesus to be the head of the church with all his

Notes

power and authority. Ask the children what role the head plays for a body.

Conclude the teaching time by helping the children commit Question 49 and the answer to memory.

(These notes are just for guidance. Please expand or amend them to suit your own children and context. Write out your talk in your own words and include illustrations and applications that you know will connect with your children.)

Activity

Give a copy of Q49 Seats of Power (RB) to each student.

Tell the children to write in the blank what kind of person would sit in each seat. Answers (clockwise): king, judge, Son of God, president.

Discussion and Question Time

Some questions that might arise include:

? If Jesus is in heaven, how can he be with us here on earth?

Explain to the children that, bodily, Jesus is seated at the right hand of God the Father in heaven, but he also promised to be with all Christians through the Holy Spirit.

? Has Jesus always had a body?

No. Though Jesus has always existed, he was not given a body until he became man and was born in Bethlehem. This is

why John 1:14 says, "The Word became flesh and dwelt among us."

Also use this opportunity to help the children think about their own lives and how this question and answer affects them personally.

- Ask the children if they've ever thought about where Jesus lives now.

- Ask the children if they believe in the bodily resurrection of Jesus.

- Ask if understanding Jesus's resurrection affects how they think about death.

Virtue Vision

Perseverance

Visit the website www.prisoneralert.com, *a site operated by Voice of the Martyrs. Find details about a Christian who is currently in prison for his or her faith.*

Tell the children that in Ephesians 1:18 Paul prays that the Ephesians would know the hope that they had been called to and the glorious inheritance of the saints. Explain that Paul is referring to all the blessings that

Christians have in knowing and trusting Jesus both in this life and in eternal life.

Explain to the children that understanding the Christian hope helps Christians persevere in life. We know that Jesus has not left us forever. One day he is going to return to take us to be with him forever.

Ask the children what it means for someone who has been imprisoned for his or her faith to persevere. Help them to see that not denying Christ is one way to persevere. Another is to hope in eternal life, even if you know you may never make it out of prison alive.

Spend a few minutes praying for the imprisoned Christian. Pray that he or she would know that Christ is seated at the right hand of God, and that this knowledge would lead to perseverance.

Memory Activity

You will need a ball and the memory verse or catechism question and answer on a piece of poster board. Have some pieces of paper and Sticky Tack or tape handy that you can place over the words of the verse to cover them up.

- Put the memory verse or catechism question and answer on a poster on the wall.
- Divide the children into two teams.
- Have the children read through the memory verse with you several times.
- Gradually cover up the words of the memory verse.

- Arrange the teams in two straight lines facing each other.

Throw the ball to a child, and tell him or her to say the first word of the memory verse or catechism question. That child will then throw the ball to a child on the opposite team, who is expected to say the second word of the memory verse. Continue down the line. If a child doesn't remember the word or gets it wrong, he or she should throw the ball and then sit down. The team with the most team members still standing at the end wins the game.

Closing Prayer Time

Pray that the children might rejoice that Jesus is seated at the right hand of the Father in heaven and that they might know the hope of eternity that the resurrection brings.

What does Christ's resurrection mean for us?

Answer

Christ triumphed over sin and death so that all who trust in him are raised to new life in this world and to everlasting life in the world to come.

Big Idea

The resurrection confirms God's satisfaction with Christ's substitutionary death and assures Christians of the hope of resurrection.

Aim

To help the children understand that Christians can confidently expect to be resurrected because of Jesus's triumph over death.

Bible Passage

1 Thessalonians 4:13–18

Memory Verse

"But we do not want you to be uninformed, brothers, about those who are asleep, that you may not grieve as others do who have no hope. For since we believe that Jesus died and rose again, even so, through Jesus, God will bring with him those who have fallen asleep." (1 Thess. 4:13–14)

Virtue

Hope

Leader's Notes

The resurrection is a key doctrine for Christians. We need to grasp not only the fact of Jesus's bodily resurrection but also its implications. This lesson will reinforce Question 49 and the belief that Jesus rose physically from the dead and physically ascended into heaven. It will also help the children to understand the personal implications of the resurrection, namely that God was satisfied with Jesus's substitutionary atoning death on the cross, and thus we know that Jesus's death was sufficient to pay for the sin of all who trust in him. The bodily resurrection of Jesus also confirms that all those who are in Christ will be raised.

Things to remember when planning and teaching:

- Remember that some of these concepts are fairly abstract and may take longer for the younger children to understand.

- Some children will struggle to understand eternity and the significance of the new heavens and the new earth. Be patient in helping them to understand Christian hope.

- This lesson engages with death. Be aware that this can be a difficult subject for children. Be particularly vigilant for those who have experienced the death of someone close to them.

- Remember to mix and match the activities in the lesson to fit your time frame (see p. 12 for some sample outlines). You won't have time to do them all. Feel free to adapt each activity based on your class's strengths and weaknesses.

Leader's Prayer

Almighty God, I praise you for the truth of the resurrection. Thank you that, by raising Jesus from the dead, you declared his death a satisfactory atonement for sin. I rejoice that I can joyfully anticipate my own resurrection and the hope of an eternity in your presence. Grant understanding to the children who will hear this lesson. May they fully grasp the personal significance of the resurrection. In Jesus's name. Amen.

Leader's Tool Kit

- Q50 Catechism Recap (DL)
- Candy
- Wrapping paper
- Tape

- Music that can be stopped and started
- A bunch of inflated balloons, two or three times the number of children in your class

- Markers
- Q50 Word Search (RB)
- Pictures of Joni Eareckson Tada
- Whiteboard and marker

Catechism Recap

Prepare a pass-the-present game. Wrap an assortment of candy in ten layers of paper. In between each layer put a catechism question from Q50 Catechism Recap (DL) and a small piece of candy.

Explain to the children that you're going to play pass the present. The game begins by the passing of the present in time with the music and stops with someone when the music stops playing. The child who has the present can unwrap one layer and see the candy and the question. Children get to keep the candy (to be eaten later, only with a parent's permission) if they answer the question correctly. If they are unable to answer the question, someone else can have the opportunity to answer and win the candy. The music is then restarted and so the game continues until all layers have been unwrapped.

Introduction to Question 50

Ask the children, "What one thing can every single person be certain about in life?" Let them spend some time guessing, and if they don't get it, explain to them that it is death. There may be lots of things that people would like to happen in their lives, but in reality, there is only one thing that is predictable about every human life: everyone will die.

Explain that people generally don't like thinking about death. We often try to hide death. Cemeteries are hidden behind high walls, and death is described as "passing away" or "crossing over."

Tell the children that it's very important for Christians to think about death, because what Christians believe about death affects how they think about life. People who believe this life is all there is will be concerned to make the most of it, living primarily for pleasure, success, and happiness. Christians, however, understand that this life is not all there is. Christians believe in eternal life and should live with eternity in mind. That should make them stand out among those who think that there is nothing after death.

Notes

Introduce the children to Question 50: "What does Christ's resurrection mean for us?" Explain to the children that this question will help them understand how Jesus's resurrection should shape and influence their lives.

Activity

Point out to the children that this week's catechism answer says Jesus *triumphed* over sin and death. Ask the children whether triumph means he was only slightly better than sin and death. Does it mean that he almost defeated death, but not quite? No! Triumph is a decisive defeat!

Bring out the balloons and markers. Ask the children to write SIN and DEATH on the balloons. Tell them that to help them remember how decisively Jesus triumphed over death, the class is now going to pop every single balloon! Have fun popping the balloons and celebrating the resurrection!

Teaching Outline

Begin the teaching time by asking for God's help. Ask that the lesson would be taught faithfully and that the children might listen well.

Read 1 Thessalonians 4:13–18. Provide Bibles for the children to read along.

Explain to the children that Paul writes these words to the Thessalonian Christians for three reasons, and each reason can be found in this passage.

1. So that they will not be confused about what happens to Christians who die and so that the knowledge and understanding of what does happen to Christians when they die will help them to live differently from those who aren't Christians.

2. So that they will be able to have hope even when someone they know dies.

3. So that they would be able to help each other by reminding one another about their shared hope.

Explain to the children that Paul restates the core of the gospel to the Thessalonians to encourage them to have hope. In verse 14 he says, "We believe that Jesus died and rose again." Tell the children that the way people use the word *hope* is different from the way the Bible uses the word *hope*.

Ask the children what people like to hope for. A new bike? No homework? A trip to Disney World? Explain to the children that people hope for things but they have no idea whether they will come to fruition. To have Christian hope means to have confidence God will raise us from the dead, and that hope is based on God's Word.

Explain to the children that Christians know that, one day, either Jesus will return, or they will die. All Christians can know with certainty that they will spend forever with him.

Paul says that because of Jesus's resurrection, all Christians can confidently believe that one day they too will be raised from death. Jesus provides proof that there is life beyond the grave, and his triumph over sin and death guarantees that all who put their trust in him for the forgiveness of sin will be raised to everlasting life. Explain to the children that when Jesus rose again on the third day, it was the public announcement that God was fully satisfied with the sacrificial death of his Son.

Conclude the teaching time by helping the children commit Question 50 and the answer to memory.

(These notes are just for guidance. Please expand or amend them to suit your own children and context. Write out your talk in your own words and include illustrations and applications that you know will connect with your children.)

Notes

Activity

You will need a copy of the Q50 Word Search and some markers

Give each child a copy of the word search and have them search for the words that make up the answer to Question 50.

Say the question and answer together when the children have finished the word search.

Discussion and Question Time

Some questions that might arise include:

? What happens to those who aren't Christians when they die?

Explain to the children that everyone will be resurrected, but only those who have put their faith and trust in Jesus during their life will enter into eternity with Jesus. Those who didn't put their faith and trust in Jesus will face judgment and eternal separation from God in hell.

You may want to refer back to Question 28 for any discussions that may arise about those who die apart from Christ.

? But can we really know for certain that we will be resurrected like Jesus?

Reassure the children by telling them that we can be confident that God will raise us from the dead because he has raised Jesus! Jesus is described as the firstfruits, meaning he is the first to be raised, which tells us that there will be more resurrections to come.

Also use this opportunity to help the children think about their own lives and how this question and answer affects them personally.

- Ask the children how Christian hope should affect the life of a Christian.

Should it help us face anxiety about death? Can anyone or anything threaten our eternal destiny?

- Ask the children what they think grieving with hope means.

Virtue Vision

Hope

You will need some pictures of Joni Eareckson Tada to show the children

Tell the children a little bit about Joni Eareckson Tada.

Joni is a woman who had a diving accident when she was seventeen years old that left her paralyzed from the neck down. After a significant struggle to come to terms with her paralysis, Joni finally believed that God had not forgotten her, and that he could use her for his glory. She started a Christian ministry to testify to God's grace and kindness and to point others to Jesus.

Explain to the children that one of the things Joni thinks about a lot is heaven and the new creation. Read these two quotes from Joni's book *Heaven: Your Real Home* to the children:

> I still can hardly believe it. I, with shriveled, bent fingers, atrophied

muscles, gnarled knees, and no feeling from the shoulders down, will one day have a new body, light, bright, and clothed in righteousness—powerful and dazzling. . . . It's easy for me to "be joyful in hope," as it says in Romans 12:12, and that's exactly what I've been doing for the past twenty-odd years. My assurance of heaven is so alive that I've been making dates with friends to do all sorts of fun things once we get our new bodies. . . .

> I don't take these appointments lightly. I'm convinced these things will really happen.[1]

Explain to the children that the Christian hope makes a huge difference to Joni's life. She knows that when she is raised from the dead, she will be given a new body that can do all the things her paralyzed body cannot.

Ask the children how Christian hope might affect how they live.

---

1. Joni Eareckson Tada, *Heaven: Your Real Home* (Grand Rapids, MI: Zondervan, 1995), 53, 55.

Memory Activity

You will need a large piece of paper or a whiteboard to write on.

Write out the memory verse or catechism question and answer without vowels. Invite the children to suggest where the vowels should go. Once all the vowels have been inserted, read the memory verse through several times with the children.

Closing Prayer Time

Invite the children to pray, giving thanks for the resurrection and for Christian hope.

Question 51

Of what advantage to us is Christ's ascension?

Answer

Christ is now advocating for us in the presence of his Father and also sends us his Spirit.

Big Idea
The risen and ascended Christ is enthroned in heaven and acts on behalf of his people.

Aim
To help the children understand what Jesus is doing now.

Bible Passage
Romans 8:3–39

Memory Verse
"Who is to condemn? Christ Jesus is the one who died—more than that, who was raised—who is at the right hand of God, who indeed is interceding for us." (Rom. 8:34)

Virtue
Hope

Leader's Notes

When children think about the work of the triune God, they usually think about God the Father rather than the ongoing work of God the Son. They may have some understanding of the work of the Holy Spirit, but are perhaps slightly confused about where the risen and ascended Jesus fits in. This lesson will help the children understand what Jesus Christ is doing now in heaven. It will begin to help them understand the role that God the Son now occupies in the world and in the lives of individual Christians. This lesson aims to equip the children with a fuller understanding of the work of the ascended Christ.

Things to remember when planning and teaching:

- Some of these concepts are abstract and will need to be explained well for the children to understand.

- Emphasize the importance of the work of the ascended Christ; help the children to see why this doctrine matters.

- The lesson should bring great confidence and joy to Christian children as they understand more fully the role and work of the ascended Christ in their lives.

- Remember to mix and match the activities in the lesson to fit your time frame (see p. 12 for some sample outlines). You won't have time to do them all. Feel free to adapt each activity based on your class's strengths and weaknesses.

Leader's Prayer

Loving God, thank you that when Jesus Christ ascended back into heaven, you sent the Holy Spirit to indwell each believer. Thank you that Jesus is intimately involved in my life both through the work of the Spirit and also his ongoing work on my behalf from his seat at the right hand of the Father. Grant understanding to the children who will hear this lesson. May they understand the work of the risen and ascended Christ and rejoice in the knowledge that he is their Advocate and Intercessor. In Jesus's Name. Amen.

Leader's Tool Kit

- Q51 Catechism Recap (DL)

- Paper

- Markers

- A bowl

- A waste basket or bucket

- Q51 Advocate Required! (RB)
  (If you have more than eighteen
  children, you will need two copies.)

Notes

🕙 **Catechism Recap**

Have paper and markers ready, along with a bucket or waste basket. Print out Q51 Catechism Recap (DL).

Divide the children into small groups. Give each group eight pieces of paper and a marker.

Explain to the children that in the bowl are the answers to eight catechism questions. The aim of the game is for them to quickly write down the question that goes with the answer. Draw one of the eight answers from the bowl and read it aloud. Give the teams two minutes to write down the question. Once the two minutes is up, read out the question. The teams that have correctly identified the question may send a representative to a marked point in the classroom to crumple up their piece of paper and shoot for the basket. Repeat until all answers have been drawn from the bowl. The team with the most scores in the basket wins the game.

🕔 **Introduction to Question 51**

Explain to the children that whenever a country receives a new king or queen, there is an enthronement ceremony when the monarch is given the charge to rule the country and care for the people. Tell the children that Jesus's ascension results in his enthronement as heavenly King. He has completed the mission that God set for him on earth and now reigns as Lord while seated at the right hand of God the Father. Introduce Question 51: "Of what advantage to us is Christ's ascension?" Explain to the children that just as a human king or queen strives to look after his or her people, so Jesus works tirelessly to care for his people. Tell the children that this question will help them understand a little more about what Jesus is doing right now.

Activity

Ask the children if they've ever heard the expression "friends in high places." Ask them what it means. It means that you know someone in a position of power, who can get things done. If you need something, you could call on your friends in high places, and they would have the power to help you.

Tell the children you are going to tell them about some friends in high places. Give them the following clues:

- I have a friend who works in an important place. A high fence surrounds it. She doesn't live in this place, but someone else does. She sees the president nearly every day. Where does my friend work? (Answer: The White House)

- I have a friend who gets to see movies before they come to theaters. He is very good at drawing and works with lots of actors. He also works with a large mouse. What company does my friend work for? (Answer: Disney)

- I have a friend who wears a uniform to work. He wears stars on his shoulder. He could send an army to rescue me if I were captured. What is my friend? (Answer: An Army General)

- I have a friend who can fly across the country any time she wants. She can get into the cockpit of a plane, even during takeoff and landing. What is my friend? (Answer: A Pilot)

- I have a friend who can hear and see everything in the world. He is always ready to help me. He is seated beside his Father, who is the King of everything. Who is my friend? (Answer: Jesus!)

Teaching Outline

Begin the teaching time by asking for God's help. Ask that the lesson would be taught faithfully and that the children might listen well.

Explain to the children that Jesus is actively ruling with full authority from the right hand of God the Father in heaven. Jesus is Lord over all and is working unceasingly for the good of his people and the glory of God.

Ask the children if they know what an advocate is. Explain that it is a person who fights for the rights of another. Give the children some examples: people who fight for unborn children are advocates for the unborn; people who fight for those who are bullied are advocates for victims of bullying. Highlight that Jesus acts as an advocate for all Christians, representing them to God. Ask the children how having the King of the universe speak on their behalf makes them feel. Highlight for the children that Jesus is intimately involved in the lives of his people.

Read Romans 8:31–39. Provide Bibles for the children to read along.

Tell the children that Paul writes this passage to give the Roman Christians confidence of all that they have in Christ Jesus. He says to them, "If God is for us, who can be against us?" This passage should encourage every Christian to keep trusting God and living for his glory.

Emphasize verse 34 and ask the children what Paul says Jesus is doing for his people in heaven. Paul says that Jesus, while seated at the right hand of the Father, is interceding for every Christian. Explain to the children that interceding is simply praying. Ask the children how the knowledge that Jesus is praying for them should affect Christians here on earth.

Remind the children that Jesus also sent the Holy Spirit to his people after he ascended into heaven. The Holy Spirit now lives in all those who trust in Jesus and helps them to become more like Jesus as they read and understand God's Word.

Ask the children if they can see all the different ways that Jesus's ascension is good news for his people. He is an advocate. Jesus, the one who satisfied God's wrath, speaks to God on behalf of Christians. The fact that Jesus is in heaven, having triumphed over sin and death, means Christians never need to worry about being punished by God (what a hopeful thought!). He is praying for every spiritual blessing for his people, and he is ensuring that his people are equipped to walk with him and become more like him by sending his Spirit.

Conclude the teaching time by helping the children commit Question 51 and the answer to memory.

(These notes are just for guidance. Please expand or amend them to suit your own children and context. Write out your talk in your own words and include illustrations and applications that you know will connect with your children.)

Activity

Cut out the six different scenarios from Q51 Advocate Required! (RB), and fold each slip in half.

Divide children into groups of three. In each group, appoint one person to be the advocate, one to be the judge, and one to read the scenario (see example below). After the scenario has been read, the advocate should make a persuasive case to the judge. After they finish, ask the judge if he or she was convinced.

When a group finishes, if there's time, have them swap scenarios with another group and change roles so that a different child is the advocate.

After a couple of advocacy sessions, ask the class why having someone else speak on your behalf may be more effective in some situations.

Notes

Reader: Fourth grader

Advocate: Son or daughter of the school principal

Judge: School principal

Pretend that you live in a place where it hardly ever snows. You just listened to the weatherman forecast snow for tomorrow. He says that some schools may close. Your good friend is the child of the principal of your school. Ask your friend to convince the principal to close school tomorrow.

After the advocate is finished, ask the judge if the advocacy worked.

---

⑤ Discussion and Question Time

Some questions that might arise include:

? **Why do we need an advocate if Jesus dealt fully with our sins?**

> Explain to the children that Jesus's presence in heaven means that sin and death have been defeated and his death has satisfied God's wrath. God has accepted his sacrifice on our behalf. Even though this saving work has been accomplished, Jesus still intercedes for us, asking God to grant us what we need on his behalf.

? **How can I know what Jesus is praying for me?**

> John 17 is a good example of the kind of prayers Jesus prays for his people.

Also use this opportunity to help the children think about their own lives and how this question and answer affects them personally.

- Ask the children if they are excited to know that Jesus is always working for his people from heaven.

- Ask the children how they might explain what Jesus is doing now to someone who is not a Christian.

---

⑩ Virtue Vision

Hope
Read this story to the children:

> Carlos loved to read. When he was lost in a book, he had no idea what was going on around him. One day, Carlos started reading a new adventure book on the bus home from school. Suddenly, he heard the bus driver say, "Last stop. Everybody off!" Carlos had missed his stop! Normally when this happened, Carlos told the bus driver,

which was the right thing to do. But today, there was a new driver, and Carlos was too embarrassed. He picked up his backpack and got off the bus.

The other children had already scattered. Carlos didn't recognize any of the houses. He had no idea where he was! He felt totally hopeless. He sat down on the curb with his head in his hands.

Then, he remembered that he had learned at church that Jesus is his advocate in heaven, interceding on his behalf. This made him feel less alone. Surely, Jesus could get him home. And Jesus had given him the Holy Spirit to guide him. Carlos felt hope rise in his heart, even though he still didn't know how to get home.

He picked up his backpack and started walking. In the distance, he could see a playground. As he got closer, he recognized the swing set with the bright orange swings. That was the playground across from his grandmother's house! He ran across the playground and, sure enough, there was his grandmother's house. Carlos prayed a prayer of thanksgiving as he looked both ways and crossed the street. He could see his grandmother through the window. He was not lost anymore!

Ask the children what thought gave Carlos hope.

Notes

Memory Activity

Read the memory verse or catechism question and answer with the children a few times. Then work together to develop actions for the memory verse or question and answer. Allow the children to be creative and come up with actions for as many words as possible. Say the memory verse through with the actions several times.

Closing Prayer Time

Invite the children to give thanks to God for enthroning Christ as King and ruler over all. Encourage them to rejoice in the knowledge that Jesus is their advocate and is interceding on their behalf in heaven.

Question 52

What hope does ever-lasting life hold for us?

Answer

That we will live with and enjoy God forever in the new heaven and the new earth, where we will be forever freed from all sin in a renewed, restored creation.

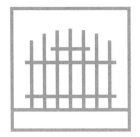

Big Idea
Those who have been redeemed by Christ have the confident hope of spending eternity with the triune God free from sin.

Aim
To help the children anticipate eternal life confidently.

Bible Passage
Revelation 21:1–4

Memory Verse
"Then I saw a new heaven and a new earth, for the first heaven and the first earth had passed away, and the sea was no more. And I saw the holy city, new Jerusalem, coming down out of heaven from God, prepared as a bride adorned for her husband. And I heard a loud voice from the throne saying, 'Behold, the dwelling place of God is with man. He will dwell with them, and they will be his people, and God himself will be with them as their God. He will wipe away every tear from their eyes, and death shall be no more, neither shall there be mourning, nor crying, nor pain anymore, for the former things have passed away.'" (Rev. 21:1–4)

Virtue
Hope

Leader's Notes

Children have varying awareness of their own mortality depending on their cultural context, age, and previous experiences with death. Most will be aware that some plants, animals, and people die, but they may have questions about what happens next. This lesson will help the children begin to understand that Scripture reveals the promise of eternal life for those who have been redeemed through Christ. It should clarify some of the misconceptions the children have about the Christian's final destination and give them a clearer picture of the beauty of eternity. This lesson should also show the children that in contrast to many other religions, Christians have a firm belief about life after death. This lesson aims to help the children anticipate eternal life confidently.

Things to remember when planning and teaching:

- Children struggle to realize their own mortality.

- The afterlife is often talked about in abstract terms, but the Bible speaks of it in concrete terms. Help the children see that the new heavens and earth will be real, physical places.

- Some children may have suffered a bereavement and subsequently may be sensitive about discussions of death. On the other hand, they may be eager to talk about it because of their experience.

- Be aware that some children may have non-Christian family members and could find the thought of being separated eternally from loved ones distressing.

- Remember to mix and match the activities in the lesson to fit your time frame (see p. 12 for some sample outlines). You won't have time to do them all. Feel free to adapt each activity based on your class's strengths and weaknesses.

Leader's Prayer

Eternal God, I praise you for the hope of spending eternity with you in the new heavens and new earth. Thank you that you have promised to give eternal life to all those who love you. May the hope of forever living in your presence spur me on each day to live for your glory. Grant understanding to the children who will hear this lesson. May they have their eyes lifted from the temporal to the eternal, and may they too be filled with the hope of everlasting life. In Jesus's name. Amen.

Leader's Tool Kit

- Whiteboard and two whiteboard markers
- Large sheets of paper
- Markers
- Timer (cell phone timer will do)

- Travel brochures
- Paper and pens
- Q52 Memory Activity (DL), one per child

Catechism Recap

You will need a whiteboard and two whiteboard markers.

Divide the children into two teams and line each team up facing the whiteboard. Explain to the children that this is a head-to-head challenge! The children should come to the whiteboard in pairs; the first children from each team, followed by the second children from each team, etc.

Read a catechism question out to the children. Tell them that the first to write the first word of the answer on the whiteboard wins a point for their team. (The rest of the team should remain silent rather than calling out the answers.) Play until every child has had a turn going head-to-head to write the first word of an answer.

Introduction to Question 52

Tell the children that different religions have different beliefs about what happens to a person after death, and those who don't have any kind of faith may believe that this life is all there is.

Explain to the children that the Bible clearly teaches that all Christians will receive the gift of eternal life. Most people think only of heaven when they think about eternal life, but actually the Bible describes eternity in terms of the new heavens and the new earth. Explain to the children that the souls of Christians who die go to be with God

in heaven, but when Jesus returns, he will give them new, resurrected bodies. God will then make all things new. In fact, he will make the earth new.

Ask the children if it comes as a surprise to them that eternity won't be lived only in heaven, but on a new earth as well?

Introduce the children to Question 52: "What hope does everlasting life hold for us?" Explain that this question will help them to discover a little bit more about what eternal life means for a Christian.

⑩ Activity

You will need large sheets of paper and markers. Have the following list written down on a piece of paper:

- *Bride*
- *No tears*
- *No death*
- *Husband*
- *New heaven*
- *New earth*
- *Loud voice*
- *Holy city*

Divide the children into small teams and give each team some large sheets of paper and markers. Explain that someone from each team will come up and receive a word or phrase from the leader. The team members then have to rush back to their teammates and try to draw the word for them. The draw-er should not speak! Once the team correctly guesses the word, the next team member runs up to the leader, tells the leader the word that they've just guessed, and unlocks the next word. Set a timer for ten minutes. The team that has correctly guessed the most words wins the game.

Explain that the Bible teaches a lot about the new heavens and the new earth. However, highlight that it is sometimes hard to fully understand what the new heavens and the new earth will be like because we think in limited human terms. The passages in the Bible that refer to the new heavens and the new earth use imagery the people will be familiar with (bride, city, tears), and those images help us better understand what eternity will be like.

⑮ Teaching Outline

You will need some travel brochures.

Begin the teaching time by asking for God's help. Ask that the lesson would be taught faithfully and that the children might listen well.

Show the children the travel brochures. Explain that travel brochures only give a glimpse of what a vacation destination will actually be like. It's not until people experience the vacation and the destination that they can fully appreciate the wonder and beauty of the place.

Tell the children that by reading the Bible, Christians can get some understanding and appreciation of what eternity in God's presence will be like. God gives his people enough information to help them look forward to eternity, but there's no doubt that it will be even better and more wonderful than anyone can imagine.

Read Revelation 21:1–4. Provide Bibles for the children to read along.

Explain to the children that this passage is written by a man called John. God gave him the ability to see what the future will be like and record it for Christians.

One day, God's people will live forever on a new and beautiful earth. God will allow the first heaven and the first earth to pass away, and there will be a new heaven and a new earth. Tell the children that most Christians think only about heaven, but that's not the end of the story. Remind the children that those who have been saved by God through Jesus will have new resurrected bodies, and they will live forever in God's perfect place.

Explain to the children that this is a wonderful hope! But even more wonderfully, the passage reveals in verse 3 that God will live with his people. Ask the children what they think about the promise that one day God will live with his people in the new creation.

Next, invite the children to look at verse 4. There will be no more crying or death or mourning or pain! Ask the children what causes these things. Ultimately, they can all be traced back to sin, and because there will be no sin in the new creation, there will be no more consequences of sin. Christians who are freed from sin will be able to perfectly enjoy God forever.

The hope of everlasting life is amazing for the Christian! There is so much to look forward to, and the hope of living with God forever should help Christians to live courageously here and now.

Conclude the teaching time by helping the children commit Question 52 and the answer to memory.

(These notes are just for guidance. Please expand or amend them to suit your own children and context. Write out your talk in your own words and include illustrations and applications that you know will connect with your children.)

Notes

Activity

Give each child a sticky note and a pen.

First, ask the children to write their name at the top of their sticky note. Next, ask them to write down the name of one living person they would most like to meet if given the chance. It could be a sports star, a movie star, an author, a singer, or someone they love who lives far away. Give them a few minutes, then ask them to write down the name of their favorite restaurant. The leaders should write their own answers down!

Collect the sticky notes. One by one, formulate a question for each child based on his answers. For example, "David, would you rather have dinner with LeBron James at your own house or eat dinner without him at Chuck E. Cheese's?" The choice should always be meeting their hero at their own house or going to their favorite restaurant without that person. Hopefully, many of the children will choose meeting their heroes. End by asking the leaders the same question.

Notes

Explain to the children that some places are really great, but getting to meet some people is even better! The presence of God will be the very best thing about the life to come. We will get to experience the very best place in the very best company!

---

⑤ Discussion and Question Time

Some questions that might arise include:

? Will eternity be boring?

> No! Explain to the children that those who think eternity will be boring have a wrong understanding of who God is and what he is like. Nothing could be further from the truth. God created this world full of pleasure and excitement, and the new heavens and new earth will be even better!

? So, will we be walking around in bodies?

> Yes! The new earth will be a real physical place and everyone will have a real physical body. There will be no one floating around like ghosts. These new bodies won't get sick.

? Do people turn into angels when they die?

> No! Although movies sometimes suggest people turn into angels, the Bible teaches that angels existed before the world was created. They are a different category of creature altogether rather than something that was once human. Likewise, humans will be human for all eternity— we cannot become angels.

Also use this opportunity to help the children think about their own lives and how this question and answer affects them personally.

- Ask the children if they're excited about the prospect of spending forever with God in the new creation.

- Ask the children if anything worries them about the new heavens and the new earth.

- Ask the children if they are confident that they will spend eternity with God. Have they been forgiven of their sin through Jesus?

---

⑩ Virtue Vision

Hope

Give each child paper and a pen.

Explain to the children that many people in the world believe that after death, we will cease to exist. As Christians, we have the confident hope that we will not only continue to live, but that we will live in a much better place than our current, fallen world.

Although we can't *fully* imagine what life will be like without any sin, sickness, or death, thinking about what it would be like can fill us with hope!

Invite the children to write a letter from their future self to their present self. They can use their imagination to describe what the new heavens and the new earth will be like.

Also ask the children to write advice to their present self based on knowing about this new earth in the future. When the children have had some time to write, ask for a few volunteers to read their letters aloud.

Remind the children that the way the Bible talks about hope is not wishful thinking. Our hope is a confidence based on God's Word!

Memory Activity

Give each child a copy of Q25 Memory Activity (DL). Pass out crayons or colored pencils.

This is more of a memory passage than a memory verse. Rather than trying to get the children to learn the verse in the lesson,

read through it with them a few times, and then encourage them to meditate on it by drawing pictures of what the verses describe. Encourage them to take the verse home and work on memorizing it.

Closing Prayer Time

Invite the children to give thanks for the hope of eternal life and the anticipation of spending forever with God the Father, Son, and Holy Spirit.

Notes

141

Acknowledgments

We are grateful to Crossway for publishing this curriculum and would like to extend special thanks to Tara Davis for her keen editorial eye, and to Dave DeWit and Josh Dennis for their oversight.

Redeemer City to City and Redeemer Presbyterian Church gave The Gospel Coalition permission to develop *The New City Catechism*, originally the work of Timothy Keller and Sam Shammas, into *The New City Catechism Curriculum*.

The project was made possible in part through a generous grant to The Gospel Coalition from the John Templeton Foundation. Thanks to Richard Bollinger and Sarah Clement who believed in the character and virtue potential of this project early on. Thanks also to TGC's Ben Peays and Dan Olson, who worked closely with the John Templeton Foundation when this project was just an idea.

We are grateful for the input and ideas of Sarah Schnitker and Kimberly Griswold of Fuller Theological Seminary on virtue development, educator Caitlin Nunery on classroom activities, and psychologist Brent Bounds on psychological development of children.

Betsy Howard of the Gospel Coalition served as managing editor of *The New City Catechism Curriculum*, and Collin Hansen provided theological oversight.

Most importantly, this curriculum would never have come to fruition without its chief writer, Melanie Lacy of Oak Hill Theological College. Melanie's years of experience as a proponent of catechesis and as a practitioner of children's ministry in the church shaped the curriculum and enriched each lesson.

It took many people to produce *The New City Catechism Curriculum*. Together, we hope it will be used to raise up a generation of children who place their only hope, in life and death, in Jesus Christ.

Build a framework for understanding core Christian beliefs.

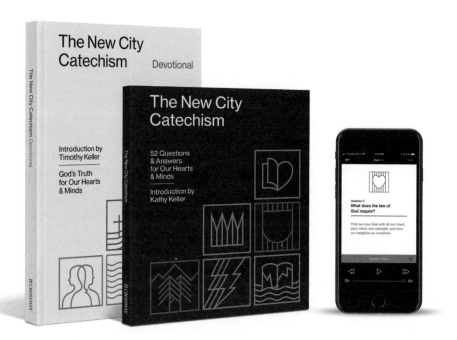

Designed to be memorized over the course of a year, *The New City Catechism* is a valuable resource for building a foundation of important concepts in the minds and hearts of children and adults alike.

For more information, visit
newcitycatechism.com

The New City Catechism

Curriculum

52 Questions
& Answers
for Our Hearts
& Minds

The New City Catechism

Curriculum

Volume 4 – Resource Book

WHEATON, ILLINOIS

The New City Catechism Curriculum: Vol. 4, Resource Book

Copyright © 2018 by The Gospel Coalition

Published by Crossway
        1300 Crescent Street
        Wheaton, Illinois 60187

This publication was made possible through the support of a grant from the John Templeton Foundation. The opinions expressed in this publication are those of the publisher and do not necessarily reflect the views of the John Templeton Foundation.

Cover design: Matt Wahl & Micah Lanier

First printing 2018

Printed in China

Scripture quotations are from the ESV® Bible (The Holy Bible, English Standard Version®), copyright © 2001 by Crossway, a publishing ministry of Good News Publishers. Used by permission. All rights reserved.

Trade paperback ISBN: 978-1-4335-6139-9

Crossway is a publishing ministry of Good News Publishers.

RRDS			29	28	27	26	25	24	23	22	21	20	19
16	15	14	13	12	11	10	9	8	7	6	5	4	3	2

This Resource Book is a companion to books 1, 2, and 3 of *The New City Catechism Curriculum*. Teachers may photocopy resources from the book or download them at **www.newcitycatechism.com/resourcebook**. The directions for how to use each resource can be found in the corresponding lesson. Some resources are worksheets that accompany the activities, and you will need one per child. Others are visual aids for classroom discussion. It would be helpful to enlarge these photos and illustrations before you print or as you photocopy them.

Contents

✂ ···

Eternal: *God has no beginning or end.*

✂ ···

Righteous: *God is right in everything he says, does, and thinks.*

✂ ···

Sovereign: *God rules over and is in control of all things.*

✂ ···

✂ ....

Holy: *God is perfect and separate from sin.*

✂ ....

Gracious: *God is kind.*

✂ ....

Infinite: *God knows no bounds.*

✂ ....

✂ ....

Omniscient: *God knows all things.*

✂ ....

Wise: *God never makes mistakes.*

✂ ....

Faithful: *God always keeps his promises.*

✂ ....

✂ ⋯⋯⋯

Omnipotent: *God is all-powerful.*

✂ ⋯⋯⋯

Omnipresent: *God is everywhere, all the time.*

✂ ⋯⋯⋯

Immutable: *God never changes.*

✂ ⋯⋯⋯

✂ ....

Self-sufficient: *God does not need anything or anyone.*

✂ ....

Merciful: *God is compassionate.*

✂ ....

Incomprehensible: *God is more than humans can understand.*

✂ ....

✂ ....

Never-tiring: *God never needs to sleep.*

✂ ....

Patient: *God is slow to become angry.*

✂ ....

Victorious: *God always wins.*

✂ ....

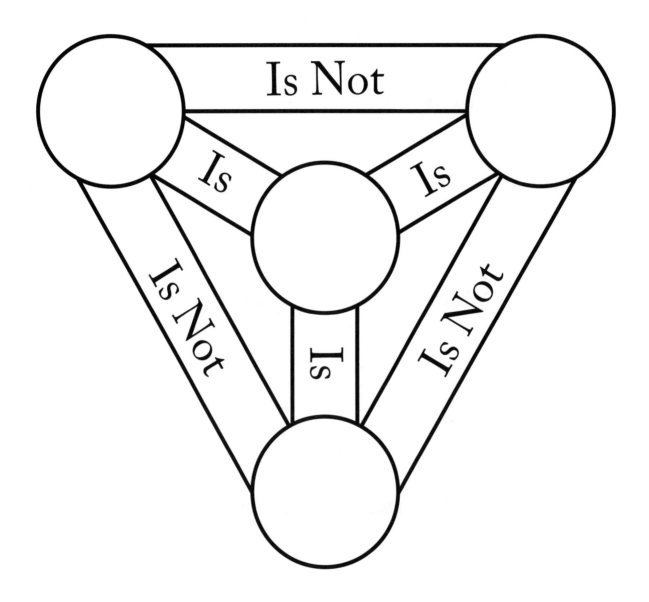

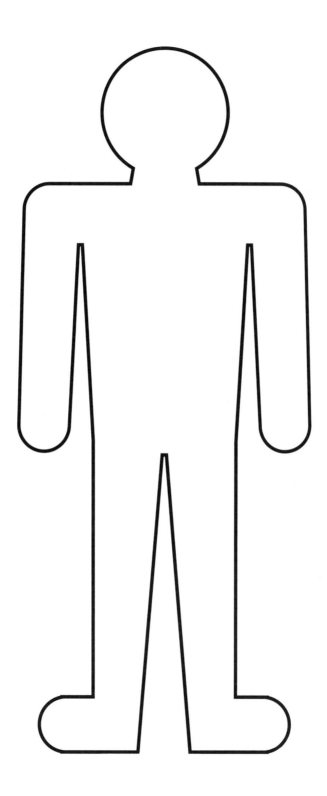

Baal

Marduk

Isis

Ishtar

1.   What is the deadliest animal in the world?

2.   What is the largest member of the cat family?

3.   What is the fastest land animal in the world?

4.   Name an animal that eats standing up.

5.   What animal can see through its eyelids?

6.   What animal does not have eyelids?

7.   Because of its bright color, this bird was named after fire.

8.   This animal can carry up to one thousand times its own body weight.

9.   Because of its speed and sense of direction, this animal has been used to carry important messages.

10.   If this animal loses a body part, that part will regenerate on its own.

Cake Recipe

Ingredients:

2 cups sugar
1 cup butter, softened
5 eggs
2 teaspoons vanilla
3 cups flour
1 teaspoon baking powder
1 cup milk

Heat oven to 350° F

Mix sugar, butter, eggs, and vanilla in large bowl. Beat on low to mix ingredients well. Beat on high for 5 minutes.

On low, add flour and baking powder alternately with milk.

Beat well after each addition.

Spoon batter into greased and floured 10-inch tube pan.

Bake for 65-75 minutes

Day 1

Separation of
Light and Darkness

Day 2

Separation of
Heavens and Earth

Day 3

Dry Land
and Vegetation

Day 4

Sun, Moon,
and Stars

Day 5

Fish and Birds

Day 6

Animals and Man

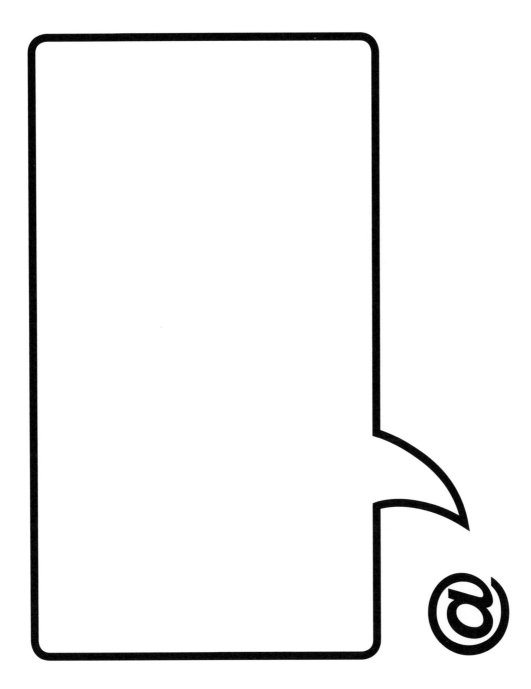

Make up a handle for yourself and write it beside the @.

1

2

3

4

5

6

7

8

Use the code below to decipher the symbols in sentences 1 and 2.

A=♣ B=ɣ C=* D=↓ E=÷ F=# G=ς H=√
I=♥ J=□ K=< L=+ M=Θ N=ß O=∞ P=≈
Q=♫ R=$ S=Δ T=† U=♦ V=∏ W=% X=!
Y=¶ Z=∫

1.

†√♣† ∞ß †√÷ Δ♣ɣɣ♣†√ ↓♣¶ %÷

Δ≈÷ß↓ †♥Θ÷ ♥ß %∞$Δ√♥≈ ∞# ς∞↓

2.

†√♣† %÷ +∞∏÷ ♣ß↓ ↓∞ß∞$ ∞♦$

#♣†√÷$ ♣ß↓ Θ∞†√÷$

1. _____ Last name of someone in the room

2. _____ Noun

3. _____ First name of boy in the room

4. _____ Plural noun

5. _____ Type of vehicle

6. _____ Type of bird

7. _____ Body of water

8. _____ Plural noun

"Tomorrow is the field trip to the zoo," said the teacher, Mrs. _____.
                                                                    1

"Whatever you do, don't forget to bring your _____."
                                              2

_____ was so excited about the field trip, he couldn't sleep. All night long he thought
       3

about how he couldn't wait to see the _____ at the zoo.
                                        4

When he got to school, Mrs. _____ asked, "_____, where is your
                              1   3

_____?" _____ had forgotten his _____!
       2   3   2

He didn't tell the teacher the truth. Instead, he said, "I had my _____ when I left home,
                                                                    2

but unfortunately, our _____ crashed on the way to school. I jumped out, holding
                         5

my _____, but a _____ swooped down and snatched it out of my hand. It
       2   6

dropped the _____ into _____, never to be seen again."
               2   7

"_____," Mrs. _____ said. "How do you expect me to believe that?
       3   1

A _____ would never steal your _____. Everyone knows they only eat
       6   2

_____."
       8

Hatw is our yoln peoh ni efli nda daeth?

Thaw Gdo si?

Woh mnay epsorns rae theer ni Gdo?

Owh nda wyh idd oGd rceate su?

Ahtw eesl idd oGd eraetc?

Owh cna ew oifglry odG?

Awth dose het alw of oGd erqeuir?

Hatw si het wla fo oGd sttdae ni het enT mCemndmtnoas?

Wath odes Gdo eirqrue ni eth sfirt, cesnod, nda thrid emsmnnandmotc?

Waht sode Gdo erueiqr ni het ofruth dan ifthf madmtosenmnc?

Thwa sode doG uerqier ni teh xthsi, ensethv, dan iegthh mdmosmnnaetc?

Tahw dose Gdo qrreiue ni teh nitnh dan etnth mndmmocaenst?

Nac eanyno kpee het lwa fo odG perfcetyl?

Idd dGo carete su nuaelb ot ekpe ish alw?

Isenc on eno cna eekp teh awl, athw si sit uprpeos?

Hwat si ins?

Hwat si oidtlary?

Liwl oGd olalw uor oicdnideesbe nda diatoyrl ot og unpunihdse?

Si rteeh nay wya ot epcsae hpuinsmten dan eb ubrgtoh bcak itno odG's avofr?

Ohw si eht demReeer?

You have entered a painting in the school art show. It is the best painting you've ever done. You're hoping to win first prize! Instead, you get an honorable mention. The first prize goes to a girl who lives across the street from you and rides your bus.	You are an excellent reader. Your cousin, who is in the same grade as you, is excited to tell you that he read a book that was more than one hundred pages. You've been reading much longer books for a couple of years.	You have won the school spelling bee! The final round was down to you and your best friend, who happens to be coming over to your house after school. When the two of you get in the car, your dad asks how the spelling bee went.
Your baseball team is up against the best team in the league. It's a close game, but your team loses because the left fielder fails to catch a fly ball. Afterward, some of your teammates are giving him a hard time.	The girls in your class are talking about what they will be wearing in the school choir program. Most of them are getting new dresses. When you ask your parents for a new dress, they say they cannot afford a new dress, but you can wear one that your sister has outgrown.	You are playing checkers with your grandfather. He wants to teach you his game strategy, but you aren't really interested. You're pretty sure that you are better at checkers than he is.
A new family comes to your church. You overhear someone say they are living in a homeless shelter. One of the kids comes to your Sunday school class. You notice that her clothes have stains on them, and her hair is messy.	On his way out the door, your dad asks you to tell your mom that all the milk is gone. Later in the day, your mom is surprised to discover that your dad drank the last of the milk and didn't mention it. You realize you forgot to give her the message.	Your daily chore assignment is to make your bed and take out the trash. You have done both of these things. Your mother has a headache and needs to lie down, so she asks you to load the dishwasher. This is not one of your chores.

Look up each verse reference. If the passage describes Jesus's divinity, write *D* in the blank. If it's about Jesus's humanity, write *H*. If it's about both, write *DH*.

_____ John 1:14   _____ Titus 2:13

_____ 1 Timothy 2:5   _____ Matthew 28:18

_____ John 11:35   _____ John 1:1

_____ Galatians 4:4   _____ Luke 11:17

_____ Hebrews 4:15   _____ Luke 2:7

_____ John 4:6   _____ Matthew 4:2

Islam

Hinduism

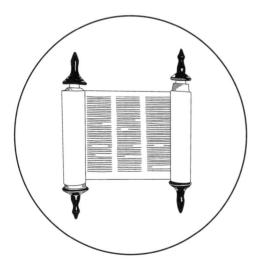

Judaism

Buddhism

In each square, write a part of the human body.

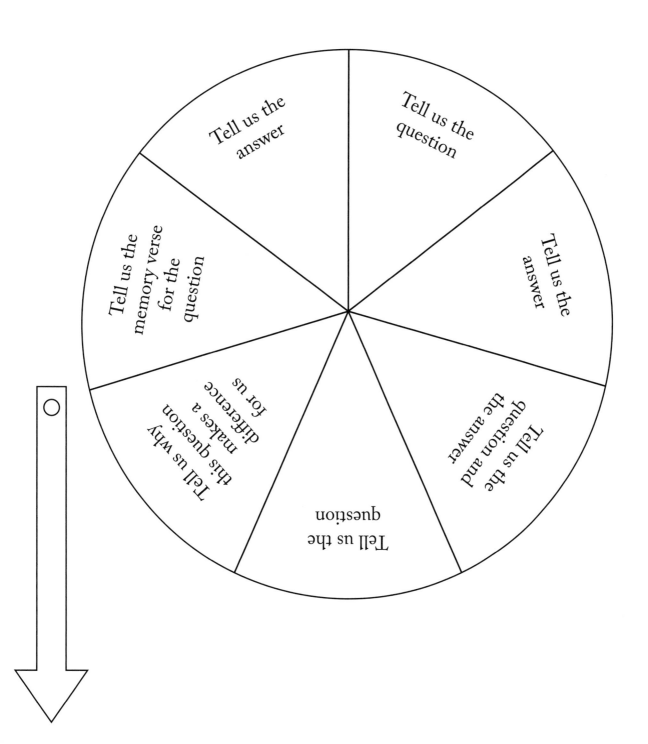

Find the path to the center of the maze.
There is only *one* way!

START

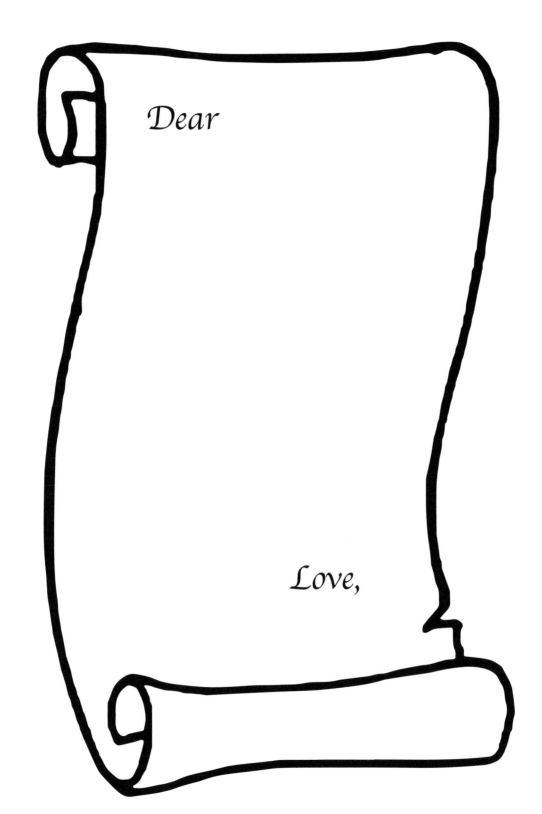

Dear

Love,

Does Christ's death mean all our sins can be forgiven?	Yes, because Christ's death on the cross fully paid the penalty for our sin, God will remember our sins no more.	**Why was it necessary for Christ, the Redeemer, to die?**	Christ died willingly in our place to deliver us from the power and penalty of sin and bring us back to God.
Why must the Redeemer be truly God?	That because of his divine nature his obedience and suffering would be perfect and effective.	**Why must the Redeemer be truly human?**	That in human nature he might on our behalf perfectly obey the whole law and suffer the punishment for human sin.
What sort of Redeemer is needed to bring us back to God?	One who is truly human and also truly God.	**Who is the Redeemer?**	The only Redeemer is the Lord Jesus Christ.
Is there any way to escape punishment and be brought back into God's favor?	Yes, God reconciles us to himself by a Redeemer.	**Will God allow our disobedience and idolatry to go unpunished?**	No, God is righteously angry with our sins and will punish them both in this life, and in the life to come.

What is idolatry?	Idolatry is trusting in created things rather than the Creator.	**What is sin?**	Sin is rejecting or ignoring God in the world he created, not being or doing what he requires in his law.
Since no one can keep the law, what is its purpose?	That we may know the holy nature of God, and the sinful nature of our hearts; and thus our need of a Savior.	**Did God create us unable to keep his law?**	No, but because of the disobedience of Adam and Eve we are all born in sin and guilt, unable to keep God's law.
Can anyone keep the law of God perfectly?	Since the fall, no human has been able to keep the law of God perfectly.	**What does the law of God require?**	That we love God with all our heart, soul, mind, and strength; and love our neighbor as ourselves.
How can we glorify God?	By loving him and by obeying his commands and law.	**What is our only hope in life and death?**	That we are not our own but belong to God.

CODE:
A=1 B=2 C=3 D=4 E=5 F=6 G=7 H=8 I=9 J=! K=@ L=# M=$
N=% O=* P=& Q=^ R=(S=) T=? U=> V=< W=~ X=+ Y=/ Z=0

1.

1%4   4*   %*?   651(?8*)5   ~8*   @9##   ?85   2*4/   2>?

31%%*?   @9##   ?85   )*># (1?85(651(89$ ~8*   31%

45)?(*/   2*?8   ?85)*>#   1%4   2*4/   9%   85##.

2.

~89#5   ?85   )*%)   *6   ?85   @9%74*$ ~9##   25   ?8(*~%

9%?*   ?85   *>?5(41(@%5)).   9%   ?81?   &#135   ?85(5

~9##   25   ~55&9%7   1%4   7%1)89%7   *6   ?55?8.

3.

29%4   89$ 81%4 1%4 6**? 1%4 31)? 89$ 9%?*   ?85   *<?5(

41(@%5)).   9%   ?81?   &#135   ?85(5   ~9##   25   ~55&9%7

1%4   7%1)89%7   *6   ?55?8.

1.
- I work in a team with other people.
- I wash my hands often.
- I often use a scalpel in my work to save people.
- I'm used to seeing lots of blood.
- Nurses work with me.
- I am a **surgeon**!

2.
- Sometimes I sit around for hours without anything to do.
- I wear a helmet.
- I have an axe in case I need to break down a door.
- I use a large hose.
- I drive a red truck.
- I am a **firefighter**!

3.
- I work in the summer months.
- I don't get out of my chair often.
- I wear sunscreen.
- I watch people.
- I swim really well.
- I am a **lifeguard**!

4.
- I am a good driver.
- I don't follow the normal traffic rules.
- I use a siren.
- I respond when you call 9-1-1.
- Paramedics ride with me.
- I am an **ambulance driver**!

5.
- I wear a uniform.
- Sometimes I work in other countries.
- My job is very dangerous.
- I am trained to fight.
- My uniform is camouflage.
- I am a **soldier**!

6.
- I save lives without leaving my office.
- I tell other people what to do.
- I answer the phone all day.
- I can trace your call even if you don't know your address.
- My phone number is 9-1-1.
- I am a **9-1-1 dispatcher**!

The Apostles' Creed

We believe in God the Father Almighty, Maker of heaven and earth; and in Jesus Christ his only Son our Lord, who was conceived by the Holy Spirit, born of the virgin Mary, suffered under Pontius Pilate, was crucified, died, and was buried. He descended into hell. The third day he rose again from the dead. He ascended into heaven, and is seated at the right hand of God the Father Almighty; from there he will come to judge the living and the dead. We believe in the Holy Spirit, the holy catholic church, the communion of saints, the forgiveness of sins, the resurrection of the body, and the life everlasting.

The Apostles' Creed

We believe in God the Father Almighty, Maker of heaven and earth; and in Jesus Christ his only Son our Lord, who was conceived by the Holy Spirit, born of the virgin Mary, suffered under Pontius Pilate, was crucified, died, and was buried. He descended into hell. The third day he rose again from the dead. He ascended into heaven, and is seated at the right hand of God the Father Almighty; from there he will come to judge the living and the dead. We believe in the Holy Spirit, the holy catholic church, the communion of saints, the forgiveness of sins, the resurrection of the body, and the life everlasting.

The Apostles' Creed

We believe in God the Father Almighty, Maker of heaven and earth; and in Jesus Christ his only Son our Lord, who was conceived by the Holy Spirit, born of the virgin Mary, suffered under Pontius Pilate, was crucified, died, and was buried. He descended into hell. The third day he rose again from the dead. He ascended into heaven, and is seated at the right hand of God the Father Almighty; from there he will come to judge the living and the dead. We believe in the Holy Spirit, the holy catholic church, the communion of saints, the forgiveness of sins, the resurrection of the body, and the life everlasting.

We believe in God the Father Almighty	"One God and Father of all, who is over all and through all and in all." (Ephesians 4:6)
Maker of heaven and earth	"In the beginning, God created the heavens and the earth." (Genesis 1:1)
Who was conceived by the Holy Spirit	"And the angel answered her, 'The Holy Spirit will come upon you, and the power of the Most High will over-shadow you; therefore the child to be born will be called holy—the Son of God.'" (Luke 1:35)
He ascended into heaven	"While he blessed them, he parted from them and was carried up into heaven." (Luke 24:51)
He is seated at the right hand of God	"He is the radiance of the glory of God and the exact imprint of his nature, and he upholds the universe by the word of his power. After making purification for sins, he sat down at the right hand of the Majesty on high." (Hebrews 1:3)
We believe in the life everlasting	"For God so loved the world, that he gave his only Son, that whoever believes in him should not perish but have eternal life." (John 3:16)

The Burning of Latimer and Ridley

Cranmer's Martyrdom

Put a *J* beside words that relate to *Justification*
and an *S* beside words that relate to *Sanctification*.
Write *JS* if it relates to both *Justification* and *Sanctification*.

Once for all time	Holiness	Not guilty
Obedience	Punishment	Become
External	Gradual	Grow
Transform	Law	Declared
Judge	Internal	One day at a time

Find and circle the words listed below.

```
D  A  E  N  V  Y  X  S  Q  Y  L  W
W  Z  L  I  S  C  C  J  Y  L  P  P
L  L  M  J  B  L  T  Q  D  Y  B  K
A  B  M  K  D  Q  A  J  G  H  U  M
O  G  V  V  Q  V  H  V  S  V  H  A
D  I  S  O  B  E  D  I  E  N  T  L
K  I  B  H  F  E  L  Z  C  S  S  I
M  J  E  D  K  O  D  Y  Q  G  S  C
L  S  F  I  O  A  H  A  T  E  D  E
U  G  Y  F  I  E  D  F  A  H  F  H
S  V  H  A  T  I  N  G  Y  A  G  U
A  S  T  R  A  Y  Q  H  B  D  T  J
```

ASTRAY	HATED
DISOBEDIENT	HATING
ENVY	MALICE
FOOLISH	SLAVES

In the circles below, design four different emoticons showing four different attitudes.

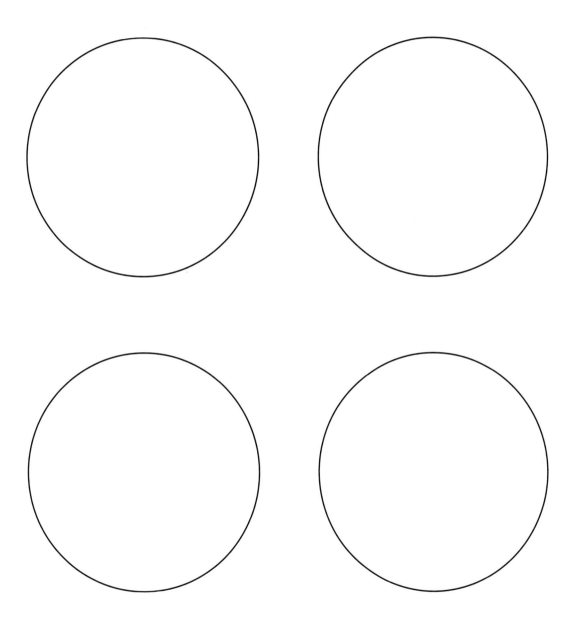

"All we like sheep have gone astray;
      we have turned—every one—to his own way;
and the Lᴏʀᴅ has laid on him
      the iniquity of us all." (Isaiah 53:6)

"The Spirit himself bears witness with our spirit that we are children of God, and if children, then heirs—heirs of God and fellow heirs with Christ, provided we suffer with him in order that we may also be glorified with him." (Romans 8:16–17)

"And my God will supply every need of yours according to his riches in glory in Christ Jesus." (Philippians 4:19)

"If any of you lacks wisdom, let him ask God, who gives generously to all without reproach, and it will be given him." (James 1:5)

"Do all things without grumbling or disputing." (Philippians 2:14)

"If we confess our sins, he is faithful and just to forgive us our sins and to cleanse us from all unrighteousness." (1 John 1:9)

The Lord's Prayer

Our Father in heaven,
hallowed be your name,
your kingdom come,
your will be done,
on earth as it is in
heaven. Give us today
our daily bread. And
forgive us our debts, as
we also have forgiven
our debtors. And lead us
not into temptation but
deliver us from evil.

The Lord's Prayer

Our Father in heaven,
hallowed be your name,
your kingdom come,
your will be done,
on earth as it is in
heaven. Give us today
our daily bread. And
forgive us our debts, as
we also have forgiven
our debtors. And lead us
not into temptation but
deliver us from evil.

The Lord's Prayer

Our Father in heaven,
hallowed be your name,
your kingdom come,
your will be done,
on earth as it is in
heaven. Give us today
our daily bread. And
forgive us our debts, as
we also have forgiven
our debtors. And lead us
not into temptation but
deliver us from evil.

Nate and Marj Saint in Ecuador with their children Kathy and Steve (Photo courtesy of MAF)

Baptism of Steve and Kathy Saint in the river where their father was killed (Photo used with the permission of Steve Saint)

Dear _____,

I hope you're very well and continuing to love the Lord Jesus. I know that you've been learning about the Lord's Supper in your class, and I want to warn you that some people are teaching wrong things about the Lord's Supper—please be sure to tell the children!

Some people are making a big mistake by believing that eating and drinking the bread and wine will make them Christians! This is definitely wrong—it says so in the Bible. The Lord's Supper will not save anyone, nor bring forgiveness to those who have not put their trust in Jesus. Be sure to tell the children that the Lord's Supper is a sacrament for those who believe; it will not bring belief.

There's no doubt that the Lord's Supper is of great help to Christians; it strengthens and encourages believers in their faith. It will bring a Christian closer into fellowship with Jesus as the Holy Spirit deepens his or her faith. But the Lord's Supper can add nothing to what Jesus achieved on the cross—his death was perfect and sufficient. Remind the children that there is nothing we can humanly do to make ourselves right with God. Our only hope is to trust in Jesus Christ who died once for all.

I hope you have a great class. Don't forget to tell the children about the false things people are teaching about the Lord's Supper.

I pray that you may trust fully in Jesus who died once for all!

In the grace and peace of God,

Your concerned friend

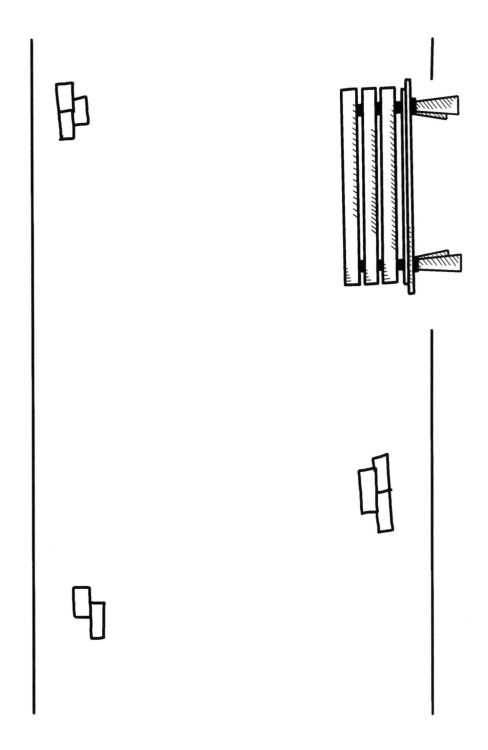

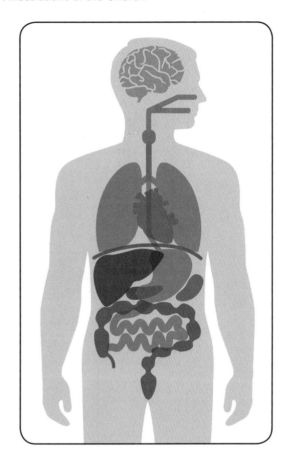

Fold on the dotted lines. Cut on the solid lines.

Write in the blank who sits in each of these seats of power.

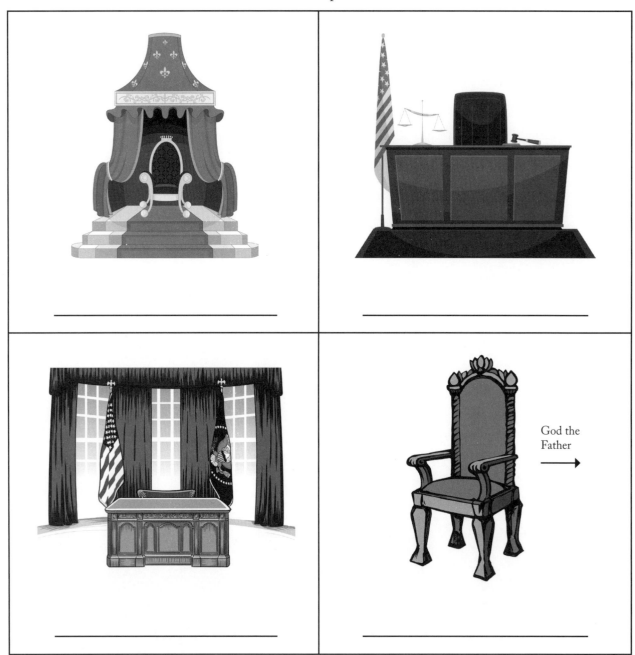

God the
Father
→

Find and circle the words from the answer to Question 50. Words appear horizontally, vertically, and diagonally, but not backwards. Words that appear twice in the answer will be found only once in the word search.

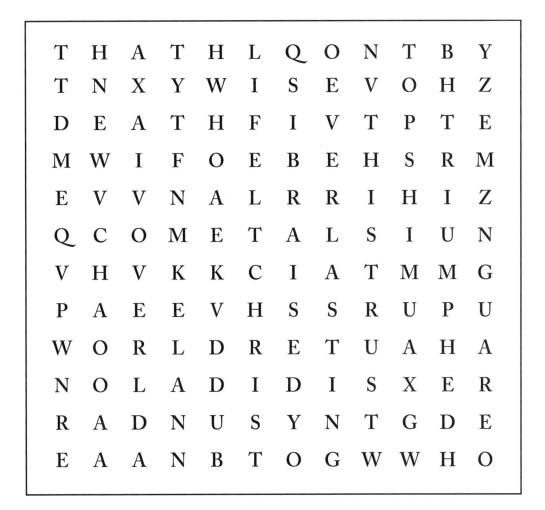

T	H	A	T	H	L	Q	O	N	T	B	Y
T	N	X	Y	W	I	S	E	V	O	H	Z
D	E	A	T	H	F	I	V	T	P	T	E
M	W	I	F	O	E	B	E	H	S	R	M
E	V	V	N	A	L	R	R	I	H	I	Z
Q	C	O	M	E	T	A	L	S	I	U	N
V	H	V	K	K	C	I	A	T	M	M	G
P	A	E	E	V	H	S	S	R	U	P	U
W	O	R	L	D	R	E	T	U	A	H	A
N	O	L	A	D	I	D	I	S	X	E	R
R	A	D	N	U	S	Y	N	T	G	D	E
E	A	A	N	B	T	O	G	W	W	H	O

Words to find:

CHRIST TRIUMPHED OVER SIN AND DEATH SO THAT ALL WHO TRUST IN HIM ARE RAISED TO NEW LIFE IN THIS WORLD AND TO EVERLASTING LIFE IN THE WORLD TO COME.

1. **Reader:** Fourth grader
Advocate: Son or daughter of the school principal
Judge: School principal

Pretend you live in a place where it hardly ever snows. You just listened to the weatherman forecast snow for tomorrow. He says that some schools may close. Your good friend is the child of the principal of your school. Call your friend and ask him or her to convince the principal to close school tomorrow.
After the advocate is finished, ask the judge if the advocacy worked.

2. **Reader:** Younger sibling
Advocate: Older sibling
Judge: A librarian

Pretend you lost a library book. Ask the advocate, your older sibling, to use his or her imagination to explain to the librarian what happened to the book and explain why you should not have to pay a fine.
After the advocate is finished, ask the judge if the advocacy worked.

3. **Reader:** Baseball card collector
Advocate: Best friend
Judge: Classmate who does not collect baseball cards

Pretend you collect baseball cards. One of your classmates brings a baseball card to school that he or she found as a prize in a cereal box. Your classmate asks if it is a good card. It happens to be your favorite baseball player of all time! Your classmate is not interested in giving or selling it to you. Ask the advocate, your best friend, to persuade your classmate why he or she should give up the card to you, the baseball card collector.
After the advocate is finished, ask the judge if the advocacy worked.

4. **Reader:** Third grader
Advocate: The parent of the third grader
Judge: The third-grade teacher

Pretend you arrived at school thirty minutes late. Ask the advocate, your parent, to use his or her imagination to explain to your teacher why you were late and to convince him or her that you should not be punished.
After the advocate is finished, ask the judge if the advocacy worked.

"Then I saw a new heaven and a new earth, for the first heaven and the first earth had passed away, and the sea was no more. And

I saw the holy city, new Jerusalem, coming down out of heaven from God, prepared as a bride adorned for her husband. And I heard a loud voice from the throne saying, 'Behold, the dwelling place of God is with man. He will dwell with them, and they will be his people, and God himself will be with them as their God. He will wipe away every tear from their eyes, and death shall be no more, neither shall there be mourning, nor crying, nor pain anymore, for the former things have passed away.'"

Revelation 21:1–4

Solutions

Q3 Trinity Diagram

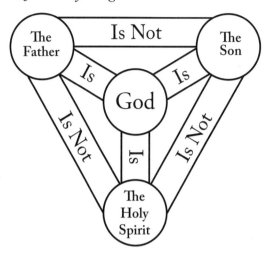

Q35 What We Were Word Search

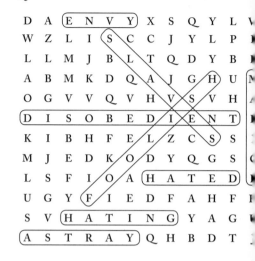

Q5 Animals in Creation Quiz

1. Mosquito 2. Tiger 3. Cheetah 4. Horse, Cow, Giraffe 5. Shark 6. Snake 7. Flamingo 8. Ant 9. Pigeon 10. Jellyfish

Q24 One-Way Maze

Q50 Word Search

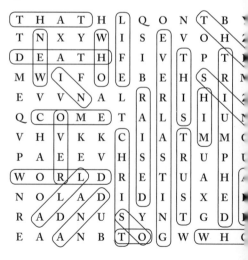

Q1 Illustrations, courtesy of iStock

Q4 Illustrations of Ancient Near East Statues, by Robert Johnson

Q5 Days of Creation Illustrations, by Robert Johnson

Q9 Images of False Gods

- Golden calf, courtesy of James Steidl/Shutterstock.com
- Artemis, Wikimedia Commons
- Shiva, Wikimedia Commons
- Shango, Wikimedia Commons
- Ancestor worship, Wikimedia Commons
- Self, courtesy of S-F/Shutterstock.com
- Shopping, courtesy of 5 second studio/Shutterstock.com
- Family, courtesy of JGA/Shutterstock.com

Q21 Illustrations of World Religions, by Robert Johnson

Q27 Illustrations

- John Calvin, modified from an image, courtesy of Solomnikov/Shutterstock.com
- Paul, by Robert Johnson
- Augustine, by Robert Johnson

Q31 Martyr Illustrations

- The Burning of Latimer and Ridley, from *Foxe's Book of Martyrs*, 1563, artist unknown, Wikipedia, https://en.wikipedia.org/wiki/Oxford_Martyrs#/media/File:Latimer_Ridley_Foxe_burning.jpg
- Thomas Cranmer's Martyrdom, burning in 1556, courtesy of Pictorial Press LTD/Alamy Stock Photo

Q33 Picture of Martin Luther, Martin Luther by Lucas Cranach der Ältere, 1529, Wikimedia Commons

Q37 Roman Armor, courtesy of tsuneomp/Shutterstock.com

Q41 Illustrations of Learned Skills

- Skiing, courtesy of ostill/Shutterstock.com
- Cellist, courtesy of grafvision/Shutterstock.com
- Skydiver, courtesy of germanskydiver/Shutterstock.com
- Fencer, courtesy of wavebreakmedia/Shutterstock.com
- Student driver, courtesy of iStock

Q43 Picture Clues

- Sack, courtesy of sedmi/Shutterstock.com
- Ram, courtesy of Karl_Sonnenberg/Shutterstock.com
- Small tin, courtesy of nelik/Shutterstock.com

Q44 Photos, courtesy of MAF and used by permission of Steve Saint

Q44 What do these signs mean?

- FBI Badge, Wikimedia Commons
- Purple heart, courtesy of Gary Blakeley/Shutterstock.com
- Baby sign, courtesy of Haryadi CH/Shutterstock.com
- Danger, courtesy of stas11/Shutterstock.com

Q47 Mural Template, by Robert Johnson

Q48 Illustrations of the Church

- Human body, courtesy of eveleen/Shutterstock.com
- Bride, courtesy of sanneberg/Shutterstock.com

- Family, courtesy of Monkey Business Images/Shutterstock.com
- Sheep, courtesy of Budimir Jevtic/Shutterstock.com
- Church, courtesy of aastock/Shutterstock.com

Q49 Illustration of Famous Homes

- White House, courtesy of Orhan Cam/Shutterstock.com
- Cinderella Castle at Magic Kingdom, photo by ShajiA, Wikimedia Commons
- Candy house, courtesy of Paul Michael Hughes/Shutterstock.com
- Rapunzel's tower, courtesy of Elliotte Rusty Harold/Shutterstock.com

Q49 Seats of Power

- King, courtesy of iStock
- Judge, courtesy of Macrovector/Shutterstock.com
- Oval Office desk, courtesy of pantid123/Shutterstock.com
- Jesus, courtesy of iStock

Build a framework for understanding core Christian beliefs.

Designed to be memorized over the course of a year, *The New City Catechism* is a valuable resource for building a foundation of important concepts in the minds and hearts of children and adults alike.

For more information, visit
newcitycatechism.com

Question 51

Of what advantage to us is
Christ's ascension?

Answer

Christ is now advocating for us in the
presence of his Father and also sends
us his Spirit.

Question 52

What hope does everlasting life hold for us?

Answer

That we will live with and enjoy God
forever in the new heaven and the
new earth, where we will be forever
freed from all sin in a renewed,
restored creation.

The New City Catechism

for Kids

The New City Catechism for Kids

Copyright © 2018 by The Gospel Coalition and Redeemer Presbyterian Church

Published by Crossway
        1300 Crescent Street
        Wheaton, Illinois 60187

This publication was made possible through the support of a grant from the John Templeton Foundation. The opinions expressed in this publication are those of the publisher and do not necessarily reflect the views of the John Templeton Foundation.

Cover design: Matt Wahl & Micah Lanier

First printing 2018

Printed in China

Scripture quotations are from the ESV® Bible (The Holy Bible, English Standard Version®), copyright © 2001 by Crossway, a publishing ministry of Good News Publishers. Used by permission. All rights reserved.

Trade paperback ISBN: 978-1-4335-6129-0

Library of Congress Cataloging-in-Publication Data

Names: Crossway Books.
Title: The new city catechism for kids.
Description: Wheaton : Crossway, 2018.
Identifiers: LCCN 2017048083 | ISBN 9781433561290 (tp)
Subjects: LCSH: Presbyterian Church—Catechisms—English—Juvenile
    literature. | Reformed Church—Catechisms—English—Juvenile literature. |
    Westminster Assembly (1643-1652). Shorter catechism—Juvenile literature.
Classification: LCC BX9184 .N49 2018 | DDC 238/.51—dc23
LC record available at https://lccn.loc.gov/2017048083

Crossway is a publishing ministry of Good News Publishers.

RRDS		29	28	27	26	25	24	23	22	21	20	19
15	14	13	12	11	10	9	8	7	6	5	4	3	2

The New City Catechism
for Kids

52 Questions
& Answers
for Our Hearts
& Minds

CROSSWAY®

WHEATON, ILLINOIS

God,
Creation & Fall,
Law

Question 1

What is our only hope in life and death?

Answer

That we are not our own but belong to God.

Question 2

What is God?

Answer

God is the creator of everyone and everything.

How many persons are there in God?

Answer

There are three persons in one God: the Father, the Son, and the Holy Spirit.

Question 4

How and why did God create us?

Answer

God created us male and female in his own image to glorify him.

Question 5

What else did God create?

Answer

God created all things, and all his
creation was very good.

Question 6

How can we glorify God?

Answer

By loving him and by obeying his commands and law.

Question 7

What does the law of God require?

Answer

That we love God with all our heart, soul, mind, and strength; and love our neighbor as ourselves.

What is the law of God stated in the Ten Commandments?

Answer

You shall have no other gods before me. You shall not make for yourself an idol. You shall not misuse the name of the LORD your God. Remember the Sabbath day by keeping it holy. Honor your father and your mother. You shall not murder. You shall not commit adultery. You shall not steal. You shall not give false testimony. You shall not covet.

What does God require in the first, second, and third commandments?

Answer

First, that we know God as the only true God.
Second, that we avoid all idolatry. Third, that we
treat God's name with fear and reverence.

Question 10

What does God require in the
fourth and fifth commandments?

Answer

Fourth, that on the Sabbath day we spend time in
worship of God. Fifth, that we love and honor our
father and our mother.

Question 11

What does God require in the sixth, seventh, and eighth commandments?

Answer

Sixth, that we do not hurt or hate our neighbor. Seventh, that we live purely and faithfully. Eighth, that we do not take without permission that which belongs to someone else.

What does God require in the ninth and tenth commandments?

Answer

Ninth, that we do not lie or deceive. Tenth, that we are content, not envying anyone.

Question 13

Can anyone keep the law of
God perfectly?

Answer

Since the fall, no human has been able to keep
the law of God perfectly.

Question 14

Did God create us unable to keep his law?

Answer

No, but because of the disobedience of Adam and Eve, we are all born in sin and guilt, and unable to keep God's law.

Question 15

Since no one can keep the
law, what is its purpose?

Answer

That we may know the holy nature of God,
and the sinful nature of our hearts; and thus
our need of a Savior.

Question 16

What is sin?

Answer

Sin is rejecting or ignoring God in the world he created, not being or doing what he requires in his law.

Question 17

What is idolatry?

Answer

Idolatry is trusting in created things rather
than the Creator.

Question 18

Will God allow our disobedience
and idolatry to go unpunished?

Answer

No, God is righteously angry with our sins
and will punish them both in this life, and in
the life to come.

Question 19

Is there any way to escape
punishment and be brought
back into God's favor?

Answer

Yes, God reconciles us to himself by
a Redeemer.

Question 20

Who is the Redeemer?

Answer

The only Redeemer is the Lord Jesus Christ.

Part 2

Christ,
Redemption,
Grace

What sort of Redeemer
is needed to bring us back
to God?

Answer

One who is truly human and also truly God.

Question 22

Why must the Redeemer be
truly human?

Answer

That in human nature he might on our behalf
perfectly obey the whole law and suffer the
punishment for human sin.

Question 23

Why must the Redeemer be truly God?

Answer

That because of his divine nature his obedience and suffering would be perfect and effective.

Question 24

Why was it necessary for Christ, the Redeemer, to die?

Answer

Christ died willingly in our place to deliver us from the power and penalty of sin and bring us back to God.

Question 25

Does Christ's death mean all our sins can be forgiven?

Answer

Yes, because Christ's death on the cross fully paid the penalty for our sin, God will remember our sins no more.

Question 26

What else does Christ's
death redeem?

Answer

Every part of fallen creation.

Are all people, just as they
were lost through Adam,
saved through Christ?

Answer

No, only those who are elected by God and
united to Christ by faith.

Question 28

What happens after death
to those not united to Christ
by faith?

Answer

They will be cast out from the presence of God,
into hell, to be justly punished, forever.

Question 29

How can we be saved?

Answer

Only by faith in Jesus Christ and in his substitutionary atoning death on the cross.

Question 30

What is faith in Jesus Christ?

Answer

Receiving and resting on him alone for
salvation as he is offered to us in the gospel.

Question 31

What do we believe by true faith?

Answer

We believe in God the Father Almighty, Maker of heaven and earth; and in Jesus Christ his only Son our Lord, who was conceived by the Holy Spirit, born of the virgin Mary, suffered under Pontius Pilate, was crucified, died, and was buried. He descended into hell. The third day he rose again from the dead. He ascended into heaven, and is seated at the right hand of God the Father Almighty; from there he will come to judge the living and the dead. We believe in the Holy Spirit, the holy catholic church, the communion of saints, the forgiveness of sins, the resurrection of the body, and the life everlasting.

Question 32

What do justification and
sanctification mean?

Answer

Justification means our declared
righteousness before God. Sanctification
means our gradual, growing righteousness.

Should those who have faith in Christ seek their salvation through their own works, or anywhere else?

Answer

No, everything necessary to salvation is found in Christ.

Question 34

Since we are redeemed by grace alone, through Christ alone, must we still do good works and obey God's Word?

Answer

Yes, so that our lives may show love and gratitude to God; and so that by our godly behavior others may be won to Christ.

Question 35

Since we are redeemed by grace alone, through faith alone, where does this faith come from?

Answer

From the Holy Spirit.

Spirit, Restoration, Growing in Grace

Question 36

What do we believe about
the Holy Spirit?

Answer

That he is God, coeternal with the Father
and the Son.

Question 37

How does the Holy Spirit
help us?

Answer

The Holy Spirit convicts us of our sin,
and he enables us to pray and to
understand God's Word.

Question 38

What is prayer?

Answer

Prayer is pouring out our hearts to God.

Question 39

With what attitude should
we pray?

Answer

With love, perseverance, and gratefulness.

Question 40

What should we pray?

Answer

The whole Word of God directs us in what we should pray.

Question 41

What is the Lord's Prayer?

Answer

Our Father in heaven, hallowed be your name, your kingdom come, your will be done, on earth as it is in heaven. Give us today our daily bread. And forgive us our debts, as we also have forgiven our debtors. And lead us not into temptation, but deliver us from evil.

Question 42

How is the Word of God to be
read and heard?

Answer

With diligence, preparation, and prayer;
so that we may accept it with faith and
practice it in our lives.

Question 43

What are the sacraments or ordinances?

Answer

Baptism and the Lord's Supper.

Question 44

What is baptism?

Answer

Baptism is the washing with water in the name of the Father, the Son, and the Holy Spirit.

Question 45

Is baptism with water the washing away of sin itself?

Answer

No, only the blood of Christ can cleanse us from sin.

Question 46

What is the Lord's Supper?

Answer

Christ commanded all Christians to eat
bread and to drink from the cup in
thankful remembrance of him.

Question 47

Does the Lord's Supper
add anything to Christ's
atoning work?

Answer

No, Christ died once for all.

Question 48

What is the church?

Answer

A community elected for eternal life and united by faith, who love, follow, learn from, and worship God together.

Question 49

Where is Christ now?

Answer

Christ rose bodily from the grave on the
third day after his death and is seated
at the right hand of the Father.

Question 50

What does Christ's resurrection mean for us?

Answer

Christ triumphed over sin and death so that all who trust in him are raised to new life in this world and to everlasting life in the world to come.

Question 51

Of what advantage to us is Christ's ascension?

Answer

Christ is now advocating for us in the presence of his Father and also sends us his Spirit.

Question 52

What hope does everlasting life hold for us?

Answer

That we will live with and enjoy God forever in the new heaven and the new earth, where we will be forever freed from all sin in a renewed, restored creation.

The New City Catechism

for Kids

This publication was made possible through the support of a grant from the John Templeton Foundation. The opinions expressed in this publication are those of the publisher and do not necessarily reflect the views of the John Templeton Foundation.

Cover design: Matt Wahl & Micah Lanier

First printing 2018

Printed in China

Trade paperback ISBN: 978-1-4335-6129-0

Library of Congress Cataloging-in-Publication Data

Names: Crossway Books.
Title: The new city catechism for kids.
Description: Wheaton : Crossway, 2018.
Identifiers: LCCN 2017048083 | ISBN 9781433561290 (tp)
Subjects: LCSH: Presbyterian Church—Catechisms—English—Juvenile
    literature. | Reformed Church—Catechisms—English—Juvenile literature. |
    Westminster Assembly (1643-1652). Shorter catechism—Juvenile literature.
Classification: LCC BX9184 .N49 2018 | DDC 238/.51—dc23
LC record available at https://lccn.loc.gov/2017048083

Crossway is a publishing ministry of Good News Publishers.

RRDS		29	28	27	26	25	24	23	22	21	20	19
15	14	13	12	11	10	9	8	7	6	5	4	3	2

The New City Catechism
for Kids

52 Questions
& Answers
for Our Hearts
& Minds

WHEATON, ILLINOIS

God, Creation & Fall, Law

Question 1

What is our only hope in life
and death?

Answer

That we are not our own but belong to God.

Question 2

_____

What is God?

Answer

_____

God is the creator of everyone and everything.

Question 3

How many persons are there
in God?

Answer

There are three persons in one God: the Father,
the Son, and the Holy Spirit.

Question 4

How and why did God create us?

Answer

God created us male and female in his own image to glorify him.

Question 5

What else did God create?

Answer

God created all things, and all his
creation was very good.

Question 6

How can we glorify God?

Answer

By loving him and by obeying his commands and law.

Question 7

What does the law of God require?

Answer

That we love God with all our heart, soul, mind, and strength; and love our neighbor as ourselves.

Question 8

What is the law of God stated in the Ten Commandments?

Answer

You shall have no other gods before me. You shall not make for yourself an idol. You shall not misuse the name of the Lord your God. Remember the Sabbath day by keeping it holy. Honor your father and your mother. You shall not murder. You shall not commit adultery. You shall not steal. You shall not give false testimony. You shall not covet.

What does God require in the first, second, and third commandments?

Answer

First, that we know God as the only true God. Second, that we avoid all idolatry. Third, that we treat God's name with fear and reverence.

Question 10

What does God require in the fourth and fifth commandments?

Answer

Fourth, that on the Sabbath day we spend time in worship of God. Fifth, that we love and honor our father and our mother.

Question 11

What does God require in the sixth, seventh, and eighth commandments?

Answer

Sixth, that we do not hurt or hate our neighbor. Seventh, that we live purely and faithfully. Eighth, that we do not take without permission that which belongs to someone else.

Question 12

What does God require in the ninth and tenth commandments?

Answer

Ninth, that we do not lie or deceive. Tenth, that we are content, not envying anyone.

Question 13

Can anyone keep the law of God perfectly?

Answer

Since the fall, no human has been able to keep the law of God perfectly.

Question 14

Did God create us unable to keep his law?

Answer

No, but because of the disobedience of Adam and Eve, we are all born in sin and guilt, and unable to keep God's law.

Question 15

Since no one can keep the law, what is its purpose?

Answer

That we may know the holy nature of God, and the sinful nature of our hearts; and thus our need of a Savior.

Question 16

What is sin?

Answer

Sin is rejecting or ignoring God in the world he created, not being or doing what he requires in his law.

Question 17

What is idolatry?

Answer

Idolatry is trusting in created things rather
than the Creator.

Question 18

Will God allow our disobedience
and idolatry to go unpunished?

Answer

No, God is righteously angry with our sins
and will punish them both in this life, and in
the life to come.

Question 19

Is there any way to escape punishment and be brought back into God's favor?

Answer

Yes, God reconciles us to himself by a Redeemer.

Question 20

Who is the Redeemer?

Answer

The only Redeemer is the Lord Jesus Christ.

Christ, Redemption, Grace

Question 21

What sort of Redeemer
is needed to bring us back
to God?

Answer

One who is truly human and also truly God.

Question 22

Why must the Redeemer be truly human?

Answer

That in human nature he might on our behalf perfectly obey the whole law and suffer the punishment for human sin.

Question 23

Why must the Redeemer be truly God?

Answer

That because of his divine nature his obedience and suffering would be perfect and effective.

Question 24

Why was it necessary for
Christ, the Redeemer, to die?

Answer

Christ died willingly in our place to deliver us
from the power and penalty of sin and bring
us back to God.

Question 25

Does Christ's death mean all our sins can be forgiven?

Answer

Yes, because Christ's death on the cross fully paid the penalty for our sin, God will remember our sins no more.

Question 26

What else does Christ's
death redeem?

Answer

Every part of fallen creation.

Question 27

Are all people, just as they were lost through Adam, saved through Christ?

Answer

No, only those who are elected by God and united to Christ by faith.

Question 28

What happens after death
to those not united to Christ
by faith?

Answer

They will be cast out from the presence of God,
into hell, to be justly punished, forever.

Question 29

How can we be saved?

Answer

Only by faith in Jesus Christ and in his substitutionary atoning death on the cross.

Question 30

What is faith in Jesus Christ?

Answer

Receiving and resting on him alone for
salvation as he is offered to us in the gospel.

Question 31

What do we believe by true faith?

Answer

We believe in God the Father Almighty, Maker of heaven and earth; and in Jesus Christ his only Son our Lord, who was conceived by the Holy Spirit, born of the virgin Mary, suffered under Pontius Pilate, was crucified, died, and was buried. He descended into hell. The third day he rose again from the dead. He ascended into heaven, and is seated at the right hand of God the Father Almighty; from there he will come to judge the living and the dead. We believe in the Holy Spirit, the holy catholic church, the communion of saints, the forgiveness of sins, the resurrection of the body, and the life everlasting.

Question 32

What do justification and sanctification mean?

Answer

Justification means our declared righteousness before God. Sanctification means our gradual, growing righteousness.

Question 33

Should those who have faith in Christ seek their salvation through their own works, or anywhere else?

Answer

No, everything necessary to salvation is found in Christ.

Question 34

Since we are redeemed by grace alone, through Christ alone, must we still do good works and obey God's Word?

Answer

Yes, so that our lives may show love and gratitude to God; and so that by our godly behavior others may be won to Christ.

Question 35

Since we are redeemed by grace alone, through faith alone, where does this faith come from?

Answer

From the Holy Spirit.

Spirit, Restoration, Growing in Grace

Question 36

What do we believe about the Holy Spirit?

Answer

That he is God, coeternal with the Father and the Son.

Question 37

How does the Holy Spirit help us?

Answer

The Holy Spirit convicts us of our sin, and he enables us to pray and to understand God's Word.

Question 38

What is prayer?

Answer

Prayer is pouring out our hearts to God.

Question 39

With what attitude should
we pray?

Answer

With love, perseverance, and gratefulness.

Question 40

What should we pray?

Answer

The whole Word of God directs us in
what we should pray.

Question 41

What is the Lord's Prayer?

Answer

Our Father in heaven, hallowed be your name, your kingdom come, your will be done, on earth as it is in heaven. Give us today our daily bread. And forgive us our debts, as we also have forgiven our debtors. And lead us not into temptation, but deliver us from evil.

Question 42

How is the Word of God to be
read and heard?

Answer

With diligence, preparation, and prayer;
so that we may accept it with faith and
practice it in our lives.

Question 43

What are the sacraments
or ordinances?

Answer

Baptism and the Lord's Supper.

Question 44

What is baptism?

Answer

Baptism is the washing with water in the name of the Father, the Son, and the Holy Spirit.

Question 45

Is baptism with water the washing away of sin itself?

Answer

No, only the blood of Christ can cleanse us from sin.

Question 46

What is the Lord's Supper?

Answer

Christ commanded all Christians to eat
bread and to drink from the cup in
thankful remembrance of him.

Question 47

Does the Lord's Supper add anything to Christ's atoning work?

Answer

No, Christ died once for all.

Question 48

What is the church?

Answer

A community elected for eternal life and united by faith, who love, follow, learn from, and worship God together.

Question 49

Where is Christ now?

Answer

Christ rose bodily from the grave on the third day after his death and is seated at the right hand of the Father.

Question 50

What does Christ's resurrection mean for us?

Answer

Christ triumphed over sin and death so that all who trust in him are raised to new life in this world and to everlasting life in the world to come.

Question 51

Of what advantage to us is
Christ's ascension?

Answer

Christ is now advocating for us in the
presence of his Father and also sends
us his Spirit.

Question 52

What hope does everlasting
life hold for us?

Answer

That we will live with and enjoy God
forever in the new heaven and the
new earth, where we will be forever
freed from all sin in a renewed,
restored creation.

The New City Catechism

for Kids

This publication was made possible through the support of a grant from the John Templeton Foundation. The opinions expressed in this publication are those of the author and do not necessarily reflect the views of the John Templeton Foundation.

Cover design: Matt Wahl & Micah Lanier

First printing 2018

Printed in China

Trade paperback ISBN: 978-1-4335-6129-0

Library of Congress Cataloging-in-Publication Data

Names: Crossway Books.
Title: The new city catechism for kids.
Description: Wheaton : Crossway, 2018.
Identifiers: LCCN 2017048083 | ISBN 9781433561290 (tp)
Subjects: LCSH: Presbyterian Church—Catechisms—English—Juvenile literature. | Reformed Church—Catechisms—English—Juvenile literature. | Westminster Assembly (1643-1652). Shorter catechism—Juvenile literature.
Classification: LCC BX9184 .N49 2018 | DDC 238/.51—dc23
LC record available at https://lccn.loc.gov/2017048083

Crossway is a publishing ministry of Good News Publishers.

RRDS		29	28	27	26	25	24	23	22	21	20	19
15	14	13	12	11	10	9	8	7	6	5	4	3	2

The New City Catechism
for Kids

52 Questions
& Answers
for Our Hearts
& Minds

WHEATON, ILLINOIS

God,
Creation & Fall,
Law

Question 1

What is our only hope in life
and death?

Answer

That we are not our own but belong to God.

Question 2

What is God?

Answer

God is the creator of everyone and everything.

Question 3

How many persons are there in God?

Answer

There are three persons in one God: the Father, the Son, and the Holy Spirit.

Question 4

How and why did God create us?

Answer

God created us male and female in his
own image to glorify him.

Question 5

What else did God create?

Answer

God created all things, and all his
creation was very good.

Question 6

How can we glorify God?

Answer

By loving him and by obeying his commands and law.

Question 7

What does the law of God require?

Answer

That we love God with all our heart, soul, mind, and strength; and love our neighbor as ourselves.

Question 8

What is the law of God stated in the Ten Commandments?

Answer

You shall have no other gods before me. You shall not make for yourself an idol. You shall not misuse the name of the LORD your God. Remember the Sabbath day by keeping it holy. Honor your father and your mother. You shall not murder. You shall not commit adultery. You shall not steal. You shall not give false testimony. You shall not covet.

Question 9

What does God require in the first, second, and third commandments?

Answer

First, that we know God as the only true God. Second, that we avoid all idolatry. Third, that we treat God's name with fear and reverence.

Question 10

What does God require in the
fourth and fifth commandments?

Answer

Fourth, that on the Sabbath day we spend time in
worship of God. Fifth, that we love and honor our
father and our mother.

Question 11

What does God require in the sixth, seventh, and eighth commandments?

Answer

Sixth, that we do not hurt or hate our neighbor.
Seventh, that we live purely and faithfully. Eighth,
that we do not take without permission that
which belongs to someone else.

What does God require in the ninth and tenth commandments?

Answer

Ninth, that we do not lie or deceive. Tenth, that we are content, not envying anyone.

Question 13

Can anyone keep the law of
God perfectly?

Answer

Since the fall, no human has been able to keep
the law of God perfectly.

Question 14

Did God create us unable to keep his law?

Answer

No, but because of the disobedience of Adam and Eve, we are all born in sin and guilt, and unable to keep God's law.

Question 15

Since no one can keep the law, what is its purpose?

Answer

That we may know the holy nature of God, and the sinful nature of our hearts; and thus our need of a Savior.

Question 16

What is sin?

Answer

Sin is rejecting or ignoring God in the world he created, not being or doing what he requires in his law.

Question 17

What is idolatry?

Answer

Idolatry is trusting in created things rather than the Creator.

Question 18

Will God allow our disobedience
and idolatry to go unpunished?

Answer

No, God is righteously angry with our sins
and will punish them both in this life, and in
the life to come.

Question 19

Is there any way to escape
punishment and be brought
back into God's favor?

Answer

Yes, God reconciles us to himself by
a Redeemer.

Question 20

Who is the Redeemer?

Answer

The only Redeemer is the Lord Jesus Christ.

Christ, Redemption, Grace

Question 21

What sort of Redeemer
is needed to bring us back
to God?

Answer

One who is truly human and also truly God.

Why must the Redeemer be truly human?

Answer

That in human nature he might on our behalf perfectly obey the whole law and suffer the punishment for human sin.

Question 23

Why must the Redeemer be truly God?

Answer

That because of his divine nature his obedience and suffering would be perfect and effective.

Question 24

Why was it necessary for Christ, the Redeemer, to die?

Answer

Christ died willingly in our place to deliver us from the power and penalty of sin and bring us back to God.

Question 25

Does Christ's death mean all
our sins can be forgiven?

Answer

Yes, because Christ's death on the cross fully
paid the penalty for our sin, God will remember
our sins no more.

Question 26

What else does Christ's death redeem?

Answer

Every part of fallen creation.

Are all people, just as they were lost through Adam, saved through Christ?

Answer

No, only those who are elected by God and united to Christ by faith.

Question 28

What happens after death
to those not united to Christ
by faith?

Answer

They will be cast out from the presence of God,
into hell, to be justly punished, forever.

Question 29

_____

How can we be saved?

Answer

_____

Only by faith in Jesus Christ and in his
substitutionary atoning death on the cross.

Question 30

What is faith in Jesus Christ?

Answer

Receiving and resting on him alone for
salvation as he is offered to us in the gospel.

Question 31

What do we believe by true faith?

Answer

We believe in God the Father Almighty, Maker of heaven and earth; and in Jesus Christ his only Son our Lord, who was conceived by the Holy Spirit, born of the virgin Mary, suffered under Pontius Pilate, was crucified, died, and was buried. He descended into hell. The third day he rose again from the dead. He ascended into heaven, and is seated at the right hand of God the Father Almighty; from there he will come to judge the living and the dead. We believe in the Holy Spirit, the holy catholic church, the communion of saints, the forgiveness of sins, the resurrection of the body, and the life everlasting.

Question 32

What do justification and sanctification mean?

Answer

Justification means our declared righteousness before God. Sanctification means our gradual, growing righteousness.

Question 33

Should those who have faith in
Christ seek their salvation through
their own works, or anywhere else?

Answer

No, everything necessary to salvation is
found in Christ.

Question 34

Since we are redeemed by grace alone, through Christ alone, must we still do good works and obey God's Word?

Answer

Yes, so that our lives may show love and gratitude to God; and so that by our godly behavior others may be won to Christ.

Question 35

Since we are redeemed by grace alone, through faith alone, where does this faith come from?

Answer

From the Holy Spirit.

Spirit, Restoration, Growing in Grace

Question 36

What do we believe about
the Holy Spirit?

Answer

That he is God, coeternal with the Father
and the Son.

Question 37

How does the Holy Spirit
help us?

Answer

The Holy Spirit convicts us of our sin,
and he enables us to pray and to
understand God's Word.

Question 38

What is prayer?

Answer

Prayer is pouring out our hearts to God.

Question 39

With what attitude should
we pray?

Answer

With love, perseverance, and gratefulness.

Question 40

What should we pray?

Answer

The whole Word of God directs us in
what we should pray.

Question 41

What is the Lord's Prayer?

Answer

Our Father in heaven, hallowed be your name, your kingdom come, your will be done, on earth as it is in heaven. Give us today our daily bread. And forgive us our debts, as we also have forgiven our debtors. And lead us not into temptation, but deliver us from evil.

Question 42

How is the Word of God to be read and heard?

Answer

With diligence, preparation, and prayer; so that we may accept it with faith and practice it in our lives.

Question 43

What are the sacraments
or ordinances?

Answer

Baptism and the Lord's Supper.

Question 44

What is baptism?

Answer

Baptism is the washing with water in
the name of the Father, the Son, and
the Holy Spirit.

Question 45

Is baptism with water the washing away of sin itself?

Answer

No, only the blood of Christ can cleanse us from sin.

Question 46

What is the Lord's Supper?

Answer

Christ commanded all Christians to eat
bread and to drink from the cup in
thankful remembrance of him.

Does the Lord's Supper add anything to Christ's atoning work?

Answer

No, Christ died once for all.

Question 48

What is the church?

Answer

A community elected for eternal life and
united by faith, who love, follow, learn
from, and worship God together.

Question 49

Where is Christ now?

Answer

Christ rose bodily from the grave on the third day after his death and is seated at the right hand of the Father.

Question 50

What does Christ's resurrection mean for us?

Answer

Christ triumphed over sin and death so that all who trust in him are raised to new life in this world and to everlasting life in the world to come.